RELIGION AND POLITICS
IN THE ANCIENT AMERICAS

This exciting collection explores the interplay of religion and politics in the precolumbian Americas. Each thought-provoking contribution positions religion as a primary factor influencing political innovations in this period, reinterpreting major changes through an examination of how religion both facilitated and constrained transformations in political organization and status relations. Offering unparalleled geographic and temporal coverage of this subject, *Religion and Politics in the Ancient Americas* spans the entire precolumbian period, from Preceramic Peru to the Contact period in eastern North America, with case studies from North, Middle, and South America.

Religion and Politics in the Ancient Americas considers the ways in which religion itself generated political innovation and thus enabled political centralization to occur. It moves beyond a "Great Tradition" focus on elite religion to understand how local political authority was negotiated, contested, bolstered, and undermined within diverse constituencies, demonstrating how religion has transformed non-Western societies. As well as offering readers fresh perspectives on specific archaeological cases, this book breaks new ground in the archaeological examination of religion and society.

Sarah B. Barber is Associate Professor in the Department of Anthropology at the University of Central Florida, USA.

Arthur A. Joyce is Professor in the Department of Anthropology at the University of Colorado Boulder, USA.

Routledge Archaeology of the Ancient Americas
Edited by Sarah B. Barber and Arthur A. Joyce

Vernacular Architecture in the Pre-Columbian Americas
Edited by Christina Halperin and Lauren Schwartz

Settlement Ecology of the Ancient Americas
Edited by Lucas C. Kellett and Eric Jones

Religion and Politics in the Ancient Americas
Edited by Sarah B. Barber and Arthur A. Joyce

RELIGION AND POLITICS IN THE ANCIENT AMERICAS

Edited by Sarah B. Barber and Arthur A. Joyce

Routledge
Taylor & Francis Group

LONDON AND NEW YORK

First published 2018
by Routledge
2 Park Square, Milton Park, Abingdon, Oxon OX14 4RN

and by Routledge
711 Third Avenue, New York, NY 10017

Routledge is an imprint of the Taylor & Francis Group, an informa business

British Library Cataloguing-in-Publication Data
A catalogue record for this book is available from the British Library

Library of Congress Cataloging-in-Publication Data
A catalog record for this book has been requested

ISBN: 978-1-138-90788-1 (hbk)
ISBN: 978-1-138-90789-8 (pbk)
ISBN: 978-1-315-69485-6 (ebk)

Typeset in Bembo
by Apex CoVantage, LLC

In memory of Molly, who had the best definition of construction episode ever.

CONTENTS

FIGURES

TABLES

CONTRIBUTORS

Susan M. Alt is Associate Professor of Anthropology at Indiana University, Bloomington, USA. Her interests include Mississippian religion, migrations, violence, gender, and the built environment, and her current research deals with the relationships between the Emerald complex, Cahokia, and the Yankeetown culture of southwestern Indiana.

Sarah B. Barber is Associate Professor of Anthropology at the University of Central Florida in Orlando, USA. Her research interests include religion, early urbanism, ancient music, long-distance exchange, and coastal ecosystems in Mesoamerica.

David M. Carballo is Associate Professor of Archaeology at Boston University, USA. His research interests include urbanism, religion, political organization, households, and collective action in precolumbian central Mexico.

Erina Gruner is in the PhD program at the State University of New York at Binghamton, USA, and works as an Archaeological Field Director for WestLand Resources, Inc. Her research addresses prehistoric interaction, exchange, and social organization in the southwestern United States, with a focus on ethnohistoric perspectives.

Scott R. Hutson directs the Ucí-Cansahcab Regional Integration Project in Yucatan, Mexico, and teaches anthropology at the University of Kentucky. His recent books include Ancient Urban Maya (University Press of Florida) and Ancient Maya Commerce (University Press of Colorado).

Arthur A. Joyce is Professor of Anthropology at the University of Colorado Boulder, USA. His research interests include the archaeology of political life, urbanism, materiality, and ecology in ancient Mesoamerica.

Rosemary A. Joyce is the Alice S. Davis Endowed Chair in Anthropology at the University of California, Berkeley, USA. Her research centers on how the things people make shape the people who make them, recreating social relations and making them seem to be natural by associating them with the material world.

Céline C. Lamb is a PhD candidate at the University of Kentucky, USA, completing her dissertation on rural complexity in northern Yucatan. She has also worked in Belize, El Salvador, and the eastern United States, and received her master's degree from the Université Paris 1 Panthéon-Sorbonne.

David Medina Arona is an archaeologist with the Centro-INAH Campeche, in Mexico. His research interests focus on the social organization of precolumbian and modern Maya groups. He also has expertise in the study of lithic artifacts and precolumbian architecture.

Jerry D. Moore, Professor of Anthropology, California State University Dominguez Hills, USA, is an Andean archaeologist whose research focuses on prehispanic cultural landscapes and the built environment.

Timothy R. Pauketat is Professor of Anthropology and Medieval Studies at the University of Illinois, USA. His interests focus on the broad relationships between ancient cosmologies, cities, and the everyday experiences of agricultural peoples along the Mississippi river south into Mexico.

Matthew Piscitelli as a Research Associate at The Field Museum in Chicago, USA. Dr. Piscitelli uses a multi-disciplinary approach to investigate the role of religion in the development of social complexity in the ancient Americas.

Christopher B. Rodning is Professor at Tulane University in New Orleans, USA. He specializes in the archaeology of the southeastern United States, with particular interests in architecture, cultural landscapes, mortuary practices, and responses by Native American groups to encounters and entanglements with European explorers and colonists.

Edward Swenson is Associate Professor, University of Toronto, Canada. Swenson's research interests include the pre-industrial city; the emergence of social inequality; the archaeology of ritual and ideology; violence and religion; materiality theory; place-making and ancient infrastructures; and the politics of spatial experience and social memory.

John H. Walker is Associate Professor at the Department of Anthropology at the University of Central Florida in Orlando, USA. His research interests include the origins of domestication, landscape archaeology, the spatial and social organization of agriculture in the Amazon Basin, and geographic information systems (GIS).

María Nieves Zedeño, Research Professor of Anthropology, University of Arizona, Tucson, USA, is interested in the archaeology, history, and ethnography of hunter-gatherer societies, landscape theory, and ontology.

1

NEW DIRECTIONS IN THE ARCHAEOLOGY OF RELIGION AND POLITICS IN THE AMERICAS

Arthur A. Joyce

Introduction

Although religion has been a topic of interest in American archaeology since the beginnings of the discipline in the nineteenth century, it has typically been considered methodologically challenging and of secondary importance to economic factors in understanding the history of precolumbian peoples. Since the 1970s, however, archaeologists have increasingly considered how religion was important in facilitating political integration and legitimizing authority in ancient societies. Less often, religion has been considered a primary factor in major political transformations. In addition, archaeological research has traditionally focused on religion as practiced by social elites. Only recently have archaeologists begun to investigate the religious beliefs and practices of non-elites and begun to see religion as a social field through which power was negotiated and sometimes contested. One reason for downplaying the role of religion in political affairs is the common view that religion is difficult or impossible to access archaeologically. As discussed by Fogelin (2007), archaeologists have tended to view religion as underlying beliefs and ideas that motivated ritual practice. Religious belief was seen as inaccessible, while ritual action could be addressed archaeologically.

The contributors to this volume seek to develop a more nuanced approach to religion and politics in the ancient Americas through consideration of three interrelated themes:

1   To move beyond a focus on political integration by considering how religion was involved in the creation, negotiation, and contestation of political authority. This theme seeks to challenge the view of religion as epiphenomenal to political change. Authors in the volume reinterpret political change in precolumbian complex societies by explicitly considering how religious practice,

paraphernalia, and belief facilitated and constrained transformations in political authority and organization. Authors also move beyond the "Great Tradition" of elite religion to understand the ways that political authority in complex societies was negotiated, contested, bolstered, and undermined among diverse constituencies via religious idioms.

2   To consider the recent ontological turn in archaeology (e.g., Zedeño 2009) and how an understanding of Native American ontologies informs our view of precolumbian religion and its relationship to politics. Since most Native American ontologies are relational, they also challenge the Cartesian dualisms in which Western scholarship is embedded, including the binary of religious belief and ritual practice that has been central to archaeological approaches to religion.

3   To consider recent theories of materiality (e.g., Latour 2005; Miller 2005) and how these can provide new insights into the entities – simultaneously social, material, and spiritual – that made a difference in political life. By considering the involvement of religious practices, materials, and beliefs in the entanglements through which political formations were constituted, the authors provide a more comprehensive view of the relationship between religion and politics in precolumbian America.

This chapter provides an overview of each of the themes that organize the volume beginning with a brief history of research on the relationship between religion and politics in American archaeology as background. As discussed in the final section of this chapter, each of the contributions to the volume addresses at least one of these themes. The authors also consider the themes from a diversity of perspectives, which provides for a more thoughtful approach to the problem of religion and politics.

A brief history of research on religion and politics in American archaeology

In American archaeology, religion has been a topic of research since the beginnings of the discipline in the nineteenth century. Through much of the history of the discipline, religion was viewed as unimportant to social change. Until the 1960s, religion was viewed as difficult to address archaeologically as exemplified by Hawkes' ladder of inference. The majority of research involved typologies of religious art, architecture, and artifacts as well as descriptions of discoveries such as tombs and temples. General syntheses that addressed ancient religion typically relied on ethnohistoric and ethnographic evidence and assumptions of continuity with the pre-contact past to interpret archaeological data and construct narratives on religious life in the ancient Americas (Rowe 1948; Tello 1929, 1942; Thompson 1954; Vaillant 1941; Waring and Holder 1945). The most significant work on religion during this period dealt with Maya writing, especially the prehispanic calendar as well as the identification of deities on inscriptions and iconography (Morley 1920, 1932–1938; Thompson 1929). Based on the epigraphic work, many archaeologists believed that ancient Maya society was integrated through religious ideologies focused on ceremonial centers and theocratic rulers (Thompson 1942; Willey 1956). Research on prehispanic religion was also almost entirely focused on elites at this time.

With the advent and optimism of the New Archaeology in the 1960s, religion was seen as potentially accessible due to its systemic connections to archaeologically visible dimensions of culture (Binford 1962; Fritz 1978). Until the 1980s, however, research on the relationship between religion and politics lagged behind studies of economy and ecology. Exceptions to this generalization include Drennan's (1976, 1983) model, drawing on Rappaport (1968), of the role of religion in the origins of social complexity. Drennan argued for the importance of religious rituals of sanctification as a means through which the decisions of emerging administrative institutions were accepted (also see Flannery 1968). Drawing from both structuralism and ecological systems theory, Isbell (1978) argued that Andean cosmology provided a highly stable reservoir for information of adaptive significance. Another important study, although not linked explicitly to political concerns, was Flannery's and Marcus's (1976; Flannery 1976) examination of religious artifacts from low-status houses in the Formative-period Valley of Oaxaca. Research on "commoner ritual" would not become a major focus until the 2000s (see below).

Research on religion and politics in American archaeology increased greatly during the 1980s and 1990s. Many studies of religion and politics were based on the neoevolutionary and ecological functionalism that had dominated American archaeology since the 1960s, and tended to focus on the role of ritual and religion in the integration of sociocultural systems (Lipe and Hegmon 1989; Morris 1998; Morris and Thompson 1985). New approaches also emerged at this time; many inspired by considerations of postprocessual and Marxist theory (Ashmore 1991; Conrad and Demarest 1984; Janusek 2006; Jennings 2003; Joyce and Winter 1996; McGuire and Saitta 1996; Moore 1996; Pauketat and Emerson 1991; Potter 2000). Much of this research focused on how religion and ritual operated as a form of ideology through which political authority and elite interests in complex societies were realized and legitimated. In Mesoamerican archaeology, an even more important factor in the linkage of religion to politics was the revolution in the decipherment of Maya writing, which in conjunction with iconographic, ethnohistoric, ethnographic, and archaeological data led to the recognition that religion figured prominently as a basis of rulership (Freidel and Schele 1988; Houston 1993; Stuart 1984).

Stemming from both the focus on integration and legitimation as well as the prevalence of data speaking to the religious practices of the elite, archaeological research has tended to focus on forms of high culture dominated by elites and their interests. Studies of the religious life of common people in both complex and small-scale societies has only become an important topic of research in the past 20 years (Aldenderfer 1993; Cutright 2013; Emerson 1997; Gonlin and Lohse 2007; Janusek 2009; Plunket 2002). Despite this focus, few scholars have considered the possibility that religion could impede social change or that the religious practices of non-elites, local leaders, and lesser nobility could influence political history (Hutson et al., Chapter 8; Janusek 2005; Joyce et al. 2001; R. Joyce,

Chapter 7; Lohse 2007; Wilson 2008; Yaeger 2003). More recently, archaeologists have begun to consider religion as a social field through which power and political authority were negotiated and sometimes contested (Barber and Joyce 2007; Dillehay 2004; Janusek 2004; A. Joyce 2010; Pauketat and Alt 2003; Swenson 2007).

At an even more basic level, American archaeologists have increasingly questioned perspectives rooted in Western Cartesian dualisms for addressing the religion of people who often held radically different ontological positions (Mock 1998; Swenson 2015; Zedeño 2008). Studies of ancient religion are also increasingly drawing on materiality theories that are likewise based on relational perspectives (Joyce and Barber 2015; Pauketat 2013; Walker 2008). These developments in approaches to religion and politics serve as a jumping off point for this volume.

Beyond integration

Archaeologists are now beginning to recognize that not only elites, but commoners as well, had rich religious lives that included rituals carried out at the individual, household, barrio, and community level. Although commoners participated in ceremonies led by rulers and elite ritual specialists, they also contacted the divine through practices that were independent of the "Great Traditions" of elite religion (e.g., Brown 2000; Brumfiel 2011; Cutright 2013; Emerson 1997; Robin 2002; Zaro and Lohse 2005), and religious specialists were not restricted to social elites (e.g., Brown et al. 2002). In many instances, elite-dominated religious institutions at the level of the polity likely developed from established practices at the local, non-elite level (Lucero 2006; McAnany 1995). Furthermore, Blackmore (2011) reminds us that commoners are not homogenous and that religious practice is one way in which households in non-elite neighborhoods were differentiated (also see Gonlin 2007; Hutson et al., Chapter 8).

Even at the level of large-scale, public ritual led by elites in complex societies, comparative research indicates that rather than acting as a means for communicating broadly understood ideological notions, religious practice and symbolism can often carry a high level of ambiguity (Bell 1992, 1997). This ambiguity affords a variety of interpretations, which on the one hand can be important in unifying diverse groups in complex societies, but on the other can be sites of struggle and contestation (Kertzer 1988). Ritualized practices are effective means of promoting solidarity because they rarely promote an explicit interpretation and instead focus more on common symbols that leave considerable room for negotiated appropriations of meaning (Bell 1992:182–187; Fernandez 1965). Religious ritual therefore is not a heavy-handed form of social control. Conversely, like ideology, ritualized acts, according to Bell (1992:195), construct an argument, creating a set of tensions and potential struggle surrounding negotiated appropriations of the beliefs and values embedded in religious symbolism and practice (also see R. Joyce, Chapter 7). Ritualized practices are therefore not simply a means through which power is legitimated, but is the very production, negotiation, appropriation, and contestation of power. Archaeological studies that have explored the political implications of the polysemy of religious objects include Van Keuren's (2011) study of ceremonial plazas and the iconography of red-slipped polychrome bowls in the late-prehispanic Southwest, and Urcid's and Joyce's (2014) examination of Late Formative period monumental art and architecture at Monte Albán.

The recognition of the plurality of religious belief and practice, along with their political and ideological implications, has opened the door for viewing religion as a site of struggle, contestation, and negotiation among differentially positioned actors and collectivities (Brumfiel 1996; Carballo 2007; Cutright 2013; Houston et al. 2003; Janusek 2004; Joyce et al. 2001; R. Joyce, Chapter 7; Pauketat and Alt 2003; Piscitelli, Chapter 9). Few studies, however, have explored in detail the fault lines along which political authority and identity were contested and negotiated via religious idioms. For example, McAnany (1995) argues that tension between the institutions of kinship and kingship were played out in rituals involving ancestor veneration and were a major force in Maya political change (also see Carmean 1998; Iannone 2002). Yaeger (2003) argues that tensions surrounding variable identities and affiliations within the Terminal Classic Maya polity of Xunantunich were worked out in religious contexts ranging from rituals at the ceremonial center, feasting in hinterland communities, and the construction of ceremonial complexes by Xunantunich's rulers at outlying sites. While most studies focus on political hierarchies as sources of social tensions that were played out in religious settings, some researchers have highlighted other dimensions of identity as sites of struggle, including gender, kinship, and ethnicity (Alt 2010; Buikstra and Charles 1999; R. Joyce 2000; Potter and Perry 2011). For example, gender was a focal point around which leadership was negotiated through the architectural settings and performance of mortuary ceremony in Mississippian and protohistoric societies of southern Appalachia (Sullivan and Rodning 2001). In Archaic-period Florida, tensions surrounding plural ethnic identities were worked out through the construction and use of ceremonial mounds (Randall and Sassaman 2010; Sassaman 2010).

Religious ritual may also have been a means through which dissatisfaction with or resistance to elite authority were expressed (Janusek 2005; Joyce and Weller 2007; Lucero 2007; Patterson 1986), and evidence from a number of regions indicates that elite and commoner rituals were not always congruent (e.g., Janusek 2004; McAnany 2002; Olson 2007; Smith 2002). For example, Janusek (2004, 2005) argues that within the Tiwanaku polity, ethnic diversity and a degree of local resistance to state authority was expressed via religious idioms that differed in subtle ways from those of the political center. These hidden transcripts of resistance became more public as political and economic conditions unraveled after ca. A.D. 1000, culminating in the ritual destruction of monuments that had assembled key aspects of Tiwanaku state religion and political authority. Rather than viewing religion as a set of social and material relations that arose to stabilize developing political hierarchies, in this volume we encourage the authors to explore religion as a fundamental component of the complex negotiations – simultaneously social, material, and spiritual – through which political life was constituted.

Defining religion/confronting ontology

One reason why American archaeologists have tended to downplay the role of religion in political affairs is the common view that religious belief is inaccessible, while ritual action can be addressed archaeologically. The dichotomy between belief and practice, however, reflects the modernist ontologies that have until recently dominated archaeology (Hodder 2012; Olsen 2010). I view religion as inherently lived, experienced, and practiced such that it cannot be conceptualized as disembodied ideas or beliefs (Aldenderfer 2012; Alt and Pauketat, Chapter 3; Barber, Chapter 5; Hodder 2014; Joyce and Barber 2015; R. Joyce 2011, Chapter 7; Keane 2008; Pauketat 2013; Zedeño, Chapter 13). From this perspective, religious belief and practice as well as the material items and settings in which religion was enacted are inseparable.

Given the lived nature of religion, it is not surprising that many researchers have found it to be a difficult concept to define (Donovan 2003; Fogelin 2007; Insoll 2004:6–7; Rowan 2012:2; Salamone 2006). Universal definitions of religion have been rejected (e.g., Asad 1993), with some scholars suggesting that the concept is a Western construct imposed on non-Western peoples (Fitzgerald 2000; Fowles 2013). Fowles (2013), in his provocative study of Pueblo archaeology and the history of encounters with Euroamericans, embraces the "nontranslatability" of modern, Western definitions of religion and instead explores Puebloan ceremony using the indigenous concept of "doings" (also see Walker, Chapter 11). In particular, authors have critiqued definitions that depend on Western Cartesian dualisms that view religious ritual as irrational, symbolic, and non-functional as opposed to secular, practical actions (Brück 1999). This dichotomy imposes Western views of rationality and Cartesian dualities onto all times and places and ignores other cultural logics that do not distinguish distinct spheres of sacred and profane thought and action (Fowles 2013; Hutson and Stanton 2007; Walker 2002). Many scholars now argue that religion must be addressed in particular historical and cultural settings, although using concepts that allow for comparative study (Bloch 2007:77; Keane 2008; Swenson 2010).

Such a non-Cartesian perspective is exemplified by the relational ontologies of many Native Americans that view humans and most other-than-human entities as animated by a sacred, life-giving force, often referred to in the literature as the "soul" (Barber and Olvera Sánchez 2012; Bray 2009, 2015; Furst 1995; Mills and Ferguson 2008; Sillar 2009; Viveiros de Castro 2004; Zedeño 2009). This existential unity blurs the boundaries between the natural, cultural and divine worlds in contrast to their differentiation in Western worldviews (e.g., Latour 1993; Walker, Chapter 11). People are therefore able to communicate with animate soul-bearing beings that are of relevance to human affairs, including earth, rain, maize, ancestors, animals, mountains, rock outcrops, buildings, time, and myriad other phenomena/ entities. Important transformations in the life cycles of humans and other beings result from ongoing relations among all sorts of animate entities (e.g., Janusek 2012; Joyce and Barber 2015). For example, ceremonial offerings can activate, deactivate, and reactivate humans (Duncan and Hofling 2011; Stross 1998:37–38) and other beings such as buildings (Kunen et al. 2003; Mock 1998; Stanton et al. 2008; Swenson 2015, Chapter 10; Walker 2002; Walker and Lucero 2000). The clothing or covering of objects such as figurines and buildings was also part of animating rituals (e.g., Bray 2009; Stross 1998). Animating actions are not dependent solely on humans in that other-than-human agents, or what Zedeño (2009, Chapter 13) terms, index objects, can also activate or ensoul entities. These index objects include dripping water, blood, red paint, tobacco, spit, breath, marine shells, figurines, wind, jade, ceramic vessels, obsidian, and speleotherms (Barber and Olvera Sánchez 2012; Bray 2009; Brown and Emery 2008; Harrison-Buck 2012; Stross 1998:32–35; Zedeño 2009, 2013:127). Sacred bundles that assemble index objects together with other potent items hold a special significance and power for many Native American groups (Guernsey and Reilly 2007; Hall 1997; Pauketat 2013; Zedeño 2008, Chapter 13). Bundles activated and connected people to sacred forces including those of divinities and ancestors.

Given such a worldview, rituals involving the enactment of a sacred covenant with divinities (e.g., Hamann 2002; A. Joyce 2000; Monaghan 1990), the opening of medicine bundles (Pauketat 2013:47–56), the persecution of witches (Walker 2008), or the ensoulment of buildings (Mock 1998) can clearly be considered examples of rational, practical activity while simultaneously being deeply sacred and symbolic. Likewise, seemingly mundane and practical activities such as farming, trash disposal, and house construction involve communication and negotiation with the divine (Hutson and Stanton 2007; Stross 1998; Swenson 2007). Therefore, religious belief, experience, and practice are difficult to disentangle from most aspects of daily life, including agriculture (Hanks 1990; Monaghan 1990; Swenson 2007), trade and exchange (Foias 2007; Mills 2004), craft production (Bray 2008; Hruby 2007), domesticity (Cutright 2013; Plunket 2002; Robin 2012), rubbish disposal (Hutson and Stanton 2007; Walker 1995), identity (Hendon 2000; Janusek 2004; R. Joyce 2000; Randall and Sassaman 2010), and most importantly for this volume, politics (Alt 2010; Dillehay 2004; Inomata 2006; Janusek 2012; Joyce and Barber 2015; R. Joyce, Chapter 7; Love 1999; Pauketat 2013). There is therefore a decided blurring of the mundane and sacred in the lives of Native Americans.

Following Bell (1992, 1997), I see variation in the degree to which practices strategically and overtly involve communication and negotiation with divinities, regardless of the degree to which they may also be wrapped up in seemingly mundane activities like farming, commensalism, and the disposal of refuse. Bell (1992, 1997) prefers the term ritualization, which she defines as a form of practice that strategically distinguishes itself relative to other actions and through which the sacred and the profane may be differentiated. In her view, however, sacred and profane are situational and are differentiated in the performing of ritualized activities rather than the product of absolute categorical distinctions (Bell 1992:91). Using Bell's terminology, one can then think of both different forms and degrees of ritualization. Like other authors (e.g., Hutson 2010; Hutson and Stanton 2007; Walker 2002), I still see a use for the term ritual to emphasize those practices that are most overtly and strategically focused on the divine, even if the boundary between what is ritual and what is not is decidedly fuzzy. This perspective also allows us to view the distinction between habitual and discursive practices as a continuum, rather than a dichotomy as is sometimes the case in practice-inspired approaches (Swenson 2015:706).

Furthermore, even though Native American ontologies can be generally described as relational and animistic, based primarily on ethnographic and ethnohistoric evidence (Alt and Pauketat, Chapter 3; Rodning, Chapter 4; Viveiros de Castro 2004; Zedeño 2009, Chapter 13), this does not mean that they are invariable or static. Instead, ontologies vary across or even within societies and through time (e.g., Barber, Chapter 5; Harrison-Buck 2012; Swenson 2015; Walker, Chapter 11). As argued by Swenson (2015), ontic constructions are products of social negotiation, including political manipulation, and are not determinative of materialities, ideologies, religious practices, or political formations. Swenson (2015:707) urges that "we must be cautious in ascribing primacy to any one of our categories or in assuming that distinct materialities transparently translate to distinct ontologies or even distinct 'materialisms.'"

A second theme of this volume is to consider the relationship between religion and politics from the perspective of indigenous ontologies, keeping in mind that we cannot assume that any one of these categories is causally primary.

Materiality and the archaeology of religion and politics

The ontologies of Native Americans, which recognize the social and agential potential of both the other-than-human and human worlds, can be effectively explored through theoretical approaches that likewise take a relational perspective to people and things (e.g., Hodder 2012; Miller 2005; Olsen 2010; Tilley et al. 2006). Drawing on the works of phenomenological philosophers (Heidegger 1962; Merleau-Ponty 1962, 1968), studies of the social dimensions of things (Appadurai 1986; Gell 1998; Keane 2005, 2007), and the Actor-Network-Theory of Latour (1993, 2005), scholars have developed relational approaches that challenge the ontological dualisms of modernity (Barad 2007; Henare et al. 2007; Hodder 2012; Miller 2005; Olsen 2010; Olsen et al. 2012; Tilley et al. 2006). These approaches are often glossed as materiality theory, although they include a range of ideas and differences of opinion regarding the degree to which modernist positions should or even can be overcome (cf. Fowles 2013; Meskell 2004; Miller 2005; Olsen 2010:103–104, 154–157; Swenson 2015; Thomas 2004; Webmoor and Witmore 2008). In these perspectives, social life is the outcome of complex networks of relations among people and things that already coexist and are in process rather than emerging from an interaction of distinct entities such as agency and structure (Giles 2010; Joyce and Barber 2015; R. Joyce 2004; Pauketat and Alt 2005). In this view, the central position of humans as social actors is decentered and destabilized through a more serious engagement with the role of things. Instead of a product solely of human relations, social life is seen as a collective in which people and things collaborate and coexist in mixed, hybrid relations (Latour 1993, 2005). Although the practices of human actors as well as issues of power and identity continue to be important in such a perspective, agency, or the ability to make a difference in the world, is dispersed among an array of people and things (Gell 1998; Latour 2005; Strathern 1988; Swenson 2015) that are dynamic and always in motion (Ingold 2011).

Although much of the writing on materiality has emphasized the relationality and mutual constitution of humans and other-than-human entities (e.g., Latour 1993, 2005), it is also crucial to recognize that things have intrinsic properties that are not the result of their place in a relational web (Gibson 1986; Ingold 2007, 2011; Olsen 2010:154–157; Webmoor and Witmore 2008). The material properties of things, their weight, color, form, physicality, and chemical properties exist independent of their relations with people. These properties are crucial for how things are incorporated in relational networks and the agencies that are made possible by human-thing entanglements (Bray 2009; Lechtman 1993; Luke 2012). For example, the physical properties of obsidian afford its usage as a cutting instrument and the properties of fired clay enable its usage as containers and cooking vessels.

Considerations of Peircean semiotics demonstrate that the physical properties of things also enable their semiotic affordances (Keane 2005). Although materials can act as symbols whereby their properties stand in an arbitrary relationship to what they signify, they more frequently take on meanings as indexes and icons where their intrinsic properties make a difference (Peirce 1932). Indexes are signs that are in some way directly connected to or are affected by their referents. For example, the physical scale of monumental buildings indexes the labor involved in their construction (Joyce et al. 2013; Moore 1996). In the case of icons, the sign and the referent bear some degree of sensory resemblance to one another, and hence physical form, color, texture, smell, taste, and other properties in part determine what is signified. Carved stone monuments in Mesoamerica were iconic in that they bore images that physically represented the rulers, deities, and ancestors that they were signifying. Since monuments were often seen as imbued with the vital essence of these beings, they were simultaneously indexical of the things they signified (Houston and Stuart 1998; Just 2005). Yet as discussed by Keane (2005), these semiotic affordances are also inherently political since they require some guidance in terms of what constitutes a sign and how signs function in the world. Keane (2005:190–191) terms these assumptions semiotic ideologies, which include such fundamental and politically significant issues as what kinds of agents are able to author signs (e.g., humans, deities, ancestors) and the role of intentionality in signification.

From this perspective, humans and other-than-human things have a symmetrical relationship such that things take on a more active role in social change than in previous approaches. Things, including people, are viewed as mediators in social processes rather than as passive reflections of forms of social organization, social relations, or cultural ideas. Things individually and in their interrelationships with people and other things afford, enable, transform, and persuade different possibilities of action and meaning (Hodder 2012; Webmoor and Witmore 2008). The durability and persistence of things also provide a degree of stability and concreteness to social life. Things can facilitate certain actions and meanings as well as gather and sediment different pasts that condition social life in the present (Swenson, Chapter 10). For example, in both greater Cahokia and Chaco, ruins of earlier ceremonial constructions still visible on the landscape allowed eleventh century communities to establish connections with the past through the construction of ceremonial alignments and roadways (Pauketat 2013:155–159; Van Dyke 2003). These connections entangled the present day with powerful places and people from the past in ways that contributed to the constitution of inequality and social power (also see Hamann 2002). Things can not only afford, but also object to and constrain human projects, thereby drawing attention to the ways in which things, including people, can be considered actors in social life. Joyce and Barber (2015) argue that the emplacement of human bodies and ceremonial offerings in public buildings were fundamental to the instantiation of community in later Formative period coastal Oaxaca. The physical entrapment of these things within public buildings at multiple communities in the region constrained the ability of rulers at the urban center of Río Viejo to extend multi-community links and political influence in ways that elsewhere created regional polities. From this perspective, networks of human and other-than-human things constitute social entities such as agency, community, and society that have often been reified and essentialized in archaeological theorizing.

Material things therefore play an indispensable role in the constitution, stabilization, and transformation of social life (Gell 1998; Hodder 2012:26; Olsen 2010:139–149; Strathern 1990), and hence are inextricably caught up in the kinds of political formations and transformations that the authors examine in this book. In the ancient Americas, complex societies were co-produced, materially anchored, and given a degree of stability and persistence through the work of many things linked to religious belief and practice, such as public plazas and buildings, carved stone monuments, burials and tombs, sacred bundles, divinities, macaws, ancestor shrines, and musical instruments (Alt and Pauketat, Chapter 3; Barber, Chapter 5; Barber and Joyce 2007; Barber and Olvera 2012; Gruner, Chapter 2; Hendon 2000; Hutson et al., Chapter 8; A. Joyce 2009; R. Joyce 2004; Joyce et al. 1991; Love 1999; Pauketat 2013). Political power, dominance, and social distinctions depended on people's access to these materials as well as cooperation, competition, and conflict surrounding their joint production, consumption, transformation, holding, storage, exchange, and disposal. Although many of the items mentioned above certainly represented social distinctions and institutions that were fundamental to the constitution of social life, things were more than simply symbols of a pre-existing social reality: through entanglements with people, they were co-producers of that society (Latour 1993, 2005). For example, certain things continuously draw attention to themselves because they are exotic, rare, highly valued, or have unusual properties (Kopytoff 1986; Olsen 2010:74; Miller 1998), and this may be especially true for many items categorized as religious in nature. These items may require special care or become inalienable or aestheticized (Barber et al.

2014). Items such as *Spondylus* shells, monumental carved stones, ceramic figurines, clay masks, ceremonial censers, post-shrines, and prayer sticks are among some of the objects that we will discuss in this volume that undoubtedly by their very nature drew people's attention and reflection.

In addition to the exotic or rare qualities of things, the context in which an item is encountered can make otherwise mundane things semiotically and emotionally charged in ways that bring them toward discursive reflection and reorient them within new relational fields. This is particularly true for ritual settings, religious or otherwise. For example, using Bell's (1992) terminology, strategies of ritualization vary greatly but usually involve proper staging, performance, and material actors, and may also involve ritual specialists who have special knowledge and abilities. Ritualization can transform the agency of otherwise mundane things into sacred objects that in turn establish other relational networks and activate other agencies. For example, in the ancient Americas, even mundane items like ceramic vessels, breath, or spit could in certain ritualized contexts act as index objects that animated other things like buildings, sacred bundles, and even people (Joyce and Barber 2015; Mock 1998; Zedeño 2008, 2009). Human bodies as well as other-than-human things are also transformed through ritualized action (Bell 1992:98–101; R. Joyce, Chapter 7). For example, at the site of Las Canoas, Honduras, the use of objects like anthropomorphic figurines and restricted ceremonial spaces by religious specialists produced ritualized bodies that dominated these settings and contributed to the ability of these specialists to negotiate a degree of prestige and political authority (Stockett 2007). The bodies of participants in ceremonies were in turn subordinated through their exclusion from certain spaces, acts, and knowledge. Ritualization therefore appropriates and culturally schools the social body, although in ways that are open to negotiation and resistance (Bell 1992:215).

The third theme of this volume is to consider the implications of theories of materiality for how we understand the interrelationship of religion and politics in the ancient Americas. By considering the involvement of religious practices, objects, and beliefs in the entanglements through which political formations were instantiated, the chapter authors consider both the ways in which politics were negotiated and the ontological implications of their approaches to precolumbian religion. In the next section, I summarize the contents of the volume and discuss how the chapters approach the themes of integration, ontology, and materiality.

Volume overview

Each of the chapters focuses on at least one of the three themes that organize the volume: (1) To move beyond a focus on religion as a means of political integration; (2) to consider Native American religion from the perspective of indigenous ontologies; and (3) to consider the archaeology of religion and politics from the perspective of theories of materiality.

The chapters in the volume move beyond traditional archaeological approaches that view religion as either unrelated to politics or as fulfilling a largely passive,

secondary role as an aspect of dominant ideologies through which political authority was legitimated. Instead, chapter authors view religion as inseparable from
political life in the ancient Americas, and many of the authors provide case studies
for the ways in which religion was at the center of political life. This perspective is exemplified by Susan Alt and Timothy Pauketat (Chapter 3), who argue
that religion more than politics *per se* was central to the rapid development of
Cahokia into an urban center that reshaped the history of large parts of the American Midwest. The complex entanglements of religious festivals, pilgrimage circuits,
shrines, smoking-pipe bowls, divinities, and other animate beings that converged
on Cahokia reshuffled powers, simultaneously divine and worldly, in ways that
transformed political life. Through the effective use of analogies with modern
Puebloan religion, Erina Gruner (Chapter 2) shows how religion was central to
post-Chacoan social and political change in the American Southwest. She suggests that members of prominent lineages empowered by religious knowledge and
sacred objects left Chaco Canyon to establish themselves as founders at important outlier communities in ways that resembled earlier founders' cults at Pueblo
Bonito. Although premised on material assemblages through which the earlier
founders' cults were based, these post-Chacoan communities differed from Chaco
in patterns of political authority and long-distance trade. Jerry Moore (Chapter 12)
argues that after A.D. 300, political responses by ancient Andean peoples to periods of drought involved a suite of entangled practices, including hydraulic rituals
as well as changes in agriculture, settlement, and land use. Christopher Rodning
(Chapter 4) argues that political decisions in contact-period Cherokee communities were negotiated during council meetings held in townhouses built on the
summits of platform mounds. These meetings stressed consensus and compromise,
concepts that were central to Cherokee religion, particularly as manifest by the
"everlasting fires" that burned within townhouse hearths and which were sources
of spiritual power and stability. As discussed by Zedeño (Chapter 13), religious
changes across the Great Plains were closely tied to community needs, particularly
surrounding bison hunting, and hence were fundamentally political. No need was
perhaps as critical and transformative as responding to the arrival of Europeans and
the novel commodities, trade relations, and epidemic diseases that they brought.
The result included both religious innovations, such as the Ghost Dance Religion,
and dramatic political transformations.

Sarah Barber (Chapter 5) argues that religious authority in initial Early Formative period Soconusco may have been fundamental to the constitution of political
authority and created social distinctions and opportunities that eventually led to
economic inequalities. At Paso de la Amada, variation in access to the divine is seen
in five residences that were significantly larger than typical ones, but which were
not unusual in terms of quantities of social valuables. Most of these residences were
elevated on low platforms and included high frequencies of objects such as hollow
figurines that were likely conduits through which residents communicated with
divine beings and forces. These houses also had formal, cleared spaces, where people likely gathered for ritual performances. Another indication of social distinctions

surrounding access to the divine was solid ceramic figurines depicting elaborately dressed individuals, usually elders, seated on stools and often wearing masks. Barber suggests that, over time, the distinction between the authority of divine beings and that of the people responsible for communicating with those beings diminished, endowing certain individuals or lineages with enduring political authority.

Several of the chapters exemplify Bell's (1992) arguments that the polysemy of ritualized practices and entities has the potential to both forge social solidarity and create points of difference with the potential for creating social tension and conflict. In two case studies from the ancient Maya of the Yucatan Peninsula, Scott Hutson, Céline Lamb, and David Medina Arona (Chapter 8) make the important point that people in complex societies engage in political relations on a variety of scales, multiplying the complexity of the intersection between religion and politics. In the case of Late Preclassic communities linked by the Ucí-Cansahcab causeway, similarities were found in ceremonial caching practices across the political spectrum. Rather than indicating that the people at the bottom of the political hierarchy were duped by a dominant ideology, Hutson and colleagues argue that people were empowered by their knowledge of principles that guided the ensoulment of buildings. Subordinates were therefore capable of evaluating the ceremonial performances of rulers in ways that increased their leverage in negotiations with leaders. In contrast, at the Classic-period city of Chunchucmil, Hutson and colleagues argue that the uniqueness of ancestor shrines across commoner households indicates inter-household competition in ceremonial displays of status and identity. Paradoxically, this competition undercut possibilities for forming strong political coalitions that could have enhanced the ability of commoners to negotiate or contest relations with elites.

Similarly, David Carballo (Chapter 6) considers variability in religious belief and practice with a focus on the site of La Laguna, Tlaxcala. He finds that public buildings and spaces, as well as a water/fire dualism in conceptualizations of important deities, both integrated and differentiated Central Mexican society. Over time, Carballo finds strong continuities in ceremonies involving cosmogenesis, existential dualisms, and fertility cycles that fostered group solidarity, while rituals that instantiated group divisions based on lineage, status, and community were more variable. He also documents the ways in which specific deity complexes could be appropriated for political ends in Central Mexico's urban centers. This contrast between integration and differentiation is also present in Matthew Piscitelli's chapter (Chapter 9) on the Mound B2 platform at the Late Archaic period site of Huaricanga on the coast of Peru. In contrast to large public buildings that were a focus of ceremonies that instantiated centralized authority, several small ceremonial buildings on Mound B2 were a locus for religious practices through which different social groups negotiated status and identity. Rosemary Joyce (Chapter 7) argues that the emergence of more exclusionary and unequal forms of political authority in Formative-period Honduras was promoted through religious innovations involving participation of select families in far-reaching networks of ritualized practices and objects. Joyce argues that the nature of Formative-period religion made it easier to promote political change via religious innovation than through political strategizing sanctioned after-the-fact by religious ideology. That claims to status and political power created social tensions that eventually led to the failure of hierarchy shows that religion can also be a site of social tension and struggle.

Most of the chapters in the volume exemplify the recent "ontological turn" in archaeology and the ways in which scholars are moving beyond Cartesian dualities that differentiate religion from ritual, belief from practice, idea from material, and sacred from profane. As emphasized by Alt and Pauketat (Chapter 3), the relational ontologies of many Native American groups view power as imbuing relations among humans and other-than-human entities. All sorts of human and other beings were seen as animated by a life-giving force, and the most powerful among these could act as index objects with the ability to animate other beings (Zedeño 2009) or as witnesses with the ability to communicate and mediate between people and other animate beings (Pauketat 2013). Such objects included young women, animals, and copper artifacts offered as sacrifices to animate or close Moche ceremonial buildings at Huaca Colorada (Swenson, Chapter 10); *Spondylus* shells in the Andes (Moore, Chapter 12); Chacoan founders and the macaws, prayer sticks, turquoise, and other sacred objects curated with them (Gruner, Chapter 2); and clay masks in Early Formative Soconusco (Barber, Chapter 5). María Nieves Zedeño (Chapter 13) reminds us that evidence of these animistic forces has great historical depth, dating to as early as the Paleoindian period, and so these forces may have been fundamental to the religious lives of the earliest Amerindian peoples. Since all living beings share an animating force, distinctions among them are more fluid, such as among the Amazonian peoples discussed by John Walker (Chapter 11), where domesticated plants as well as human offspring were considered children. This relationality also allows beings to transform from one state of being to another, such as in practices of nahualism, tonalism, and life-cycle ceremonies across the Americas (Gutiérrez and Pye 2010; R. Joyce, Chapter 7).

Likewise, people, places, and things could be focal nodes or bundles (see Zedeño, Chapter 13) that concentrated animate powers. For example, ceremonial buildings were often considered to be powerful animate beings that assembled varied entities such as people, divinities, ancestors, celestial bodies, life, death, and time. Examples discussed by the authors include Mississippian shrines (Alt and Pauketat, Chapter 3), Moche ceremonial buildings (Swenson, Chapter 10), Chacoan Kivas (Gruner, Chapter 2), Cherokee townhouses (Rodning, Chapter 4), Mojo forest islands (Walker, Chapter 11), and small ceremonial structures in Peru (Piscitelli, Chapter 9). In the Early Formative Soconusco, elaborate houses bundled people, sacred objects, and ceremonial practices in ways that brought forth divinities (Barber, Chapter 5). The assemblages through which divinities were manifest were gradually transferred from special houses to public spaces in ways that expanded the scale and reach of these communities of religious practice. As discussed by Moore (Chapter 12), in the ancient Andes, *Spondylus* shells assembled water, hydraulic systems, agricultural fertility, and divinities. *Spondylus* shells were powerful mediators deployed in rituals designed to bring rain and fertility as well as perhaps to animate buildings and other entities. In addition to sacred objects and ceremonial buildings, people including Mississippian religious specialists (Alt and Pauketat, Chapter 3) and participants in far-reaching religious networks in Formative-period Honduras (R. Joyce, Chapter 7) could be powerful mediators assembling and concentrating animate beings and forces. Ancestors as well as the "living" were seen as animate beings with abilities to impact the world, including Chacoan founders (Gruner, Chapter 2), Maya ancestors worshipped in household shrines (Hutson et al., Chapter 8), and perhaps burials associated with Cherokee townhouses (Rodning, Chapter 4).

Several authors draw on the work of Catherine Bell (1992, 1997) in viewing ritualized practices as strategically set off from other activities. As discussed in most of the chapters, rituals often involve special staging and knowledge, and can assemble an array of animate beings that together have the potential to affect the world in powerful ways. Through ritualized practices and settings, relations among animate beings may be negotiated and transformed such as in the ritual animation of buildings (see Gruner, Chapter 2; Hutson et al., Chapter 8; Swenson, Chapter 10) and in Mesoamerican rituals that petitioned divinities for fertility and well-being (Carballo, Chapter 6; Hutson et al., Chapter 8). Likewise, ritualized practices are often settings where distinctions among humans are negotiated and transformed in ways that are inherently political. Depending on factors such as specialized knowledge and experience, familial ties, and ancestry, people's relations with other animate beings often varied, and this generated the potential for the creation and transformation of social distinctions, including unequal ones. For example, as discussed by Rosemary Joyce (Chapter 7) for Formative-period Honduras, families that established ties to an extensive religious community that reached as far as Central Mexico gained access to ritualized practices, animate objects, and religious knowledge that included distinctive costuming, monumental architecture, and human figural sculpture. These objects and practices differentiated members of this cosmopolitan religious community from other people in their villages and began to support claims to power and authority.

Yet as discussed by Hutson and colleagues (Chapter 8), Swenson (Chapter 10), and Walker (Chapter 11), animate beings and forces pervade social life ranging from the sorts of ceremonial performances that archaeologists have traditionally thought of as religious to everyday practices involving farming, trash disposal, craft production, and domestic chores. Therefore, all practices, whether ritualized or not, involve relations with other-than-human animate beings. Thus, as discussed in many of the chapters, religion is inherently lived and experienced and so is inseparable from other dimensions of social life traditionally viewed as distinct, including politics (see Barber, Chapter 5; Hutson et al., Chapter 8; R. Joyce, Chapter 7; Rodning, Chapter 4; Swenson, Chapter 10). For example, ritual feasts carried out on ceremonial architecture at Late Moche sites were examples of the kinds of dramatic ritual performances that we typically associated with religion (Swenson, Chapter 10). These rituals, however, also entangled a far-reaching array of more quotidian practices, including the scheduling of seasonal movements, food preparation, craft production, weaving, waste disposal, and llama breeding. Likewise, drawing on the work of Charles Peirce, Rosemary Joyce (Chapter 7) traces how people, objects, and practices in Formative-period Honduras were entangled and ritualized through semiotic associations involving iconicity and indexicality. She shows how the ritualized burial of shell belts, obsidian, pottery vessels, and human remains below house floors indexed and extended the effect of ritualization to everyday practices, such as the sharing of meals, bodily ornamentation, and the knapping of obsidian.

The relationality of Native American ontologies is also congruent with approaches emanating from materiality theory, which constitutes the third theme of the volume. As discussed by several authors, rather than solely the result of human relationships; communities, polities, and political institutions in the Americas were co-produced, materially anchored, and given a degree of stability and persistence through the work of many things linked to religious belief and practice. These authors exemplify the emphasis in materiality theory on moving away from representational perspectives that view material culture as simply representing social institutions, societal types, political strategies, or shared meanings. Instead, material things are given an active role in constituting social life via their entanglements with people.

For example, Alt and Pauketat (Chapter 3) show how shrine sites, found throughout the Cahokian world, were centered on an array of lunar-aligned earthen ceremonial buildings that brought together pilgrims and powerful animate forces or beings such as earth, sky, and moon during ceremonies tied to lunar events. Cahokia was the centerpiece of this cosmic convergence with its massive ceremonial architecture, which hosted rituals that drew in thousands of people. Shrine sites were likely connected to Cahokia via a ceremonial circuit, and in some cases through processional pathways. Since these shrine sites were established very early in the history of Cahokia, they could not have simply represented Cahokia's political institutions already formed. Instead, Cahokia and its network of shrines assembled a vast array of people, practices, experiences, and things that came to constitute a shared vision of the cosmos and a broader Cahokian identity that facilitated the creation of political authority and inequality.

Perhaps distantly related to the Cahokian shrines, the Cherokee townhouses discussed by Rodning (Chapter 4) were also *axis mundi* that brought together earth, sky, and underworld. Like at Cahokia, these ceremonial buildings were focal points for the constitution of community through the bundling of people, labor, time, ancestors, offerings, and sacred fire. The evidence for cycles of rebirth and renewal of the townhouses indicates that they were viewed as animate beings. Townhouses were sources of spiritual power, particularly as manifest in the constant fire that burned in their hearths, conferring balance and stability to the community. Like the ceremonial buildings discussed in these North American examples, the Amazonian forest islands considered by John Walker (Chapter 11) were also focal points in the constitution of communities, consisting of people, plants, animals, spirits, ancestors, mounds, and fields.

Gruner (Chapter 2) shows that the ability of certain lineages to establish themselves as founders and solidify their authority in Chacoan and post-Chacoan communities was dependent on the assemblage of a variety of powerful entities emplaced with burials of possible founding ancestors. These entities included the remains of the ancestors, effigy bows and arrows, prayer sticks, and exotic imported items, including macaws and shell ornaments. These items may have been assembled as sacred bundles that empowered founding lineages through time.

Several chapters discuss the ways in which the material and spatial configuration of ceremonial architecture can facilitate and stabilize social differences. For example, Carballo (Chapter 6) describes the ways in which paired temple-plaza complexes in Central Mexico drew people together in large-scale ritual. At the same time, the spatial separation of those with access to elevated and restricted temples could differentiate participants, subordinating those denied access. Likewise, restricted rituals carried out in small ceremonial buildings at Huaricanga discussed by Piscitelli (Chapter 9) may have instantiated social divisions while empowering factions in negotiations with polity leaders. In their discussion of ancestor veneration at Chunchucmil, Hutson and colleagues (Chapter 8) show that variability in ancestor shrines were more than simply representations of differences in status and identity. Instead, the style and elaboration of the shrines, as well as the ceremonies staged within them, were central to the constitution and transformation of these distinctions.

Swenson (Chapter 10) shows that temporal regimes were stabilized and politicized through ritualized practices and objects involved in large-scale feasting, and building dedication and termination ceremonies periodically staged at Huaca Colorada. These ceremonies in turn synchronized, ritualized, and entangled an array of quotidian practices required in the preparation and aftermath of ceremonies that are not usually seen as religious, such as food preparation, craft production, and waste disposal. The monumental buildings as well as sacrificial victims and copper offerings emplaced within them during ceremonies of rebirth and renovation therefore charted, communicated, and regulated temporal cycles extending far beyond the ceremonies at Huaca Colorada. This temporal regime was profoundly political as well in that it exerted control over the activities and lifecycles of people throughout the region. In fact, Swenson shows that these temporal structures persisted long after the decline of the political and religious elites who had staged the large-scale ceremonies, as people continued to return periodically to the site to carry out more modest feasting events. Swenson's study shows that public ceremony can affect political life in ways that result in historical continuity, rather than transformation.

In the final chapter, Zedeño (Chapter 13) takes stock of the volume and identifies five themes that demonstrate the inseparability of religion and politics as exemplified by the volume's contributions: essence and experience, dynamics of religious practice, religious communities, contexts of religious practice, and objects of religious practice. Her synthetic treatment of the chapters further highlights the innovative perspectives that are emerging in the archaeology of religion and politics in the Americas.

Acknowledgments

The editors would like to thank The Historical Society for a Religion and Innovation in Human Affairs Grant (funded by the Templeton Foundation) that contributed to the completion of this volume.

References

Aldenderfer, Mark 1993 Ritual, Hierarchy and Change in Foraging Societies. *Journal of Anthropological Archaeology* 12(1): 1–40.

———. 2012 Envisioning a Pragmatic Approach to the Archaeology of Religion. In *Beyond Belief: The Archaeology of Religion and Ritual*, edited by Yorke M. Rowan, pp. 23–36. Archeological Papers of the American Anthropological Association 21, Arlington, VA.

Alt, Susan M. 2010 Complexity in action(s): Retelling the Cahokia story. In *Ancient Complexities: New Perspectives in PreColumbian North America*, edited by Susan M. Alt, pp. 119–137. University of Utah Press, Salt Lake City.

Appadurai, Arjun 1986 Introduction: Commodities and the Politics of Value. In *The Social Life of Things: Commodities in Cultural Perspective*, edited by Arjun Appadurai, pp. 64–91. Cambridge University Press, Cambridge.

Asad, Talal 1993 *Genealogies of Religion: Discipline and Reasons of Power in Christianity and Islam*. John Hopkins University Press, Baltimore.

Ashmore, Wendy 1991 Site-Planning Principles and Concepts of Directionality Among the Ancient Maya. *Latin American Antiquity* 2: 199–226.

Barad, Karen 2007 *Meeting the Universe Halfway*. Duke University Press, Durham.

Barber, Sarah B., and Arthur A. Joyce 2007 Polity Produced and Community Consumed: Negotiating Political Centralization in the Lower Río Verde Valley, Oaxaca. In *Mesoamerican Ritual Economy*, edited by E. Christian Wells and Karla L. Davis-Salazar, pp. 221–244. University Press of Colorado, Boulder.

Barber, Sarah B., and Mireya Olvera Sánchez 2012 A Divine Wind: The Arts of Death and Music in Terminal Formative Oaxaca. *Ancient Mesoamerica* 23(1): 9–24.

Barber, Sarah B., Andrew Workinger, and Arthur Joyce 2014 Situational Inalienability and Social Change in Formative Period Coastal Oaxaca. In *Inalienable Possessions in the Archaeology of Mesoamerica*, edited by Brigitte Kovacevich and Michael G. Callaghan, pp. 38–53. American Anthropological Association, Washington, DC.

Bell, Catherine 1992 *Ritual Theory, Ritual Practice*. Oxford University Press, New York.

———. 1997 *Ritual: Perspectives and Dimensions*. Oxford University Press, Oxford.

Binford, Lewis R. 1962 Archaeology as Anthropology. *American Antiquity* 28: 217–225.

Blackmore, Chelsea 2011 Ritual Among the Masses: Deconstructing Identity and Class in an Ancient Maya Neighborhood. *Latin American Antiquity* 22: 159–177.

Bloch, Maurice 2007 Durkheimian Anthropology and Religion: Going In and Out of Each Other's Bodies. In *Religion, Anthropology, and Cognitive Science*, edited by Harvey Whitehouse and James Laidlaw, pp. 63–80. Carolina Academic Press, Durham.

Bray, Tamara L. 2008 Exploring Inca State Religion through Material Metaphor. In *Religion, Archaeology and the Material World*, edited by Lars Fogelin, pp. 118–138. Center for Archaeological Investigations, Southern Illinois University, Carbondale.

———. 2009 An Archaeological Perspective on the Andean Concept of *Camaquen*: Thinking Through Late Precolumbian Ofrendas and Huacas. *Cambridge Archaeological Journal* 19: 357–368.

———. 2015 Andean Wak'as and Alternative Configurations of Persons, Power, and Things. In *The Archaeology of Wak'as: Explorations of the Sacred in the Precolumbian Andes*, edited by Tamara L. Bray, pp. 3–19. University Press of Colorado, Boulder.

Brown, Linda A. 2000 From Discard to Divination: Demarcating the Sacred Through the Collection and Curation of Used and/or Discarded Objects. *Latin American Antiquity* 11: 319–333.

Brown, Linda A., Scott Simmons, and Payson Sheets 2002 Household Production of Extra-Household Ritual at the Cerén Site, El Salvador. In *Domestic Ritual in Mesoamerica*, edited by Patricia Plunket, pp. 83–92. University of California Press, Los Angeles.

Brown, Linda A., and Kitty F. Emery 2008 Negotiations With the Animate Forest: Hunting Shrines in the Guatemalan Highlands. *Journal of Archaeological Method and Theory* 15: 300–337.

Brück, Joanna 1999 Ritual and Rationality: Some Problems of Interpretation in European Archaeology. *European Journal of Archaeology* 2: 313–344.

Brumfiel, Elizabeth M. 1996 Figurines and the Aztec State: Testing the Effectiveness of Ideological Domination. In *Gender and Archaeology*, edited by Rita T. Wright, pp. 143–166. University of Pennsylvania Press, Philadelphia.

———. 2011 Technologies of Time: Calendrics and Commoners in Postclassic Mexico. *Ancient Mesoamerica* 22: 53–70.

Buikstra, Jane E., and Douglas K. Charles 1999 Centering the Ancestors: Cemeteries, Mounds, and Sacred Landscapes of the Ancient North American Midcontinent. In *Archaeologies of Landscape*, edited by Wendy Ashmore and A. Bernard Knapp, pp. 201–228. Blackwell Publishers, Malden.

Carballo, David M. 2007 Effigy Vessels, Religious Integration, and the Origins of the Central Mexican Pantheon. *Ancient Mesoamerica* 18: 53–67.

Carmean, Kelli 1998 Leadership at Sayil: A Study of Political and Religious Decentralization. *Ancient Mesoamerica* 9: 259–270.

Conrad, Geoffrey W., and Arthur A. Demarest 1984 *Religion and Empire: The Dynamics of Aztec and Inca Expansionism*. Cambridge University Press, Cambridge.

Cutright, Robyn E. 2013 Assessing Household and Community Ritual at a Late Intermediate Period Village, Jequetepeque Valley, Peru. *Ñawpa Pacha* 33(1): 1–21.

Dillehay, Tom D. 2004 Social Landscape and Ritual Pause: Uncertainty and Integration in Formative Peru. *Journal of Social Archaeology* 4: 239–268.

Donovan, James M. 2003 Defining Religion. In *Selected Readings in the Anthropology of Religion: Theoretical and Methodological Essays*, edited by Stephen D. Glazier and Charles A. Flowerday, pp. 61–98. Praeger, Westport, CT.

Drennan, Robert D. 1976 Religion and Social Evolution in Formative Mesoamerica. In *The Early Mesoamerican Village*, edited by Kent V. Flannery, pp. 345–368. Academic Press, New York.

———. 1983 Ritual and Ceremonial Development at the Early Village Level. In *The Cloud People: Divergent Evolution of the Zapotec and Mixtec Civilization*, edited by Kent V. Flannery and Joyce Marcus, pp. 46–50. Academic Press, New York.

Duncan, William N., and Charles Andrew Hofling 2011 Why the Head? Cranial Modification as Protection and Ensoulment Among the Maya. *Ancient Mesoamerica* 22: 199–210.

Emerson, Thomas E. 1997 *Cahokia and the Archaeology of Power*. The University of Alabama Press, Tuscaloosa.

Fernandez, James W. 1965 Symbolic Consensus in a Fang Reformative Cult. *American Anthropologist* 67: 902–929.

Fitzgerald, Timothy 2000 *The Ideology of Religious Studies*. Oxford University Press, New York.

Flannery, Kent V. 1968 The Olmec and the Valley of Oaxaca: A Model for Interregional Interaction in Formative Times. In *Dumbarton Oaks Conference on the Olmec*, edited by Elizabeth P. Benson, pp. 79–117. Dumbarton Oaks Research Library and Collection, Washington, DC.

———. 1976 Contextual Analysis of Ritual Paraphernalia From Formative Oaxaca. In *The Early Mesoamerican Village*, edited by Kent V. Flannery, pp. 333–345. Academic Press, New York.

Flannery, Kent V., and Joyce Marcus 1976 Formative Oaxaca and the Zapotec Cosmos. *American Scientist* 64: 374–83.

Fogelin, Lars 2007 The Archaeology of Religious Ritual. *Annual Review of Anthropology* 36: 55–71.

Foias, Antonia E. 2007 Ritual, Politics, and Pottery Economics in the Classic Maya Southern Lowlands. In *Commoner Ritual and Ideology in Ancient Mesoamerica*, edited by Nancy Gonlin and Jon C. Lohse, pp. 167–194. University Press of Colorado, Boulder.

Fowles, Severin M. 2013 *An Archaeology of Doings: Secularism and the Study of Pueblo Religion*. SAR Press, Santa Fe.

Freidel, David A., and Linda Schele 1988 Kingship in the Late Preclassic Maya Lowlands. *American Anthropologist* 90: 547–567.

Fritz, John 1978 Paleopsychology Today: Ideational Systems and Human Adaptation in Prehistory. In *Social Archeology, Beyond Subsistence and Dating*, edited by Charles L. Redman, Mary Jane Berman, Edward V. Curtin, William T. Langhorne, Jr., Nina M. Versaggi, and Jeffrey C. Wanser, pp. 303–313. Academic Press, New York.

Furst, Jill L. 1995 *The Natural History of the Soul in Ancient Mexico*. Yale University Press, New Haven, CT.

Gell, Alfred 1998 *Art and Agency: An Anthropological Theory*. Clarendon, Oxford.

Gibson, James J. 1986 *The Ecological Approach to Visual Perception*. Lawrence Erlbaum, Hillsdale, NJ.

Giles, Bretton 2010 Sacrificing Complexity: Renewal Through Ohio Hopewell Rituals. In *Ancient Complexities: New Perspectives in PreColumbian North America*, edited by Susan M. Alt, pp. 73–95. University of Utah Press, Salt Lake City.

Gonlin, Nancy 2007 Ritual and Ideology Among Classic Maya Rural Commoners at Copán, Honduras. In *Commoner Ritual and Ideology in Ancient Mesoamerica*, edited by Nancy Gonlin and Jon C. Lohse, pp. 83–121. University Press of Colorado, Boulder.

Gonlin, Nancy, and Jon C. Lohse, eds. 2007 *Commoner Ritual and Ideology in Ancient Mesoamerica*. University Press of Colorado, Boulder.

Guernsey, Julia, and F. Kent Reilly III, eds. 2007 *Sacred Bindings of the Cosmos: Ritual Acts of Bundling and Wrapping in Ancient Mesoamerica*. Boundary End Archaeology Research Center Press, Barnardsville, NC.

Gutiérrez, Gerardo, and Mary E. Pye 2010 The Iconography of the Nahual: Human-Animal Transformations in Preclassic Guerrero and Morelos. In *The Place of Sculpture in Mesoamerica's Preclassic Transition: Context, Use, and Meaning*, edited by John Clark, Julia Guernsey, and Barbara Arroyo, pp. 27–54. Dumbarton Oaks Research Library and Collection, Washington, DC.

Hall, Robert L. 1997 *An Archaeology of the Soul: North American Indian Belief and Ritual*. University of Illinois Press, Urbana.

Hamann, Byron Ellsworth 2002 The Social Life of Pre-Sunrise Things. *Current Anthropology* 43: 351–382.

Hanks, William F. 1990 *Referential Practice: Language and Lived Space Among the Maya*. University of Chicago Press, Chicago.

Harrison-Buck, Eleanor 2012 Architecture as Animate Landscape: Circular Shrines in the Ancient Maya Lowlands. *American Anthropologist* 114: 64–80.

Heidegger, Martin 1962 *Being and Time*. Harper and Row, New York.

Henare, Amiria, Martin Holbraad, and Sari Wastell, eds. 2007 *Thinking Through Things: Theorizing Artefacts Ethnographically*. Routledge, London.

Hendon, Julia A. 2000 Having and holding: Storage, Memory, Knowledge, and Social Relations. *American Anthropologist* 102: 42–53.

Hodder, Ian 2012 *Entangled: An Archaeology of the Relationship Between Humans and Things*. Wiley-Blackwell, Malden, MA.

Hodder, Ian, ed. 2014 *Religion at Work in a Neolithic Society: Vital Matters*. Cambridge University Press, Cambridge.

Houston, Stephen 1993 *Hieroglyphs and History at Dos Pilas: Dynastic Politics of the Classic Maya*. University of Texas Press, Austin.

Houston, Stephen, Héctor Escobeda, Mark Child, Charles Golden, and René Muñoz 2003 The Moral Community: Maya Settlement Transformation at Piedras Negras, Guatemala. In *The Social Construction of Ancient Cities*, edited by Monica L. Smith, pp. 212–253. Smithsonian Books, Washington and London.

Houston, Stephen D., and David Stuart 1998 The Ancient Maya Self: Personhood and Portraiture in the Classic Period. *RES Anthropology and Aesthetics* 33: 73–101.

Hruby, Zachary X. 2007 Ritualized Chipped-Stone Production at Piedras Negras, Guatemala. In *Rethinking Craft Specialization in Complex Societies: Archaeological Analyses of the Social Meaning of Production*, edited by Zachary X. Hruby and Rowan K. Flad, pp. 68–87. Archeological Papers of the American Anthropological Association vol. 17. American Anthropological Association, Arlington, VA.

Hutson, Scott R. 2010 *Dwelling, Identity, and the Maya: Relational Archaeology at Chunchucmil*. Altamira Press, Lanham, MD.

Hutson, Scott R., and Travis W. Stanton 2007 Cultural Logic and Practical Reason: The Structure of Discard in Ancient Maya Houselots. *Cambridge Archaeological Journal* 17: 123–144.

Iannone, Gyles 2002 Annales History and the Ancient Maya State: Some Observations on the "Dynamic Model". *American Anthropologist* 104(1): 68–78.

Ingold, Tim 2007 Materials Against Materiality. *Archaeological Dialogues* 14(1): 1–16.

———. 2011 *Being Alive: Essays on Movement, Knowledge and Description*. Routledge, London.

Inomata, Takeshi 2006 Plazas, Performers, and Spectators: Political Theaters of the Classic Maya. *Current Anthropology* 47: 805–842.

Insoll Timothy 2004 *Archaeology, Ritual, Religion*. Routledge, London.

Isbell, William J. 1978 Cosmological Order Expressed in Ceremonial Centers. In *Actes du XLIIe Congrés International des Américanistes*, vol. IV, pp. 269–297. Musée de l'Homme, Paris.

Janusek, John Wayne 2004 *Identity and Power in the Ancient Andes*. Routledge Press, New York.

———. 2005 Collapse as Cultural Revolution: Power and Identity in the Tiwanaku to Pacajes Transition. In *Foundations of Power in the Prehispanic Andes*, edited by Kevin J. Vaughn, Dennis Ogburn, and Christina A. Conlee, pp. 175–209. Archaeological Papers of the American Anthropological Association 14, Washington, DC.

———. 2006 The Changing 'nature' of Tiwanaku Religion and the Rise of an Andean State. *World Archaeology* 38: 469–492.

———. 2009 Residence and Ritual in Tiwanaku: Hierarchy, Specialization, Ethnicity, and Ceremony. In *Domestic Life in Prehispanic Capitals: A Study of Specialization, Hierarchy, and Ethnicity*, edited by Linda R. Manzanilla and Claude Chapdelaine, pp. 149–169. Memoirs of the Museum of Anthropology University of Michigan Number 46, Ann Arbor.

———. 2012 Understanding Tiwanaku Origins: Animistic Ecology in the Andean Altiplano. In *The Past Ahead: Language, Culture, and Identity in the Neotropics*, edited by Christian Isendahl, pp. 111–138. Uppsala University, Uppsala.

Jennings, Justin 2003 The Fragility of Imperialist Ideology and the End of Local Traditions, an Inca Example. *Cambridge Archaeological Journal* 13(1): 107–120.

Joyce, Arthur A. 2000 The Founding of Monte Albán: Sacred Propositions and Social Practices. In *Agency in Archaeology*, edited by Macia-Anne Dobres and John Robb, pp. 71–91. Routledge Press, London.

————. 2009 The Main Plaza of Monte Albán: A Life History of Place. In *The Archaeology of Meaningful Places*, edited by Brenda Bowser and María Nieves Zedeño, pp. 32–52. University of Utah Press, Salt Lake City.

————. 2010 *Mixtecs, Zapotecs, and Chatinos: Ancient Peoples of Southern Mexico*. Wiley-Blackwell, Malden, MA.

Joyce, Arthur A., Laura Arnaud Bustamante, and Marc N. Levine 2001 Commoner Power: A Case Study From the Classic Period Collapse on the Oaxaca Coast. *Journal of Archaeological Method and Theory* 8: 343–385.

Joyce, Arthur A., and Sarah B. Barber 2015 Ensoulment, Entrapment, and Political Centralization: A Comparative Study of Religion and Politics in Later Formative Oaxaca. *Current Anthropology* 56: 819–847.

Joyce, Arthur A., Marc N. Levine, and Sarah B. Barber 2013 Place-Making and Power in the Terminal Formative: Excavations on Río Viejo's Acropolis. In *Polity and Ecology in Formative Period Coastal Oaxaca*, edited by Arthur A. Joyce, pp. 135–164. University Press of Colorado, Boulder.

Joyce, Arthur A., and Erin T. Weller 2007 Commoner Rituals, Resistance, and the Classic-to-Postclassic Transition. In *Commoner Ritual and Ideology in Ancient Mesoamerica*, edited by Nancy Gonlin and Jon C. Lohse, pp. 143–184. University Press of Colorado, Boulder.

Joyce, Arthur A., and Marcus Winter 1996 Ideology, Power, and Urban Society in Prehispanic Oaxaca. *Current Anthropology* 37: 33–86.

Joyce, Rosemary A. 2000 *Gender and Power in Prehispanic Mesoamerica*. University of Texas Press, Austin.

————. 2004 Unintended Consequences? Monumentality as a Novel Experience in Formative Mesoamerica. *Journal of Archaeological Method and Theory* 11: 5–29.

————. 2011 What Should an Archaeology of Religion Look Like to a Blind Archaeologist? In *Beyond Belief: The Archaeology of Religion and Ritual*, edited by Yorke M. Rowan, pp. 180–188. Archeological Papers of the American Anthropological Association vol. 21. American Anthropologial Association, Arlington, VA.

Joyce, Rosemary, Richard Edging, Karl Lorenz, and Susan Gillespie 1991 Olmec Bloodletting: An Iconographic Study. In *The Sixth Palenque Round Table, 1986*, Volume VIII, edited by Merle Greene Robertson and Virginia Fields, pp. 143–150. University of Oklahoma Press, Norman.

Just, Bryan R. 2005 Modifications of Ancient Maya Sculpture. *RES: Anthropology and Aesthetics* 48: 69–82.

Keane, Webb 2005 Signs Are Not the Garb of Meaning: On the Social Analysis of Material Things. In *Materiality*, edited by Daniel Miller, pp. 182–205. Duke University Press, Durham.

————. 2007 *Christian Moderns: Freedom and Fetish in the Mission Encounter*. University of California Press, Los Angeles.

————. 2008 The Evidence of the Senses and the Materiality of Religion. *Journal of the Royal Anthropological Institute* 14(1): 110–127.

Kertzer, David 1988 *Ritual, Politics, and Power*. Yale University Press, New Haven.

Kopytoff, Igor 1986 The Cultural Biography of Things: Commoditization as Process. In *The Social Life of Things: Commodities in Cultural Perspective*, edited by Arjun Appadurai, pp. 64–91. Cambridge University Press, Cambridge.

Kunen, Julie L., Mary Jo Galindo, and Erin Chase 2003 Pits and Bones: Identifying Maya Ritual Behavior in the Archaeological Record. *Ancient Mesoamerica* 13: 197–211.

Latour, Bruno 1993 *We Have Never Been Modern*. Harvard University Press, Cambridge.

————. 2005 *Reassembling the Social: An Introduction to Actor-Network-Theory*. Oxford University Press, Oxford.

Lechtman, Heather 1993 Technologies of Power – the Andean Case. In *Configurations of Power in Complex Society*, edited by John S. Henderson and Patricia J. Netherly, pp. 244–80. Cornell University Press, Ithaca.

Lipe, William D., and Michelle Hegmon 1989 *The Architecture of Social Integration in Prehistoric Pueblos*. Occasional Papers, Crow Canyon Archaeological Center, Cortez, Colorado.

Lohse, Jon C. 2007 Commoner Ritual, Commoner Ideology: (Sub-)alternate Views of Social Complexity in Prehispanic Mesoamerica. In *Commoner Ritual and Ideology in Ancient Mesoamerica*, edited by Nancy Gonlin and Jon C. Lohse, pp. 1–32. University Press of Colorado, Boulder.

Love, Michael 1999 Ideology, Material Culture, and Daily Practice in Pre-Classic Mesoamerica: A Pacific Coast perspective. In *Social Patterns in Pre-Classic Mesoamerica*, edited by David C. Grove and Rosemary A. Joyce, pp. 127–154. Dumbarton Oaks Research Library and Collection, Washington, DC.

Lucero, Lisa J. 2006 *Water and Ritual: The Rise and Fall of Classic Maya Rulers*. University of Texas Press, Austin.

———. 2007 Classic Maya Temples, Politics, and the Voice of the People. *Latin American Antiquity* 18: 407–427.

Luke, Christina. 2012 Materiality and Sacred Landscapes: Ulúa Style Marble Vases in Honduras. In *Beyond Belief: The Archaeology of Religion and Ritual*, edited by Yorke M. Rowan, pp. 114–129. Archeological Papers of the American Anthropological Association vol. 21. American Anthropological Association, Arlington, VA.

McAnany, Patricia A. 1995 *Living With the Ancestors*. University of Texas Press, Austin.

———. 2002 Rethinking the Great and Little Tradition Paradigm From the Perspective of Domestic Ritual. In *Domestic Ritual in Mesoamerica*, edited by Patricia Plunket, pp. 115–120. University of California Press, Los Angeles.

McGuire, Randall H., and Dean Saitta 1996 Although They Have Petty Captains They Obey Them Badly: The Dialectics of Prehispanic Western Pueblo Social Organization. *American Antiquity* 61: 197–216.

Merleau-Ponty, Maurice 1962 *The Phenomenology of Perception*. Routledge and Kegan Paul, London.

———. 1968 *The Visible and the Invisible*. Northwestern University Press, Evanston.

Meskell, Lynn 2004 *Object Worlds in Ancient Egypt: Material Biographies Past and Present*. Berg, Oxford.

Miller, Daniel, ed. 2005 *Materiality*. Duke University Press, Durham.

Miller, Daniel 1998 Why Some Things Matter. In *Material Cultures: Why Some Things Matter*, edited by Daniel Miller, pp. 3–21. University College London Press, London.

Mills, Barbara J. 2004 The Establishment and Defeat of Hierarchy: Inalienable Possessions and the History of Collective Prestige Structures in the Pueblo Southwest. *American Anthropologist* 106: 238–251.

Mills, Barbara J., and T. J. Ferguson 2008 Animate Objects: Shell Trumpets and Ritual Networks in the Greater Southwest. *Journal of Archaeological Method and Theory* 15: 338–361.

Mock, Shirley B., ed. 1998 *The Sowing and the Dawning: Termination, Dedication, and Transformation in the Archaeological and Ethnographic Record of Mesoamerica*. University of New Mexico Press, Albuquerque.

Monaghan, John 1990 Sacrifice, Death, and the Origins of Agriculture in the Codex Vienna. *American Antiquity* 55: 559–569.

Moore, Jerry 1996 *Architecture and Power in the Ancient Andes: The Archaeology of Public Buildings*. Cambridge University Press, Cambridge.

Morley, Sylvanus G. 1920 *The Inscriptions of Copán*. Carnegie Institution of Washington, Publication 219, Washington, DC.

———— 1932–1938 *The Inscriptions of Petén*, 5 vols. Carnegie Institution of Washington, Publication 437, Washington DC.

Morris, Craig 1998 Inka Strategies of Incorporation and Governance. In *Archaic States*, edited by Gary M. Feinman and Joyce Marcus, pp. 293–310. School of American Research Press, Santa Fe.

Morris, Craig, and Donald E. Thompson 1985 *Huánuco Pampa: An Inka City and Its Hinterland*. Thames and Hudson, London.

Olsen, Bjornar 2010 *In Defense of Things: Archaeology and the Ontology of Objects*. Altamira Press, Lanham.

Olsen, Bjornar, Michael Shanks, Timothy Webmoor, and Christopher Witmore 2012 *Archaeology: The Discipline of Things*. University of California Press, Los Angeles.

Olson, Jan 2007 A Socioeconomic Interpretation of Figurine Assemblages From Late Postclassic Morelos, Mexico. In *Commoner Ritual and Ideology in Ancient Mesoamerica*, edited by Nancy Gonlin and Jon C. Lohse, pp. 251–279. University Press of Colorado, Boulder.

Patterson, Thomas C. 1986 Ideology, Class Formation, and Resistance in the Inca State. *Critique of Anthropology* 6(1): 75–85.

Pauketat, Timothy R. 2013 *An Archaeology of the Cosmos: Rethinking Agency and Religion in Ancient America*. Routledge, London and New York.

Pauketat, Timothy R. and Susan M. Alt 2003 Mounds, Memory, and Contested Mississippian History. In *Archaeologies of Memory*, edited by Ruth Van Dyke and Susan Alcock, pp. 151–179. Blackwell Press, Oxford.

————. 2005 Agency in a Postmold? Physicality and the Archaeology of Culture-Making. *Journal of Archaeological Method and Theory* 12: 213–236.

Pauketat, Timothy R., and Thomas E. Emerson 1991 The Ideology of Authority and the Power of the Pot. *American Anthropologist* 93: 919–941.

Peirce, Charles Sanders 1932 *Collected Papers of Charles Sanders Peirce. II: Elements of Logic.* Harvard University Press, Cambridge.

Plunket, Patricia, ed. 2002 *Domestic Ritual in Ancient Mesoamerica*. Cotsen Institute of Archaeology Press Monographs, vol. 46. University of California, Los Angeles.

Potter, James M. 2000 Pots, Parties, and Politics: Communal Feasting in the American Southwest. *American Antiquity* 65: 471–492.

Potter, James M. and Elizabeth M. Perry 2011 Mortuary Features and Identity Construction in an Early Village Community in the American Southwest. *American Antiquity* 76: 529–546.

Randall, Asa R., and Kenneth E. Sassaman 2010 (E)mergent Complexities During the Archaic Period in Northeast Florida. In *Ancient Complexities: New Perspectives in PreColumbian North America*, edited by Susan M. Alt, pp. 8–31. University of Utah Press, Salt Lake City.

Rappaport, Roy A. 1968 *Pigs for the Ancestors: Ritual in the Ecology of a New Guinea People*. Yale University Press, New Haven.

Robin, Cynthia 2002 Outside of Houses. *Journal of Social Archaeology* 2: 245–267.

————. 2012 *Chan: An Ancient Maya Farming Community*. University Press of Florida, Gainesville.

Rowan, Yorke M. 2012 Beyond Belief: The Archaeology of Religion and Ritual. In *Beyond Belief: The Archaeology of Religion and Ritual*, edited by Yorke M. Rowan, pp. 1–10. Archeological Papers of the American Anthropological Association vol. 21. American Anthropological Association, Arlington, VA.

Rowe, John H. 1948 The Kingdom of Chimor. *Acta Americana* 6(1–2): 26–59.

Salamone, Frank 2006 In Search of Religion. *Reviews in Anthropology* 35: 155–167.

Sassaman, Kenneth E. 2010 *The Eastern Archaic, Historicized*. Altamira Press, Lanham.

Sillar, Bill 2009 The Social Agency of Things? Animism and Materiality in the Andes. *Cambridge Archaeological Journal* 19: 367–377.

Smith, Michael E. 2002 Domestic Ritual at Aztec Provincial Sites in Morelos. In *Domestic Ritual in Mesoamerica*, edited by Patricia Plunket, pp. 93–114. University of California Press, Los Angeles.

Stanton, Travis W., M. Kathryn Brown, and Jonathan B. Pagliaro 2008 Garbage of the Gods? Squatters, Refuse Disposal, and Termination Rituals Among the Ancient Maya. *Latin American Antiquity* 19: 227–247.

Stockett, Miranda K. 2007 Performing Power: Identity, Ritual, and Materiality in a Late Classic Southeast Mesoamerican Crafting Community. *Ancient Mesoamerica* 18: 91–105.

Strathern, Marilyn 1988 *The Gender of the Gift: Problems With Women and Problems With Society in Melanesia*. University of California Press, Los Angeles.

———. 1990 Artifacts of History: Events and the Interpretation of Images. In *Culture and History in the Pacific*, edited by Jukka Siikala, pp. 25–44. Finnish Anthropological Society, Helsinki.

Stross, Brian 1998 Seven Ingredients in Mesoamerican Ensoulment. In *The Sowing and the Dawning: Termination, Dedication, and Transformation in the Archaeological and Ethnographic Record of Mesoamerica*, edited by Shirley B. Mock, pp. 31–39. University of New Mexico Press, Albuquerque.

Stuart, David S. 1984 Royal Auto-Sacrifice Among the Maya: A Study in Image and Meaning. *RES Anthropology and Aesthetics* 7/8: 6–20.

Sullivan, Lynne P., and Christopher B. Rodning 2001 Power Relationships in Southern Appalachian Chiefdoms. In *The Archaeology of Traditions: Agency and History Before and After Columbus*, edited by Timothy R. Pauketat, pp. 107–120. University Press of Florida. Gainesville.

Swenson, Edward R. 2007 Adaptive Strategies or Ideological Innovations? Interpreting Sociopolitical Developments in the Jequetepeque Valley of Peru During the Late Moche Period. *Journal of Anthropological Archaeology* 26: 253–282.

———. 2010 Revelation and Resolution: Anthropologies of Religion, Cognition, and Power. *Reviews in Anthropology* 39: 173–200.

———. 2015 The Materialities of Place-Making in the Ancient Andes: A Critical Appraisal of the Ontological Turn in Archaeological Interpretation. *Journal of Archaeological Method and Theory* 22: 677–712.

Tello, Julio C. 1929 *Antiguo Perú: Primera Época*. Comisión Organizadora del Segundo Congreso Turismo, Lima.

———. 1942 *Orígen y desarrollo de las civilizaciones prehistóricas andinas*. Actas y trabajos científicos del XXVII Congreso Internacional de Americanistas (Lima, 1939), vol. 1, pp. 589–720.

Thomas, Julian 2004 *Archaeology and Modernity*. Routledge, London.

Thompson, J. Eric S. 1929 Maya Chronology: Glyph G of the Lunar Series. *American Anthropologist* 31: 223–231.

———. 1942 *Maya Arithmetic*. Carnegie Institution of Washington, Publication 528, Washington, DC.

———. 1954 *The Rise and Fall of Maya Civilization*. University of Oklahoma Press, Norman.

Tilley, Chris, Webb Keane, Susanne Kuchler, Mike Rowlands, and Patricia Spyer, eds. 2006 *Handbook of Material Culture*. Sage, London.

Urcid, Javier, and Arthur A. Joyce 2014 Early Transformations of Monte Albán's Main Plaza and Their Political Implications, 500 BC-AD 200. In *Mesoamerican Plazas*, edited by Kenichiro Tsukamoto and Takeshi Inomata, pp. 149–167. University of Arizona Press, Tucson.

Vaillant, George C. 1941 *Aztecs of Mexico*. Garden City Press, Garden City.

Van Dyke, Ruth M. 2003 Memory and the Construction of Chacoan Society. In *Archaeologies of Memory*, edited by Ruth M. Van Dyke and Susan E. Alcock, pp. 180–200. Blackwell Press, Oxford.

Van Keuren, Scott 2011 The Materiality of Religious Belief in East-Central Arizona. In *Religious Transformation in the Late Pre-Hispanic Pueblo World*, edited by Donna M. Glowacki and Scott Van Keuren, pp. 175–195. University of Arizona Press, Tucson.

Viveiros de Castro, Eduardo 2004 Exchanging Perspectives: The Transformation of Objects Into Subjects in Amerindian Ontologies. *Common Knowledge* 10: 463–85.

Walker, William H. 1995 Ceremonial Trash? In *Expanding Archaeology*, edited by James M. Skibo, William H. Walker, and Axel E. Nielsen, pp. 67–79. University of Utah Press, Salt Lake City.

———. 2002 Stratigraphy and Practical Reason. *American Anthropologist* 104: 159–177.

———. 2008 Practice and the Afterlife Histories of Witches and Dogs. In *Memory Work: Archaeologies of Material Practices*, edited by Barbara M. Mills and William Walker, pp. 137–158. School of American Research Press, Santa Fe.

Walker, William H., and Lisa Lucero 2000 The Depositional History of Ritual and Power. In *Agency in Archaeology*, edited by Marcia-Anne Dobres and John Robb, pp. 130–147. Routledge, London.

Waring, Antonio J., Jr. and Preston Holder 1945 A Prehistoric Ceremonial Complex in the Southeastern United States. *American Anthropologist* 47: 1–34.

Webmoor, Timothy, and Christopher L. Witmore 2008 Things Are Us! A Commentary on Human/Things Relations Under the Banner of a 'Social' Archaeology. *Norwegian Archaeological Review* 41(1): 53–70.

Willey, Gordon 1956 The Structure of Ancient Maya Society: Evidence From the Southern Lowlands. *American Anthropologist* 58: 777–782.

Wilson, Gregory D. 2008 *The Archaeology of Everyday Life at Early Moundville*. University of Alabama Press, Tuscaloosa.

Yaeger, Jason 2003 Untangling the Ties That Bind: The City, the Countryside, and the Nature of Maya Urbanism at Xunantunich, Belize. In *The Social Construction of Ancient Cities*, edited by Monica L. Smith, pp. 121–155. Smithsonian Books, Washington and London.

Zaro, Gregory, and Jon C. Lohse 2005 Agricultural Rhythms and Rituals: Ancient Maya Solar Observation in Hinterland Blue Creek. *Latin American Antiquity* 16: 81–98.

Zedeño, María Nieves 2008 Bundled Worlds: The Roles and Interactions of Complex Objects From the North American Plains. *Journal of Archaeological Method and Theory* 15: 362–78.

———. 2009 Animating by Association: Index Objects and Relational Taxonomies. *Cambridge Archaeological Journal* 19: 407–417.

———. 2013 Methodological and Analytical Challenges in Relational Archaeologies: A View From the Hunting Ground. In *Relational Archaeologies: Humans, Animals, Things*, edited by Christopher Watts, pp. 117–134. Routledge, London.

2

THE MOBILE HOUSE

Religious leadership at Chacoan and Chacoan revival centers

Erina Gruner

Introduction

Chaco Canyon is unique among prehistoric political centers in the North American Southwest. The fluorescence of the Chaco phenomenon in present-day northwest New Mexico, during the eleventh and twelfth centuries A.D., united dispersed communities across the four corners region in a shared expression of religious practice, characterized by highly formalized monumental "great houses," a centralized settlement pattern, and participation in the extensive trade networks centered on Chaco Canyon itself (Figure 2.1). At the height of the Chaco phenomenon during the late eleventh century, Chaco's great house communities commanded trade networks stretching to Mesoamerica and the Gulf of California, and their unique architectural signature was emulated as far as northeastern Arizona and southwestern Colorado (Kantner and Kintigh 2006). This regional interaction sphere differed dramatically in scale from both the localized settlements which preceded it, and the autonomous village societies which followed it during the late prehistoric and early historic periods.

Many scholars position the Chaco phenomenon as fundamentally divorced from the decentralized theocratic villages documented by early ethnographers among Puebloan descendant communities (Lekson 2006; Wilcox 1993; Wills 2000). They conceive of Chaco as a hierarchically ranked, centralized polity, integrated by an ideology and social organization which must necessarily be radically different from the insular and communalistic ethos of the historic Pueblos.

However, examination of the rare perishable assemblages from Chacoan centers reveals ritual objects nearly identical to those used by modern Puebloan priesthoods (Vivian et al. 1978; Webster 2006, 2011). Likewise, burial data from these centers suggests systems of hereditary control over religious roles and associated material privileges that are strikingly similar to those documented in historic

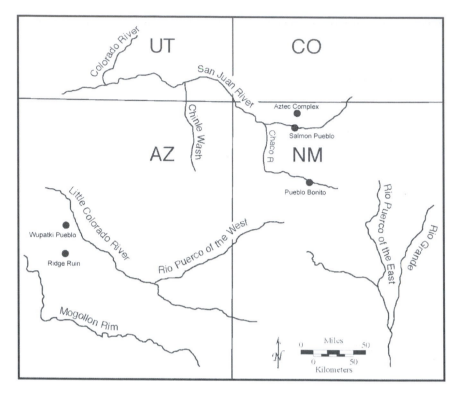

FIGURE 2.1 Map of Archaeological sites mentioned in this chapter. Redrawn from Gruner 2015, Fig. 3.1, drafted by Ann Hull.

Pueblos (Gruner 2012; Plog and Heitman 2010). These patterns continue in post-Chacoan centers that eclipsed the canyon itself during the late twelfth century. I argue that during the post-Chacoan period, the material foundations of Chacoan theocracy – including heirloom Chacoan ritual paraphernalia, and Chacoan patterns of ritual consumption – were co-opted by leaders of peripheral communities to create continuity in a time of political rupture. The priesthoods that emerged from these revitalizations developed into the backbone of theocratic leadership in the autonomous Pueblo villages of later periods.

Social organization during the Chacoan period

The Chaco phenomenon is defined primarily by the size and formality of its public ceremonial structures, the monumentality of which stood in stark contrast to the 5–20 room domestic structures common to this period. Great houses within Chaco Canyon reached up to four stories and over 400 rooms (Chaco Research Archive Searchable Database 2014). Excavations of some of these structures uncovered evidence of ritual activities such as feasting, ritual paraphernalia and costume, and votive deposits of rare materials (Judd 1981 [1954]; Pepper 1996 [1920]). Most appear to have been built to monumental proportions, yet used for activities that left minimal material traces (Durand 2003:150).

Some archaeologists hypothesize that Chaco lay at the center of an integrated political system, with outlier great houses throughout the four corners exerting Chacoan control at the local level and the canyon serving as a redistributive center for outlier communities (Judge 1979; Wilcox 1993, 2002). Chaco drew resources from an extensive radius of supporting outlier communities: corn and raw chert were regularly transported from the Chuskan and Zuni mountains (over 50 km away), and turquoise was procured from sources as distant as the Cerillos Mountains (190 km away). Indeed, the very construction of great houses would not have been possible without main-beam timbers transported from Chuskan territories, or labor parties that exceeded the size of local populations (Sebastien 1992; Toll 2006). The scale and apparent centralization of these networks contrasts dramatically with the organization of descendent communities in the modern Pueblos, where economic activity is coordinated primarily at the family level and political activity by autonomous villages (Ware 2014).

However, archaeologists increasingly argue that Chacoan outlier communities interacted with Chaco Canyon to varying degrees – some regularly contributing labor and materials to Chaco's program of ritual activity and monumental construction – while others emulated aspects of its architectural (and presumably ideological) paradigm with minimal direct interaction (Kantner 2003; Kantner and Kintigh 2006; Van Dyke 2003). These models position Chaco as a ceremonial center of extraordinary influence and significance, rather than a centralized polity capable of directly overseeing outlier communities.

This perspective is implicitly rooted in the Puebloan ethnohistoric record. Some anthropologists argue that the fluorescence of Chaco Canyon represents the rise of priestly sodalities analogous to the moieties and ritual societies that govern modern pueblo villages, and anchored interactions between politically autonomous communities during the historic period (Heitman and Plog 2005; Vivian 1970; Ware 2014). Elizabeth Brandt (1980) notes that councils of religious specialists exerted a hegemonic authority within Pueblo communities, where hierarchical control over secret ritual knowledge allowed initiates into high-ranking priesthoods to regulate the behavioral standards of their neighbors. The scope of their authority was simultaneously religious, political, military, and economic.

As Severin Fowles (2013:63) observes, "esoteric knowledge, ritual objects, and the rights to engage in ceremony were conceptualized not only as means of cultural reproduction and worldly maintenance, but simultaneously as forms of wealth which marked the distinction between haves and have-nots." Indeed, although the communalistic ethos of historic Pueblo villages proscribed ostentatious displays of personal wealth, these villages were nonetheless stratified because of the nature of ritual leadership: hereditary curation of ritual objects and leadership of the priesthoods associated with them fell to the prime lineages of important clans in some Pueblo descendent groups (Parsons 1996 [1939]; Fox 1967), and to important households in others (see Fowles 2013:55). Likewise, households with ceremonial status did accrue precious materials: rare resources including minerals, shell, feathers, animal parts, and herbs, which were procured, used, and distributed in specific ritual contexts (Parsons 1996 [1939]).

Great house as "household"

Of the small number of Chacoan great houses that have been extensively excavated, most have both notably low density of domestic refuse and an absence of cemetery areas: evidence that during the height of Chaco Canyon, the primary use of these structures was non-domestic (Sebastien 1992). Elements of dance costume found in great houses such as Chetro Ketl and Pueblo Bonito suggest these structures housed mass spectacles to rival the elaborate dances of modern Pueblo ceremonials (Judd 1981 [1954]; Pepper 1996 [1920]; Vivian et al. 1978). However, it is in the inaccessible interior and subterranean rooms of Chacoan great houses that caches of ritual paraphernalia and concentrations of votive deposits are found – suggesting that the most intense forms of ritual practice within the Chacoan sphere were witnessed only by a select cadre of individuals.

While most great houses appear to have been non-residential, a handful of Chacoan great houses contain burial chambers, as well as residential "suites" with artifact assemblages indicating domestic activities (Durand 2003). Significantly, great houses with apparent residential populations are always among the oldest in their respective areas, and thus have been hypothesized to represent "founding" populations of Chacoan cultists. Uniquely rich assemblages of exotic materials, finely crafted ornaments, and ritual objects also indicate that this primacy differentiated these great houses and their occupants from others in the Chacoan world. Materials sourcing some types of ritual objects only found in Chacoan great houses shows that they were in fact manufactured in dispersed communities throughout the Chacoan world for use or disposal within this specific social context (Toll 2006).

Stephen Plog and Carrie Heitman (2010) suggest that a productive way to view Chacoan great houses is according to the "house society" model developed by Claude Lévi-Strauss. In this model, corporate groups structure their identity and prestige according to enduring collective residence in a shared "house," rather than exclusively according to principles of lineal descent:

> When communities and land ownership are sustained, more successful groups may legitimize . . . their productive success by claiming greater access to ancestors and cosmological powers. Moreover, material culture is often used to show both access to and sanction from these cosmological referents. Particular groups or houses, thus, may create origin structures laden with greater quantities of particular materials that show their access to ancestral origins and powers vis a vis other houses . . . layered through time with the bones of ancestors and material manifestations of places of origin.
>
> *(Plog and Heitman 2010:19624)*

As manifestations of collective origins and identity, great houses are explicitly symbolically laden, with generations of organizational, ideological, and cosmological
principles inscribed into their construction and layout. They are spaces in which
the collectively owned estate of the house is used, stored, and disposed of, including corporately allocated resources and heirloom objects such as ritual costume,
altars, and totems and staves of office – and ancestral remains that were placed
within the house to be curated by successive generations.

To date, human burials from Pueblo Bonito are the only thoroughly studied great house burial populations from Chaco Canyon. Pueblo Bonito's human
remains sort into a western burial group and a northeastern burial group, totaling
approximately 123 to 131 individuals (Akins 2003:95).

Each burial group is spatially associated with a rear, interior section of rooms
within the great house. While both groups include rich burial furnishings, the
rarest and most finely crafted artifacts concentrate in the burial chambers of the
northeastern burial group, suggesting higher sociopolitical status. Artifacts associated with both burial clusters include ritual paraphernalia of types that are not
found at Chacoan small house sites, including flutes and conch trumpets, prayer
sticks, special basketry, and painted boards. Mortuary offerings and associated
artifacts recovered from room 33, the richest burial chamber in the structure,
included over 25,000 pieces of turquoise, over 22,000 intact and fragmentary shell
ornaments, and carved wooden artifacts including nine flutes, "rabbit sticks" and
over two dozen ceremonial staves. Adjacent rooms also contained quantities of
apparent ritual objects, often broken or disassembled (Judd 1981 [1954]; Pepper
1996 [1920]).

Craniometric studies by Michael Schillaci and Christopher Stojanowski (2003)
indicate a degree of genetic relatedness shared by individuals within each of Pueblo
Bonito's burial groups. Recent archaeogenomic studies confirm that the northeastern group is indeed a kin group, with direct lineal descent from a single matriline
(Kennett et al. 2017). However, the demographics of these burial groups do not
conform to the mortality rates which would be expected were these burial chambers
simply cemetery areas for two resident households. Subadults and children, which
should comprise approximately half of a Neolithic burial population, are notably
absent in the northeastern burial group (Marden 2011:211). Males exhibit statistically anomalous height, traumatic injuries consistent with hand-to-hand combat,
and unusually robust muscular attachments, suggesting that status for men buried in
this group was ascribed by heredity, but also achieved in war (Harrod 2012).

The western burial cluster, unlike the northeastern one, contains individuals
of all ages, including children (Akins 2003). However, the demographics of this
group are nonetheless unusual, with approximately twice as many women as men,
and approximately twice as many adults as subadults and children (Akins 2003).
Finally, these burials comprise a strikingly small number of individuals for the 400-
year occupation of this structure, indicating that while some people were being
distinguished by placement within the great house's rooms in death, the great
majority of its occupants were being interred elsewhere.[1]

Significantly, death did not end the active role of these individuals within the religious practice of their community: rather, it was a transition point. Taphonomic studies of the Pueblo Bonito inhumations provide further information about the social life of ancestral remains after death. Keriann Marden (2011) notes that the term "burial" is a misnomer when applied to great house mortuary chambers. Great house internments were typically wrapped in mats and left exposed in the interior rooms of the great house to mummify in the arid desert environment. Further, she notes that remains show post-mortem cut marks and they are often distributed within or between rooms, suggesting that these bundles were opened and bodies manipulated post-mortem (Marden 2011). A common pattern seems to be the removal of crania (Marden 2011:298). In the richest burial chambers, remains appear to have been disturbed repeatedly over extended periods of time. For example, bones from the two richest inhumations, two men interred in a vault in room 33, were found both above and below the plank floor of their vault (Marden 2011:278–279). These burials appear to be the oldest in the great house, and may represent cult founders in this community. Recent radiocarbon dating of the remains and re-dating of associated artifacts indicate that the offerings found within this vault were deposited over a period of up to 400 years (Plog and Heitman 2010:19623). This pattern is not unique to Pueblo Bonito: human remains from Penasco Blanco, another large, early Chacoan great house, show similar signatures of post-mortem disarticulation (Perez 2012).

Overall, the impression given is that the human remains in Pueblo Bonito are a select group of individuals, of an age and physical type to have achieved a status through fulfilling specific social roles in life, which granted them particular significance to their kin groups after death. Their remains thus served as an ongoing focus of ritual activity for successive generations. The demographics and richness of burials within Pueblo Bonito's northeastern and western burial groups differ, indicating differing social roles fulfilled by men and women within these two kin groups.

The richness of the artifacts associated with Chacoan great house burials is frequently cited as evidence that Chacoan society was more hierarchical, its elite stratum more aggrandizing than modern Puebloan theocrats (Akins 2003; Lekson 2006; Neitzel 2003; Plog and Heitman 2010). While this may be the case, it is not clear whether the bulk of offerings left in great house burial chambers consecrated the individuals interred in these chambers, signaling their personal prestige in life, or whether both human bodies and materials consecrated the space itself, signaling associations with the larger corporate identity of the house.

These materials strikingly resemble deconstructed altar assemblages of modern Puebloan ritual societies, which also contain quantities of exotic materials and finely crafted objects – the majority of which are corporately, rather than individually, owned. While such assemblages are in some sense a display of wealth, they are more importantly a cosmogram in which representations of people, places, and things significant to the corporate groups that used them were laid out, each in their particular order.

Each Pueblo ritual reassembles altars from diverse constituent objects, each of which carries a distinct object biography. Likewise, each animal, vegetable, or mineral used to build a single ritual object indexes a suite of symbolic relations, including directional symbolism; color symbolism; association with seasonal, astrological, or meteorological phenomena; and association with ancestral persons or territories (Parsons 1996 [1939]). The reordering of these parts is intended to actively effect changes in the relations between natural, cultural, and spiritual forces that they index. In modern Puebloan ritual societies, founders of cults and deceased society leaders are represented symbolically on altars, and they are conceived of as active participants in these rituals (Parsons 1996 [1939]:163). Chacoan ritual practice may represent a similar principle carried out in more literal fashion: by using human remains as index objects for the deceased ancestors of the kin group.

Ethnographic analogy and Chacoan ritual

Recent anthropological considerations of complex heirlooms such as altars, medicine bundles, staves of office, and "clan houses" have emphasized the capability of such artifacts to serve as agents in the societies that curate them, due both to their perceived animacy and to their ability to enchain social actors to one another, and to other places and objects (see Bernardini 2012; Zedeño 2008; Pauketat 2013; Gell 1998). Zedeño (2008:363) observes that archaeology's overarching concern with classification places us in an ideal position to address the interactive capabilities of such complex assemblages through addressing the culturally specific practices and conceptions associated with their constituent parts.

The burial of the Magician

Indigenous ontologies are best addressed through immediate reference to an emic perspective. Fortunately, many of the materials found in Chacoan great houses have been interpreted in other archaeological contexts by Pueblo descendants. One of the more famous instances in which traditional knowledge identified ritual objects in the archaeological record is the so-called "burial of the Magician," the inhumation of an adult male excavated from the twelfth-century site of Ridge Ruin, near Flagstaff, Arizona. This man was laid to rest with over 600 objects, making this the most elaborate single burial excavated in the American Southwest (McGregor 1943). The contents of this burial were not only interpreted, but also preemptively predicted by Hopi cultural consultants, who, when shown certain prayer sticks from the burial, were able to accurately describe other prayer sticks and elements of ritual costume (McGregor 1943:295–296).

Hopi men consulted by the excavator identified this individual as a War Chief, and also the leader of a war priesthood which had recently stopped initiating members on the Hopi mesas. This identification is consistent with biological indicators of his life history: as with the most venerated male burials in Pueblo Bonito, the

Magician was an unusually robust male with a possible healed traumatic injury (McGregor 1943:296). Cultural consultants identified objects, including inlaid and painted prayer sticks, a beaded cap, and mountain lions' claws, as the costume and paraphernalia of this cult. They noted that many of these were typically owned by the priesthood and curated for many generations, rather than buried with individuals. They hypothesized that these objects were buried with this individual because his priesthood had died out in this village. Thus, its last initiated leader curated its sacred possessions in death (McGregor 1943:296).

Recent consultations with a second group of Hopi advisors identified additional items from this burial as those used in ritual practice, including artifacts such as effigy bows, a bowl with bear paw designs, inlaid awls, painted basketry, an inlay bow guard, shell-rattle leggings, arrow bundles, and altar pieces. They also identified ritually significant raw materials such as turquoise, malachite, hematite, quartz, and shell. Consultants characterized this priesthood as a "proto-Hopi ancestral religious society" (Ferguson and Loma'omvaya 2011:173). However, it should be noted that analogous priesthoods were recorded by early ethnographers at other Pueblo villages, where they were observed using many of the same objects and materials (Gruner 2012:86–96). The ethnographic record preserves hints of specific rights membership in this group entailed. For example, at Laguna, this society controlled access to precious pigments within the village (Parsons 1920:99). The prestigious lineages that contributed leaders to these societies at Zuni and Hopi villages also composed the leadership stratum of other politically powerful priesthoods, and curated the sacred objects of multiple societies within their residences (for review, see Gruner 2012:99–100).

Ridge Ruin is not a Chacoan great house – in fact, it lies just beyond the boundaries of the Chaco phenomenon, both spatially and temporally. Ridge Ruin is approximately a hundred miles west of the nearest Chacoan great houses (Chaco Research Archive Searchable Database 2014), and was built during the half century of social upheaval following the unraveling of Chacoan networks on the Colorado Plateau. The structure has stylistic citations to Chacoan architecture,[2] but was clearly built by people who had not participated in Chaco's monumental construction regime. Nonetheless, excavator John McGregor noted strong stylistic and technological resemblance between material culture from Ridge Ruin and assemblages from the great houses of Chaco Canyon (McGregor 1941:280–282).

Elsewhere (Gruner 2012), I demonstrated strong technological and stylistic similarities between material culture from Ridge Ruin and from Chacoan great houses. However, the resemblance was only seen in ritual objects (prayer sticks and special basketry), and ornaments that might be elements of ritual costume (painted and inlay shell and turquoise jewelry), almost all of which were found in the Magician's burial. These stylistic similarities to Chacoan artifacts include low-visibility aspects of the construction of complex objects, which could only be learned through direct tutelage: for example, the construction of joins and interior layers in complex artifacts such as lacquered painted basketry or inlay jewelry (Figure 2.2) (NMAI Object Reports n.d.; McGregor 1941; Webster 2008). I hypothesized that

FIGURE 2.2   Stylistically similar ritual objects from Chaco Canyon, the Totah, and the Wupatki area. (a) reed bundle container from Aztec West (image courtesy Laurie Webster, with permission of the American Museum of Natural History); (b) reed bundle container from Pueblo Bonito (image courtesy Laurie Webster, with permission of the American Museum of Natural History); (c) prayer stick from the Magician's burial (image from McGregor 1943 Plate II); (d) prayer stick from Wupatki Pueblo (image from Fewkes 1927); (e) mosaic arm band from Pueblo Bonito (image courtesy the American Museum of Natural History); (f) mosaic arm band from the Magician's burial (image from McGregor 1943 Plate I); (g) asphaltum plugged *Haliotis* shell from Pueblo Bonito (image courtesy the American Museum of Natural History); (h) asphaltum plugged *Haliotis* shell from the Magician's burial (image from McGregor 1943 Fig. 10).

this assemblage showed the introduction of Chacoan priesthoods into new culture areas following large-scale population movements in the mid-twelfth century. Many of the materials buried with the Magician were probably heirlooms – for example, the elaborate turquoise mosaic ornaments and prayer stick heads were not manufactured at Ridge Ruin, where there is no evidence of turquoise production debris.

The elaborate burial treatment of the Magician supports the hypothesis that he may have brought Chacoan cult to Ridge Ruin. For example, the Magician was interred in a wood-roofed vault grave in the northeastern kiva at Ridge Ruin, with offerings laid across his pelvis and to the four corners of the vault: an arrangement strikingly similar to the arrangement of "founder" burials in Pueblo Bonito.

TABLE 2.1 Distribution of artifacts and materials similar to those in the Magician's burial within the western and northeastern room suites. Modified from Stein et al. 2003: Figure 4.5.

	Bonito Northeast		Bonito West		Courtyard Kiva	
	Number of Items	*Room Number*	*Number of Items*	*Room Number*	*Number of Items*	*Room Number*
Ritual Paraphernalia						
"Swallowing sticks" (long-pointed prayer sticks)	1	6	0		0	
Effigy bow (prayer stick)	4	209a	0		0	
Painted coated basketry	2	13, 300	0		0	
Inlay bow guard	1	33	0		0	
Mosaic ornaments and lignite buttons	24	32, 33, 28, 38	3	330, 348	0	
Arrow bundles	2	32, 10	2	330, 25	0	
Reed cylinders	3	110	0		0	
Exotic Materials						
Macaws	28	38, 71, 78, 249, 306, 309, east mound	0		0	
Murex, Melongena, or Strombus shell (conchs)	10	10, 13, 33, 38, 42, 201, 3a	0		2	Kiva R, Kiva A
Haliotis and bivalve shell (unprocessed)	5	33, Kiva D	0		1	Kiva Q

Moreover, multiple layers of offerings within and above the vault suggest that, as with the Bonito burials, sacred materials may have been deposited within this chamber over an extended period of time (Museum of Northern Arizona [MNA], Flagstaff, AZ, NA site file NA1785, unpublished manuscript and notes, "*Ridge Ruin Burial.*").

The resemblance to Pueblo Bonito's northeastern burial group is also reflected in artifact types. Ritual paraphernalia like artifacts from the Magician's burial concentrate in the northern and eastern sections of Pueblo Bonito: the roomblocks associated with the founding kin group (see Table 2.1 and Figure 2.3). These include painted coated basketry, effigy bows, hoof-headed prayer sticks, and bundled reed tube containers. An inlay turquoise bow guard similar to that buried with the Magician was found only in the "founder" vault grave at Pueblo Bonito. Mosaic inlay pendants similar to the Magician's costume were mostly found in the northeastern wing, although this association was not exclusive. Overall, it appears that the ritual paraphernalia of the Magician's priesthood was overwhelmingly curated by one kin group at Pueblo Bonito – its founders.

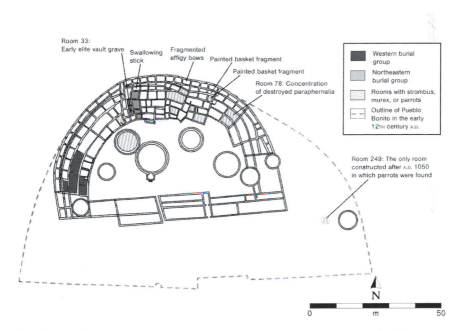

FIGURE 2.3   Distribution of artifacts and materials similar to those in the Magician's burial within Pueblo Bonito. Artifact distributions based on collections research and examination of inventories on file at the American Museum of Natural History (AMNH 2014), photographic inventories on file at the National Museum of the American Indian (NMAI 2013), and the Chaco Research Archive (CRI 2014). Drafted by Andrew Saiz, courtesy Statistical Research, Inc.

Ceremony, materials, and exchange

The association between a founding kin group and ritually significant materials is also reflected in the distribution of rare raw material types within Pueblo Bonito. The kiva in which the Magician was buried contained two scarlet macaws (*Aris macao*). Two more were excavated within Ridge Ruin's roomblocks (McGregor 1941:258). Macaws, prized for their dramatic plumes used in prayer sticks and dance costume, were raised in captivity at a small number of prehistoric sites in the American Southwest – however, they did not breed and thus were imported as fledglings from Mesoamerica (Vokes and Gregory 2009:328). The Magician was also buried with quantities of turquoise and worked shell, jet ornaments, a conch shell (*Melongena sp.*), three cockle shells (*Laevicardium sp.*), and an abalone (*Haliotis sp.*); the shells are imports from the Pacific coast and the Gulf of California (McGregor 1943).

Some of these materials were precious but not unusual in the American Southwest. Others were traded within extremely restricted networks. During the fluorescence of the Chaco Phenomenon, macaws were found on the upper Colorado Plateau only within Chaco Canyon great houses: 31 at Pueblo Bonito and five at nearby Pueblo Del Arroyo (Vokes and Gregory 2009). The fact that Pueblo Bonito's macaws were only found in the northeastern rooms and the northeastern midden mound of Pueblo Bonito (see Table 2.1) suggests that access to this trade network was the exclusive domain of Bonito's founding kin group. Recent accelerator mass spectrometry (AMS) dating of macaw remains from Pueblo Bonito confirms that macaws were procured during the earliest occupations of the site, with the oldest dating to the late eighth or early ninth century. Indeed, by the presumed fluorescence of Chaco during the Classic Bonito phase, importation of macaws had significantly decreased (Watson et al. 2015:8241).

Likewise, conch species were found above the Mogollon Rim only at Pueblo Bonito (12 specimens) and two small residential sites in its immediate area (one shell was found at each) (Vokes and Gregory 2009). As with macaws, Pueblo Bonito's 12 conch shells are all in the northeastern areas of the structure associated with the founding kin group. Unprocessed jet, fossil shell, *Halotis* shell, and *Laevicardiaum* shell also concentrate in Pueblo Bonito's northern wings (Gruner 2012:138; Neitzel 2003). The distance between these centers and the nearest potential trade partner for goods like macaws or conchs (approximately 200 miles) suggests participants in these networks journeyed extraordinary distances in order to procure their goods. Participation in these trade networks facilitated communication between otherwise isolated elites from discrete cultural backgrounds across the southwestern United States and Northern Mexico, and also reinforced the special status of religious initiates through providing physical tokens of arduous journeys. During the historic period, similar pilgrimages to gather sacred materials – which could take weeks or months – continued to be an important status marker for initiates of Puebloan religious societies (Parsons 1996 [1939]).

The association of particular materials with particular kin groups and their priesthoods also reflects a totemic logic similar to that of modern Puebloans. Puebloan

sodalities such as clans and moieties are generally named after the primary natural object or principle that their ceremonies affect, constituting a core of group
identity. The totems for which the group is named are in turn linked to a suite of
other plants, animals, and materials, meaning that "descent groups have conceptual
'rights' over ethnotaxonomic classes of natural objects" (Whiteley 1998:75). This
symbolic identification structures resource procurement and allocation: for example, Neil Judd noted that his Zuni Macaw Clan excavators were pleased to receive
a live macaw, because their clan distributed parrot feathers to their village (Judd
1981 [1954]:263).

One of the more elaborate examples of this principle is the moiety system
of the eastern Pueblos, where every member of the community belongs to one
of two "houses" (moiety kivas) associated with winter or summer. Each moiety
commands control of the ceremonial cycle during their respective season. A given
moiety also claims particular priesthoods, cardinal or semicardinal directions (structuring residence within the village), and is also associated with a variable host of
plants, animals, minerals, and phenomena associated with warm or cold (Fox 1967;
Ortiz 1969; Parsons 1996 [1939]). The burial demographics and distribution of
materials in Pueblo Bonito suggests an asymmetrical moiety system similar to that
of the Pueblo of Cochiti – wherein the Cacique, the War Captain, and leaders of
the most politically important priesthoods are drawn exclusively from the Winter
moiety (Fox 1967:65; Ortiz 1969).

Significantly, although the social organization of Hopi and Zuni is not structured by a division between summer and winter moieties, origin myths that sanction clan ownership of specific priesthoods suggest that rituals were inherited from
a society that *was* organized in this manner. Hopi tradition divides leadership of
Chaco between two founding clans, Parrot and Crow/Katsina (Kuwanwisiwma
2004:45).[3] Zuni origin stories recall that in the first days, they were organized into
two "houses": the Summer People, the people of the macaw; and the Winter
People, the people of the raven. The less populous but more powerful of these
houses, that of the Macaw, supplied the Sun Priest and his sisters, "keeper and giver
of precious things and commandments . . . the seed of all priests . . . the House of
Houses" (Cushing 1988:22).

The Summer and Winter People were divided into clans, each of which was
given the "seed" of a particular priesthood. So, for example, among the Summer
People, Badger clan was given "the great [conch] whose core has an affinity for
fire" and thus became the wardens of fire (Cushing 1988:26). The fact that distribution of macaws, conchs, shells, and ornamental jet (i.e. coal, rock that makes fire)
was controlled by one "house" at Chaco suggests that these traditions recall totemic
associations that structured the actual domains of prehistoric corporate kin groups.

The mobile house: founders on the Chacoan periphery

How did the totemic associations of Chaco's ritual economy become embedded
in the social fabric of historic communities as distant as the Hopi Mesas or the

Rio Grande Pueblos? Tracking the distribution of Chacoan trade goods and ritual paraphernalia during the post-Chacoan interval begins to answer this question. Exclusive Chacoan control over materials such as macaws and conchs persisted until the early twelfth century A.D., when trade shifted to two new regions: the Totah north of Chaco, where macaws are found at Salmon Pueblo and Aztec West; and near the San Francisco Mountains west of Chaco, where macaws are found at Wupatki Pueblo, Ridge Ruin, Winona, the Pollock Site, and Nalakihu, and conchs at Wupatki and Ridge Ruin (Vokes and Gregory 2009).

This shift reflects larger changes in the regional politics. Monumental construction at Chaco slowed during the early 1100s, then halted around A.D. 1140 (Kantner and Kintigh 2006:182–183). However, as Chaco's power waned, its ideological program was adopted and adapted in the Totah and San Francisco Peaks, at centers which persisted until the early 1300s. It may seem strange that Chacoan ritual flourished along the periphery even as it died out in its place of origin. However, as noted by Elizabeth Brandt (1980:144), when factional disputes arise within Pueblo communities, it is the "conservative" theocrats (those empowered with ritual paraphernalia and knowledge) that are most empowered to migrate: "They have the ability . . . to reconstitute a complete new village, but those who are left behind are in the same position as the American community might be if the utilities were abandoned."

As Chacoan hegemony unraveled, members of ritually empowered lineages may have taken their ritual objects, and the hereditary authority they entailed, elsewhere. Mortuary and artifactual patterns from Salmon Pueblo, Aztec West, and Wupatki Pueblo show how rising elites within these communities established themselves as founders in their own right, using continuity with the established material icons of Chacoan authority to anchor their own authority locally.

The Totah great houses

The earliest outlier great house in the Totah to be established as a rival polity to Chaco Canyon was Salmon Pueblo, founded along the banks of the San Juan River in the 1070s A.D. In size and formality, Salmon Pueblo equals Classic Bonito-phase great houses at Chaco. Plentiful domestic features such as hearths, storage bins, trash deposits, and mealing bins suggest that Salmon, unlike most outlier great houses, had a resident population (Reed 2008). Many archaeologists suggest that Salmon was founded by Chacoan migrants who established themselves among a local population (Irwin-Williams 2008; Reed 2006, 2008).

While Salmon has a sizable burial population, only five Chaco-period burials were recovered. Most of these cluster to the northeast of the great house (Reed 2006:56–57), echoing the semi-cardinal association of Pueblo Bonito's founding group. For the most part, they lack the elaborate ritual objects and exotic materials found at Pueblo Bonito. However, a man dubbed the "Bow Priest" was buried with a bow, effigy arrows, carved and painted prayer sticks, a "rabbit stick," and a bundle of cane tube containers (Irwin-Williams 2008:283; Webster 2006:906,

1010): an assemblage that echoes the founder graves of Pueblo Bonito. Rich post-Chacoan burials from this room and one immediately west of it contained offerings of bows and arrows (Webster 2006:906–916), suggesting continuity in the material markers of leadership after the fall of Chaco.

Salmon's founders were not able to mobilize the local materials or labor to craft the quantities of ornaments found at Chaco Canyon great houses. However, they evidently still participated in pan-Southwestern prestige trade networks. This is most clearly evident in the presence of seven macaws recovered from the northern and eastern wings (Durand and Durand 2006, 2008), two of which were buried near the "Bow Priest" (Durand and Durand 2006:105). While it is unclear if Salmon's burials sort into two kin groups, other materials show the familiar asymmetrical bilateral division between residents of Salmon's north/eastern and western wings: for example, purple-red pigment, which was exclusively recovered from the northern and eastern wings (Webster 2006:1007).

Aztec West

If Salmon represented the first attempt to establish a Chacoan polity in the Totah, the Aztec Complex fulfilled that ideal. Construction began around A.D. 1085 at Aztec West Ruin, a great house of approximately 400 rooms. During the thirteenth century A.D., the center was expanded with two additional monumental structures (Chaco Research Archive Searchable Database 2014). Aztec West contains domestic refuse and elite burials, along with quantities of finely crafted ornaments and ritual objects (Morris 1919, 1924).

As at Salmon and Pueblo Bonito, an asymmetrical bilateral division is evident in both burial patterns and the deposition of ritual paraphernalia within Aztec West. Internments within Aztec West's richest ossuaries were left exposed, and were heavily disturbed and comingled (Morris 1924:151–153, 155–161), suggesting post-mortem manipulation similar to Chacoan mortuary rites. While the eastern and northern wings contained burial chambers with ritual paraphernalia, ornaments, and quantities of shell and jet, a far greater number of burials were uncovered from the western wing with few accompanying mortuary offerings (Morris 1924). Other northeastern rooms, such as room 72, contained caches of painted dance paraphernalia and altar parts (Morris 1919). Several classes of ritual paraphernalia that were also found in the Magician's burial and at Pueblo Bonito concentrate in this area of the structure (Figure 2.4).

However, Aztec elites do not seem to have been able to command exotic trade networks in the fashion of their predecessors. Aztec's northern wing contains three macaw skulls, a feather, a fragmentary carcass (possibly stuffed), and no conchs (American Museum of Natural History [AMNH], Accessions List, Aztec Ruins macaws 2014). One macaw skull may be associated with the western burial group. This shift may be due to Aztec's more localized networks of alliance. The appearance of copious shells in Chaco Canyon's great houses coincides with the construction of outliers south of Chaco, which provide a travel corridor toward the

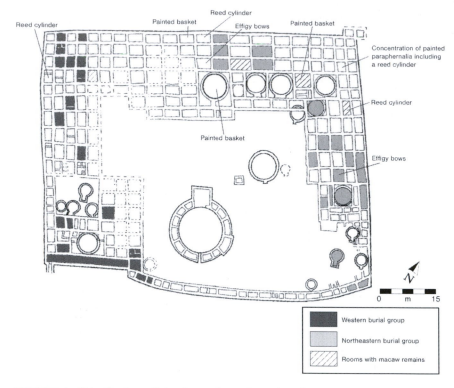

Reed cylinder

Reed cylinder

Painted basket

Effigy bows

Painted basket

Concentration of painted
paraphernalia including
a reed cylinder

Reed cylinder

Painted basket

Effigy bows

N

0   m   15

Western burial group

Northeastern burial group

Rooms with macaw remains

FIGURE 2.4   Distribution of ritual paraphernalia and trade goods within Aztec West. Artifact distributions based on collections research and examination of inventories on file at the American Museum of Natural History (AMNH 2014), photographic inventories on file at the National Museum of the American Indian (NMAI 2013), and the Chaco Research Archive (CRI 2014). Drafted by Andrew Saiz, courtesy Statistical Research, Inc.

Gulf of California (Kantner and Kintigh 2006:183). These territories fell outside the radius of the Totah great houses. It is also of note that macaw remains at Aztec were not articulated skeletons. While this may reflect analytical bias, it could also indicate that Aztec's "macaws" were heirloom objects such as feathers, bones, and mounted skins, rather than living birds. These may have been curated as markers of corporate identity, in the absence of the cosmopolitan connections that live macaws attested.

Wupatki and the western frontier

There is no universal agreement among archaeologists about whether Wupatki Pueblo constitutes a Chacoan great house. As with great houses, Wupatki is large (three stories and 110 rooms) (Adler and Johnson 1996). The oldest sections of its southern unit were built with Chacoan veneers that indicate that, despite great

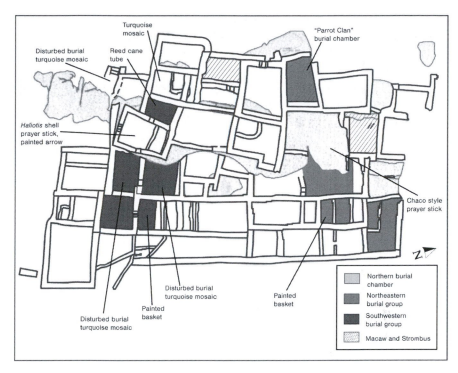

FIGURE 2.5 Distribution of ritual paraphernalia and trade goods in Wupatki Pueblo's southern unit. Distribution is based on examination of archived field notes (MNA 1785) and perishable collections curated at the Museum of Northern Arizona. Drafted by Andrew Saiz, courtesy Statistical Research, Inc.

geographic distance from Chaco Canyon, its founders participated in Chaco's regime of monumental construction (Gruner 2012:57). However, this core of early construction is surrounded by agglomerative roomblocks lacking the formalism of Chacoan architecture.[4] Additionally, the site shows influence from the Hohokam culture, including hybrid ritual architecture. Most likely, Wupatki's founders began to build a Chaco style great house in the early 1100s A.D., but the project was abandoned by their successors in favor of local innovations in ritual practice.

Wupatki's weak commitment to Chacoan monumentality is counterbalanced by a far stronger command of exotic trade networks than the more orthodox Totah great houses. Excavations at Wupatki Pueblo found no less than 41 macaws and two conch shells, with a minimum of two conch shells and seven parrots recovered from nearby smaller settlements, including Ridge Ruin (Vokes and Gregory 2009; McGregor 1941, 1943). Several types of Chacoan ritual paraphernalia were recovered from Wupatki, including painted basketry and reed tubes, a hoof-headed prayer stick, and a type of prayer stick also recovered from Pueblo Bonito's founder burial chamber (Fewkes 1927; Museum of Northern Arizona [MNA],

Flagstaff "Artifact Inventory NA405," records search on 13 June 2012; Museum of Northern Arizona [MNA], Flagstaff, site file NA405).

As with Chacoan great houses, macaws and conch shells were clustered in the northern roomblocks at the rear of the structure (Figure 2.5). One room, room 35, contained the disturbed remains of a child and an adult male, along with five parrots and isolated human skeletal elements. A Hopi tradition about Wupatki details specifics about this burial, which was interpreted as a revered leader of the Macaw clan (Ferguson and Loma'omvaya 2011:171).

In many ways, this burial seems like a good candidate for a Chacoan cult founder. We can only speculate as to how individuals with knowledge particular to elite kin groups in the San Juan basin arrived at Wupatki. They may have been local people who travelled to Chaco, then returned to their community with exotic knowledge. Alternately, they may have been actual relations of Chaco Canyon elites: Puebloan archaeology and ethnohistory shows frequent migrations over such distances during times of social upheaval. Either way, these founders successfully recruited their own "outliers": nearby small settlements like Ridge Ruin.

However, the fact that only two burials were placed in room 35 suggests reorganization shortly after the introduction of this cult. During later periods, the most elaborate burials were placed in the western half of the structure (MNA NA405).[5] Patterned disturbance within the western cluster includes the disarticulation of human crania, suggesting continuity with Chacoan elite mortuary ritual – and indeed, this group seems to have inherited many trappings of Chacoan elites, including fine turquoise mosaic burial offerings, painted basketry, and *Haliotis* shell (MNA NA405).

The social reorganization indicated by shifting burial patterns may pertain to the fact that ceremonially empowered households in the western Pueblos do not fall under the centralized control of moieties (Fox 1967) – an organizational trend which likely originated prior to the twelfth century. In this region, the kin-based principle of ceremonial leadership can be deceptively flexible, and control of ritual paraphernalia and important ceremonies can transfer between clans during crises of succession (Bernardini 2012; Whiteley 1998).

Discussion and conclusions

Comparing the corporately owned ritual paraphernalia and resource rights of modern Puebloan priesthoods with those held by Chacoan cult leaders suggests that basic ideological and organizational principles of Chacoan priesthoods transcended Chaco, to become the building blocks of modern Puebloan theocracies. However, this does not imply a static structuralist interpretation, wherein the social fabric of these societies remained stable through the Chacoan, post-Chacoan, and ethnohistoric periods through the adoption of shared symbolic constructs. The paradox of leaders who premise their power on material tokens of ancestral authority is that actual continuity is less important to maintaining their prestige than the public perception of ancestral precedent.

Chacoan society had a clear settlement hierarchy where religious leaders in core sites such as Pueblo Bonito drew on the labor pool and resources of broad regions. The sacred authority of elites was naturalized through the creation of persistent spaces within Chacoan great houses, in which the remains of founding kin groups were deposited among material indices of the most venerated natural and supernatural powers of the Chacoan world. Repetitive ritual practice, in which ancestral remains and sacred materials were deposited or manipulated by successive generations, entangled cultural conceptions of elite families with the natural domains they claimed through totemic association.

In the Totah, a post-Chacoan "revivalist" faction maintained heirloom ritual objects, Chacoan mortuary rites, and material symbols of Chacoan orthodoxy to reinforce local authority – including exotica such as parrots, which suggested influence over regions that had abandoned Chacoan networks. Conversely, migrant founders at Wupatki cultivated trade networks to gather materials associated with the traditional domains of Chacoan priesthoods – parrots, conch shells, jet, et cetera – despite operating within a hybrid religious milieu that was as Western Puebloan as it was Chacoan. Finally, the leaders of priesthoods in the ethnohistoric Pueblos drew exclusively on the collective resources of their own villages. Nonetheless, the same objects and materials remained salient symbols of corporate identity, signaling the authenticity of ancestral rights and responsibilities.

The immutability of material symbols creates continuity, even during times of dramatic change. Ritual objects can be resituated in physical space, and thus in the social matrix in which they are embedded. The relationships they anchor are constantly shifting – yet constantly tied to that which came before through the life history of the object itself, and the repetition of associated practices. In noting the radical changes that have taken place in Puebloan religious and political organization since the fall of Chaco, we must also note that this change is premised on an essential core of continuity.

Acknowledgments

I would like to thank the people whose time, energy, and insights contributed to this chapter: Ruth Van Dyke and Randy McGuire for support and guidance throughout the research process, and Kelley Hays-Gilpin, who enabled me to research collections and archival documents housed at the Museum of Northern Arizona. Andrew Saiz of Statistical Research, Inc. (SRI), graciously drafted final architectural maps, and I would like to thank SRI for their support. Thanks also to Anibal Rodriguez and Lorann Thomas at the American Museum of Natural History for providing access to accessions lists, and to Patricia Nietfield for providing object reports from the National Museum of the American Indian. A number of people also contributed data or background from their own ongoing research which proved invaluable in shaping my own ideas. I also would like to thank Laurie Webster, Adam Watson, Ryan Harrod, Michael Schillaci, and Erika Basseraba for sharing data and helping me to understand their areas of expertise.

Notes

1 Wesley Bernardini estimates approximately 70 individuals in residence at Pueblo Bonito in any given period, based on the construction and abandonment of residential suites.
2 Early sections of Ridge Ruin have spall-chinked sandstone walls evoking Chacoan veneers, unlike the basalt rubble walls typical of the area. However, they lack the core-veneer construction of true Chacoan masonry.
3 Kuwanwisiwma writes that the "Katsina" clan co-ruled Chaco, but in Katsina clan origin myths, the Katsina clan was part of Crow clan before their founder introduced novel ceremonies near the San Francisco Peaks.
4 The relative dating of rooms in Wupatki follows the construction sequence published by Northern Arizona University Anthropology Labs (Downum 2004).
5 All burial data was gathered from room excavation descriptions. Detailed photographic and descriptive information pertaining to burials remains redacted per the wishes of descendant communities.

References

Adler, Michael, and Amber Johnson 1996 Mapping the Puebloan Southwest. In *The Prehistoric Pueblo World A.D. 1150–1350*, edited by Michael Adler, pp. 255–272. University of Arizona Press, Tucson.

Akins, Nancy J. 2003 The Burials of Pueblo Bonito. In *Pueblo Bonito: Center of the Chacoan World*, edited by Jill Neitzel, pp. 94–106. Smithsonian Books, Washington DC.

American Museum of Natural History Accession list, Pueblo Bonito. Downloaded February 14, 2014, Courtesy Anibal Rodriguez.

Bernardini, Wesley 2012 Hopi Clan Traditions and the Pedigree of Ceremonial Objects. In *Enduring Motives: The Archaeology of Tradition and Religion in Native America*, edited by John E. Clark and Arlene Colman, pp. 172–184. University of Alabama Press, Tuscaloosa.

Brandt, Elizabeth 1980 On Secrecy and the Control of Knowledge: Taos Pueblo. In *Secrecy: A Cross-Cultural Perspective*, edited by Stanton K. Tefft, pp. 123–146. Human Sciences Press, New York.

Cameron, Catherine 2008 Comparing Great House Architecture: Perspectives From the Bluff Great House. In *Chaco's Northern Prodigies: Salmon, Aztec, and the Ascendency of the Middle San Juan After A.D. 1100*, edited by Paul F. Reed, pp. 251–272. University of Utah Press, Salt Lake City.

Chaco Research Archive Searchable Database 2014 *Query the Database*. Electronic document, www.chacoarchive.org/cra/query-the-database/, accessed December 20, 2014.

Cushing, Frank H. 1988 *The Mythic World of the Zuni*, edited and illustrated by Barton Wright. University of New Mexico Press, Albuquerque.

Downum, Christian E. 2004 Dating Wupatki Pueblo: Tree Ring Evidence. Excerpted and adapted from *An Architectural Study of Wupatki Pueblo (NA 405)*, by Christian E. Downum, Ellen Brennan, and James P. Holmlund. Northern Arizona University Archaeological Report 1175, Flagstaff. Electronic document, jan.ucc.nau.edu/~d-antlab/Wupatki/tree ring.htm, accessed January 22, 2012.

Durand, Kathy Roler 2003 Function of Chaco Era Great Houses. *Kiva* 69: 141–169.

Durand, Kathy Roler, and Stephen R. Durand 2006 Variation in Economic and Ritual Fauna at Salmon Ruins. In *Thirty-Five Years of Archaeological Research at Salmon Ruins, New Mexico. Volume Three: Archaeobotanical Research and Other Analytical Studies*, edited by Paul F. Reed, pp. 1079–1100. Center for Desert Archaeology, Tucson.

———. 2008 Animal Bone From Salmon Ruins and Other Great Houses: Faunal Exploitation in the Chaco World. In *Chaco's Northern Prodigies: Salmon, Aztec, and the Ascendency of the Middle San Juan After A.D. 1100*, edited by Paul F. Reed, pp. 96–112. University of Utah Press, Salt Lake City.

Ferguson, T.J., and Micah Loma'omvaya 2011 Nuvatukya'ovi, Palatsmo, Niqw Wupatki: Hopi History, Culture, and Landscape. In *Sunset Crater Archaeology: Prehistoric Settlement in the Shadow of the Volcano*, edited by Mark Elson, pp. 143–186. Anthropological Papers No. 37, Center for Desert Archaeology, Tucson.

Fewkes, Jesse W. 1927 *Archaeological Studies of the Wupatki National Monument*. Smithsonian Miscellaneous Collections vol. 78, pp. 100–105. Smithsonian Institution, Washington, DC.

Fowles, Severin M. 2013 *An Archaeology of Doings: Secularism and the Study of Pueblo Religion*. School for Advanced Research Press, Santa Fe.

Fox, Robin 1967 *The Keresan Bridge: A Problem in Pueblo Ethnography*. Humanities Press Inc., New York.

Gell, Alfred 1998 *Art and Agency: An Anthropological Theory*. Clarendon Press, Oxford.

Gruner, Erina 2012 *Post-Chacoan Ceremonial Societies on the Chaco Periphery*. Unpublished Master's thesis, Department of Anthropology, Binghamton University, Binghamton.

———. 2015 Replicating Things, Replicating Identity: The Movement of Chacoan Ritual Paraphernalia Beyond the Chaco World. In *Practicing Materiality*, edited by Ruth Van Dyke, pp. 56–78. University of Arizona Press, Tucson.

Harrod, Ryan P. 2012 Centers of Control: Revealing Elites Among the Ancestral Pueblo During the "Chaco Phenomenon." *International Journal of Paleopathology* 2: 123–135.

Heitman, Carolyn, and Stephen Plog 2005 Kinship and the Dynamics of the House: Rediscovering Dualism in the Pueblo Past. In *A Catalyst for Ideas: Anthropological Archaeology and the Legacy of Douglas Schwartz*, edited by Vernon L. Scarborough, pp. 69–100. School for Advanced Research Press, Santa Fe.

Irwin-Williams, Cynthia 2008 Chacoan Society: The View from Salmon Ruins. In *Chaco's Northern Prodigies: Salmon, Aztec, and the Ascendency of the Middle San Juan*, edited by Paul F. Reed, pp. 273–283. University of Utah Press, Salt Lake City.

Judd, Neil 1981 *The Material Culture of Pueblo Bonito*. Reprints in Anthropology, vol. 23. J. & L Reprint Company, Lincoln. Originally published 1954, Smithsonian Miscellaneous Collections 124, Smithsonian Institution, Washington, DC.

Judge, W. J. 1979 The Development of a Complex Cultural Ecosystem in the Chaco Basin, New Mexico. In *Proceedings of the First Conference on Scientific Research in the National Parks*, vol. II, edited by R. M. Linn, pp. 901–906, Transactions and Proceedings Series 5. National Park Service, US Department of the Interior, Washington, DC.

Kantner, John 2003 Rethinking Chaco as a System. *Kiva* 69: 207–227.

Kantner, John W., and Keith W. Kintigh 2006 The Chaco World. In *The Archaeology of Chaco Canyon: An Eleventh-Century Pueblo Regional Center*, edited by Stephen Lekson, pp. 153–188. School of American Research Advanced Seminar Series, James F. Brooks, general editor, School for Advanced Research Press, Santa Fe.

Kennett, Douglas, Stephen Plog, Richard J. George, Brendan J. Culleton, Adam S. Watson, Pontus Skoglund, Nadin Rohland, Swapun Mallick, Kristen Stewardson, Logan Kistler, Stephen A. LeBlanc, Peter M. Whiteley, David Reich and George H. Perry 2017 Archaeogenomic evidence reveals prehistoric matrilineal dynasty. *Nature Communications* 8: 1–9.

Kuwanwisiwma, Leigh J. 2004 Yupkoyvi: The Hopi Story of Chaco Canyon. In *In Search of Chaco: New Approaches to an Archaeological Enigma*, edited by David Grant Noble, pp. 41–47. School for Advanced Research Press, Santa Fe.

Lekson, Stephen H. 2006 Chaco Matters. In *The Archaeology of Chaco Canyon: An Eleventh-Century Pueblo Regional Center*, edited by Stephen H. Lekson, pp. 3–44. School for Advanced Research Press, Santa Fe.

Marden, Keriann 2011 *Taphonomy, Paleopathology and Mortuary Variability in Chaco Canyon: Using Archaeological and Forensic Methods to Understand Ancient Cultural Practices*. Ph.D. dissertation, Department of Anthropology, Tulane University, New Orleans.

McGregor, John C. 1941 *Winona and Ridge Ruin, Part I: Architecture and Material Culture*. Museum of Northern Arizona Bulletin 18. Northern Arizona Society of Science and Art, Flagstaff.

———. 1943 Burial of an Early American Magician. *Proceedings of the American Philosophical Society* 82: 270–289.

Morris, Earl H. 1919 *The Archer M. Huntington Survey of the Southwest: The Aztec Ruin*. Anthropological Papers of the Museum of Natural History, Volume XXVI. American Museum Press, New York.

———. 1924 *Burials in the Aztec Ruin, The Aztec Ruin Annex. Anthropological Papers of the American Museum of Natural History, vol. XXVI, parts III and IV*. American Museum Press, New York.

National Museum of the American Indian Pueblo Bonito object reports and photographic documentation. Downloaded December 2013, courtesy Patricia Nietfeld.

Neitzel, Jill 2003 Artifact Distributions at Pueblo Bonito. In *Pueblo Bonito: Center of the Chacoan World*, edited by Jill Neitzel, pp. 107–126. Smithsonian Books, Washington, DC.

Ortiz, Alfonso 1969 *The Tewa World: Space, Time, Being and Becoming in a Pueblo Society*. University of Chicago Press, Chicago.

Parsons, Elsie C. 1920 *Notes on Ceremonialism at Laguna*. Anthropological Papers of the American Museum of Natural History, vol. XIX, part IV. American Museum Press, New York.

———. 1996 *Pueblo Indian Religion*. 2 vols. University of Nebraska Books, Lincoln. Originally published 1939, University of Chicago Press, Chicago.

Pauketat, Timothy R. 2013 *An Archaeology of the Cosmos: Rethinking Agency and Religion in Ancient America*. Routledge, New York.

Pepper, George 1996 *Pueblo Bonito*. University of New Mexico Press, Albuquerque. Originally published 1920, Anthropological Papers of the American Museum of Natural History, vol. XXVII, American Museum of Natural History, New York.

Perez, Ventura R. 2012 The Taphonomy of Violence: Recognizing Variation in Disarticulated Skeletal Assemblages. *The International Journal of Paleopathology* 2: 156–165.

Plog, Stephen, and Carrie Heitman 2010 Hierarchy and Social Inequality in the American Southwest, A.D. 800–1200. *Proceedings of the National Academy of Sciences* 107: 19619–19626.

Reed, Paul F. 2006 *Thirty-Five Years of Archaeological Research at Salmon Ruins, New Mexico*. 2 vols. Center for Desert Archaeology, Tucson.

———. 2008 Salmon Pueblo as Ritual and Residential Chacoan Great House. In *Chaco's Northern Prodigies: Salmon, Aztec, and the Ascendency of the Middle San Juan*, edited by Paul F. Reed, pp. 42–64. University of Utah Press, Salt Lake City.

Sebastien, Lynn 1992 Chaco Canyon and the Anasazi Southwest: Changing Views of Sociopolitical Organization. In *Anasazi Regional Organization and the Chaco System*, edited by David Doyel, pp. 23–34. Maxwell Museum of Anthropology Papers No. 5. University of New Mexico, Albuquerque.

Schillaci, Michael A., and Christopher M. Stojanowski 2003 Postmarital Residence and Biological Variation at Pueblo Bonito. *American Journal of Physical Anthropology* 120: 1–15.

Stein, John, Dabney Ford, and Richard Freidman 2003 Reconstructing Pueblo Bonito. In *Pueblo Bonito: Center of the Chacoan World*, edited by Jill Neitzel, pp. 33–60. Smithsonian Books, Washington, DC.

Toll, H. Wolcott 2006 Organization of Production. In *The Archaeology of Chaco Canyon: An Eleventh-Century Pueblo Regional Center*, edited by Stephen Lekson, pp. 117–152. School of American Research Advanced Seminar Series, James F. Brooks, general editor. School for Advanced Research Press, Santa Fe.

Van Dyke, Ruth M. 2003 Bounding Chaco: Great House Architectural Variability Across Time and Space. *Kiva* 69: 117–139.

Vivian, R. Gwinn 1970 An Inquiry Into Prehistoric Social Organization in Chaco Canyon, New Mexico. In *Reconstructing Prehistoric Pueblo Societies*, edited by William A. Longacre, pp. 59–83. School of American Research Press, Albuquerque.

Vivian, R. Gwinn, Dulce N. Dodgen, and Gayle H. Hartmann 1978 *Wooden Ritual Artifacts From Chaco Canyon, New Mexico: The Chetro Ketl Collection*. Anthropological Papers of the University of Arizona No. 32. University of Arizona Press, Tucson.

Vokes, Arthur W., and David A. Gregory 2009 Exchange Networks for Exotic Goods in the Southwest and Zuni's Place in Them. In *Zuni Origins: Towards a New Synthesis of Southwestern Archaeology*, edited by David A. Gregory and David R. Wilcox, pp. 318–357. University of Arizona Press, Tucson.

Ware, John A. 2014 *A Pueblo Social History: Kinship, Sodality, and Community in the Northern Southwest*. School for Advanced Research Press, Santa Fe.

Watson, Adam S., Stephen Plog, Brendan J. Culleton, Patricia A. Gilman, Stephen A. LeBlanc, Peter M. Whiteley 2015 Early Procurement of Scarlet Macaws and the Emergence of Social Complexity in Chaco Canyon, NM. *Proceedings of the National Academy of Sciences* 112(27): 8238–8243.

Webster, Laurie D. 2006 Worked Fiber Artifacts From Salmon Pueblo. In *Thirty-Five Years of Research at Salmon Ruins, New Mexico. Volume Three: Archaeobotanical Research and Other Analytical Studies*, edited by Paul F. Reed, pp. 893–1012. Center for Desert Archaeology, Tucson.

———. 2008 An Initial Assessment of Perishable Relationships Among Salmon, Aztec, and Chaco Canyon. In *Chaco's Northern Prodigies: Salmon, Aztec, and the Ascendancy of the Middle San Juan Region after A.D. 1100*, edited by Paul F. Reed, pp. 167–189. University of Utah Press, Salt Lake City.

———. 2011 Perishable Ritual Artifacts at the West Ruin of Aztec, New Mexico: Evidence for a Chacoan Migration. *Kiva* 77: 139–171.

Whiteley, Peter 1998 *Rethinking Hopi Ethnography*. Smithsonian Institution Press, Washington, DC.

Wilcox, David R. 1993 The Evolution of Chacoan Polity. In *The Chimney Rock Archaeological Symposium, October 20–21, 1990, Durango, CO*, edited by J. McKim Malville and Gary Matlock, pp. 76–90. United States Department of Agriculture, Rocky Mountain Forest and Range Experiment Station. Forest Service General Technical Report RM-227, Fort Collins.

———. 2002 The Wupatki Nexus: Chaco-Hohokam-Chumash Connectivity, A.D. 1150–1225. In *The Archaeology of Contact: Processes and Consequences. Proceedings of the Twenty-fifth Annual Conference of the Archaeological Association of the University of Calgary. The Archaeology of Contact: Processes and Consequences*, edited by Kurtis Lesick, Barbara Kulle, Christine Cluney, and Meaghan Peuramaki-Brown, pp. 218–234. University of Calgary, Calgary.

Wills, W. H. 2000 Political Leadership and the Construction of Chacoan Great Houses. In *Alternative Leadership Strategies in the Prehispanic Southwest*, edited by Barbara Mills, pp. 19–44. University of Arizona Press, Tucson.

Zedeño, Maria Nieves 2008 Bundled Worlds: The Roles and Interactions of Complex Objects from the North American Plains. *Journal of Archaeological Method and Theory* 15: 362–378.

3

THE ELEMENTS OF CAHOKIAN SHRINE COMPLEXES AND BASIS OF MISSISSIPPIAN RELIGION

Susan M. Alt and Timothy R. Pauketat

Introduction

Decreasingly few archaeologists are willing to treat religion as if it was a set of shared beliefs, official myths, or established institutions that fulfilled some greater societal purpose (A. Joyce, Chapter 1; Shaw 2013). To do so is both to overlook the locus of change in the past – people's continuous, practical engagement in the world – and to assume that religious places, practices, and objects are mere representations of fixed beliefs, unchanging metaphors, and static institutions. Opposed to this standard approach to religion are those that discuss religiosity as a dynamic, experiential dimension of social life (Hodder 2014; Insoll 2004, 2011; see also A. Joyce, Chapter 1). From such viewpoints, religion is lived, which is to say ontological, involving people's fundamental ways of relating to their worlds. In other words, religion is more about what people do and how they do it (Geertz 1973; Morgan 2005). For that reason, one might even question whether the word "religion" is necessary or appropriate in all cases (Fowles 2013).

None of this means that these same archaeologists would deny the existence of important long-term historical patterns involving religious or ontological change (Robb and Pauketat 2013). Clearly, the ways in which people relate to a wider world change through time. Precisely how human beings become self-aware persons, how people become "a people," or how certain persons emerge to govern others, for instance, depends on their entangled relationships with non-human beings, powers, substances, or phenomena (for a variety of approaches, see Descola 2013; Ingold 2000; Malafouris 2013). Following that line of thought further, it is true that the personification (or politicization) of cosmic forces on earth was (and is) doubtless a significant human development (e.g., Wheatley 1971). However, that process is a historical one (not a one-time evolutionary transformation), and is driven by the continuous engagement of human bodies with other non-human agencies, powers, or beings. It continues to this day.

More to the present point, such processes were and are closely linked to the assembling, bundling, or gathering of non-human forces and phenomena with and among people. These are processes with a spatial dimension. They happen in space and, in so doing, define religious places. For such reasons, Fustel de Coulanges' (1980), writing in 1864, noted that early cities had spiritual and cosmological underpinnings. They did not merely transform religion; they were in some sense founded because of religion. Simply stated, the causal relationships between places, peoples, identities, and religion(s), among other things, remain key in our explanations of human history; and they are simultaneously relevant to any understanding of contemporary social and geopolitical dynamics.

Our present purpose consists of showing *how* places – namely the city of Cahokia and later Mississippian centers in precolumbian eastern North America – were products of lived, religious experience. They were not, first or foremost, political capitals. The production process was doubtless political, involving the contested negotiations with or over sacred, otherworldly power(s). But the power of such negotiations was not *primarily* political nor was it simply human. This is because power, in precolumbian America and elsewhere, was inherent to human–human, human–non-human, and nonhuman–nonhuman relationships of all kinds. Power imbued and defined various phenomena, substances, things, places, and people, and it becomes the object of our concern as it was "bundled" (Pauketat 2013a) – which is to say assembled, enchained, gathered, entangled, or emplaced in and as them (see DeLanda 2006; Heidegger 1996; Hodder 2011; Strathern 1988). This understanding by necessity alters how we approach and think about Mississippian phenomena (ca. 1050–1600 CE).

In the following sections, we first highlight the ontologies of mid-continental Prairie-Plains peoples in a historical and material sense, recognizing that these were lived and not held in the mind or uniformly shared. We then outline the bundling process as it pertains to religion and the ancient city by recognizing the experiential dimensions of four Cahokia-related "shrine complexes": Emerald, Pfeffer, Angel, and Trempealeau. Especially important in this regard are the intersections of human bodies with non-human elements, landforms, materials, substances, and moving celestial bodies. Finally, we extend the inferences to the greater history of the Mississippian world as it speaks to the larger relationships between religion and politics.

Woodland ontologies

By the final two to three centuries of the Late Woodland era (ca. A.D. 400–1050), the forested hills, river bottoms, and tall-grass prairies of the American Midwest and mid-South were carved up into the territories of horticultural peoples (Figure 3.1). Settlements of clustered wooden pole-frame homes, outdoor processing facilities, and storage pits filled with foodstuffs were surrounded by gardens of squash, sunflower, and native grasses in most valleys and along waterways. The seasons could be extreme, with snows in winters and heat waves in summers. The ninth-century

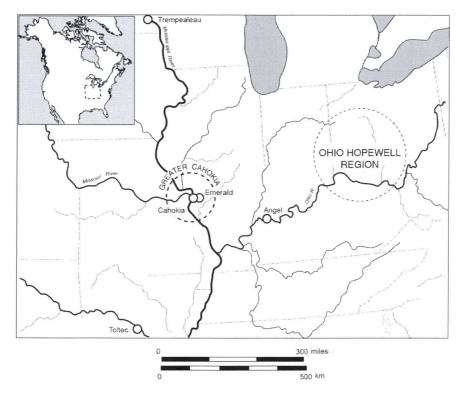

FIGURE 3.1　Map of mid-continental North America showing sites or complexes mentioned in the text

adoption of the foreign crop, maize, from the Southwest or Mesoamerica by some in the Midwest was probably part and parcel of a significant ontological shift.

In some regions, especially in present-day Ohio, Illinois, Arkansas, Louisiana, and western Tennessee, some horticultural peoples would have identified with yet-visible Hopewell earthworks (ca. 150 B.C.–A.D. 400). Up until the eleventh century A.D., other maize-less people communed with earth, sky, and water spirits in what is today Wisconsin through their constructions of modest effigy mounds in the shapes of bear and bird spirits and water beings (Birmingham and Eisenberg 2000). Far to the south, in Mississippi, Arkansas, and Louisiana, their "Coles Creek" contemporaries, also maize-free, built four-sided packed-earth pyramids around plazas, some complexes covering 10 ha and featuring isolated upright posts (Steponaitis et al. 2015). Their pottery serving-wares were decorated with likely wind or water motifs (see Cummings 2015; Emerson 1989).

Centuries later, the Prairie-Plains and Southeastern descendants of these Late Woodland progenitors sensed that mysterious disembodied life forces might imbue some people, places, things, substances, and phenomena with spiritual power, continuously creating a host of subjects that mediated social relationships. The most powerful among these mediators were the most elemental: earth, sky, sun, moon, stars, water, fire, and smoke. Such fundamental forces were thought by many to be able to "witness" that which people did on earth (Pauketat 2013b).

For these later people, the specific arrays of witnesses defined in no uncertain terms one's relationships in life and in death. They were, that is, the basis of relational, animic ontologies – ways of being-in-the-world in which one's senses of self and other rested to some significant degree on the configuration of the non-human elemental forces across entire *fields* of experience (Ingold 2000). Similar fields probably characterized the earlier Late Woodland world of the Midwest and mid-South, bearing in mind that these fields were themselves relational ontologies. In other words, the latter were not uniformly cognized and shared, slow-to-change worldviews that might be reflected in art, imagery, or settlement patterns (Harris and Robb 2012). Instead, they were multi-dimensional (material, experiential, and phenomenal) landscapes and skyscapes open to change and filled with human and non-human beings, forces, and moving entities (Pauketat 2013a).

Importantly, such experiential fields in the Late Woodland era seem to have been regionally isolated or "parochial" (Anderson and Mainfort 2002; Emerson, et al. 2000). Archaeologists surmise this based on the modest scale of most Late Woodland places and the general lack of elaborate artifacts or exotic materials. We might also hypothesize that this parochial quality indicates that the animate powers of the greater Woodland world were not highly concentrated in people, places, or things, but were widely dispersed before A.D. 1050 (see Spielmann 2013).

There were exceptions. Certain mounded Late Woodland complexes in the mid-South epitomize a centralization of animate forces. For example, the central Arkansas site of Toltec had 18 platform mounds and a semi-circular embankment rigidly aligned to both a watery bayou and a maximum moonrise, an event that took place during one out of every 18.6 years (Romain 2015). In this configuration, Toltec harkened back to the great Hopewell sites of the Ohio and Mississippi Valleys, which were built, it seems, to position human bodies in the midst of convergences of non-human powers: earth, water, sky, sun, and moon.

Besides the historical, commemorative qualities of earthworks, all such sites would also have been experienced as places of power, engaging one's auditory, visual, tactile, and olfactory senses. In experiencing them, the human bodies, materials, and practices positioned together and put into contact with each other would have been wrapped, at least momentarily, in cosmic associations. Such a cosmic bundle might have done more than serve local people. It may have attracted people from far away, as some assume the earlier Ohio Hopewell sites had done (Pacheco 2006), and as historic-era "revitalization movements" were known to have done (Pauketat 2013b).

Shrine complexes

Such attractors included both ancient mounded landscapes and natural places: caves, springs, cliffs, and hills (Basso 1996; Bradley 2000). At the beginning of the eleventh century A.D., one hill – the future location of the Emerald Acropolis – lay 24 km east of the future city of Cahokia (Figure 3.2). Situated in the midst of a great expanse of prairie, the hill is one of a series of Pleistocene-era glacial drift ridges in the uplands east of the Mississippi River bottoms. In the early eleventh century, its linear shape by coincidence was oriented to about 53 degrees of azimuth. It rose some 15 m above the surrounding glacial plain with an unobstructed view of the treeless eastern horizon.

Cahokians would later enhance its azimuth alignment by flattening the hill, adding fill to its sides, and building 12 mounds in rows atop the acropolis, all emphasizing the 53-degree angle if not the elongate rectangularity of the hill (Pauketat and Alt 2015). That angle was potentially powerful because, given a flat eastern horizon, the Emerald ridge and mound-rows also coincided precisely with a maximum northern moonrise. Other powerful moonrise angles at this latitude and with Emerald's near-zero horizon include 67, 115, and 129 (Pauketat 2013a). Given that the earliest known archaeological feature at the Emerald site seems

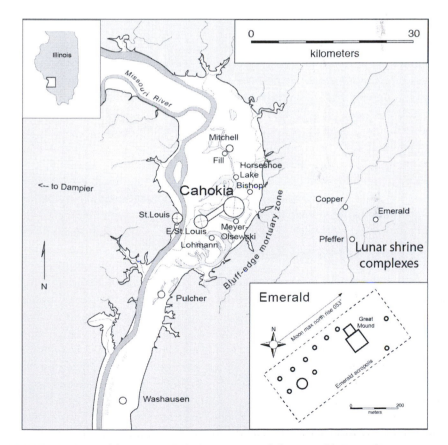

FIGURE 3.2 Map of the greater Cahokia region and the Emerald Acropolis

to have been a pre-Mississippian (i.e., Terminal Late Woodland) lunar-aligned "shrine house" dating to about A.D. 1000 (Alt 2013), the earthly and lunar alignment at this location appears to have been recognized before the abrupt mid-eleventh-century transition of the Late Woodland village of Cahokia into a city, discussed at length elsewhere (Alt 2012; Pauketat 2004). That is, the motivations that produced the Emerald lunar shrine complex were not political, but religious. The religious genesis of Cahokia needs to be seriously entertained.

At the start of the eleventh century, a thousand or more residents probably occupied the sprawling village areas of old Cahokia that stretched out along an oxbow lake in the Mississippi river bottom. In short order and by A.D. 1050, Cahokian designers laid out a new Mississippian city design over this pre-Mississippian village (Pauketat, Alt, and Kruchten 2015). That design, which included three major precincts, extended out into the rural landscape. Each major precinct built at this time, during the Lohmann phase (A.D. 1050–1100), had its own orthogonal layout. Redesigned outlying complexes within a 50-km radius presumably did as well. The regional effect may have been that Cahokia was the center of a constellation of various cosmic and phenomenal referents, alignments, and layouts. The population of the Cahokia site increased four- to ten-fold, and the regional population did likewise.

Central to the new reorganized regional landscape seems to have been central Cahokia's large pyramids, a great 20-plus hectare plaza, and a kilometer-long causeway that extended from the plaza south through watery swampland to a ridge-top-shaped burial mound (Baires 2014a, b). The latter feature established a cosmic axis, currently interpreted to align the movements of living human bodies with those of dead souls, the moon and, perhaps, the Milky Way's "Path of Souls" (Baires, et al. 2013; Pauketat 2015; Pauketat et al. 2015; Romain 2015). At or shortly after this time, many people moved into the region and to the new city, as argued in the past based on pottery, housing, and isotopic measures (Alt 2006a, 2012; Pauketat 2003; Slater et al. 2014). They came from the east and south, although the reasons why have been, up to this point, difficult to discern.

The Emerald and Pfeffer Acropolises

Emerald is perhaps the most visually distinctive of the regional outliers owing to its acropolis and the absence of a permanent water source save a large spring to the northeast. Its occupation spans the period A.D. 1000–1300, with a possible hiatus in the twelfth century. A smaller version of it, known as the Pfeffer site, sits 5 km away and dates exclusively to the period A.D. 1050–1100. Excavations there in 2000 and 2007–2008, and at Emerald beginning in 2012, have established in broad outlines the site histories relative to Cahokia's other precincts and outliers (Table 3.1).

Unlike most of the others, Emerald and Pfeffer appear to have been intermittently occupied *shrine complexes*. The shrine complex designation is new to Mississippian studies and captures the essence of these sites. Both consist of multiple

TABLE 3.1 Mid-eleventh-century constructions of greater Cahokia precincts, outliers, and shrine complexes*

Site	Straight-line distance from Cahokia's central pyramid (km)	Constructions at ca. 1050 CE
Central Cahokia Precinct	<1	Causeway, plazas, and initial earthen pyramids constructed over old Terminal Late Woodland village areas
Horseshoe Lake	5	Lohmann-phase wall-trench buildings and platform mound without earlier occupation indicates founding event
East St. Louis Precinct	6–9	Expansive ritual-residential areas composed of large buildings and upright wooden posts built over and beyond old Terminal Late Woodland village
Lohmann	9	Lohmann-phase wall-trench buildings without earlier occupation indicates founding event
Pfeffer	22	Temporary Lohmann-phase wall-trench housing established around modest hilltop mound-and-plaza complex
Emerald	24	Dense stands of religious architecture and temporary housing built atop re-contoured acropolis
Washausen	24	Lohmann-phase wall-trench buildings indicate conversion of extant pre-Mississippian center
Pulcher	39	Lohmann-phase wall-trench buildings indicate conversion of extant pre-Mississippian center
Dampier	53	Lohmann-phase wall-trench buildings and ritual deposits without earlier occupation indicates founding event

* (Betzenhauser 2011; Emerson 1997a; Esarey and Pauketat 1992; Fortier 2007; Harl et al. 2011; Kelly 2002; Pauketat 2005, 2013a; Pauketat and Alt 2015; Pauketat et al. 2015; Pauketat et al. 1998)

shrines, holy places associated with or dedicated to one or more spiritual powers or gods (see Scarre 2008). But neither appears to have had a dense, year-round residential occupation. As defined based on excavations, the Emerald and Pfeffer shrine complexes minimally consist of a complement of non-domestic Cahokian architectural forms, some on earthen platforms or mounds, and all atop and on the slopes of prominent modified hilltops. The earthen platforms include great flat-topped and rectangular sub-structural pyramids that were carefully built using colored and specially mixed earthen fills. Other mounds include modest circular tumuli. Several of these at Emerald were platforms that probably elevated circular pole-and-thatch buildings. At least one at Pfeffer elevated a lone upright post which may have been a post-shrine of sorts (Pauketat 2009). Posts and earth among Mississippian descendants might contain or manifest spirits (Skousen 2012). As such, both they and the mounds were more than merely commemorative; they were future-oriented "imaginaries" that allowed people to engage otherworldly powers and, thereby, construct alternative futures (Pauketat 2014; Scarre 2011). They were opportunities for the spiritual powers to witness people's movements.

The same applies to the non-domestic architecture at both sites, including:

1 Oversized council houses or temples that might accommodate two or three dozen congregants (Alt 2006b; Emerson 1997a);
2 T-shaped "medicine lodges" with a small alcove or interior shrine area (Alt 2006b; Collins 1990; Pauketat et al. 2012);
3 Individual- to group-sized circular rotundas (Mehrer 1995); and
4 Small, semi-subterranean and rectangular buildings with yellow-plastered floors, interior hearths, and small niche-like pits that Alt (2013) has dubbed "shrine houses."

Together, these religious-administrative buildings make up what Thomas Emerson (1997a) labeled Cahokia's "architecture of power," in part since "medicine lodges" and circular rotundas, described in the list above, were constructed only within the period A.D. 1050–1200. At Cahokia, the largest such buildings include great halls, temples, or council chambers that are 24 or more meters across (Figure 3.3). Of special importance is one of Cahokia's circular rotundas, Feature 238/389, which had some exceptional characteristics (Figure 3.3, right). Besides having a pair of human long bones buried in the floor and another yellow-plastered pit to one side, the building seems to have been closed and buried using a specially mixed yellow and black earth, inferred based on color photos from 1960 (Pauketat 2013b:82).

At Emerald, smaller versions of these same religious-administrative buildings comprise 27 percent (N = 22) of the total identified in the 2012 and 2013 excavations (Table 3.2). The other 60 buildings are simple rectangular structures, most of which appear to have been temporary residences, an inference based on the absence of the attributes of domiciles: semi-subterranean basins, interior hearths, roof support posts, storage pits, and significant accumulations of refuse. For all intents and purposes, these were empty rectangular shells likely built by work crews in conjunction with major ceremonial events at the Emerald Acropolis (Pauketat and Alt 2015). Those events were presumably focused on the site's shrine houses, all of which are lunar aligned (Figure 3.4). Possibly, these lunar-aligned buildings were built in anticipation of a specific maximum or minimum moonrise, one of which happens every 9.3 years (Pauketat 2013a:73–75).

At least one of these shrine houses, known as Feature 157, pre-dates the Lohmann phase. Two or three others that feature single-set post walls may have been built initially before the Lohmann phase, which is to say during the final years of the Edelhardt phase (A.D. 1000–1050), but these probably lasted or were rebuilt during the early decades of the Lohmann phase as well. All of the rest were built and later dismantled during that late eleventh-century phase (A.D. 1050–1100), with one or two at Emerald possibly lasting into the initial decade of the subsequent

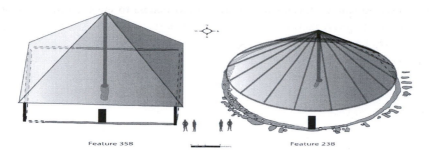

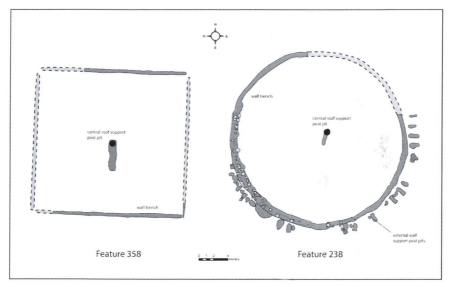

FIGURE 3.3 Oversized buildings at Cahokia. Adapted from Pauketat 2013b with permission of the Illinois State Archaeological Survey.

TABLE 3.2 Buildings identified and excavated at the Emerald site, 2012–2013. Adapted from Pauketat and Alt 2015.

Building form	N of wall-trench constructions (post-1050 CE)	N of single-post constructions (pre- and post-1050 CE)	Total
Shrine houses	2	6	8
Temples/council houses	6	0	6
Rotundas/sweat lodges	8	0	8
T-shaped medicine lodges	2	0	2
Rectangular houses	55	3	58
Total	73	9	82

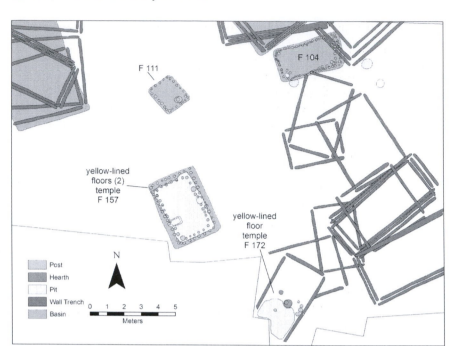

FIGURE 3.4   Plan view of shrine houses (Features 157 and 172) and other wall-trench buildings in block 2, Emerald 2012 excavations

Early Stirling phase (A.D. 1100–1150). Given that the 2012–2013 excavations covered 3,931 m² of the site's total area of at least 150,000 m², and allowing for an open 3,000 m² plaza on the acropolis summit, the minimum number of buildings constructed during any one of eight hypothesized late-Edelhardt through Lohmann phase pulses (every 9.3 years over 7.5 decades) is 380. At 27 percent of the buildings, some 100 of these would have been shrine houses.

What specifically was being co-associated or bundled as part of the construction of these shrines and other religious-administrative architecture at either Emerald or Pfeffer? Minimally, the answer includes earth, sky, water, moon, sun, night, day, life, death, and feminine life forces. To explain, we note that all eight of the Emerald and both of the Pfeffer shrine houses, along with many of the other buildings at both sites, were lunar aligned. Moreover, such alignments were reoriented successively with each major construction event. For instance, sequential buildings at Emerald and Pfeffer alternated between maximum and minimum northern and southern moonrise angles. Similarly, an unusual linear depression on the floor of one Pfeffer shrine house suggests that the floor was partially re-exposed during an ancient excavation in order to commemorate a maximum moonrise event 9.3 years (or some multiple of 9.3 years) after the original lunar-aligned construction (Pauketat 2008, 2013a).

Assuming that the lunar alignments indicate that people gathered at Emerald and Pfeffer on the occasion of maximum or minimum moonrises, then the buildings, builders, or other human or non-human associations of the shrine houses would likely have included the powers of the sun, sky, night, and day as well, since the full moon that rises at its extremes begins its ascent at or just after sunset – the interface of night and day – and takes 18.6 years (or about one human generation) to repeat. The connections between earth and moon, and earth and sky, are also evident in other deposits associated with the floor and later fill of each of the shrine houses. For instance, people expended great amounts of energy excavating earth, both to re-contour the natural ridges and to dig scores of meter-deep shrine house basins. In addition, preparing and slathering thin layers of yellow clayey-silt plaster on the floors of these lunar-aligned buildings and nearby pits (and to the bases or surfaces of platform mounds) would have been an intimate and tactile experience of earth and water for at least a person or two, the substance possibly also being a metaphor of the moon.

Further linkages between earth and sky can be seen in the decommissioning and removal of the shrine-house basins. At those moments, the open basins were the sites of incinerations, sometimes filled with burned debris and ash in alternation with specially prepared and packed construction fill and water-laid silts. Of particular concern here are the water-laid silts, which may have originated from the sky – which is to say from natural precipitation events – or might have referenced the groundwater that gurgled up in the nearby spring. They might also have been created by people pouring water into the open basin (Baltus 2014). Either way, water from above or below was an integral part of the depositional process.

As with Prairie-Plains descendants, these watery, nightly, lunar, and earthly powers may all have been feminine life forces or witnesses (Emerson 1989; Prentice 1986). Thus, it may be no coincidence that a human offering, probably a young female, was placed into an open post pit at the Emerald site (Pauketat and Alt 2015). The post had likely projected up through the roof of a solar-aligned council house or temple that was, in turn, located on one of the Emerald site's principal lunar axes (Pauketat et al. 2017). Once the building was decommissioned and the post removed, the body was laid in a flexed position into the pit. Next, water-laid silt was allowed to cover her exposed body before human beings returned to fill in the hole with earth. Such female offerings were integral components of theatrical mortuary displays in Cahokia's central precincts (Alt 2008, 2015; Pauketat 2013b; Romain 2015).

All may have been timed to astronomical events and, hence, the overriding experience of Emerald and Pfeffer was probably overwhelmingly visual. But the visual experience entailed positioning one's body in the moment and at the interface between moving luminous celestial orbs and the earth. Presumably, people would have positioned themselves inside, alongside, or behind mounds, upright posts, and religious buildings as the sun set in the west and, minutes later, the full moon rose on the eastern horizon. The simultaneous experience of earthly, atmospheric, and astronomical phenomena was no doubt heightened by the ingestion of hallucinogenic substances, such as morning glory, known from some of Emerald's deposits (Kathryn Parker, personal communication 2014). Under such conditions, the heavenly and earthly powers at the complexes, especially those at the earliest levels of Emerald, bundled people to Cahokia and enabled the mid-continental transformative events that followed ca. A.D. 1050 (see p. 64). To appreciate the trans-regional effects of this process, we turn to two other shrine complexes.

Angel and Trempealeau

Elsewhere, Alt and Watts (2012) have argued that the ubiquitous occurrence of non-local Terminal Late Woodland "Yankeetown" pottery styles, common to southwestern Indiana, in pre-Mississippian and early Mississippian refuse at and around Cahokia, in southwestern Illinois, identifies some of Cahokia's pilgrims and immigrants as non-local Wabash and Ohio valley natives. They also imply that such a connection may have been critical in the expansion of Mississippianism out of the greater Cahokia region. After all, one of the earliest Mississippian centers founded after Cahokia was the Angel site, located in the heart of the Yankeetown homeland.

Three lines of circumstantial evidence suggest that Angel was founded as a shrine complex. First, the extensive mound, plaza, and palisade complex date to the late eleventh century A.D. (Monaghan and Peebles 2010; Monaghan et al. 2013). The pyramidal constructions appear to have been frequent, though the periodicity is unknown. Second, the site initially appears to have been underpopulated (Peterson 2011). Finally, Angel's earliest pyramids and the surmounting architecture were lunar aligned (Figure 3.5); the positioning of the complex relative to the waters of the Ohio and an adjacent Woodland-era burial mound doubtless was equally significant.

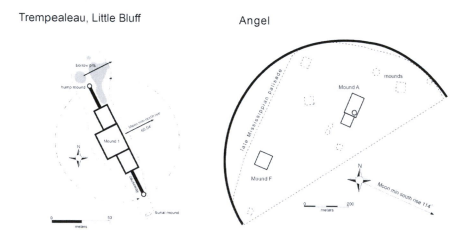

FIGURE 3.5   Schematic maps of Trempealeau's Little Bluff and Angel site complexes

Some of the large buildings atop Angel's pyramidal mounds are usually termed "temples," with the implications being that everything from ancestral bones to ritual accouterments were kept inside (Black 1967; Holley 1999). However, the Angel temples date later within the Mississippian period. Earlier, at Cahokia, the platform mounds themselves seem to have elevated the full complement of Cahokian religious architecture (Pauketat 1993), making them shrine complexes unto themselves (Figure 3.6). Evidence for this exists in the form of a likely Cahokian shrine house atop a sculpted acropolis-style hilltop complex at Trempealeau, in western Wisconsin.

Dating to the early- to mid-eleventh century A.D., the same as Emerald and Pfeffer, Trempealeau consists of a collection of Cahokian wall-trench buildings in a 10-ha settlement area around the base of "Little Bluff" and at least one other nearby platform mound (Pauketat, Boszhardt, and Benden 2015). Little Bluff is a bilaterally terraced bluff top centered on a rectangular platform 30 m above the surrounding landscape. The hilltop complex is, in this case, aligned to a minimum north moonrise (Figure 3.5). Importantly, both the platform mound and the shrine building on its summit were built using yellow and black fills during the first or second decade of the Lohmann phase (A.D. 1050–1100). The principal platform had been built in one fell swoop using the colored construction fills, while the floor and central hearth of the small, semi-subterranean building (Features 5 and 7) had been slathered with yellow plaster followed by black silt.

Also apparent from Trempealeau and a nearby Cahokian settlement, this northern shrine complex – almost 900 km north of Cahokia – was intrusive, not indigenous, to the region (Pauketat, Boszhardt, and Benden 2015). Besides everyday supplies, Cahokian colonists, missionaries, or pilgrims appear to have imported the necessary ritual articles for use at the site. To the best of our knowledge, the location's special properties – an unusual landform and associated natural phenomena and Woodland-era burial and effigy mounds – appear to have been that which attracted Cahokians to the spot. Like Emerald, Trempealeau too might have immediately preceded the urban-scale expansion of Cahokia far to the south into a city at circa A.D. 1050. Like Angel, this northern Cahokian shrine complex – situated

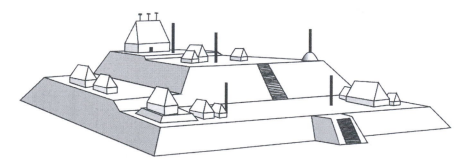

FIGURE 3.6 Oblique schematic view of Monks Mound, Cahokia

in the midst of a local Late Woodland territory – may well have forever altered the history of the region.

Discussion

There were doubtless other such Cahokian shrine complexes, with candidates including northern and southern archaeological sites identified based on unusual platform mounds, early Cahokian pottery, or early Cahokian ritual-microlithic technologies (Johnson 1987; Mainfort 1996; Perino 1967). The distant shrines may have varied in terms of both their history and historical effect, but we may presume that those connected in some way with Cahokia were places where Cahokians, if not also locals, might commune with spirits and non-human elemental properties, landforms, materials, substances, and moving celestial bodies.

Of these, Cahokia itself was doubtless the most impactful attractor, helping to explain its dramatic population surge during the eleventh century A.D. As argued repeatedly by Alt (2001, 2002, 2006b, 2008), the city and its hinterland settlements were populated by significant numbers of immigrants from diverse backgrounds. Recent isotopic evidence from Cahokia proper suggests that as many as 30 percent of the city's population at any given point in its history was made up of people from outside the greater Cahokia region (Slater, et al. 2014). That figure was doubtless higher during the decades immediately before and after 1050 A.D. Something was attracting people. What was it and what were its long-term effects?

The archaeological findings surrounding Cahokia's shrine complexes lead us to two primary inferences. First, religion as it was lived (if not also as an emergent orthodoxy) in the greater Cahokia region was lived *through* the region and its shrines. That is, people regularly moved from site to site and probably from shrine to shrine within sites – minimally from Cahokia to Emerald or Pfeffer on a 9.3- to 18.6-year basis. Some presumably made pilgrimages far up the Mississippi at the founding moments of their city (Pauketat, Boszhardt, and Benden 2015). At Emerald, the first shrine building pre-dates Cahokia's reconstruction as a city, the latter currently dated to about A.D. 1050. Most other yellow-plastered, anachronistic shrine buildings date immediately afterwards to the Lohmann phase, when the Emerald acropolis itself was re-contoured, along with Cahokia and many of its outlier complexes. Certainly, the first circular buildings and T-shaped medicine lodges appeared only after 1050, indicative of great religious if not also administrative change during the Lohmann phase.

A second primary inference is that Cahokian religious experience was the realization of a distinct vision of the cosmos. The vision, of course, might also have been experienced through multiple senses that were, on the one hand, routine – taking place every day and night, perhaps with some exclusionary aspects (the shrine houses and some circular buildings were tiny; pyramid summits were likely restricted) – and, on the other hand, theatrical, taking place outside buildings, atop acropolises, and in spacious plazas. Both sorts of experience were also phenomenal and generational, emplaced on the ground at Emerald, Pfeffer, Angel, Trempealeau, and beyond. The senses would have converged most clearly in or through the shrine house, which was in turn a bundle of relationships that tethered past with present, night with day, living with dead, and earth with sky, moon, and water. Those shrines and shrine complexes, in turn, were part of a much more encompassing Cahokia bundle that was a great cosmic center place that likely embodied all of the powers of the known universe due to its multiply aligned precincts, elevated religious architecture, and elaborate all-inclusive ceremonies of life and death.

Three kinds of archaeological deposits in the very center of the Cahokia precinct give us some sense of the experience of Cahokia in those years. One is the massive 100 × 19 × 3 m borrow pit, initially used to obtain earth to build the central pyramids, found alongside the Grand Plaza (Pauketat et al. 2002). In it are dense deposits of butchered animals, spilled soups, craft debris, and sumptuary articles indicative of religious festivals attended by many thousands. Another sort of buried deposit consists of the elaborate ridge-top-mound mortuaries, where prominent people, mythic impersonators, and sacrificial victims were buried (Alt 2008; Fowler et al. 1999; Pauketat 2008, 2010; Porubcan 2000). The latter happened with some unknown multi-year periodicity, though they may have been timed to the same lunar events celebrated at Emerald, Pfeffer, Angel, and Trempealeau. Indeed, a third deposit – the yellow-and-black fill used to seal the large Lohmann-phase rotunda, noted above, may indicate that Cahokia articulated directly with the lunar-related buildings at Emerald, Pfeffer, and beyond, entangling locals, visitors, and immigrants alike.

Moreover, a historically recorded ancient pathway – probably a processional avenue – connected Emerald to Cahokia (Snyder 1962; Thomas 1985) and may indicate that all of the various shrine complexes and Cahokian ceremonies were experienced as part of extended ceremonial occasions (Skousen 2015). The entire region, as transformed and expanded at circa A.D. 1050, might have been an entangled series of shrine complexes, such that pilgrims and visiting dignitaries might engage in a ritual circuit every few years or once in a lifetime, or such that immigrants might attach themselves to one or another locale depending on the qualities and disposition of shrines in the vicinity.

The result would have been a complex, centralized, trans-regional, and multi-dimensional relational field ripe with emergent human-to-human political possibilities. Priests or other ritual specialists, for instance, would have been positioned to administer all major ceremonials. Such specialists may have possessed shamanic qualities, enabling them to transcend physical and spiritual boundaries in powerful ways and, thus, affording them political clout; sculpted stone smoking pipes depict these individuals (Emerson 2003). Certainly the evidence from one or more of the Cahokian shrine complexes – most notably that of Trempealeau – points to the long-distance travel of religious personages who, presumably, oversaw the construction of shrine complexes in these distant locations. We may presume that they returned home from such journeys empowered in ways that lent them both religious and political authority (Helms 1988). In the process, the associations and powers surrounding these religious leaders could have taken on new and inherently political associations.

Few would have been better placed to oversee the massive construction projects back home at Cahokia than those who had traveled to shrines in distant lands. The Cahokian projects, in turn, probably saw thousands of pilgrims and devotees moving from one location to another over the course of prolonged ritual seasons. The same workers might have moved earth at, say, Emerald before moving onto Cahokia, first witnessing the rising full moon in an extreme position and later seeing young people sacrificed and laid into the ground, all over the course of a single circuit. In so doing, moving human bodies, dead and alive, would have converged and aligned with those animate beings, elemental forces, and spirits who moved with and, thus, witnessed the movements of people. In the process, diverse groups of locals and pilgrims may have become "a people" as their own sense of self was re-bundled around the increasingly centralized powers emplaced in the landscape and, in moments, embodied by powerful priests and other ritual specialists.

Conclusion

It remains unlikely that politics alone was a force that might explain the expansive Mississippianization of the American mid-continent and Southeast in the centuries after Cahokia's rise. Yes, it seems likely that human bodies increasingly articulated and centralized the agentic powers that had previously been dispersed across a Late Woodland world. Even at Cahokia, those powers took form as anthropomorphized spirit or human beings by A.D. 1100, when carvings of a humanoid goddess are known in association, it turns out, with twelfth-century versions of shrine houses (Emerson and Jackson 1984; Jackson et al. 1992). The Cahokian goddess is routinely shown in association with crops, baskets of ancestral bones, and a serpentine earth monster (Emerson 1989, 1997b). Her stone carvings are most often found at and around Cahokia (Alt and Pauketat 2007). Male characters shown in such Cahokian carvings, which usually doubled as smoking-pipe bowls, appear not to have been gods but priests, shamans, culture heroes, or demi-gods, and were frequently exported or carried away from greater Cahokia (Emerson 2003; Emerson et al. 2003).

But the lessons of Cahokia's shrine complexes suggest that these carvings were not mere representations of pan-Mississippian religious themes. That view of Mississippian religion is based in a functionalist approach to the past (see A. Joyce, Chapter 1), where "cult institutions" integrated Mississippian society and revolved around the ancestor/temple-mound complex and warrior ideologies (Knight 1986), and where anthropomorphic imagery is thought to symbolize ancestors or other mythic characters (Dye and King 2007; Knight 1986; Lankford et al. 2011;

Smith and Miller 2009). Such interpretations have led archaeologists to exaggerate political dynamics and the personification of spiritual powers over matters onto-logical and experiential.

But we should now recognize that Mississippian complexes themselves medi-ated human–non-human and non-human–non-human relationships as well. These were sensuous, spectacular religious gatherings of a sort that built Emerald and places like it, and that changed human–non-human relationships fundamentally, perhaps helping to explain what may otherwise be inexplicable in political terms: the "remarkably homogeneous" Mississippian civilization that extended across the North American Southeast (see Yoffee et al. 1999). Such great movements had in fact begun around the soon-to-be city of Cahokia just before A.D. 1050, as demonstrated by the late Edelhardt and Lohmann phase dates of the first shrine complexes at Emerald and Trempealeau. These earliest of shrine complexes pre-date the later, largely thirteenth-century evidence of politicians of the sort typi-cally assumed by Mississippianists to be among those who founded Mississippian polities. But the causal powers of even these politicians have probably been over-blown, and later Mississippian capitals or towns were likely also shrine complexes where human beings, other-than-human beings, and various other powers might converge. And so recent reanalyses of the iconography, architecture, and object assemblages from Moundville, Alabama, for instance, indicate that it was first and foremost a place from whence souls might travel into the night sky (Knight and Steponaitis 2011; Wilson 2008).

The existence of Cahokia's shrine complexes as emplacements of religion at the very inception of the Mississippian era should also impel us to recognize that, similar to the complexes themselves, imagery and sumptuary objects were never simply representational of religious beliefs. The carved-stone goddess statuettes and the masculine characters of Cahokia were neither depictions of deities nor mythic characters objectified in stone. Rather, they too were witnesses who, through their materiality, bundled and concentrated the otherwise dispersed powers of the cosmos and who, as mediators of such forces, might see that which people did on earth. The goddess's position at the interstices of cosmic forces may be sensed in the carvings themselves, one of which finds her digging a hand-held hoe into the back of the earth, a great monster, from which crops spring and grow up her back (Figure 3.7). Likewise, the masculine-character smoking-pipe bowls would have afforded the human user a direct connection with the spirits embodied therein, aided of course by the hallucinogenic properties of native tobacco.

In this way, the stone images presenced the spiritual powers of the stone and conducted the powers of tobacco, which further entangled the earth from which it grew, the fire that converted it to smoke, and the sky into which the smoke drifted and disappeared (Baires et al. 2013; Baltus and Baires 2012). They actively bundled these, much like the shrine complexes and their monumental and archi-tectural alignments and constructions. Mound and acropolis construction, house basin excavation, floor plastering, wood cutting and post emplacement or removal,

FIGURE 3.7 Carved red stone goddess, BBB Motor site, Cahokia. Photo by Linda Alexander. Courtesy of the Illinois State Archaeological Survey, University of Illinois.

house construction, procession, female sacrifice – these were the elements of Cahokian shrine complexes and the basis of Mississippian religion. Cahokia and any number of Mississippian places may be proof of Fustel de Coulanges' (1980) point that the ancient city had spiritual and cosmological underpinnings. Cahokian shrine complexes show us how.

Acknowledgments

The authors' research at the Emerald and Pfeffer Acropolises has been funded by the Religion and Innovation in Human Affairs program at the Historical Society of Boston and by the John Templeton Foundation (grant 51485). Pauketat's work at the Trempealeau site was funded by the National Science Foundation (BCS-0924138). Additional funding for excavations at Pfeffer was provided by the National Science Foundation (SBR-9996169), the National Geographic Society (grant 6319–98), and the University of Illinois. Alt's research at and around the Yankeetown site in Indiana was funded by Indiana University and the Indiana State Historic Preservation agency. We also thank the Illinois State Archaeological Survey for permission to use the base map in Figure 3.3 and the image in Figure 3.7. Finally, we are grateful to a host of field consultants and graduate supervisors on the Emerald, Pfeffer, and Trempealeau projects: Sarah Baires, Rebecca Barzilai, Melissa Baltus, Danielle Benden, Erin Benson, Ernie Boszhardt, Meghan Buchanan, Amanda Butler, Leslie Drane, Michael Kolb, Jeff Kruchten, Joel Lennen, Gregory Lautz, Kathryn Parker, Jake Pfaffenroth, Jake Reib, Jacob Skousen, Adam Sutherland, Christopher Wallace, and Thomas Zych.

References

Alt, Susan M. 2001 Cahokian Change and the Authority of Tradition. In *The Archaeology of Traditions: Agency and History Before and After Columbus*, edited by Timothy R. Pauketat, pp. 141–156. University Press of Florida, Gainesville.

———. 2002 Identities, Traditions, and Diversity in Cahokia's Uplands. *Midcontinental Journal of Archaeology* 27: 217–236.

———. 2006a The Power of Diversity: The Roles of Migration and Hybridity in Culture Change. In *Leadership and Polity in Mississippian Society*, edited by Brian M. Butler and Paul D. Welch, pp. 289–308. Center for Archaeological Investigations Occasional Paper No. 33. Southern Illinois University, Carbondale.

———. 2006b *Cultural Pluralism and Complexity: Analyzing a Cahokian Ritual Outpost*. Ph.D. dissertation, Department of Anthropology, University of Illinois, Urbana.

———. 2008 Unwilling Immigrants: Culture, Change, and the "Other" in Mississippian Societies. In *Invisible Citizens: Slavery in Ancient Pre-State Societies*, edited by Catherine M. Cameron, pp. 205–222. University of Utah Press, Salt Lake City.

———. 2012 Making Mississippian at Cahokia. In *The Oxford Handbook of North American Archaeology*, edited by Timothy R. Pauketat, pp. 497–508. Oxford University Press, Oxford.

———. 2013 *A Tale of Two Temples*. Paper presented at the 57th Annual Meeting of the Midwestern Archaeological Conference, Columbus, Ohio.

———. 2015 Human Sacrifice at Cahokia. In *Medieval Mississippians: The Cahokian World*, edited by Timothy R. Pauketat and Susan M. Alt, pp. 27. School for Advanced Research Press, Santa Fe.

Alt, Susan M., and Timothy R. Pauketat 2007 Sex and the Southern Cult. In *The Southeastern Ceremonial Complex*, edited by Adam King, pp. 232–250. University of Alabama Press, Tuscaloosa.

Alt, Susan M., and Elizabeth L. Watts 2012 Enchained, Entangled, Engaged: Building Mississippian Society. Paper presented at the 69th Annual Meeting of the Southeastern Archaeological Conference. Baton Rouge, Louisiana.

Anderson, David G., and Robert C. Mainfort, eds. 2002 *The Woodland Southeast.* University of Alabama Press, Tuscaloosa.

Baires, Sarah E. 2014a *Cahokia's Origins: Religion, Complexity and Ridge-Top Mortuaries in the Mississippi River Valley.* Ph.D. dissertation, Department of Anthropology, University of Illinois, Urbana.

———. 2014b Cahokia's Rattlesnake Causeway. *Midcontinental Journal of Archaeology* 39(1): 1–19.

Baires, Sarah E., Amanda J. Butler, B. Jacob Skousen, and Timothy R. Pauketat 2013 Fields of Movement in the Ancient Woodlands of North America. In *Archaeology After Interpretation*, edited by Benjamin Alberti, Andrew M. Jones, and Joshua Pollard, pp. 197–218. Left Coast Press, Walnut Creek.

Baltus, Melissa R. 2014 *Transforming Material Relationships: 13th Century Revitalization of Cahokian Religious-Politics.* Ph.D. dissertation, Department of Anthropology, Unviersity of Illinois, Urbana.

Baltus, Melissa R., and Sarah E. Baires 2012 Elements of Power in the Cahokian World. *Journal of Social Archaeology* 12: 167–192.

Basso, Keith H. 1996 *Wisdom Sits in Places: Landscape and Language Among the Western Apache.* University of New Mexico Press, Albuquerque.

Betzenhauser, Alleen M. 2011 *Creating the Cahokian Community: The Power of Place in Early Mississippian Sociopolitical Dynamics.* Ph.D. dissertation, Department of Anthropology, University of Illinois, Urbana.

Birmingham, Robert A., and Leslie E. Eisenberg 2000 *Indian Mounds of Wisconsin.* University of Wisconsin Press, Madison.

Black, Glenn A. 1967 *Angel Site: An Archaeological, Historical, and Ethnological Study.* Indiana Historical Society, Indianapolis.

Bradley, Richard 2000 *An Archaeology of Natural Places.* Routledge, London.

Collins, James M. 1990 *The Archaeology of the Cahokia Mounds ICT-II: Site Structure.* Illinois Cultural Resources Study No. 10. Illinois Historic Preservation Agency, Springfield.

Cummings, Marisa Miakonda 2015 An Umonhon Perspective. In *Medieval Mississippians: The Cahokian World*, edited by Timothy R. Pauketat and Susan M. Alt, pp. 43–46. School for Advanced Research Press, Santa Fe.

DeLanda, Manuel 2006 *A New Philosophy of Society: Assemblage Theory and Social Complexity.* Bloomsbury, London.

Descola, Philippe 2013 *Beyond Nature and Culture.* University of Chicago Press, Chicago.

Dye, David H., and Adam King 2007 Desecrating the Sacred Ancestor Temples: Chiefly Conflict and Violence in the American Southeast. In *North American Indigenous Warfare and Ritual Violence*, edited by Richard J. Chacon and Rubén G. Mendoza, pp. 160–181. University of Arizona Press, Tucson.

Emerson, Thomas E. 1989 Water, Serpents, and the Underworld: An Exploration Into Cahokia Symbolism. In *The Southeastern Ceremonial Complex: Artifacts and Analysis*, edited by Patricia Galloway, pp. 45–92. University of Nebraska Press, Lincoln.

———. 1997a *Cahokia and the Archaeology of Power.* University of Alabama Press, Tuscaloosa.

———. 1997b Cahokian Elite Ideology and the Mississippian Cosmos. In *Cahokia: Domination and Ideology in the Mississippian World*, edited by Timothy R. Pauketat and Thomas E. Emerson, pp. 190–228. University of Nebraska Press, Lincoln.

———. 2003 Materializing Cahokia Shamans. *Southeastern Archaeology* 22: 135–154.

Emerson, Thomas E., Randall E. Hughes, Mary R. Hynes, and Sarah U. Wisseman 2003 The Sourcing and Interpretation of Cahokia-Style Figurines in the Trans-Mississippi South and Southeast. *American Antiquity* 68: 287–313.

Emerson, Thomas E., and Douglas K. Jackson 1984 *The BBB Motor Site (11-Ms-595).* American Bottom Archaeology, FAI-270 Site Reports No. 6. University of Illinois Press, Urbana.

Emerson, Thomas E., Dale L. McElrath, and Andrew C. Fortier, eds. 2000 *Late Woodland Societies: Tradition and Transformation Across the Midcontinent*. University of Nebraska Press, Lincoln.

Esarey, Duane, and Timothy R. Pauketat 1992 *The Lohmann Site: An Early Mississippian Center in the American Bottom*. American Bottom Archaeology, FAI-270 Site Reports, vol. 25. University of Illinois Press, Urbana.

Fortier, Andrew C., ed. 2007 *The Archaeology of the East St. Louis Mound Center, Part II: The Northside Excavations*. Illinois Transportation Archaeological Research Program, Transportation Archaeological Research Reports No. 22. University of Illinois, Urbana.

Fowler, Melvin L., Jerome C. Rose, Barbara Vander Leest, and Steven R. Ahler 1999 *The Mound 72 Area: Dedicated and Sacred Space in Early Cahokia*. Reports of Investigations, No. 54. Illinois State Museum, Springfield.

Fowles, Severin M. 2013 *An Archaeology of Doings: Secularism and the Study of Pueblo Religion*. School for Advanced Research Press, Santa Fe.

Fustel de Coulanges, Numa Denis 1980 *The Ancient City*. Johns Hopkins University Press, Baltimore.

Geertz, Clifford 1973 *The Interpretation of Cultures*. Basic, New York.

Harl, Joe, Sophie Kohn, Lucretia S. Kelly, and Marjorie B. Schroeder 2011 *Data Recovery Investigations at the Dampier Site (23SL2296): A Mississippian Center in the City of Chesterfield, St. Louis County, Missouri*. Unpublished report submitted to the U.S. Corps of Engineers, St. Lous District, and the Missouri Department of Natural Resources, St. Louis.

Harris, Oliver J. T., and John Robb 2012 Multiple Ontologies and the Problem of the Body in History. *American Anthropologist* 114: 668–679.

Heidegger, Martin 1996 *Being and Time*. Translated by J. Stambaugh. State University of New York Press, Albany.

Helms, Mary W. 1988 *Ulysses' Sail: An Ethnographic Odyssey of Power, Knowledge, and Geographical Distance*. Princeton University Press, Princeton.

Hodder, Ian 2011 *Entangled: An Archaeology of the Relationships between Humans and Things*. Wiley-Blackwell, Malden, MA.

———. 2014 *Religion at Work in a Neolithic Society*. Cambridge University Press, Cambridge.

Holley, George R. 1999 Late Prehistoric Towns in the Southeast. In *Great Towns and Regional Polities in the Prehistoric American Southwest and Southeast*, edited by Jill E. Neitzel, pp. 22–38. Amerind Foundation and the University of New Mexico Press, Albuquerque.

Ingold, Tim 2000 *The Perception of the Environment: Essays in Livelihood, Dwelling and Skill*. Routledge, London.

Insoll, Timothy 2004 *Archaeology, Ritual, Religion*. Routledge, London.

———. 2011 *The Oxford Handbook of the Archaeology of Ritual and Religion*. Oxford University Press, Oxford.

Jackson, Douglas K., Andrew C. Fortier, and Joyce Williams 1992 *The Sponemann Site 2 (11-Ms-517): The Mississippian and Oneota Occupations*. American Bottom Archaeology, FAI-270 Site Reports No. 24. University of Illinois Press, Urbana.

Johnson, Jay K. 1987 Cahokia Core Technology: The View From the South. In *The Organization of Core Technology*, edited by Jay K. Johnson and Carol A. Morrow, pp. 187–206. Westview Press, Boulder.

Kelly, John E. 2002 The Pulcher Tradition and the Ritualization of Cahokia: A Perspective From Cahokia's Southern Neighbor. *Southeastern Archaeology* 21: 136–148.

Knight, Vernon J., Jr. 1986 The Institutional Organization of Mississippian Religion. *American Antiquity* 51: 675–687.

Knight, Vernon James, Jr. and Vincas P. Steponaitis 2011 A Redefinition of the Hemphill Style in Mississippian Art. In *Visualizing the Sacred: Cosmic Visions, Regionalism, and the*

Art of the Mississippian World, edited by George E. Lankford, F. Kent Reilly, III, and James F. Garber, pp. 201–239. University of Texas Press, Austin.

Lankford, George E., F. Kent Reilly, III and James F. Garber, eds. 2011 *Visualizing the Sacred: Cosmic Visions, Regionalism, and the Art of the Mississippian World*. University of Texas Press, Austin.

Mainfort, Robert C., Jr. 1996 The Reelfoot Lake Basin, Kentucky and Tennessee. In *Prehistory of the Central Mississippi Valley*, edited by Charles H. McNutt, pp. 77–96. University of Alabama Press, Tuscaloosa.

Malafouris, Lambros 2013 *How Things Shape the Mind: A Theory of Material Engagement*. The MIT Press, Cambridge.

Mehrer, Mark W. 1995 *Cahokia's Countryside: Household Archaeology, Settlement Patterns, and Social Power*. Northern Illinois University Press, DeKalb.

Monaghan, G. William, and Christopher S. Peebles 2010 The Construction, Use and Abandonment of Angel Site Mound A: Tracing the History of a Middle Mississippian Town through its Earthworks. *American Antiquity* 75: 935–953.

Monaghan, G. William, Timothy Schilling, Anthony Michal Krus, and Christopher S. Peebles 2013 Mound Construction Chronology at Angel Mounds: Episodic Mound Construction and Ceremonial Events. *Midcontinental Journal of Archaeology* 38: 155–170.

Morgan, David 2005 *The Sacred Gaze: Religious Visual Culture in Theory and Practice*. University of California Press, Berkeley.

Pacheco, Paul J., ed. 2006 *A View From the Core: A Synthesis of Ohio Hopewell Archaeology*. Ohio Archaeological Council, Columbus.

Pauketat, Timothy R. 1993 *Temples for Cahokia Lords: Preston Holder's 1955–1956 Excavations of Kunnemann Mound*. Memoirs of the University of Michigan Museum of Anthropology, No. 26. University of Michigan, Ann Arbor.

———. 2003 Resettled Farmers and the Making of a Mississippian Polity. *American Antiquity* 68: 39–66.

———. 2004 *Ancient Cahokia and the Mississippians*. Cambridge University Press, Cambridge.

———. 2008 Founders' Cults and the Archaeology of Wa-kan-da. In *Memory Work: Archaeologies of Material Practices*, edited by Barbara Mills and William H. Walker, pp. 61–79. School for Advanced Research Press, Santa Fe.

———. 2009 *Identification of the Kruchten Mound in 2000, Pfeffer Site (11-S-204/205), St. Clair County, Illinois*. Illinois Historic Preservation Agency, Springfield.

———. 2010 The Missing Persons in Mississippian Mortuaries. In *Mississippian Mortuary Practices: Beyond Hierarchy and the Representationist Perspective*, edited by Lynne P. Sullivan and Robert C. Mainfort, pp. 14–29. University Press of Florida, Gainesville.

———. 2013a *An Archaeology of the Cosmos: Rethinking Agency and Religion in Ancient America*. Routledge, London.

———. 2013b *The Archaeology of Downtown Cahokia II: The 1960 Excavation of Tract 15B*. Studies in Illinois Archaeology 8. Illinois State Archaeological Survey, Urbana.

———. 2014 From Memorials to Imaginaries in the Monumentality of Ancient North America. In *Approaching Monumentality in Archaeology*, edited by James F. Osborne, pp. 431–446. State University of New York Press, Albany.

———. 2015 Illuminating Triangulations: Moonlight and the Mississippian World. In *The Oxford Handbook of Light in Archaeology*, edited by Costas Papadopoulos and G. Earl, in press. Oxford University Press, Oxford.

Pauketat, Timothy R., and Susan M. Alt 2015 Religious Innovation at the Emerald Acropolis: Something New Under the Moon. In *Religion and Innovation: Antagonists or Partners?*, edited by Donald Yerxa, pp. 43–55. Bloomsbury, London.

Pauketat, Timothy R., Susan M. Alt, and Jeffery D. Kruchten 2015 City of Earth and Wood: Cahokia and Its Material-Historical Implications. In *Early Cities in Comparative Perspective, 4000 BCE–1200 CE*, The Cambridge World History, vol. III, edited by Norman Yoffee, pp. 437–454. Cambridge University Press, Cambridge.

Pauketat, Timothy R., Susan M. Alt, and Jeffery D. Kruchten 2017 The Emerald Acropolis: Elevating the Moon and Water in the Rise of Cahokia. *Antiquity* 91: 207–222.

Pauketat, Timothy R., Robert F. Boszhardt, and Danielle M. Benden 2015 Trempealeau Encounters: An Ancient Colony's Causes and Effects. *American Antiquity* 80: 260–289.

Pauketat, Timothy R., Thomas E. Emerson, Michael G. Farkas, and Sarah E. Baires 2015 An American Indian City. In *Medieval Mississippians: The Cahokian World*, edited by Timothy R. Pauketat and Susan M. Alt. School for Advanced Research Press, Santa Fe.

Pauketat, Timothy R., Lucretia S. Kelly, Gayle J. Fritz, Neal H. Lopinot, Scott Elias and Eve Hargrave 2002 The Residues of Feasting and Public Ritual at Early Cahokia. *American Antiquity* 67: 257–279.

Pauketat, Timothy R., Jeffery D. Kruchten, Melissa R. Baltus, Kathryn E. Parker and Elizabeth Kassly 2012 An Ancient Medicine Lodge in the Richland Complex. *Illinois Archaeology* 24: 159–183.

Pauketat, Timothy R., Mark A. Rees, and Stephanie L. Pauketat 1998 *An Archaeological Survey of Horseshoe Lake State Park, Madison County, Illinois*. Report of Investigations, No. 55. Illinois State Museum, Springfield.

Perino, Gregory 1967 *The Cherry Valley Mounds and Banks Mound 3*. The Central States Archaeological Societies, Inc., Memoir No. 1. The Central States Archaeological Societies, Inc., St. Louis.

Peterson, Staffan 2011 *Townscape Archaeology at Angel Mounds, Indiana: Mississippian Spatiality and Community*. Ph.D. dissertation, Department of Anthropology, Indiana University, Bloomington.

Porubcan, Paula J. 2000 Human and Nonhuman Surplus Display at Mound 72, Cahokia. In *Mounds, Modoc, and Mesoamerica: Papers in Honor of Melvin L. Fowler*, edited by Steven R. Ahler, pp. 207–225. Scientific Papers vol. XXVIII. Illinois State Museum, Springfield.

Prentice, Guy 1986 An Analysis of the Symbolism Expressed by the Birger Figurine. *American Antiquity* 51: 239–266.

Robb, John E., and Timothy R. Pauketat, eds. 2013 *Big Histories, Human Lives: Tackling Problems of Scale in Archaeology*. School for Advanced Research Press, Santa Fe.

Romain, William F. 2015 Moonwatchers of Cahokia. In *Medieval Mississippians: The Cahokian World*, edited by Timothy R. Pauketat and Susan M. Alt. School for Advanced Research Press, Santa Fe, New Mexico.

Scarre, Chris 2008 Shrines of the Land and Places of Power: Religion and the Transition to Farming in Western Europe. In *Belief in the Past: Theoretical Approaches to the Archaeology of Religion*, edited by David S. Whitley and Kelley Hays-Gilpin, pp. 209–226. Left Coast Press, Walnut Creek.

———. 2011 Monumentality. In *The Oxford Handbook of the Archaeology of Ritual and Religion*, edited by Timothy Insoll, pp. 9–23. Oxford University Press, Oxford.

Shaw, Julia 2013 Archaeology of Religious Change: Introduction. *World Archaeology* 45(1): 1–11.

Skousen, B. Jacob 2012 Posts as Ancestors: New Insights into Monumental Posts in the American Bottom. *Southeastern Archaeology* 31: 57–69.

Skousen, B. Jacob 2015 Moonbeams, Water, and Smoke: Tracing Otherworldly Relationships at the Emerald Site. In *Tracing the Relational: The Archaeology of Worlds, Spirits, and Temporalities*, edited by M. E. Buchanan and B. J. Skousen, pp. 38–53. University of Utah Press, Salt Lake City.

Slater, Philip A., Kristin M. Hedman, and Thomas E. Emerson 2014 Immigrants at the Mississippian Polity of Cahokia: Strontium Isotope Evidence for Population Movement. *Journal of Archaeological Science* 44: 117–127.

Smith, Kevin, and James V. Miller 2009 *Speaking With the Ancestors: Mississippian Stone Statuary of the Tennessee-Cumberland Region.* University of Alabama Press, Tuscaloosa.

Snyder, John Francis 1962 Certain Indian Mounds Technically Considered. In *John Francis Snyder: Selected Writings,* edited by Clyde C. Walton, pp. 230–273. The Illinois Historical Society, Springfield.

Spielmann, Katherine A. 2013 The Materiality of Spiritual Engagement: Art and the End of Ohio Hopewell. *World Art* 3(1): 141–162.

Steponaitis, Vincas P., Megan C. Kassabaum, and John W. O'Hear 2015 Cahokia's Coles Creek Predecessors. In *Medieval Mississippians: The Cahokian World,* edited by Timothy R. Pauketat and Susan M. Alt, pp. 13–19. School for Advanced Research Press, Santa Fe.

Strathern, Marilyn 1988 *The Gender of the Gift: Problems With Women and Problems With Society in Melanesia.* University of Califorina Press, Berkeley.

Thomas, Cyrus 1985 *Report on the Mound Explorations of the Bureau of Ethnology.* Smithsonian Institution Press, Washington, DC.

Wheatley, Paul 1971 *The Pivot of the Four Quarters.* Aldine, Chicago.

Wilson, Gregory D. 2008 *The Archaeology of Everyday Life at Early Moundville.* University of Alabama Press, Tuscaloosa.

Yoffee, Norman, Suzanne K. Fish, and George R. Milner 1999 Comunidades, Ritualities, Chiefdoms: Social Evolution in the American Southwest and Southeast. In *Great Towns and Regional Polities in the Prehistoric American Southwest and Southeast,* edited by Jill E. Neitzel, pp. 261–271. University of New Mexico Press, Albuquerque.

4

CHEROKEE RELIGION AND EUROPEAN CONTACT IN SOUTHEASTERN NORTH AMERICA

Christopher B. Rodning

Introduction

At the point of early Spanish exploration and colonization of the Americas during the late 1400s and 1500s, complex societies that were part of the broader Mississippian cultural tradition were present across what is now the southeastern United States and parts of the Midwest. Mississippian peoples were farmers. Mississippian groups lived in permanent settlements, including large towns and rural farmsteads. Surpluses of food and other resources within the Mississippian political economies contributed to the construction of monumental earthworks, the acquisition of raw materials for the production of valuable items such as copper plates and engraved marine shell, and the circulation of prestige goods (Anderson 1994; Muller 1997; Steponaitis 1986, 1991). Major geopolitical centers, such as Cahokia and Moundville, had large earthen mounds and plazas (Knight 1997, 1998; Pauketat 1994, 1998, 2004; Steponaitis 1983), although these and other major Mississippian mound centers were abandoned or diminished in importance at the point of European contact. As evident from sites like Fatherland, Mississippi (Brown 1990), and Etowah, Georgia (King 2003), pyramidal platform mounds formed settings for the placement of elite residences, charnel houses, and temples, although there were other forms of religious and ceremonial architecture present at sites without mounds. Across the Mississippian Southeast, religion was closely associated with the practice of political power (Knight 1986), and careful adherence to alignments in the placement of earthworks and ceremonial structures, including alignments to reference points on the ground and in the sky, demonstrates the importance of pathways and place to religious thought and practice (Pauketat 2013). Mississippian religious thought and practice emphasized themes of balance, world renewal, center symbolism, and dualism (Emerson 1989, 1997a, 1997b, 2003; Hall 1989; Pauketat and Emerson 1991, 1999). Mississippian religion was more a way of experiencing the animistic powers of the cosmos than it was a discrete set of beliefs (Emerson and Pauketat 2008). As Timothy Pauketat (2013:190) has put it:

> Native Americans knew and yet know that religion is not a set of beliefs per se, but a way of living with the past in the present toward the future. Beliefs are there, in the hands of people and in the alignments of moving agents on the land and in the sky. They bind time and experience with the powers of the cosmos.

These general perspectives and principles of religious thought were practiced by Mississippian groups across the Southeast at the points of early encounters with Europeans, including contacts with mid-sixteenth-century Spanish conquistadores, and French and English explorers and traders in the late 1600s and early 1700s (Ethridge 2010). Religious thought and practice related to balance, world renewal, and center symbolism guided the responses by Native American groups to encounters and entanglements with European colonists and European goods. Archaeologists have not yet explored the challenges posed by colonialism to these aspects of Native American spirituality and cosmology as much as they should.

Mississippian societies are ancestral to several historically known Native American peoples of the Eastern Woodlands, including the Cherokee, whose towns were situated in the southern Appalachians, in eastern Tennessee, northern Georgia, and the western Carolinas (Figure 4.1; Boulware 2011; Dickens 1967, 1976, 1978, 1979; Goodwin 1977; Greene 1999; Keel 1976; King 1979; Duncan and Riggs 2003). Ethnologists and ethnohistorians have recorded many aspects of traditional Cherokee religious thought and practice (Gearing 1958, 1962; Hudson 1976, 1984; Mooney 1891, 1900). Archaeological evidence from late prehistoric and postcontact Cherokee sites in the southern Appalachians demonstrates overarching similarities between religious thought and practice in Cherokee town areas and elsewhere in the Southeast (Rodning 2009a, 2010a, 2012, 2015a).

This chapter summarizes basic tenets of Cherokee religion, relationships between religion and politics in Cherokee towns, and some of the ways in which religious principles were manifested in architecture and in select forms of material culture, with particular focus on the Coweeta Creek site in southwestern North Carolina (Figure 4.2; Keel et al. 2002; Rodning and VanDerwarker 2002; Ward and Davis 1999:183–190). At this site, as at other Cherokee town sites, there were domestic structures and domestic activity areas situated around a large plaza, with a community structure known as a townhouse adjacent to the plaza (Rodning 2002, 2007, 2009a, 2009b, 2013). Townhouses and adjacent plazas were landmarks for Cherokee towns; they were settings for ceremonial events, and just as Mississippian platform mounds in the Southeast were "earth icons" and world symbols (Knight 1986, 2004, 2006), so too were Cherokee townhouses manifestations of the Cherokee cosmos. The series of townhouses at the Coweeta Creek site, built and rebuilt in place, formed a mound, encompassing burned and buried remnants of several stages of this community structure, and encompassing other architectural

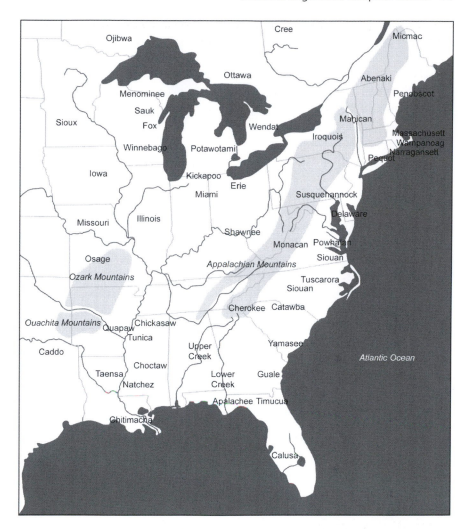

FIGURE 4.1 Locations of Cherokee and other native peoples of eastern North America. Drafted by the author.

elements and deposits related to religious thought and practice within the town, including hearths and burials. This architectural history anchored the surrounding town to a particular place. From this perspective, the Coweeta Creek townhouse, dating from the 1600s through the early 1700s, created stability and permanence within an unstable geopolitical landscape, in the aftermath of early episodes of European contact and colonialism in the Southeast.

From another perspective, the townhouse mound at Coweeta Creek is a bundle, and, arguably, other examples of townhouses and earthen mounds in southeastern North America may also have been created and conceptualized as bundles. Cultural practices of bundling, and ceremonialism associated with bundles, are prevalent

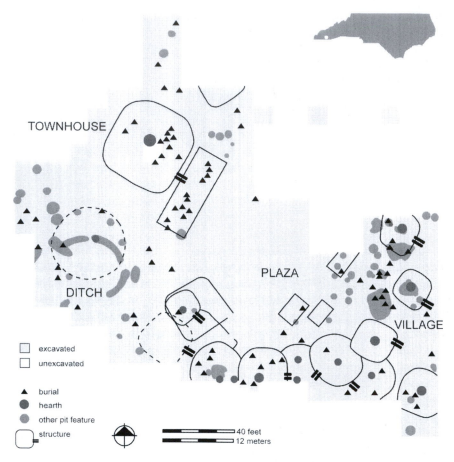

FIGURE 4.2   Schematic map of the Coweeta Creek site in southwestern North Carolina (after Rodning 2002:12; 2009a:629; 2015a:5).

in Native American societies of the Great Plains (Zedeño 2009), although bundling is also evident within Native American landscapes and lifeways in the Eastern
Woodlands (Pauketat 2013). A bundle is a collection of diverse items that have
a shared life history (Zedeño 2008a:364), that are brought together in efforts to
harness "cosmic power contained in the material and spiritual worlds" to achieve
specific goals (Zedeño 2008a:367), and that create binding compacts between bundle holders and the other-than-human forces from which they originate (Zedeño
2008a:368). Bundles are associated with knowledge about specific rites, and this
knowledge is only known to individuals entitled to possess such knowledge and to
keep the bundles associated with it (Zedeño 2008a:364). Bundles can accumulate
new elements, especially when they are passed from one holder to another, and
bundles can also be split into separate bundles that then accumulate their own
life history (Zedeño 2008a:365). A key dimension in keeping bundles, at least

for Native American groups of the Great Plains, is the "conceptual trilogy" of animacy, transfer, and transmutation (Zedeño 2008a:366). Animacy is the perspective that diverse forms of power, including spiritual power, reside within people and within the natural environment, and spiritual forces are activated and managed through interaction between persons and other-than-human agents (Zedeño 2008b:265). This viewpoint and animistic ontology is widespread among peoples of Native North America (Zedeño 2009:408), including the Cherokee. Transfer is the property by which animating power can move between people, and between human and nonhuman actors and agents, as in the case of the Water Spider delivering fire to the Cherokee people (Mooney 1900:240–242), and the actions of the first mythical Cherokee man (Kana'tĭ) and woman (Selu) that shaped the life cycles and habits of game and crops (Mooney 1900:243–249, 262). Transmutation is the phenomenon of human or nonhuman actors transforming from one being to another, as in the cases from Cherokee oral tradition and cosmogonic myths of people turning into bears (Mooney 1900:264, 325–327), or people turning into stars and trees (Mooney 1900:258–259). Bundling, as such, is not as prevalent, or at least not as well known, in Cherokee culture as it is for other Native Americans, especially within groups of the Great Plains. Nevertheless, several aspects of bundling – including the concepts of animacy, transfer, and transmutation – are indeed elements of Cherokee cosmology and ontology, and interpretive frameworks for studying bundles and bundling are applicable to considerations of archaeological evidence from the southern Appalachians.

The sequence of townhouses and related deposits at the Coweeta Creek site, and similar sequences at other Cherokee town sites in the southern Appalachians, effectively bundle together material elements of the spiritual vitality of past and present generations of Cherokee towns. Mounds encompass remnants of earthen mantles and mound stages, ruins of structures, and symbolically powerful deposits, including burials. They represent the world itself in microcosm; they encompass ruins and remnants of ancestral generations; they connect the past to the present; and, by extrapolation, they connect the present to the future.

Principles of Cherokee religion

Important evidence about traditional Cherokee religion comes from books kept by Cherokee healers and keepers of sacred knowledge during the mid- to late-nineteenth century. This knowledge was preserved through oral tradition during antiquity, but after the development of the Cherokee syllabary by Sequoyah during the early nineteenth century, ritual practitioners began writing down what they knew, and they wrote down the sacred formulas they would recite to heal people, to restore balance, to cure disease and illness, and to bring about success in love, hunting, warfare, and the ballgame. During the late nineteenth century, James Mooney (1891, 1900), an affiliate of the Bureau of American Ethnology at the Smithsonian Institution, collected sacred formulas and other oral traditions during consultations with Cherokee elders in western North Carolina.

His compilations have greatly influenced the study of Native American religion in southeastern North America, in general, and Cherokee religion and culture in the southern Appalachians, in particular (Hudson 1976; Mooney 1891, 1900; Swanton 1946, 1952). As is the case for other Native North American groups, the spiritual beliefs and practices of the Cherokee can be characterized as an animistic form of religion. Spiritual and sacred powers reside within the landscape, the sky, water, animals, and plants. Religious specialists and healers have harnessed these powers through reciting sacred formulas (Mooney 1891). References to these powerful properties are also incorporated into oral traditions (Mooney 1900).

Ritual specialists in Cherokee towns, known as "conjurors" or as "priests" in some primary and secondary sources, conducted rites related to agricultural cycles, purification, renewal, and preparation for warfare and related activities. They conducted rites of purification and preparation for warriors in townhouses before and after groups of warriors were away from their towns on the war path (Fogelson 1980; Gearing 1962:60), and they conducted rituals to prepare players and teams for ballgames (Gearing 1962:61; Zogry 2010), in which teams from different towns played each other. Families called upon a priest when a member of a family or a household died, and the priest made plans and preparations for handling and burying the deceased, and often burning or burying his or her possessions (Corkran 1969:26–27; Gearing 1962:28). Priests conducted ceremonies related to planting and harvesting, and they conducted ceremonies related to hunting (Corkran 1969:14–26; Gearing 1962:28). Many of these ceremonial activities emphasized balance and stability, including properly sending the dead to the afterlife, preparing warriors (and ballplayers) for the different demands and expectations for conducting themselves on the war path (or in ballgames) or at home, and ensuring the sustainability of producing and acquiring food through farming, gardening, gathering, and hunting.

Ethnohistorian Charles Hudson (1984:11–15) has outlined the following major characteristics of Cherokee cosmological knowledge and religious beliefs in his introduction to religious thought and practice in the Native American Southeast.

1   There is a mythical past, during which the world was formed, and this mythical past preceded the "prehistory" and "history" of the Cherokee people themselves. The "earth island" was formed when a mythical beetle brought mud up from the bottom of the waters that had covered the entire world (Mooney 1900:239–240). The "first fire" was delivered to the Cherokee people by a spider (Mooney 1900:240–242). After attempts by owls and other animals, a spider crossed the water to retrieve a live coal in a sycamore tree on a nearby island. The spider brought this fire in a basket on its back to give to people, a mythical event that is depicted on engraved shell gorgets, found at Mississippian sites throughout the southern Appalachians, with cross-in-circle motifs (symbols of the sun and of fire) depicted on the backs of spiders (Lankford 1987).

2   The Cherokee cosmos includes this world (the earth), the upper world (the sky), and the underworld (below the ground and below water). Rivers and

streams are pathways to the underworld, springs were portals connecting the underworld and the earth, and perhaps caves were, as well. Many spirits are thought to dwell in the upper world, above the sky vault.

3 The Cherokee homeland is situated at the center of the world, the four cardinal directions emanate outward from this center place, and there are different symbolic characteristics and colors attached to the north (blue), the south (white), the east (red), and the west (black). Cherokee ritual practices involve blowing smoke in each of the cardinal directions. Cherokee townhouses, and the earthen mounds present at the sites of some towns, may have been aligned with the cardinal directions.

4 There is an emphasis on balance in Cherokee religion and culture, including the principle of vengeance, which stipulates that groups and individuals victimized by violence are expected and even obligated to seek revenge, in efforts to restore balance within the world.

5 "The microcosm resembles the macrocosm" (Hudson 1984:12), or, alternatively, there is symmetry in the world of people and the world of other animate powers (A. Joyce, Chapter 1). The macrocosm encompasses the earth island, the sky vault, and the myriad forces animating these domains of the cosmos. The microcosm here refers to public and domestic architecture, and to ritual observances and social relations within Cherokee towns that paralleled conceptual models of the cosmos. Architectural manifestations of these concepts of the Cherokee cosmos include earthen mounds, which are earth icons (Knight 1986, 2006), and the architecture of household dwellings and townhouses (Rodning 2009a, 2009b, 2010a, 2015b), all of which include central hearths and four posts spaced around them, connecting earth (floors) to the sky (roofs). Manifestations of Cherokee cosmograms in portable material culture include engraved shell gorgets depicting four corners, crosses inside circles, and symbolically powerful animals such as woodpeckers, water spiders, and rattlesnakes (Figure 4.3; Rodning 2012), and, perhaps, pottery depicting similar motifs in complicated stamping and incising (Figure 4.4; Rodning 2008).

6 "All things possess spirit" (Hudson 1984:12), including human and nonhuman actors (A. Joyce, Chapter 1). Symbolic and sacred powers emanate from the sun, fire, water, and rock. Fire is an earthly manifestation of the sun, and sacred fire is prevalent within Cherokee oral tradition and traditional Cherokee religious practice. Male elders tended constant fires in the hearths of Cherokee townhouses, and everlasting fires are said to burn inside some of the large earthen mounds at old Cherokee towns, such as those at Kĭtu'hwa (Kituhwa) and Nĭkwăsĭ' (Nequassee), both located in southwestern North Carolina, not far from the Coweeta Creek site (Mooney 1900:395–397). The fires in Cherokee townhouses were rekindled during annual community renewal rituals, and they were transported from those townhouses to the hearths in household dwellings nearby and to houses in lesser settlements between towns (Mooney 1900:502–503).

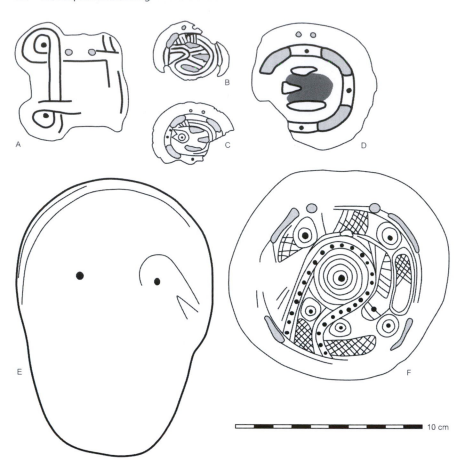

FIGURE 4.3 Engraved shell gorgets from the Warren Wilson, Garden Creek, and Coweeta Creek sites in southwestern North Carolina (after Rodning 2012:38–40; see also Dickens 1976:166; Rodning 2011a:163–164).

7 All people, plants, and animals fit within categories, and those categories encompassed discrete sets of species, powers, and characteristics. For example, raptors possess characteristics that are beneficial to hunters and warriors. Not surprisingly, mythical hawks are invoked in ritual preparations for warfare and the Cherokee ballgame (Mooney 1891:396–397); falcon eye surrounds on engraved marine shell gorgets and copper plates are thought to have been related to warfare and hunting (Smith 1989; Smith and Smith 1989), and falcons are depicted on embossed copper plates found at Mississippian sites across the Southeast (Hudson 1984:10–11). For similar reasons, woodpeckers and turkeys are depicted on some engraved marine shell gorgets (Brain and Phillips

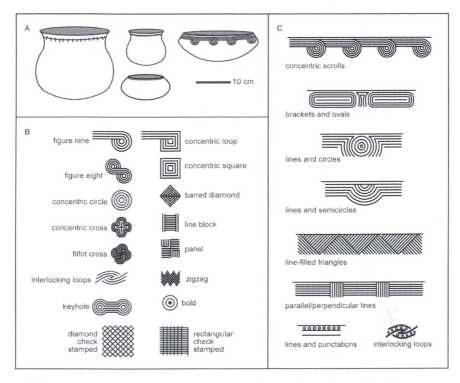

FIGURE 4.4   Complicated stamped patterns and incised motifs on Cherokee pottery from southwestern North Carolina (after Rodning 2008:7–8; see also Dickens 1976:184; 1979:25, 27; Rodning 2015a:24).

1996; Hally 2007; Muller 1989; Sullivan 2007). Bald eagles are regarded as chiefs in the world of birds by many peoples in Native North America (Hudson 1984:13–14), including the Cherokee, and only "the greatest warriors" are allowed to wear or to carry eagle feathers during Cherokee eagle dances (Mooney 1900:281–294).

8   Animals with characteristics belonging to more than one cosmological domain are treated with special consideration. Bears, for example, resemble both animals and people. Frogs, turtles, and otters are both land dwellers and water dwellers, and kingfishers, bats, and flying squirrels dwell in both the sky and in the earth, and (in the case of the kingfisher) in the water.

Hudson (1984:15–18) demonstrates that Cherokee concepts of health and disease, and Cherokee curing practices, emphasize balance and the diverse activities by which people can maintain and restore balance, as needed. Eventually, neither trade, nor politics, nor Cherokee medicine and religion, could restore balance to Cherokee towns upended by the myriad forces of change unleashed by European contact and colonialism. However, basic tenets of Cherokee religion must have guided Cherokee responses to early encounters and entanglements with European explorers and colonists, and the material goods acquired from them.

Religion and Cherokee politics

Similar to the emphasis in Cherokee religion on balance and equilibrium, so also has there been an emphasis in Cherokee politics on mechanisms to maintain and to restore balance and equilibrium within Cherokee towns. Historically, the major components of Cherokee social and political organization have been clans and towns (Gilbert 1943; Perdue 1998; Persico 1979). There were and are seven matrilineal Cherokee clans. The permanent members of matrilocal households were members of the same clan. Men moved from the households of their mothers to the households of their wives upon marriage. During the eighteenth century, all seven clans were represented by one or more households in each major Cherokee town, and representatives of each clan were members of town councils. All community members could speak during town council deliberations that took place within townhouses, although the voices of older men and women typically carried more weight, as did, in some cases, the voices of warriors and war chiefs. Town councils sought consensus and compromise in decisions affecting all townspeople, but clans or other segments of Cherokee towns could choose to dissent and to withdraw from town council decisions. Leaders of Cherokee towns had the power to persuade opinion, but they did not have power to coerce, or at least could only do so when making war on enemy groups. Although ties of clan kinship, shared cultural heritage, and common interest connected Cherokee towns to each other, towns were independent, and there was no overarching mode of political organization above the level of individual towns until the formation of the Cherokee Republic in the early nineteenth century, just before the period leading to Cherokee Removal in the 1820s and 1830s. Historically, annual rites of community renewal, referred to collectively as Green Corn Ceremonialism, involved dancing and feasting, rekindling the fires in the hearths of townhouses and dwellings, and forgiveness of wrongs that had been done to community members during the past year.

This emphasis on balance and equilibrium is echoed in dual leadership roles within Cherokee towns and the differentiation between town leaders in war and peace (Gearing 1958, 1962). Often, this distinction followed generational lines, with younger men as warriors and older men as war leaders or peace chiefs. Meanwhile, this distinction was often symbolized by the colors of red, for war, and white, for peace. During the eighteenth century, when Cherokee towns were at war, those towns flew red flags on posts outside townhouses, and when they were at peace, they flew white flags. There is even some evidence to indicate that red and white symbolism was present within the architecture of Cherokee townhouses themselves, with red emanating from fires in townhouse hearths, white smoke emanating upward, and white clay placed around the edges of at least some townhouses (Rodning 2010a, 2011b).

The hearths inside townhouses are particularly important to consider here, as an intersection between politics and religion in Cherokee towns. Selected male elders within Cherokee towns kept fires burning constantly within the hearths inside townhouses (Gearing 1962:23–24). Fire from these hearths never left townhouses, except in instances when it was taken to nearby houses or nearby settlements to rekindle fires in those places, and in cases in which warriors transported fire with them on the warpath (Corkran 1969:44–47). Fires in townhouse hearths were only put out when they were rekindled during annual community renewal rituals. These fires – sometimes known in Cherokee oral tradition as "constant fire" or "everlasting fire" – were tangible and visible manifestations of towns themselves. Cherokee people conceptualized fire as an earthly manifestation of the sun, and fires in Cherokee townhouse hearths symbolized this concept. Cherokee religion encouraged balance, as did Cherokee politics, and fires kept within townhouse hearths were sources of spiritual power and stability.

Materiality of Cherokee spirituality

Aspects of Cherokee spirituality and religion, as summarized above, are manifested at archaeological sites in earthen mounds, townhouses, hearths, arrangements of posts around hearths, deposits of ash from townhouse hearths, burials, engraved shell gorgets, and probably in other material forms that we do not yet recognize as having sacred and spiritual significance. Clear examples of these archaeological clues about Cherokee religious thought and practice are present at the Coweeta Creek site, located in the upper Little Tennessee Valley of southwestern North Carolina (Rodning 2010b, 2012, 2015a). Several houses were present at this site in the 1400s, and there are indications of cultural activity at the site before that point. After an apparent hiatus, the site was the setting for a formally planned town dating to the 1600s, with a townhouse, an adjacent plaza, and domestic houses surrounding the plaza, all situated according to shared axial alignments. At least six stages of the Coweeta Creek townhouse were built and rebuilt in place (Figures 4.5 and 4.6), forming a mound composed of the burned and buried remnants of these successive stages of the townhouse itself, as well as deposits of clay and river boulders along the outer edges of its later stages (Rodning 2002, 2010a, 2015a). The townhouse and domestic structures at Coweeta Creek were built by digging basins in the ground, placing wall posts within the edges of those structure basins, placing hearths and roof support posts near the centers, embanking the outer walls with earth, and covering wooden roof beams with earth and bark (Riggs 2008; Rodning 2009a, 2011a, 2015b; Schroedl 1986). Kaolin clay pipe fragments and glass beads are associated with some deposits of sand covering the plaza at the Coweeta Creek site, indicating that this public space was utilized through the late 1600s and early 1700s (Rodning 2010b). The site was abandoned in the early- to mid-eighteenth century. The date ranges for Coweeta Creek span the period just before European contact in the Americas, the period of Spanish exploration of the Southeast in the sixteenth century, and the spread of English and French trade networks

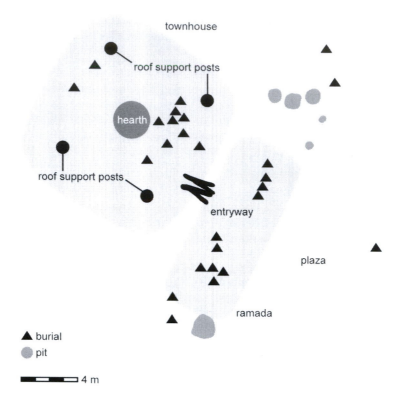

FIGURE 4.5 First stages of the Cherokee townhouse at Coweeta Creek (after Rodning 2002:13; 2009a:641); note burials beside entryways, corners aligned to cardinal directions, and pits near townhouse with concentrations of ash and charcoal

across the Southeast during the late 1600s and early 1700s (Rodning 2010b). The presence of a piece of a calumet pipe at the Coweeta Creek site (Rodning 2014), and calumet pipe fragments at the eighteenth-century Chota-Tanasee site in eastern Tennessee (Schroedl 1986), demonstrates the participation of Cherokee towns in calumet ceremonialism, involving singing, dancing, smoking, and the formation of fictive kinship among Native American and European colonial groups, all with an emphasis on creating balance and stability, particularly during the period after European contact in the Southeast (Brown 2006).

One of the core principles of Cherokee cosmology is the concept that the microcosm reflects the macrocosm (see p. 81; Hudson 1984). According to Cherokee oral tradition, the earth is an island, suspended from the sky vault by four cords at corners corresponding to the cardinal directions (Mooney 1900:239). This point is evident in the Coweeta Creek townhouse in the following ways (Rodning 2010a). First, the structure itself had a framework of wooden posts and beams, but earthen embankments and earthen components of the roof made the townhouse

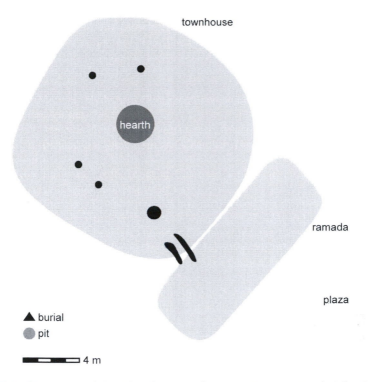

townhouse

hearth

ramada

plaza

▲ burial
● pit

━━━━ 4 m

FIGURE 4.6 Last stages of the Cherokee townhouse at Coweeta Creek (after Rodning 2002:15; 2009a:641); note continuity from preceding stages but slight
changes in townhouse size and shape, continuity in the axial alignment of
the structure itself, and the absence of burials associated with late stages of
the structure

comparable to a mound (compare with Hally 2002; Knight 2006). Second, the
four corners of the structure correspond generally to the cardinal directions. Third,
the roof support posts connecting the floor to the roof are analogous to the four
cords connecting the earth island to the sky vault (compare with Pauls 2005; Prine
2000). Fourth, the placements of the roof support posts around the central hearth
generally correspond to the cardinal directions. The architectural layout of the
townhouse at Coweeta Creek is comparable to other townhouses in the southern
Appalachians dating to the period just before and after European contact (Baden
1983; Hally 2008; Hally and Kelly 1998; Riggs 2008; Rodning 2009a, 2011a; Russ
and Chapman 1983; Schroedl 1978; Sullivan 1995). The sequence of townhouses
at Coweeta Creek is comparable to the sequence of early-eighteenth-century
townhouses at Chattooga, in northwestern South Carolina, and sequences of late
prehistoric mound stages and structures at Toqua, in eastern Tennessee (Polhemus
1987; Schroedl 2000, 2001).

Another core principle of Cherokee cosmology is the tripartite division of the
upper world, the earth, and the lower world (see p. 80; Hudson 1984). This point

is evident in the townhouses at Coweeta Creek and at other Cherokee towns in the form of roof support posts, which bounded square spaces surrounding central hearths and the fire and columns of smoke emanating upward from those hearths. Roof support posts in Cherokee townhouses connected the lower world (posts set in the ground), the earth itself (the floor), and the upper world or sky vault (the roof); and in the case of townhouses at Coweeta Creek and probably at other sites, roof support posts and hearths connected the remnants of several stages of these public structures.

Because many native groups of the Southeast conceptualize fire as an earthly manifestation of the sun, fires kept in the hearths of temples and public structures have symbolic and sacred power (Hudson 1984). Fires were kept in the Coweeta Creek townhouse hearth, and those fires were kept in successive stages of the same hearth in each of the successive stages of the townhouse. The fire probably never went out, with people keeping it burning constantly, but fire in the Coweeta Creek townhouse hearth can also be considered "constant" or even "everlasting" from the perspective that it stayed in place throughout the history of this public structure. Ash from Cherokee townhouse hearths was periodically removed and dumped into heaps or pits known as "Skeona," translated from Cherokee as "the spirits" or "place of the spirits," located close to townhouses themselves (Corkran 1969:36). Pit features close to the Coweeta Creek townhouse with high concentrations of ash and charcoal may represent archaeological examples of this phenomenon (Rodning 2015a:104; compare with Lewis et al. 1995:529–530; Sullivan 1987).

According to the principle of animacy in the cosmology of many Native American peoples, including the Cherokee and other groups from the Southeast, spiritual power resides within people, plants, animals, and other agents within the world (Hudson 1984; Sundstrom 2003; Zedeño 2008a, 2008b, 2009). The fire in the Coweeta Creek townhouse hearth, and columns of smoke emanating upward toward the roof and the sky, were sources of spiritual power, as were nearby pits where ash and embers from the townhouse hearth were placed. Spiritual power resided within the burned and buried remnants of the Coweeta Creek townhouse itself. Each stage of the townhouse was burned down, and later stages were rebuilt directly on top of them. This architectural cycle symbolized rebirth and renewal of the town itself, and world renewal more generally. Meanwhile, there were burials of people in and around the townhouse, and those burials became embedded within the Coweeta Creek townhouse mound. Most and probably all the burials in and around the townhouse correspond to its early stages (Rodning 2015a). Not all of these burials included mortuary offerings, but the items placed in some of these burials include stone discs, clay pipes, stone pipes, marine shell beads, engraved shell gorgets, and in one case, an apparent quiver of seven arrows, perhaps symbolizing the seven Cherokee clans represented in nearly all Cherokee towns (Rodning 2011b). Collectively, these burials, associated grave goods, burned and buried remnants of successive stages of a townhouse, and other elements of the Coweeta Creek townhouse mound formed a bundle, of sorts, and a bundle that anchored the community to a specific point on the landscape for several generations.

Several aspects of the Cherokee oral tradition, "The Mounds and the Constant Fire" (Mooney 1900:395–397), are consistent with the identification of the Coweeta Creek townhouse mound as a bundle. According to Mooney, the first step in building a townhouse involved clearing a space on the ground surface, placing a circle of stones around that space, and lighting a fire at the center of the stone circle. Then, one or more recently deceased elders were buried near the fire – "some say seven chief men from the different clans" (Mooney 1900:396) – along with items such as an *Uktena* scale (or marine shell gorget with an engraved rattlesnake design), an *Ulûñsû'tĭ* stone (or quartz crystal), the feathers of eagles or mythical hawks known as *tlă'nuwă*, and glass beads of seven different colors (red, black, white, purple, yellow, blue, and grayish blue). These deposits were then "conjured with disease, so that, if ever an enemy invaded the country, even though he should burn and destroy the town and the townhouse, he would never live to return home" (Mooney 1900:396). After earth was heaped atop these deposits and around the sacred fire at the center, a townhouse was built on the mounded surface. This description is broadly applicable to the successive stages of the Coweeta Creek townhouse, its central hearth, and burials associated with its early stages (Rodning 2009a). There are no glass beads in burials in the Coweeta Creek townhouse mound, nor direct evidence of raptor feathers, but there are shell beads and shell gorgets in some of those burials, including one with an engraved rattlesnake design (Rodning 2011b). Glass beads did accumulate within the townhouse mound, mostly after having been dropped on floors and then having been buried within burned architectural rubble and postholes (Rodning 2010a). These diverse elements of the Coweeta Creek townhouse mound had a shared life history; they created a binding compact between the sacred fire and the responsibility of the surrounding town to keep it burning constantly (Gearing 1958, 1962), and they manifested connections between spiritual forces and the material world – all characteristics of bundles and bundling in Native North America (Zedeño 2008a, 2008b).

In another Cherokee oral tradition, "The Spirit Defenders of Nĭkwăsĭ'," the warriors of this old and venerable Cherokee town, located beside the Little Tennessee River roughly 15 kilometers downstream from (and north of) the Coweeta Creek site, once gathered in the Nequassee townhouse as an enemy advanced on the town from the southeast (Mooney 1900:336–337). This enemy razed Cherokee towns in what is now northwestern South Carolina and northeastern Georgia, and marched into the mountains and into the upper Little Tennessee Valley, where Nequassee and other Middle Cherokee towns (including the town at Coweeta Creek) were located. At the site of Nequassee is a large earthen mound, on the summit of which was placed a townhouse (Evans and King 1977), as was the case at Cowee (Waselkov and Braund 1995:84–85), roughly 12 kilometers downstream from (north of) Nequassee. The warriors from Nequassee gathered everybody within the townhouse, they met the enemy, and they fought bravely. They were overwhelmed, until at last, hundreds of armed and painted warriors "poured out" of the Nequassee mound and drove the enemy away. These mythical warriors were Nûñnĕ'hĭ, the Cherokee "spirit folk" who dwell within the mountains and streams near Cherokee towns and who keep themselves hidden except when they are called upon or when they choose to become visible and audible (Mooney 1900:330–335). Perhaps the placement of burials and associated grave goods in and around the Coweeta Creek townhouse was a means of harnessing the kinds of spiritual power that resided within the Nequassee mound.

The stability and permanence of place evident in the Coweeta Creek townhouse would have been an important source of social, political, and spiritual stability for this Cherokee town, and others like it, during the period encompassing the aftermath of mid-sixteenth-century Spanish entradas and the spread of English and French colonial trade networks across the Southeast during the late 1600s and early 1700s. As an architectural bundle, the Coweeta Creek townhouse anchored the surrounding Cherokee town to a place and a landscape within which powerful spiritual forces were embedded. The emplacement of burials within this space, and ceremonial offerings in the form of grave goods, is broadly comparable to similar practices of emplacement and dedicatory offerings in monuments and public architecture in other world areas (Blom and Janusek 2004; Joyce and Barber 2015; Mills 2008). Maintaining the constant fire in the Coweeta Creek townhouse – from day to day, from year to year, and from one generation to another – conferred balance and stability to a community during a period of profound cultural change throughout the Americas, as the Cherokee and other native peoples became more and more deeply entangled in the complicated dynamics of life in the colonial Southeast. Townhouses themselves, and the central hearths inside them, were containers for sacred fire, and they were powerful center symbols in and of themselves (Rodning 2010a, 2012, 2015a).

Cherokee religion and European contact

The town at Coweeta Creek was probably broadly typical of the dozens of Cherokee towns that dotted the southern Appalachians during the 1600s and early 1700s (Fogelson 2004; Smith 1979), but the Cherokee landscape changed during cycles of trade, warfare, diplomacy, and alliance with English colonists and Native American groups from points to the north and south of Cherokee town areas (Goodwin 1977). During the 1600s and early 1700s, many if not all Cherokee people lived in close proximity to townhouses like those seen at Coweeta Creek (Duncan and Riggs 2003). By the late 1700s, there were fewer town centers, and most people lived in settlements that were more spatially dispersed than were towns like that at the Coweeta Creek site (Baden 1983; Russ and Chapman 1983; Schroedl 1986). During the early 1800s, townhouses were still present at major Cherokee political centers, but not in the kinds of settlements (like Coweeta Creek) that had formerly been relatively common in the Cherokee landscape. The effects of community emplacement from building, burning, burying, and rebuilding townhouses in place; from maintaining constant fires within townhouse hearths that spanned several iterations of those townhouses themselves; and from the deposits of burials and material items in the ground before townhouses were built – all evident at Coweeta Creek – were diminished.

Such changes must have had profound impacts on Cherokee religion and ritual. Indeed, archaeologists know relatively little about the effects of "spiritual contact" on native peoples of the Southeast during early stages of European contact and colonialism. Conversely, we also know relatively little about how Native American spirituality motivated responses to European contact and colonialism in the Southeast, how native people and groups made sense of encounters with European colonists and European goods from the perspectives of spirituality and animacy, or how Native American religion and ritual may have been sources of resistance to colonial hegemony.

That said, we do know that several elements of Cherokee religion were manifested in the series of public structures, known as townhouses, at the Coweeta Creek site, in southwestern North Carolina, and probably at other Cherokee town sites as well, during the 1600s and early 1700s. These townhouses, the arrangements of hearths and roof support posts within them, and burials associated with them, all demonstrate an emphasis on emplacement, and an emphasis on balance, center symbolism, and world renewal. They anchored towns to particular points on the landscape, they manifested center symbolism at several scales, and they were agents of cultural stability and balance during periods of dramatic culture change. Given the diverse components within townhouses like those at the Coweeta Creek site, they represent bundles, of a sort, encompassing a variety of elements – wood, earth, fire, burials, and various forms of material culture – that manifested the spiritual essence and vitality of Cherokee towns. From this perspective, townhouses like those at Coweeta Creek were not merely settings for religious and political activity in Cherokee towns; they were agents of religion and politics, and sources of cultural persistence and spiritual power during episodes of considerable political change.

Acknowledgments

This essay is dedicated to the late Charles Hudson, in appreciation for his contributions to the ethnohistory and archaeology of the Native American South. I am grateful to Professor Hudson, Stacy Barber, Art Joyce, María Nieves Zedeño, Ken Sassaman, David Anderson, Chester DePratter, Robert Hill, Nick Spitzer, Adeline Masquelier, Bennie Keel, Brett Riggs, Ben Steere, David Moore, Rob Beck, Tony Boudreaux, Jon Marcoux, Robbie Ethridge, Maureen Meyers, Mark Williams, Bram Tucker, Jen Birch, Greg Wilson, Amber VanDerwarker, David Watt, and Susan Chevalier for guidance, encouragement, inspiration, and patience. Thanks for support from the Louisiana Board of Regents; the Department of Anthropology, the Center for Archaeology, the Committee on Research, the School of Liberal Arts, and the New Orleans Center for the Gulf South at Tulane University; and the Research Laboratories of Archaeology, the Department of Anthropology, and the Center for the Study of the American South at the University of North

Carolina at Chapel Hill. I am, of course, responsible for any problems with this chapter.

References

Anderson, David G. 1994 *The Savannah River Chiefdoms: Political Change in the Late Prehistoric Southeast*. University of Alabama Press, Tuscaloosa.

Baden, William W. 1983 *Tomotley: An Eighteenth Century Cherokee Village*. Report of Investigations 36, Department of Anthropology. University of Tennessee, Knoxville.

Blom, Deborah E., and John W. Janusek 2004 Making Place: Humans as Dedications in Tiwanaku. *World Archaeology* 36: 123–141.

Boulware, Tyler 2011 *Deconstructing the Cherokee Nation: Town, Region, and Nation Among Eighteenth-Century Cherokees*. University Press of Florida, Gainesville.

Brain, Jeffrey P., and Philip Phillips 1996 *Shell Gorgets: Styles of the Late Prehistoric and Protohistoric Southeast*. Peabody Museum Press, Peabody Museum of Archaeology and Ethnology. Harvard University, Cambridge.

Brown, Ian W. 2006 The Calumet Ceremony in the Southeast as Observed Archaeologically. In *Powhatan's Mantle: Indians in the Colonial Southeast (Revised and Expanded Edition)*, edited by Gregory A. Waselkov, Peter H. Wood, and Tom Hatley, pp. 371–419. University of Nebraska Press, Lincoln.

Brown, James A. 1990 Archaeology Confronts History at the Natchez Temple. *Southeastern Archaeology* 9: 1–9.

Corkran, David 1969 A Small Postscript on the Ways and Manners of the Indians Called Cherokees. *Southern Indian Studies* 21: 3–49.

Dickens, Roy S., Jr. 1967 The Route of Rutherford's Expedition Against the North Carolina Cherokees. *Southern Indian Studies* 19: 3–24.

———. 1976 *Cherokee Prehistory: The Pisgah Phase in the Appalachian Summit Region*. University of Tennessee Press, Knoxville.

———. 1978 Mississippian Settlement Patterns in the Appalachian Summit Area: The Pisgah and Qualla Phases. In *Mississippian Settlement Patterns*, edited by Bruce D. Smith, pp. 115–139. Academic Press, New York.

———. 1979 The Origins and Development of Cherokee Culture. In *The Cherokee Indian Nation: A Troubled History*, edited by Duane H. King, pp. 3–32. University of Tennessee Press, Knoxville.

Duncan, Barbara R., and Brett H. Riggs 2003 *Cherokee Heritage Trails Guidebook*. University of North Carolina Press, Chapel Hill.

Emerson, Thomas E. 1989 Water, Serpents, and the Underworld: An Exploration Into Cahokian Symbolism. In *The Southeastern Ceremonial Complex: Artifacts and Analysis*, edited by Patricia Galloway, pp. 45–92. University of Alabama Press, Tuscaloosa.

———. 1997a *Cahokia and the Archaeology of Power*. University of Nebraska Press, Lincoln.

———. 1997b Cahokian Elite Ideology and the Mississippian Cosmos. In *Cahokia: Domination and Ideology in the Mississippian World*, edited by Timothy R. Pauketat and Thomas E. Emerson, pp. 190–228. University of Nebraska Press, Lincoln.

———. 2003 Materializing Cahokia Shamans. *Southeastern Archaeology* 22: 135–154.

Emerson, Thomas E., and Timothy R. Pauketat 2008 Historical-Processual Archaeology and Culture Making: Unpacking the Southern Cult and Mississippian Religion. In *Belief in the Past: Theoretical Approaches to the Archaeology of Religion*, edited by David S. Whitley and Kelley Hays-Gilpin, pp. 167–188. Left Coast Press, Walnut Creek, California.

Ethridge, Robbie F. 2010 *From Chicaza to Chickasaw: The European Invasion and the Transformation of the Mississippian World, 1540–1715.* University of North Carolina Press, Chapel Hill.

Evans, E. Raymond, and Duane H. King, eds. 1977 Memoirs of the Grant Expedition Against the Cherokees in 1761. *Journal of Cherokee Studies* 2: 272–337.

Fogelson, Raymond D. 1980 The Conjuror in Eastern Cherokee Society. *Journal of Cherokee Studies* 5(2): 60–87.

———. 2004 Cherokee in the East. In *Southeast*, edited by Raymond D. Fogelson, pp. 337–353. Handbook of North American Indians, vol. 14, William C. Sturtevant, general editor, Smithsonian Institution, Washington, DC.

Gearing, Frederick O. 1958 The Structural Poses of Eighteenth-Century Cherokee Villages. *American Anthropologist* 60: 1148–1157.

———. 1962 *Priests and Warriors: Structures for Cherokee Politics in the Eighteenth Century.* American Anthropological Association Memoir 93, Washington, DC.

Gilbert, William H., Jr. 1943 *The Eastern Cherokees.* Bulletin 133:169–413, Bureau of American Ethnology, Smithsonian Institution, Washington, DC.

Goodwin, Gary C. 1977 *Cherokees in Transition: A Study of Changing Culture and Environment Prior to 1775.* Research Paper 181, Department of Geography, University of Chicago, Chicago.

Greene, Lance K. 1999 *The Archaeology and History of the Cherokee Out Towns.* Volumes in Historical Archaeology 40. South Carolina Institute of Archaeology and Anthropology, Columbia.

Hall, Robert L. 1989 The Cultural Background of Mississippian Symbolism. In *The Southeastern Ceremonial Complex: Artifacts and Analysis*, edited by Patricia Galloway, pp. 239–278. University of Alabama Press, Tuscaloosa.

Hally, David J. 2002 "As Caves Beneath the Ground": Making Sense of Aboriginal House Form in the Protohistoric and Historic Southeast. In *Between Contact and Colonies: Archaeological Perspectives on the Protohistoric Southeast*, edited by Cameron B. Wesson and Mark A. Rees, pp. 90–109. University of Alabama Press, Tuscaloosa.

———. 2007 Mississippian Shell Gorgets in Regional Perspective. In *Southeastern Ceremonial Complex: Chronology, Content, Context*, edited by Adam King, pp. 185–231. University of Alabama Press, Tuscaloosa.

———. 2008 *King: The Social Archaeology of a Late Mississippian Town in Northwestern Georgia.* University of Alabama Press, Tuscaloosa.

Hally, David J., and Hypatia Kelly 1998 The Nature of Mississippian Towns in Georgia: The King Site Example. In *Mississippian Towns and Sacred Spaces: Searching for an Architectural Grammar*, edited by R. Barry Lewis and Charles B. Stout, pp. 49–63. University of Alabama Press, Tuscaloosa.

Hudson, Charles 1976 *The Southeastern Indians.* University of Tennessee Press, Knoxville.

———. 1984 *Elements of Southeastern Indian Religion.* E. J. Brill, Leiden.

Joyce, Arthur A., and Sarah B. Barber 2015 Ensoulment, Entrapment, and Political Centralization: A Comparative Study of Religion and Politics in Later Formative Oaxaca. *Current Anthropology* 56: 819–847.

Keel, Bennie C. 1976 *Cherokee Archaeology: A Study of the Appalachian Summit.* University of Tennessee Press, Knoxville.

Keel, Bennie C., Brian J. Egloff, and Keith T. Egloff 2002 Reflections on the Cherokee Project and the Coweeta Creek Mound. *Southeastern Archaeology* 21: 49–53.

King, Adam 2003 *Etowah: The Political History of a Chiefdom Capital.* University of Alabama Press, Tuscaloosa.

King, Duane H. 1979 Introduction. In *The Cherokee Indian Nation: A Troubled History*, edited by Duane H. King, pp. ix–xix. University of Tennessee Press, Knoxville.

Knight, Vernon J., Jr. 1986 The Institutional Organization of Mississippian Religion. *American Antiquity* 51: 675–687.

———. 1997 Some Developmental Parallels Between Cahokia and Moundville. In *Cahokia: Domination and Ideology in the Mississippian World*, edited by Timothy R. Pauketat and Thomas E. Emerson, pp. 229–268. University of Nebraska Press, Lincoln.

———. 1998 Moundville as a Diagrammatic Ceremonial Center. In *Archaeology of the Moundville Chiefdom*, edited by Vernon J. Knight, Jr., and Vincas P. Steponaitis, pp. 44–62. Smithsonian Institution Press, Washington, DC.

———. 2004 Ceremonialism Until 1500. In *Southeast*, edited by Raymond D. Fogelson, pp. 734–741. Handbook of North American Indians, vol. 14, William C. Sturtevant, general editor, Smithsonian Institution, Washington, DC.

———. 2006 Symbolism of Mississippian Mounds. In *Powhatan's Mantle: Indians in the Colonial Southeast (Revised and Expanded Edition)*, edited by Gregory A. Waselkov, Peter H. Wood, and Tom Hatley, pp. 421–434. University of Nebraska Press, Lincoln.

Lankford, George E. 1987 *Native American Legends: Southeastern Legends – Tales From the Natchez, Caddo, Biloxi, Chickasaw, and Other Nations*. August House, Little Rock.

Lewis, Thomas M. N., Madeline D. Kneberg Lewis, and Lynne P. Sullivan, eds. 1995 *The Prehistory of the Chickamauga Basin*. University of Tennessee Press, Knoxville.

Mills, Barbara J. 2008 Remembering While Forgetting: Depositional Practices and Social Memory at Chaco. In *Memory Work: Archaeologies of Material Practices*, edited by Barbara J. Mills and William H. Walker, pp. 81–108. School for Advanced Research Press, Santa Fe.

Mooney, James 1891 *Sacred Formulas of the Cherokees*. Annual Report 7: 301–397, Bureau of American Ethnology, Smithsonian Institution, Washington, DC.

———. 1900 *Myths of the Cherokee*. Annual Report 19:1–576, Bureau of American Ethnology, Smithsonian Institution, Washington, DC.

Muller, Jon D. 1989 The Southern Cult. In *The Southeastern Ceremonial Complex: Artifacts and Analysis*, edited by Patricia Galloway, pp. 11–26. University of Alabama Press, Tuscaloosa.

———. 2007 Prolegomena for the Analysis of the Southeastern Ceremonial Complex. In *Southeastern Ceremonial Complex: Chronology, Content, Context*, edited by Adam King, pp. 15–37. University of Alabama Press, Tuscaloosa.

Pauketat, Timothy R. 1994 *The Ascent of Chiefs: Cahokia and Mississippian Politics in Native North America*. University of Alabama Press, Tuscaloosa.

———. 1998 Refiguring the Archaeology of Greater Cahokia. *Journal of Archaeological Research* 6: 45–89.

———. 2004 *Ancient Cahokia and the Mississippians*. Cambridge University Press, Cambridge.

———. 2013 *An Archaeology of the Cosmos: Rethinking Agency and Religion in Ancient America*. Routledge, London.

Pauketat, Timothy R., and Thomas E. Emerson 1991 The Ideology of Authority and the Power of the Pot. *American Anthropologist* 93: 919–941.

———. 1999 The Representation of Hegemony as Community at Cahokia. In *Material Symbols: Culture and Economy in Prehistory*, edited by John Robb, pp. 302–317. Occasional Paper 26, Center for Archaeological Investigations. Southern Illinois University, Carbondale.

Pauls, Elizabeth P. 2005 Architecture as a Source of Cultural Conservation: Gendered Social, Economic, and Ritual Practices Associated With Hidatsa Earthlodges. In *Plains Earthlodges: Ethnographic and Archaeological Perspectives*, edited by Donna C. Roper and Elizabeth P. Pauls, pp. 51–74. University of Alabama Press, Tuscaloosa.

Perdue, Theda 1998 *Cherokee Women: Gender and Culture Change, 1700–1835*. University of Nebraska Press, Lincoln.

Persico, V. Richard, Jr. 1979 Early Nineteenth-Century Cherokee Political Organization. In *The Cherokee Indian Nation: A Troubled History*, edited by Duane H. King, pp. 92–109. University of Tennessee Press, Knoxville.

Polhemus, Richard, ed. 1987 *The Toqua Site: A Late Mississippian Dallas Phase Town*. Report of Investigations 41. Department of Anthropology, University of Tennessee, Knoxville.

Prine, Elizabeth P. 2000 Searching for Third Genders: Toward a Prehistory of Domestic Spaces in Middle Missouri Villages. In *Archaeologies of Sexuality*, edited by Robert Schmidt and Barbara Voss, pp. 197–219. Routledge, London.

Riggs, Brett H. 2008 *A Synthesis of Documentary and Archaeological Evidence for Early Eighteenth Century Cherokee Villages and Structures: Data for the Reconstruction of the Tsa-La-Gi Ancient Village, Cherokee Heritage Center, Park Hill, Oklahoma*. Report on file at the Research Laboratories of Archaeology, University of North Carolina, Chapel Hill.

Rodning, Christopher B. 2002 The Townhouse at Coweeta Creek. *Southeastern Archaeology* 21: 10–20.

———. 2007 Building and Rebuilding Cherokee Houses and Townhouses in Southwestern North Carolina. In *The Durable House: House Society Models in Archaeology*, edited by Robin A. Beck, Jr., pp. 464–484. Occasional Paper 35, Center for Archaeological Investigations. Southern Illinois University, Carbondale.

———. 2008 Temporal Variation in Qualla Pottery at Coweeta Creek. *North Carolina Archaeology* 57: 1–49.

———. 2009a Mounds, Myths, and Cherokee Townhouses in Southwestern North Carolina. *American Antiquity* 74: 627–663.

———. 2009b Domestic Houses at Coweeta Creek. *Southeastern Archaeology* 28: 1–26.

———. 2010a Architectural Symbolism and Cherokee Townhouses. *Southeastern Archaeology* 29: 59–79.

———. 2010b European Trade Goods at Cherokee Settlements in Southwestern North Carolina. *North Carolina Archaeology* 59: 1–84.

———. 2011a Cherokee Townhouses: Architectural Adaptation to European Contact in the Southern Appalachians. *North American Archaeologist* 32: 131–190.

———. 2011b Mortuary Practices, Gender Ideology, and the Cherokee Town at the Coweeta Creek Site. *Journal of Anthropological Archaeology* 30: 145–173.

———. 2012 Late Prehistoric and Protohistoric Shell Gorgets From Southwestern North Carolina. *Southeastern Archaeology* 31: 33–56.

———. 2013 Architecture of Aggregation in the Southern Appalachians: Cherokee Townhouses. In *From Prehistoric Villages to Cities: Settlement Aggregation and Community Transformation*, edited by Jennifer A. Birch, pp. 179–200. Routledge, London.

———. 2014 Cherokee Towns and Calumet Ceremonialism in Eastern North America. *American Antiquity* 79: 425–443.

———. 2015a *Center Places and Cherokee Towns: Archaeological Perspectives on Native American Architecture and Landscape in the Southern Appalachians*. University of Alabama Press, Tuscaloosa.

———. 2015b Native American Public Architecture in the Southern Appalachians. In *Archaeological Perspectives on the Southern Appalachians: A Multiscalar Approach*, edited by Ramie A. Gougeon and Maureen S. Meyers, pp. 105–140. University of Tennessee Press, Knoxville.

Rodning, Christopher B., and Amber M. VanDerwarker 2002 Revisiting Coweeta Creek: Reconstructing Ancient Cherokee Lifeways in Southwestern North Carolina. *Southeastern Archaeology* 21: 1–9.

Russ, Kurt, and Jefferson Chapman 1983 *Archaeological Investigations at the Eighteenth Century Overhill Cherokee Town of Mialoquo*. Report of Investigations 37, Department of Anthropology, University of Tennessee, Knoxville.

Schroedl, Gerald F. 1978 Louis-Philippe's Journal and Archaeological Investigations at the Overhill Town of Toqua. *Journal of Cherokee Studies* 3: 206–220.

———. 2000 Cherokee Ethnohistory and Archaeology From 1540 to 1838. In *Indians of the Greater Southeast: Historical Archaeology and Ethnohistory*, edited by Bonnie G. McEwan, pp. 204–241. University Press of Florida, Gainesville.

———. 2001 Cherokee Archaeology Since the 1970s. In *Archaeology of the Appalachian Highlands*, edited by Lynne P. Sullivan and Susan C. Prezzano, pp. 278–297. University of Tennessee Press, Knoxville.

Schroedl, Gerald F., ed. 1986 *Overhill Cherokee Archaeology at Chota-Tanasee*. Report of Investigations 38, Department of Anthropology, University of Tennessee, Knoxville.

Smith, Betty A. 1979 Distribution of Eighteenth-Century Cherokee Settlements. In *The Cherokee Indian Nation: A Troubled History*, edited by Duane H. King, pp. 46–60. University of Tennessee Press, Knoxville.

Smith, Marvin T. 1989 Early Historic Period Vestiges of the Southern Cult. In *The Southeastern Ceremonial Complex: Artifacts and Analysis*, edited by Patricia Galloway, pp. 142–146. University of Alabama Press, Tuscaloosa.

Smith, Marvin T., and Julie Barnes Smith 1989 Engraved Shell Masks in North America. *Southeastern Archaeology* 8: 9–18.

Swanton, John R. 1946 *The Indians of the Southeastern United States*. Bulletin 137, Bureau of American Ethnology, Smithsonian Institution, Washington, DC.

———. 1952 *The Indian Tribes of North America*. Bulletin 145, Bureau of American Ethnology, Smithsonian Institution, Washington, DC.

Steponaitis, Vincas P. 1983 *Ceramics, Chronology, and Community Patterns: An Archaeological Study at Moundville*. Academic Press, New York.

———. 1986 Prehistoric Archaeology in the Southeastern United States, 1970–1985. *Annual Review of Anthropology* 15: 363–404.

———. 1991 Contrasting Patterns of Mississippian Development. In *Chiefdoms: Power, Economy, and Ideology*, edited by Timothy K. Earle, pp. 193–228. Cambridge University Press, Cambridge.

Sullivan, Lynne P. 1987 The Mouse Creek Phase Household. *Southeastern Archaeology* 6: 16–29.

———. 1995 Mississippian Community and Household Organization in Eastern Tennessee. In *Mississippian Communities and Households*, edited by J. Daniel Rogers and Bruce D. Smith, pp. 99–123. University of Alabama Press, Tuscaloosa.

———. 2007 Shell Gorgets, Time, and the Southeastern Ceremonial Complex in Southeastern Tennessee. In *Southeastern Ceremonial Complex: Chronology, Content, Context*, edited by Adam King, pp. 88–106. University of Alabama Press, Tuscaloosa.

Sundstrom, Linea 2003 Sacred Islands: An Exploration of Religion and Landscape in the Northern Great Plains. In *Islands on the Plains: Ecological, Social, and Ritual Uses of Landscapes*, edited by Marcel Kornfeld and Alan J. Osborn, pp. 258–300. University of Utah Press, Salt Lake City.

Ward, H. Trawick, and R. P. Stephen Davis, Jr. 1999 *Time Before History: The Archaeology of North Carolina*. University of North Carolina Press, Chapel Hill.

Waselkov, Gregory A., and Kathryn E. Holland Braund, eds. 1995 *William Bartram on the Southeastern Indians*. University of Nebraska Press, Lincoln.

Zedeño, María Nieves 2008a Bundled Worlds: The Roles and Interactions of Complex Objects from the North American Plains. *Journal of Archaeological Method and Theory* 15: 362–378.

————. 2008b Traditional Knowledge, Ritual Behavior, and Contemporary Interpretations of the Archaeological Record – An Ojibway Perspective. In *Belief in the Past: Theoretical Approaches to the Archaeology of Religion*, edited by David S. Whitley and Kelley Hays-Gilpin, pp. 259–274. Left Coast Press, Walnut Creek, California.

————. 2009 Animating by Association: Index Objects and Relational Taxonomies. *Cambridge Archaeological Journal* 19: 407–417.

Zogry, Matthew J. 2010 *Anetso, the Cherokee Ball Game*. University of North Carolina Press, Chapel Hill.

5

UNSETTLED GODS

Religion and politics in the Early Formative Soconusco

Sarah B. Barber

Introduction

The Mesoamerican Early Formative period (1900–1000 cal. B.C.) was an era of remarkable innovation in a wide array of social fields. While the transition from the preceding Late Archaic period (3500–1900 cal. B.C.) is generally defined in terms of the widespread adoption of domesticated plants (i.e., Lesure 2011a:1), transformations at this time encompassed all aspects of the lived experience. The Early Formative period thus saw the beginning of sedentary communities, the adoption of fired ceramic technology, the advent of hereditary inequality, the first expressions of multi-community authority, and the development of many ideas, practices, and things that remained fundamental to Mesoamerican social relations until the arrival of the Spanish 3,000 years later (i.e., Lesure 2011a). While archaeologists have developed a number of sophisticated models to explain various aspects of Early Formative social transformation, religion is generally referenced as an integrative tool (i.e., Clark 2004b; Cyphers 2004:35) and often subordinated to other processes such as land ownership, labor deployment, aggrandizing individuals, or long-distance exchange (Clark and Blake 1994; Flannery 1968; Hill and Clark 2001). Certainly all of these phenomena were important elements of the changes that occurred during Mesoamerica's Early Formative period.

In this chapter, however, I foreground religion in order to trace the changing things and spaces through which people in the Soconusco region of Chiapas, Mexico, interacted with the divine (Figure 5.1). Focusing on the initial Early Formative period (1900–1300 B.C.), I propose that people began to encounter animate, other-than-human beings at home soon after the establishment of Mesoamerica's earliest villages in the Soconusco's Mazatán region.[1] Houses, particularly the large residences built during the Locona phase (1700–1500 B.C.) at several sites in the Mazatán, entangled people, other-than-human beings, objects of varying degrees

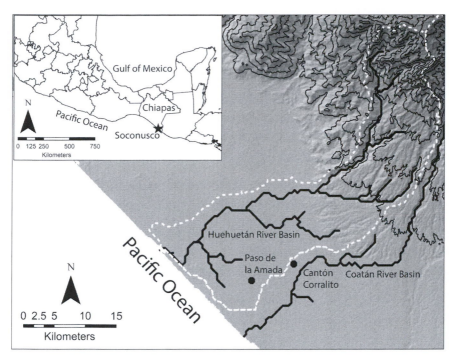

FIGURE 5.1   Map of the Huehuetán and Coatán River basins, showing sites mentioned in the text. Contour interval 250 m.

of animacy, and actions in ways that afforded the exercise of authority and the generation of inequality in novel ways that had profound implications for subsequent historical processes. Intimate, domestic encounters with the divine shifted over time to public and increasingly impersonal spaces and scales of engagement by the fifteenth century B.C. Concomitant with this spatial relocation was an expansion in the reach of authority and in the kinds of things through which social distinction was generated. By the beginning of the thirteenth century B.C., the divine had left home to become distant and exotic. Rather than making decisions directly in the mundane world in intimate settings, divine beings became remote – leaving the exercise of authority to living people whose unique status was also translated into the use and display of valued things.

Religion in the Early Formative period

Disentangling religion from other fields of social engagement has proven to be a thorny, if not fruitless, endeavor (Aldenderfer 2012; Alt and Pauketat, Chapter 3; Asad 1993; Fowles 2013). I follow other authors in this volume in viewing religion as entangled relations among people, ideas, things, other-than-human beings, places, and actions (Alt and Pauketat, Chapter 3; A. Joyce, Chapter 1; R. Joyce, Chapter 7;

Pauketat 2013a; Zedeño, Chapter 13). The insertion of other-than-human beings, divinities, or "cosmic forces" into human-thing entanglements makes certain relational fields religious (following Pauketat 2013a:42; cf. Walker, Chapter 11). Of course, people constantly engage with other-than-human beings, be they a laptop computer or a rain cloud. Treating religion as entangled human-thing relations has the potential to result in a concept so broad (e.g., "Life/Religion"; Insoll 2004:22–23) as to negate distinctions between religion and human being.

While religion may be undefinable and inherent in human experience, it is consistently intertwined with what Arthur Joyce (Chapter 1; see also Joyce and Barber 2015) calls "the divine," acknowledging a metaphysical component. What that metaphysical component might entail is again context-driven and almost certainly debatable. To avoid definitional quagmires, here I understand the divine to encompass animate essences or other-than-human beings with which living people seek (or sought) to engage as purposive entities (cf. Bennett 2010:93). In other words, the divine is comprised of other-than-human beings with which living people interact, or at least attempt to interact, based on the assumption that such beings have needs, desires, and intentions. However the divine manifests in a particular context, it has the capacity to act in the world because it is bundled with the myriad things that people create, employ, experience, and encounter when going about their lives. Religion does not rest solely in people's minds (Keane 2008). Particular people, things, actions, and places may be more or less religious in that they afford engagement with the divine more or less overtly.

There is an extensive body of literature examining the religious principles and ontological positions of Mesoamerican peoples at the time of Spanish contact and extending into the precolumbian period (Lopez Austin 2015; Monaghan 2000; Nicholson 1981). The Early Formative period, however, poses a particular challenge because it is likely that many of these principles, particularly those enmeshing political hierarchies with interaction with the divine, were first developed at this time (Clark 2004a). There is evidence that at least some elements of the much later ideas, practices, things, and places through which Mesoamerican peoples encountered the divine had very deep histories (Gutiérrez and Pye 2010). Drawing on a range of sources discussing precolumbian ontology and practices designed to encounter the divine (e.g., Lopez Austin 2015; Monaghan 2000; Morrison 2000; Nicholson 1981; Zedeño 2009), I propose that the following principles can aid in the identification of archaeological evidence for human-divine interaction in the initial Early Formative period. Notably, I suggest that Early Formative Mesoamerican peoples:

- held an ontological position recognizing sentience and intention in a wide range of other-than-human beings, from people to animals to plants to many things that would be categorized as "objects" in Western ontology (Morrison 2000);
- recognized certain geographic locations or orientations either as being animate or particularly conducive to interaction with other-than-human beings, or both (Zedeño 2009);

- held that the outer surface of animate things both determined and provided information about each thing's capacities, which helped direct how living people engaged with those things (Lopez Austin 2015; Monaghan 2000);
- combined (or bundled) different sentient things to transfer, transform, enhance, or diffuse those things' capacities (papers in Guernsey and Reilly 2006; Pauketat 2013a, 2013b; Zedeño 2008, 2009, Chapter 13).

Given the ubiquity of relational ontologies in the Americas (e.g., Viveiros de Castro 2004; Zedeño 2009) and in Mesoamerica particularly (Monaghan 2000), it is more analytically conservative to assume that precolumbian Mesoamericans interacted with most things as if they were animate, rather than the reverse.

Such an assumption brings back the specter of "Life/Religion" (Insoll 2004), potentially turning everything examined archaeologically into a facet of religion. Nonetheless, it is possible to focus on actions, things, and places that likely were entangled in potent or evocative transactions with the divine. Drawing on the importance of surfaces, I suggest that things with faces would have been part of potent transactions because they could be encountered in more human-like ways, facilitating communication between the living and other-than-humans (Barber and Olvera 2012; Furst 1995; Houston et al. 2006:74; Monaghan 2000:29). Drawing on the potential inherent in combination, I further suggest that bundled things recovered archaeologically were intended to facilitate potent transactions (Zedeño 2008, 2009, Chapter 13). Finally, drawing on the animate and/or communicative capacity of places, I suggest that locations that people significantly modified for reasons other than dwelling would also have been particularly potent for human-divine engagement. These statements are regrettably broad and could be applied to a range of examples that may have had little to do with divine encounters (e.g., marketplaces or middens; but see Hutson and Stanton 2007). They at least provide a foundation for the context-specific examples I discuss here: houses (places where a variety of things were intentionally brought together and that had specific geographic orientations); anthropomorphic ceramic figurines and masks (things with faces that also depicted, or were part of, the combination of humans and other potentially animate things); and a ceremonial center (a significantly modified place with a specific geographic orientation).

Over the following pages, I draw on the ideas outlined above to examine the radical transformations of the initial Early Formative period. As per Aldenderfer (2012), I examine what religion was doing during the development of the region's earliest expression of large-scale authority and the subsequent development of inequality. Focusing on houses, ceramic figurines and masks, and Paso de la Amada's ceremonial core, I argue that people's efforts to encounter the divine created a space first for the cohabitation of certain people and other-than-human beings in houses. Over time, those intimate sites of divine engagement were abandoned in favor of a potent, non-domestic space where large numbers of people could encounter the divine together, although at a greater remove. Large-scale authority emerged out of, rather than brought about, this movement of divine encounters from home to ceremonial center. Drawing on ontological and religious principles that were widely shared in Early Formative Mesoamerica (and probably beyond), the inhabitants of the Soconusco created a completely novel set of relations among people, things, and the divine that profoundly transformed subsequent political histories.

The gods at home: religion and authority in the Locona phase

Small-scale polities developed in the Chiapan Soconusco between the Barra (1900–1700 B.C.) and Ocós (1500–1400 B.C.) ceramic phases (see Figure 5.1). The Barra phase, which immediately followed the Late Archaic period (3500–1900 B.C.), was characterized by the region's first permanent villages as well as the adoption of pottery (Clark and Blake 1994). Unlike Archaic-period habitations (to the extent that these are known; e.g., Voorhies 2004), Barra-phase villages were long-lived: houses were built and renovated repeatedly in the same place (Clark 1994:150, 196; 2004a; Rosenswig 2010:Chapter 4). Houses were durable locations at which a range of potentially animate things became combined in new ways, enabling transformations or enhancements of the actions and things through which people engaged the divine that had not existed in earlier eras. Such things would have included people, pottery, stored foods, lithic tools, and a wide range of perishable items now lost archaeologically, such as gourd containers, nets, basketry, wooden objects, and so on. While the sentience of domestic things (other than living people) in the Barra phase is unclear, by the subsequent Locona phase (1700–1500 B.C.), at least some dwellings housed other-than-human beings in addition to human and material occupants.

By the seventeenth century B.C., the site of Paso de la Amada had surpassed 50 ha in area and had a population between 1,950 and 2,600 people (Clark 2004b:60). The majority of the site's inhabitants at this time lived in small, thatch-roofed structures built directly on the ground surface, natural elevations, or low rises (< .3 m) created by earlier refuse accumulation (Lesure 1997a; 1999b:392). These apsidal dwellings were between 4 and 8 m long (Clark 1994:Table 21; Lesure 1997a, 1999b). In contrast, five large residences (Mounds 4, 6, 13, 32, and 50) built early in the Locona phase were architecturally distinct for the size of their perishable superstructures, for their placement atop earthen platforms, for the presence of exterior gathering space, and for a few unique associated artifacts (Blake 1991, 2011; Lesure 2011c:124–125) (Figure 5.2). Paso de la Amada's five large residences (and presumably those at other large sites; e.g., Clark 1994:140–158) afforded relations among people, things, and other-than-human beings that would have generated sub-community collectivities, while also enabling the development of inequality and facilitating the exercise of authority.

All five large residences were architecturally distinct from other domestic facilities at Paso de la Amada. Four of the five (Mounds 4, 13, 32, and 50) were comprised of one or two layers of earthen fill that reached approximately 1 m

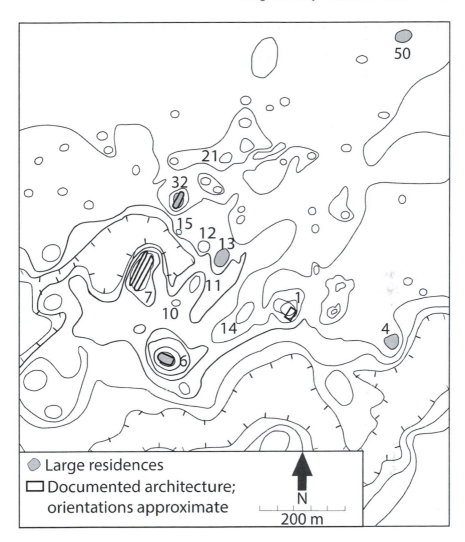

FIGURE 5.2   Map of the southwestern section of Paso de la Amada showing large residences and other mounds. Contour interval 50 cm (redrawn from Clark
and Pye 2006:Figure 3 and Lesure 2011c:Figure 6.2).

in elevation above the ancient ground surface (Lesure 2011c; Lesure and Blake
2002:3). Mound expansion was limited after 1600 B.C., although all were occupied for another century or more (Lesure 2011c:128,137). All five large platforms
supported thatch-roofed, apsidal structures ranging in size from 10–22 m long
(Blake 2011; Lesure 1999b:392). These residences were scattered across the site,
although they were built to a regionally shared orientation (35 degrees E of N or
55 degrees W of N) (Lesure 2011c:Table 6.1; Rosenswig 2010:122). The large
residences also had exterior space that could have been used for gatherings and

other interaction between inhabitants and visitors. At both Mounds 6 and 32, the only two mounds for which relevant data are available, this space was kept clear of refuse, effectively indicating a front and back to the residences (Lesure 2011c). Small residences, on the other hand, had refuse on all sides (Lesure 1999b: 397). The "formalized," cleared spaces (Lesure 1999b, 2011c) created an appropriate avenue of approach for visitors and a venue for interaction among groups of people beyond just domestic inhabitants. These spaces also left residents open to observation during ritual events and everyday life, enabling others in the community – living, dead, and other-than-human – to evaluate platform occupants' actions (Lesure 2011c:141).

Large residences also brought together a few items not found elsewhere at the site (Lesure 1999b; Lesure and Blake 2002). Large residences had a higher proportion of large (greater than 20 cm tall; Lesure 2011b:76), hollow anthropomorphic figures than did small ones, although these anthropomorphic representations were present in low quantities in off-platform domestic assemblages as well (Lesure and Blake 2002:15). Hollow figures depicted individuals in a variety of poses, with elaborately detailed faces, hair, clothing, and other ornaments (Lesure 1999a:215). They were made with far greater care than the ubiquitous solid figurines (see p. 105), probably requiring specialized knowledge to produce (Clark 1994:264). Given their detail, it seems plausible that these figures depicted people rather than divinities (Clark 2004a; Lesure 2011b). Nonetheless, they were *not* people; they were things of clay with faces, likely imbuing them with both a degree of animacy and also different capacities than those of living people. Of particular interest were the fragments of two very large ceramic statuettes found at Mounds 6 and 32 (Lesure and Blake 2002:17). Lesure (2011c:125) estimates that, when complete, the Mound 32 statuette would have been 60–70 cm high. The fact that they had faces, and were large, elaborate, and rare, suggests that statuettes, and possibly also hollow figurines, were involved in the kinds of ritualized acts through which the divine would have been encountered (Lesure 1999a:216). Additionally, a ceramic mask fragment was recovered from the Mound 6 residence (Lesure and Blake 2002:Table 2). As with other things with faces, masks were likely animate beings in their own right in Mesoamerican ontologies (see p. 106; Houston et al. 2006:74; Monaghan 2000:29). Finally, subfloor offerings at the Mound 6 residence permanently combined domestic architectural space with a range of other things. Offering contents included a human infant, a greenstone celt, a complete green heron, parts of two other birds, and a V-shaped, hematite-covered pendant carved from a deer scapula (Blake 2011:105, 107). While some of the items found in these offerings were not unusual (the celt and pendant; Lesure and Blake 2002:18), their placement beneath domestic floors would have created an enduring combination of potent things that had the potential to change the properties of the house itself.

The capacity of Paso de la Amada's platform residences to bundle things together extended beyond the living people who inhabited the buildings. Constructing and maintaining both the earthen platforms and domestic structures would have required labor beyond that of the occupants, thereby giving some subset of the community a stake in the facilities and generating sub-community collectivities. Indeed, construction of the perishable superstructures of large residences required nearly as much labor as the earthen platforms (Blake 1991:36, 2011:107). Ongoing use of the buildings reiterated the collective investment inherent in construction and maintenance, while cleared exterior spaces enabled gatherings. Events involving large groups are further supported by several of the things used and discarded at platform residences. The size of the hollow figurines and statuettes would have made these objects more easily visible from a distance than the smaller and more ubiquitous solid figures found at residences of all sizes, allowing the actions in which hollow figurines were involved to be seen from the back of a crowd (Lesure 1999a:215; Lesure and Blake 2002:17; see also Blomster 2009:144; Joyce 2009:413). The higher proportion of hollow figurines, furthermore, suggests either that such events occurred more frequently at large residences, that large-residence inhabitants had greater access to hollow figurines, and/or that more participants were involved in those events. The presence of statuettes and a mask in refuse at Mounds 32 and 6 suggests that these unusual things also inhabited platform residences and would have mediated living people's encounters with the divine there.

With five large residences at the site, entanglements of residents, non-residents, spaces, and potentially animate things were duplicated several times at Paso de la Amada. Each residence may have been enmeshed in a partially autonomous network with its own internal relations of inequality and authority (Lesure 2011c:137,142; see also Clark 1994:380, 2004b:54, proposing ten "barrios" at Paso de la Amada in the Barra and early Locona phases). While platform residences may have provided space and housed people and things that together afforded communication with other-than-human beings for both residents and visitors, the inhabitants of these buildings held a unique and more potent position in reference to the divine. Their homes were aligned to a shared axis, thereby positioning daily tasks in reference to a particular geographic orientation. They also lived in proximity to potentially potent things and benefited from the aggregated labor of other members of the community. Inequality and, at the very least, the authority to undertake certain kinds of interaction with the divine were thus vested in the occupants of platform residences. There is little evidence prior to 1600 B.C., however, that the inhabitants of any one residence had greater authority. Considering labor investment alone, no one platform residence was notably larger or more impressive than the others. The first two iterations of the Mound 6 residence were built directly on the ground surface, for instance (Blake et al. 2006). And the uniformity of domestic assemblages site-wide reiterates that no domestic group or groups had greater access to the kinds of rare and valuable things that were so important in generating inequality in later eras (e.g., Lesure and Blake 2002). The geographic orientation of the Mound 6 residence near a ballcourt (see p. 107) as well as the presence of offerings and a mask, however, may have together made Mound 6 and its occupants more effective in accessing the divine.

The solid ceramic figurine assemblage from the Locona and Ocós (1500–1400 B.C.) phases provides further insight into how encounters with the divine may have become entangled with authority and inequality. While fired clay was used exclusively for serving vessels until just prior to 1700 B.C., by the end of the Barra phase people had begun making solid anthropomorphic clay figurines for widespread use (Lesure 2011b; Rosenswig 2010:187). Domestic figurines in the Locona and Ocós phases take two forms (Lesure 1997b, 1999a; Rosenswig 2010, 2011). One subset depicts naked young-adult females, always standing, lacking arms, and sometimes represented as pregnant. A second subset consists of older figures with arms resting on or beside their protruding bellies who are seated on stools and often wear elaborate clothing, headgear, and masks (Lesure 1997b; Rosenswig 2011:253). Gender is rarely indicated in this group of figures, which could mean that they are largely male (i.e., Clark 1994:424), or that gender was less relevant than age in these depictions (Lesure 1997b:241). There were at least seven regionally standard masks worn by many of the seated figures (Rosenswig 2010:189) demonstrating the existence of collectively recognized beings whose visages likely were worn by older adults in communities across the southeastern Soconusco. While interpretations vary regarding the uses to which these figurines were put (Clark 1991; Clark and Pye 2000; Joyce 2000; Lesure 1997b, 2011b), I would argue that as things with faces, they were minimally understood as animate and could plausibly have had capacities that facilitated human encounters with the divine. What those capacities might have been or how these figures were deployed remains unclear. Regardless, there is agreement that Soconuscan figurines depict people, things, and actions that likely existed during the centuries when the artifacts were produced.

The seated figures are of particular interest because they depict a combination of two beings with faces – living people and masks. The seated position, furthermore, identifies these figures as representing individuals with a degree of authority (Clark 1991; Clark and Pye 2000; Lesure 1997b; see also Marcus and Flannery 1996:99). That seated figures wear masks and sometimes other costume elements suggests that authority at this time was not vested in individuals of a particular age or gender, but rather in other-than-human beings who were made manifest through a complex bundle of people, things, and places. Within Mesoamerican ontologies, masks were (and are) potent animate entities with significant capacity for action (Cordry 1980; Houston et al. 2006:Chapter 8). They are portraits, which in both precolumbian and ethnographic contexts have been understood by Mesoamerican peoples to contain some of the animate essence of the depicted being (Barber and Olvera 2012; Furst 1995; Houston et al. 2006:74; Monaghan 2000:29). Even more compellingly, masks are meant to be worn. By giving the wearer a new outer surface or "face," "the mask puts on the person" who then gives the depicted being a vehicle for action in the mundane realm (Monaghan 2000:29; Shulman 2006:38; see also Lopez Austin 2015). While the figurine assemblage provides the widest set of examples of masking at this time, at least two effigy vessels from the Locona phase also show masked individuals (Rosenswig 2011:255), another figurine depicts a person inside a zoomorphic costume (Lesure 1997b:237, Figure 5), and there were the aforementioned clay mask fragments from an Ocós phase midden at the Mound 6 residence (Lesure 1997b:237). While the solid figurine assemblage suggests that advanced age may have been one means by which living people became suitable vehicles for the divine, these other depictions show younger individuals. Age, therefore, was only one characteristic that might have enabled people to speak for or with the voice of the divine.

Early Formative religious principles, when enacted in the novel material contexts that existed with the advent of sedentism and the adoption of pottery, would have facilitated the generation and exercise of authority along with the initial creation of distinctions that would lead to inequality. Houses created a place where a combination of animate beings could reside in a permanent place while giving some people a privileged position – literally and figuratively – within the village of Paso de la Amada. Large residences, furthermore, drew in people beyond the immediate household, thereby creating larger, more diverse entanglements of people, things, and other-than-humans than had previously existed. The practice of masking also leveraged the principle of combination to transform certain people, allowing them to act and speak not as their mundane selves, but rather as a divine character. This combined being enabled masked individuals to extend their authority over others in a way that situated decisions outside individual bodies. Positioning certain kinds of decisions within the purview of divine beings may have made the wider reach of Early Formative authority more palatable to people newly experiencing sedentary life. Additionally, masks detached specific people from expressions of authority and would have made decisions harder to contest. Once the mask was removed, a religiously potent combination was diffused and the mask-wearer was no longer the decision-maker. The person or people affected by such decisions had no means of recourse except through someone who could manifest other-than-human authorities. At the same time, the capacity for mask-wearing would have distinguished certain people from others. Such distinctions created the potential for transference of decision-making away from other-than-humans and into the mundane realm. Mask-wearing capacity also created a space for the generation of inequality, since those who could bring forth the beings inhabiting masks were clearly unlike the rest of the population by virtue of their capacity to be transformed through combination with another animate being (the mask).

The gods in public: religion and ceremonial space

While Paso de la Amada's five large residences would have been important locations at which people encountered the divine in the Locona phase, public facilities constructed during these centuries became pivotal in a new, non-domestic entanglement of people, other-than-humans, architectural spaces, and things after 1600 B.C. The earliest of these facilities was a ballcourt (Mound 7) that was constructed concomitant with the earliest iteration of the Mound 6 residence at the very beginning of the Locona phase (Blake 2011:109; Blake et al. 2006). Mounds 6 and 7 were aligned perpendicular to each other with a level, open area in between. They thus shared an intentional geographic orientation, highlighting their potential to facilitate evocative transactions with the divine. The first phase of ballcourt construction was the largest building event in the site's history, consisting of 1,229 m³ of earthen fill forming two parallel mounds with benches extending into the playing alley (Blake et al. 2006:196). The scale of building would have required collective labor. Hill (1999:116; Hill and Clark 2001) estimates 1,375 person-days, requiring a large labor force but one that was likely available within Paso de la Amada itself. The two structures may have been renovated in tandem again around 1600 B.C. when the first large platform (397.74 m³ of fill) to elevate the Mound 6 residence was deposited, and the ballcourt mounds were lengthened and widened with another 1,135 m³ of fill (Blake 2011:112; Blake et al. 2006:196, Table 7.1). This second expansion was the last significant modification of the ballcourt, although renovations continued for more than a century at nearby Mound 6 (Blake 2011).

Paso de la Amada's ballcourt offered a novel facility at which inhabitants of the village and surrounding areas could have interacted with each other and with the divine, given its similarity to later examples (Hill and Clark 2001). Mound 7 would have been the site of public contests surrounded by a range of associated events such as feasts, gambling, and acts specifically targeting interaction with other-than-human beings (Hill and Clark 2001). Reiterating the potential of certain places to enable evocative experiences, later Mesoamerican ballcourts were liminal spaces at which the living could encounter not just other-than-humans but also gain access to locations that were outside of quotidian experience (Gillespie 1991). Like large residences, the ballcourt would have brought together people, other-than-humans, things, and actions in ways that facilitated their mutual engagement. Such entanglements were fundamentally different from those centered on large residences, however. The scale of the human element would presumably have been much larger than that at large residences, since labor was drawn from across the community. Furthermore, Mound 7 likely would not have provided a home for divine beings and the paraphernalia required to care for and access them. With its proximity to the ballcourt and the synchrony of its renovations with Mound 7, however, the Mound 6 large residence would have provided exactly those missing facilities (Blake et al. 2006; Hill and Clark 2001).

Over time, Mounds 6 and 7 became tangled within an even larger public space for encountering the divine. From just before 1500 B.C. until 1400 B.C., the southwestern corner of the site was transformed into a ceremonial complex analogous to those that characterized later Mesoamerican urban areas (Clark 2004b; Lesure 2011c). During these centuries, the Mound 6 residence was expanded at least five times with a cumulative 1,722 m³ of fill (Blake et al. 2006:Table 7.1) and topped with standing buildings of varying elaboration (Blake 1991). An area to the northwest was infilled (Mound 11) to create a level open area, and Mound 14 was built to the northeast of Mound 6 (Lesure 2011c:133–134). These construction efforts defined a plaza approximately 200 m a side that was capable of accommodating thousands of people (Clark [2004a:60] estimates as many as 10,000), and surrounded on three sides by buildings sharing the site-wide orientation (Lesure

2011c:Table 6.1). Nearly all of this space was accessible and public, although the use of Mound 14 remains unclear. The scale of building in this area far exceeded other construction efforts in the Ocós phase and indicates labor investment well beyond the scale of individual households (Clark 2004b).

Drawing on religious principles related to combination/bundling, potent places, and geographic orientation, the ceremonial complex at Paso de la Amada spatially concentrated community- and/or region-wide encounters with the divine. The potential scale of actions in the ceremonial complex would have far exceeded anything that could have taken place at large residences. The physical spaces created through decades of construction were imbued with the collective efforts of people from across the site over multiple generations. Beyond their scale, the spaces of the ceremonial complex both afforded and demanded certain kinds of actions that could not have taken place elsewhere at the site or even in surrounding villages. While appearing unstructured, the plaza was a carefully delineated space that would have allowed for very large gatherings and perhaps discouraged small ones. The axes of the surrounding buildings, furthermore, would have oriented people on the plaza to a geographic position that was clearly of importance across the village. The ballcourt was also a very specific space that dictated the kinds of actions that could take place there. The Mound 6 residence, which was probably already more effective at bringing humans and the divine together than other large residences due to its proximity to the ballcourt and the perhaps sacred things buried beneath its floors, was the anchor of this space. It entwined one lineage near the center of a new kind of entanglement with inherent inequality: the inhabitants of the residence had privileged access to the divine, given that they dwelled among potent spaces and the other-than-human beings that could manifest there. Inequality premised in this way was not unprecedented in the Mazatán zone since analogous dwelling conditions had obtained for the inhabitants of other large residences for decades. The differences in venue type and scale between Paso de la Amada's large residences and its ceremonial complex, however, demonstrate that quite different actions and encounters with other-than-humans would have occurred in public facilities. The scale of such encounters, in particular, would have been far less intimate. The exercise of authority would have been similarly impersonal.

Despite the scale and impressiveness of Paso de la Amada's public spaces, the human-thing relations that developed during the Locona and Ocós phases were short-lived. The ballcourt and the Mound 6 residence were both abandoned by the end of the Ocós phase in 1400 B.C. (Blake 2011). Large residences elsewhere at the site continued to be occupied, expanded, and built into the fourteenth century. Ongoing resurfacing at Mound 13 raised the occupational surface of the residential platform another 50 cm in the Cherla phase (1400–1300 B.C.), and a new ground-level large residence (Residence 1–2) was built (Lesure 2011c:127–128). Yet the bundling of people, other-than-humans, and things that had occurred at large residences dissolved over the course of the Ocós phase. Lesure (1999b, 2011c) describes a loss of "formalization" at Paso de la Amada's large residences from the Ocós to Cherla phases. Platforms were enlarged in asymmetrical ways, platform erosion was not repaired, cleared avenues of approach became pitted with refuse dumps, and burials and refuse pits were excavated into interior floors (Lesure 2011c:Figure 6.5). Such features made space-use at large residences resemble that at smaller residences. These changes suggest that both non-residents and some other-than-humans became detached from the entanglements that had formerly assembled these groups together with residents, things, and large residence domestic spaces.

Decoupling visitors from the entanglements centered on large residences was a process of exclusion and segregation that accelerated during the Cherla phase. Not only were large residences no longer designed to accommodate non-residents in collective events, but new things were brought into large residences that distinguished their occupants from others in the village. Middens located near mounds contained jade, iron-ore mirror fragments, and higher proportions of obsidian and ceramic earspools than contemporary contexts elsewhere at the site (Lesure 1995:246; 1999a:217–218). Several of these items (mirrors, earspools) were used for personal adornment, and may have drawn on the principle of combination to enhance the potential of individual people to engage with the divine. The abandonment of the ceremonial core represents an analogous process given that the large, accessible spaces of the plaza and ballcourt fell into disuse. While Mound 14 was expanded with the placement of at least 60 cm of fill, additional large constructions were located elsewhere – at Mounds 1 and 12 (see Figure 5.2) (Lesure 2011c). The Cherla-phase platforms were large in area (20–22 m × 26 m for Mound 12), nearly circular or nearly square in shape, and did not follow the Locona- and Ocós-phase site-wide orientation (Lesure 2011c:128–130, 132). They also lacked the pits and refuse that are characteristic of earlier residences and of Cherla-phase deposits elsewhere at the site (Lesure 2011c:140). Lesure (2011c) argues convincingly that these platforms were non-domestic. Although further research will be necessary to strengthen this interpretation, it may be that housing for some divine beings may have become fully detached from residences by the Cherla phase.

The Cherla phase represented the last gasp of occupation at Paso de la Amada. The site and several other large villages were abandoned by the beginning of the Cuadros phase (1300–1200 cal. B.C.) (Clark 2007; Pye, et al. 2011). A single large center developed at Cantón Corralito, a site of at least 25 ha located directly on the Coatán River (Cheetham and Clark 2006).[2] Evidence from the site indicates close interaction, and possibly political interference, by people from the Gulf Coast Olmec heartland (Cheetham 2010; Clark 2007).

The masks come off: religion, authority, and inequality in early Mesoamerica

In the Chiapan Soconusco, early Mesoamerican ontological positions and religious principles became entangled with architecture and specific lineages from the beginnings of sedentary life. Less than two centuries after people in the Mazatán region began building permanent houses, they had begun intertwining these spaces with people, things, and actions that connected the living with the divine (see also Clark

2004a, citing Renfrew 2001). The principle of combination or bundling, through which the religious capacities of places or things could be enhanced and transformed by being placed in physical proximity (Pauketat 2013a:Chapter 4; Zedeño 2008), was extended to houses such that certain people's homes were modified to facilitate encounters with other-than-human beings. The large residences of the Locona and Ocós phases combined living people and animate things with faces that required careful crafting, like ceramic masks, statuettes, and hollow figurines. The spaces of large residences enabled the presence of large groups of people and also provided inhabitants and visitors appropriate geographic positioning through their shared orientations. So while large residences remained houses, they were houses that had been transformed. They were significantly modified from typical homes, presumably improved in their capacities to afford encounters between living people and the divine.

Authority and inequality were an outcome – rather than a cause – of people's efforts to develop more potent things, acts, and places through which to engage with the divine. The full-time occupants of large residences would have been the primary caretakers and users of the things that brought people and other-than-humans into proximity. There is an inherent ranking in this set of relations given that large-residence occupants would have been permanent elements of the bundles created by their houses. Initially, their privileged physical and existential position did not translate into other kinds of material benefits. However, large-residence occupants almost certainly would have had a degree of authority over affiliated people who relied on the bundled people and things at large residences for interventions or decisions requiring divine action.

The modest and probably narrow authority that developed in the Locona phase was distributed across the site of Paso de la Amada, the Mazatán region, and possibly the entire southeastern Soconusco. There were multiple large residences at Paso de la Amada, and at least one is known for Cantón Corralito (e.g., Clark 1994:140–158); masked figurines were uniform over an area that encompassed the entire southeastern Soconusco, and other evidence for masking is similarly widespread (Rosenswig 2011:243, 253). The uniformity of things involved in human-divine contact demonstrates that people in many parts of the southeastern Soconusco had the capacity to manifest the authority of other-than-human beings through actions like donning masks or deploying hollow figurines and statuettes. The scale of authority at this time would have been quite modest, furthermore, extending only to the village members who congregated at large residences for events at which the divine was to be made manifest.

Like the limited intra-village authority that developed by the Locona phase, larger-scale authority was an outcome of efforts to create more effective places for encounters between humans and other-than-humans. The Mound 6-ballcourt combination in the southeastern portion of the site was likely designed from the outset to be a particularly compelling location for such encounters. Mound 6 itself bundled together the things found in other large residences (masks, statuettes) with unique items like a red-tinted ornament and a wading bird (both of which were, in later eras, important indices for divine encounters) (Schele and Miller 1986:55; Zedeño 2009). While the reasons for expanding this portion of the site remain unclear, it seems plausible that the efficacy of this place and its associated people and things for divine encounters was such that a substantial segment of the village's inhabitants saw value in further augmenting the capacity of the area (see also Clark 2004b). The ceremonial space that emerged from these enhancements drew on existing principles of combination and geographic position to create an entirely novel facility that demanded novel actions and political relations.

While probably not intended by its builders, Paso de la Amada's ceremonial center created a new bundle (both of relations [following Pauketat 2013b] and of potent humans, things, places, and other-than-humans [following Zedeño 2008]) that was utterly unlike what had existed before in Mesoamerica. The scale of the human element of this bundle, a community, incorporated most or all of the village and perhaps people from beyond the village. It is not clear the extent to which the divine component of a village-wide collectivity differed from those centered on large residences; certainly the physical spaces and things that were necessary to create the Paso de la Amada community were very different from earlier and smaller groupings. The ballcourt was unlike anything else at the site. The size of the plaza and the labor invested in the ceremonial spaces demonstrate that the scale of community events was many orders of magnitude larger than those that could have taken place at large residences. And unlike the inhabitants of other large residences, the domestic group occupying the Mound 6 residence continued to demand or merit (likely both) ongoing attention concomitant with collective building efforts. Like the spaces of the ceremonial core itself, Mound 6 was renovated and expanded multiple times.

The decision by the Soconusco's earliest villagers to invite the divine into their homes had profound consequences. The building and use of architectural spaces were central to a process through which the site's residents transformed how they engaged with the divine – and each other. By concentrating certain divine encounters first at a small number of homes and later at Paso de la Amada's ceremonial core, decisions originally made based on enduring ontological positions and religious principles afforded the development of authority and ultimately inequality. Efforts to create a more potent and effective location for encountering the other-than-humans – the ceremonial core – simultaneously made the divine more accessible and more distant. While far more people now had access to the things, spaces, and living people through which the divine was manifested, at least some divine entities were now situated at a greater remove from the quotidian, everyday contexts where they had formerly been encountered. The erosion of Lesure's (1999b, 2011c) "formalized" spaces at large residences, including Mound 6, by the Ocós phase likely traces the detachment of some elements of the divine from the domestic. In leaving home to encounter the divine, people also engaged with each other in new ways. The actions undertaken to bring the divine forth, or at least close by, were much more work: to build appropriate facilities, to assemble sufficient people, to coordinate events, to obtain needed things. Unsurprisingly, the people whose ancestors had once directly manifested the divine in their homes shouldered the increasingly onerous organizational burden of bringing the living and the divine into proximity to one another. While such efforts at first may have been understood to be of benefit to all participants, over time the material benefits to a small subset of the community included greater access to potent and precious things, often from afar. Given their home's geographic position and uniquely bundled items, occupants of the Mound 6 residence presumably were of greatest importance in navigating the relocation of and subsequent community-scale interaction with the divine. And perhaps, as proposed by Clark and colleagues (Clark and Blake 1994; Hill and Clark 2001), there was a degree of self-serving intentionality in the process.

By the Cherla phase, the accessible spaces of Paso de la Amada's ceremonial core that had provided a meeting place for the living and the divine fell into disuse. The divine did not return home, however. Instead, new spaces for divine engagement were built in several parts of the site. Those spaces lacked the geographic positioning that had been so important in earlier centuries, suggesting deeply changed understandings of how and where the divine was appropriately engaged. The Soconuscan figurine assemblage further supports the notion of profound change at this time. The masked elders found in Locona- and Ocós-phase assemblages were replaced by unmasked, seated figures with features characteristic of the pan-regional "Olmec" aesthetic (Clark 1994:424; Lesure 2011b:145). By the Cherla phase, authority had a foreign and exotic face. Following the principles laid out at the beginning of this chapter, a change of face implies a significant transformation in the capacities of individuals with authority. Current evidence is insufficient to determine the nature of those transformations, but the removal of masks suggests that living people spoke, rather than beings indexed by a mask. There are several possible interpretations for the abandonment of masks in this case. It could be that the other-than-humans who had spoken through masks were abandoned in favor of those from the Gulf Coast, a region with which the Soconusco saw increased interaction at this time (Cheetham 2010; Clark 2007; Clark and Pye 2000). It could also be that the divinities became even further removed from daily life, speaking only through human intermediaries rather than themselves through masks. It could be that qualification to serve as an intermediary became increasingly restricted and hereditary. It could be some combination of these conditions.

Regardless, authority was exercised directly by living people who were distinct because of their connections to distant beings in both the mundane and divine realms. At Paso de la Amada, the bodies of such people manifested those connections through adornments like earspools and jade beads (Lesure 2011c). The temporary distinction created when masks were worn was replaced with more permanent forms of bodily difference.

Conclusions

The changes evident at Paso de la Amada during the Cherla phase were part of a new era of accelerated transformation, both in the Mazatán and elsewhere in

Mesoamerica. Paso de la Amada was abandoned at the end of the Cherla phase, never to be reoccupied. Populations continued to expand elsewhere in the region until the end of the Jocotal phase (1200–1000 B.C.) (Pye et al. 2011). The network of small polities of which Paso de la Amada was the largest exemplar disintegrated, to be replaced by the more typical Mesoamerican pattern of large regional centers. In the Mazatán zone, this center was located first at Cantón Corralito. While very little information about the site is available at this time, in no small part because it was comprehensively buried in a catastrophic flood, it may be that the unsettled gods of the southeastern Soconusco and Paso de la Amada came to reside yet again in a new place, speaking with new voices in new, more potent spaces.

Acknowledgments

Funding for this research was provided by the Historical Society via the John Templeton Foundation. I would like to thank Arthur Joyce, Guy Hepp, and Richard Lesure for their valuable comments on an earlier draft of this chapter. All mistakes and problems are, of course, my own. Thanks to Jacklyn Rumberger for editorial assistance and to Pascale Meehan for assistance with illustrations.

Notes

1 All dates in this chapter are in calibrated years B.C.
2 Cantón Corralito's size is poorly understood because the site was buried by flooding around 1000 B.C., and thus surface remains are not reflective of site size (Gutierrez 2011).

References

Aldenderfer, Mark 2012 Envisioning a Pragmatic Approach to the Archaeology of Religion. In *Beyond Belief: The Archaeology of Ritual and Religion*, edited by Yorke M. Rowan, pp. 23–36. Archaeological Papers of the American Anthropological Association, vol. 21. American Anthropological Association, Arlington, VA.

Asad, Talal 1993 *Genealogies of Religion: Discipline and Reasons of Power in Christianity and Islam*. Johns Hopkins University Press, Baltimore.

Barber, Sarah B., and Mireya Olvera 2012 A Divine Wind: The Arts of Death and Music in Ancient Oaxaca. *Ancient Mesoamerica* 23: 9–24.

Bennett, Jane 2010 *Vibrant Matter: A Political Ecology of Things*. Duke University Press, Durham.

Blake, Michael 1991 An Emerging Early Formative Chiefdom at Paso de la Amada, Chiapas, Mexico. In *The Formation of Complex Society in Southeastern Mesoamerica*, edited by William R. Fowler, pp. 27–46. CRC Press, Boca Raton, Florida.

———. 2011 Building History in Domestic and Public Space at Paso de la Amada: An Examination of Mounds 6 and 7. In *Early Mesoamerican Social Transformations: Archaic and Formative Lifeways in the Soconusco Region*, edited by Richard G. Lesure, pp. 97–118. University of California Press, Berkeley.

Blake, Michael, Richard G. Lesure, Warren D. Hill, Luis Barba, and John E. Clark 2006 The Residence of Power at Paso de la Amada, Mexico. In *Palaces and Power in the*

Americas: From Peru to the Northwest Coast, edited by Jessice Joyce Christie and Patricia Joan Sarro, pp. 191–210. University of Texas Press, Austin.

Blomster, Jeffrey P. 2009 Identity, Gender, and Power: Representational Juxtapositions in Early Formative Figurines from Oaxaca, Mexico. In *Mesoamerican Figurines: Small-Scale Indices of Large-Scale Social Phenomena*, edited by Christina T. Halperin, Katherine A. Faust, Rhonda Taube, and Aurore Giguet, pp. 119–148. University Press of Florida, Gainesville.

Cheetham, David 2010 *America's First Colony: Olmec Materiality and Ethnicity at Canton Corralito, Chiapas, Mexico*. PhD dissertation, Department of Anthropology, Arizona State University, Tempe.

Cheetham, David, and John E. Clark 2006 Investigaciones Recientes en Cantón Corralito: Un posible enclave Olmeca en la Costa del Pacífico de Chiapas, México. In *XIX Simposio de Investigaciones Arqueológicas en Guatemala, 2005*, edited by Juan Pedro Laporte, Barbara Arroyo, and Héctor E. Mejia, pp. 1–9. Museo Nacional de Arqueología y Etnología, Guatemala City.

Clark, John E. 1991 The Beginnings of Mesoamerica: Apologia for the Soconusco Early Formative. In *The Formation of Complex Society in Southeastern Mesoamerica*, edited by William R. Fowler, pp. 13–26. CRC Press, Boca Raton, Florida.

———. 1994 The Development of Early Formative Rank Societies in the Soconusco, Chiapas, Mexico. PhD dissertation, Department of Anthropology, University of Michigan, Ann Arbor.

———. 2004a The Birth of Mesoamerica Metaphysics: Sedentism, Engagement, and Moral Superiority. In *Rethinking Materiality: The Engagement of Mind With the Material World*, edited by Elizabeth DeMarrais and Colin Renfrew, pp. 205–224. McDonald Institute for Archaeological Research, Cambridge.

———. 2004b Mesoamerica Goes Public: Early Ceremonial Centers, Leaders, and Communities. In *Mesoamerican Archaeology: Theory and Practice*, edited by Julia A. Hendon and Rosemary A. Joyce, pp. 43–72. Blackwell, Malden.

———. 2007 Mesoamerica's First State. In *The Political Economy of Ancient Mesoamerica: Transformations during the Formative and Classic Periods*, edited by Vernon L. Scarborough and John E. Clark, pp. 11–46. University of New Mexico Press, Albuquerque.

Clark, John E., and Michael Blake 1994 The Power of Prestige: Competitive Generosity and the Emergence of Rank in Lowland Mesoamerica. In *Factional Competition and Political Development in the New World*, edited by Elizabeth Brumfiel and John Fox, pp. 17–30. Cambridge University Press, Cambridge.

Clark, John E., and Mary E. Pye 2000 The Pacific Coast and the Olmec Question. In *Olmec Art and Archaeology in Mesoamerica*, edited by John Clark and Mary E. Pye, pp. 217–251. Studies in the History of Art. vol. Vol. 58. National Gallery of Art and Yale University Press, Washington, DC and New Haven.

———. 2006 Los Orígenes de Privilegio en el Soconusco, 1650 AD: Dos Décadas de Investigación. In the proceedings of the *XIX Simposio de Investigaciones Arqueológicas en Guatemala, 2005*, edited by Juan Pedro Laporte, Barbara Arroyo, and Hector E. Mejía, pp. 10–22. Ministerio de Cultura y Deportes, Instituto de Antropología e Historia, Asociación Tikal, Guatemala City.

Cordry, Donald 1980 *Mexican Masks*. University of Texas Press, Austin.

Cyphers, Ann 2004 *Escultura olmeca de San Lorenzo Tenochititlán*. Universidad Nacional Autónoma de México, Mexico City.

Flannery, Kent V. 1968 Archaeological Systems Theory and Early Mesoamerica. In *Anthropological Archaeology in the Americas*, edited by Betty J. Meggers, pp. 67–87. The Anthropological Soiety of Washington, Washington, D.C.

Fowles, Severin M. 2013 *An Archaeology of Doings: Secularism and the Study of Pueblo Religion.* School for Advanced Research Press, Sante Fe.

Furst, Jill L. M. 1995 *The Natural History of the Soul in Ancient Mexico.* Yale University Press, New Haven.

Gillespie, Susan D. 1991 Ballgames and Boundaries. In *The Mesoamerican Ballgame*, edited by Vernon L. Scarborough and David R. Wilcox, pp. 317–345. University of Arizona Press, Tucson.

Guernsey, Julia, and F. Kent Reilly, eds. 2006 *Sacred Bundles: Ritual Acts of Wrapping and Binding in Mesoamerica.* Boundary End Archaeology Research Center, Barnardsville.

Gutiérrez, Gerardo 2011 A History of Disaster and Cultural Change in the Coatán River Drainage of the Soconusco, Chiapas, Mexico. In *Early Mesomerican Social Transformations: Archaic and Formative Lifeways in the Soconusco Region*, edited by Richard G. Lesure, pp. 146–169. University of California Press, Berkeley.

Gutiérrez, Gerardo, and Mary E. Pye 2010 Iconography of the Nahual: Human-Animal Transformations in Preclassic Guerrero and Morelos. In *The Place of Stone Monuments: Context, Use, and Meaning in Mesoamerica's Preclassic Transition*, edited by Julia. Guernsey, John E. Clark, and Barbara Arroyo, pp. 27–95. Dumbarton Oaks, Washington, DC.

Hill, Warren D. 1999 *Ballcourts, Competitive Games and the Emergence of Complex Society.* PhD dissertation, Department of Anthropology and Sociology, The University of British Columbia, Vancouver.

Hill, Warren D., and John E. Clark 2001 Sports, Gambling, and Government: America's First Social Compact? *American Anthropologist* 103: 331–345.

Houston, Stephen D., David Stuart, and Karl A. Taube 2006 *The Memory of Bones: Body, Being, and Experience Among the Classic Maya.* 1st ed. Joe R. and Teresa Lozano Long series in Latin American and Latino art and culture. University of Texas Press, Austin.

Hutson, Scott R., and Travis W. Stanton 2007 Cultural Logic and Practical Reason: the Structure of Discard in Ancient Maya Houselots. *Cambridge Archaeological Journal* 17(2): 123–144.

Insoll, Timothy 2004 *Archaeology, Ritual, and Religion.* Routledge, London.

Joyce, Arthur A. and Sarah B. Barber 2015 Ensoulment, Entrapment, and Political Centralization: A Comparative Study of Religion and Politics in Later Formative Oaxaca. *Current Anthropology* 56: 819–847.

Joyce, Rosemary A. 2000 *Gender and Power in Prehispanic Mesoamerica.* 1st ed. University of Texas Press, Austin.

———. 2009 Making a World of Their Own: Mesoamerican Figurines and Mesoamerican Figurine Analysis. In *Mesoamerican Figurines: Small-Scale Indices of Large-Scale Social Phenomena*, edited by Christina T. Halperin, Katherine A. Faust, Rhonda Taube and Aurore Giguet, pp. 407–425. University Press of Florida, Gainesville.

Keane, Webb 2008 The Evidence of the Senses and the Materiality of Religion. *Journal of the Royal Anthropological Institute* 14: 110–127.

Lesure, Richard G. 1995 *Paso de la Amada: Sociopolitical Dynamis in an Early Formative Community.* PhD dissertation, Department of Anthropology, The University of Michigan, Ann Arbor.

———. 1997a Early Formative Platforms at Paso de la Amada, Chiapas, Mexico. *Latin American Antiquity* 8: 217–235.

———. 1997b Figurines and Social Identities in Early Sedentary Societies of Coastal Chiapas, Mexico, 1550–800 b.c. In *Women in Prehistory: North America and Mesoamerica*, edited by Cheryl Claassen and Rosemary A. Joyce, pp. 227–248. Regendering the Past, Cheryl Claassen, general editor. University of Pennsylvania Press, Philadelphia.

————. 1999a Figurines as Representations and Products at Paso de la Amada, Mexico. *Cambridge Archaeological Journal* 9: 209–220.

————. 1999b Platform Architecture and Activity Patterns in an Early Mesoamerican Village in Chiapas, Mexico. *Journal of Field Archaeology* 26: 391–406.

————. 2011a Early Social Transformations in the Soconusco: An Introduction. In *Early Mesoamerican Social Transformations: Archaic and Formative Lifeways in the Soconusco Region*, edited by Richard G. Lesure, pp. 1–24. University of California Press, Berkeley.

————. 2011b *Interpreting Ancient Figurines: Context, Comparison, and Prehistoric Art*. Cambridge University Press, Cambridge.

————. 2011c Paso de la Amada as a Ceremonial Center. In *Early Mesoamerican Social Transformations: Archaic and Formative Lifeways in the Soconusco Region*, edited by Richard G. Lesure, pp. 119–145. University of California Press, Berkeley.

Lesure, Richard G., and Michael Blake 2002 Interpretive Challenges in the Study of Early Complexity: Economy, Ritual, and Architecture at Paso de la Amada, Mexico. *Journal of Anthropological Archaeology* 21: 1–24.

Lopez Austin, Alfredo 2015 *The Myth of Quetzalcoatl: Religion, Rulership, and History in the Nahua World*. Translated by Russ Davisdon. University Press of Colorado, Boulder.

Marcus, Joyce, and Kent V. Flannery 1996 *Zapotec Civilization: How Urban Society Evolved in Mexico's Oaxaca Valley*. New aspects of antiquity. Thames and Hudson, New York.

Monaghan, John 2000 Theology and History in the Study of Mesoamerican Religions. In *Handbook of Middle American Indians: Ethnology Supplement*, edited by Victoria Reifler Bricker and John Monaghan, pp. 24–49. vol. 6. University of Texas Press, Austin.

Morrison, Kenneth M. 2000 The Cosmos as Inter-Subjective: Native American Other-than-Human Persons. In *Indigenous Religions: A Companion*, edited by Graham Harvey, pp. 23–36. Cassell, London.

Nicholson, Henry B. 1981 Religion in Pre-Hispanic Central Mexico. In *Handbook of Middle American Indians*, edited by Richard Wauchope, pp. 395–446. vol. 10. University of Texas Press, Austin.

Pauketat, Timothy 2013a *An Archaeology of the Cosmos: Rethinking Agency and Religion in Ancient America*. Routledge, New York.

————. 2013b Bundles of/in/as Time. In *Big Histories, Human Lives: Tackling Problems of Scale in Archaeology*, edited by John Robb and Timothy Pauketat, pp. 35–56. School for Advanced Research Advanced Seminar Series. School for Advanced Research Press, Santa Fe.

Pye, Mary E., John Hodgson, and John Clark 2011 Jocotal Settlement Patterns, Salt Production, and Pacific Coast Interactions. In *Early Mesoamerican Social Transformations: Archaic and Formative Lifeways in the Soconusco Region*, edited by Richard G. Lesure, pp. 217–241. University of Califonia Press, Berkeley.

Renfrew, Colin 2001 Commodification and Institution in Group-Oriented and Individualizing Socities. In *The Origin of Human Social Institutions*, edited by Walter G. Runciman, pp. 91–117. The British Academy, Oxford.

Rosenswig, Robert M. 2010 *The Beginnings of Mesoamerican Civilization: Inter-Regional Interaction and the Olmec*. Cambridge University Press, Cambridge.

————. 2011 An Early Mesoamerican Archipelago of Complexity. In *Early Mesoamerican Social Transformations: Archaic and Formative Lifeways in the Soconusco Region*, edited by Richard G. Lesure, pp. 242–271. University of California Press, Berkeley.

Schele, Linda, and Mary Ellen Miller 1986 *The Blood of Kings*. George Braziller, New York.

Shulman, David 2006 Toward a New Theory of Masks. In *Masked Ritual and Performance in South India*, edited by David Shulman and Deborah Thiagarajan, pp. 17–58. Centers for South and Southeast Asian Studies, University of Michigan, Ann Arbor.

Viveiros de Castro, Eduardo 2004 Exchanging Perspectives: the Transformation of Objects Into Subjects. *Common Knowledge* 10: 463–484.

Voorhies, Barbara 2004 *Coastal Collectors in the Holocene: The Chantuto People of Southwest Mexico.* University Press of Florida, Gainsville.

Zedeño, María Nieves 2008 Bundled Worlds: The Roles and Interactions of Complex Objects from the North American Plains. *Journal of Archaeological Method and Theory* 15: 362–378.

―――. 2009 Animating by Association: Index Objects and Relational Taxonomies. *Cambridge Archaeological Journal* 19: 407–417.

6

RELIGION, URBANISM, AND INEQUALITY IN ANCIENT CENTRAL MEXICO

David M. Carballo

Introduction

Within the archaeology of religion, a sustained objective has been to better elucidate those elements of religious belief and practice that bonded past peoples together in the process of forming larger social groups, including early cities. Yet we must simultaneously consider the disintegrative dimensions of religion that provide the conceptual underpinnings to regenerate social divisions, often imposed from above, or the fields of social action within which groups or individuals with less power can challenge such divisions from below. Religious systems offer visions of the cultural logic within which all other human action is to be realized, but individuals differ in their interpretations of the logic, giving rise to competing visions and actions.

As noted by Pauketat (2013:6), archaeologies of religion should strive to "understand how religion – as performed in the open, practiced on the landscape, and experienced in and through things, elements, and substances – was related to human history." In this chapter, I examine variability in the entanglements between religion, urbanism, and social inequality in precolumbian central Mexico. This variability includes synchronic considerations such as those between urban and rural populations and between elites and commoners, as well as diachronic considerations of a sequence covering approximately 3,000 years – beginning with largely autonomous villages of the Formative period and ending with imperial Aztec society during the sixteenth century A.D. I focus particularly on the first and third themes discussed by Arthur Joyce in the introductory chapter to this volume: the articulations between religion and the logic of inequality propagated by powerful elites, and a material record emphasizing the symbolism of architecture, deities, and offerings.

Religion, solidarity, and inequality

Archaeologists have noted that approaches to religion within the discipline have traditionally been divided into more functionalist perspectives emphasizing social cohesion and solidarity, and more exploitative perspectives emphasizing power and the legitimation of social asymmetry, due in no small part to the looming influences of prominent social theorists such as Durkheim and Marx (Insoll 2004:45–53; Renfrew 1994:50). Such divisions are apparent still, which Fowles (2013:30–31) attributes principally to two causes: (1) a scalar divide whereby researchers studying smaller-scale societies tend to look to Durkheim and focus on integration, whereas those studying larger-scale societies tend to look to Marx and focus on legitimation; and (2) a dominant paradigm in Anglo-American scholarship with strong secularist and Protestant influences driving narratives of an inward-focused religiosity of early small-scale societies having been corrupted by priestly classes and state ideology of later civilizations.

Scholars in religious studies are well aware of these sorts of issues and have developed more fluid frameworks for understanding ritual actions, which often have a strong material focus amenable to archaeological analysis. For instance, Grimes (2011:77) notes: "Although rituals consist of actions, it's almost impossible to discover, or even imagine, a ritual without its attendant material culture." Works by Grimes (see also Grimes 2014; Bell 1992, 1997) have drawn attention to the process of ritualization as creating a diverse arena of social action within which groups and individuals pursue varied and often conflicting interests. Such interests may be desires for integration and connectedness, or they may be more divisive, such as those enacted through politically sanctioned spectacles and the counter-hegemonic responses to such spectacles. Sometimes interests can overlap among commoners and elites, or among rural and urban constituencies; other times they conflict, especially when the normative order of institutionally sanctioned bases of inequality (social stratification, rural-urban disparities) are questioned by those with little institutional power.

Archaeologists have approached these axes of variability in the uses of religion in various ways. Building from earlier work on the corporate/network axis of political strategy (e.g., Blanton et al. 1996), Peregrine (2012) examines the intersection of religion and politics through comparative ethnography. His study illustrates that power within hierarchical societies tends to emphasize a divine mandate, with its strongest expression in historically known institutions of divine kingship; yet hierarchical societies that temper divinely sanctioned political prerogatives with more meritocratic or consensual bases of authority and greater accountability of leaders are more enduring (see also Feinman and Carballo 2017). Peregrine's illuminating study focuses primarily on the use of religion by those wielding institutional power. I suggest a comparable schema that focuses on the space and context of religious practices in order to encompass a wider population of potential actors (see also Hutson et al., Chapter 8). A first axis of variability is the spectrum of settings for action ranging from private to public, with gradations of semi-private, semi-public, and other such intermediaries as defined by Robin and Rothschild (2002). Two other axes are commonly defined spectra of societal variability: elite/commoner and urban/rural. In considering these varied socio-spatial scales, I draw inspiration from McAnany's (2002) critique and reframing of Redfield's (1956) distinction between "great" and "little" religious traditions. McAnany notes the static and pejorative connotations that the distinction has today, but sees value in evaluating differences between institutional religion propagated by political elites at urban centers and domestic religion practiced by commoners, or the public rituals of more rural communities. Multiscalar considerations of religious symbols and ritual practices – in the temple precincts of ancient urban centers, in rural households, and all places in between – are capable of illustrating how certain religious practices varied, and what proved to be more stable or enduring over time.

The spatial contexts of religion are often studied archaeologically through ritual remains, which Aldenderfer (2011) notes can run the risk of missing the forest for the trees, in that individual instantiations of religious expression are studied disconnected from the broader systems of beliefs and practices that made them meaningful. The inextricability of ritual action from religion highlights the utility of perspectives articulated by authors such as Handelman (1997; Handelman and Lindquist 2004) and Monaghan (2000): that rituals must be first studied on their own terms, as divorced from explanatory frameworks as is possible for any individual researcher to do, so that elements of underlying cultural logics can be understood in order to evaluate and modify our explanatory frameworks. By better understanding local constructions of the internal cultural logics of religious belief and practice, we strive to minimize the influence of our own interpretive biases on the archaeological record. Methodologically, this is often done in Americanist archaeology by considering the archaeological record in light of ethnography and ethnohistory, yet we must be attentive to the detrimental effects of uncritically imposing the continent's rich historical corpus from later societies on prehistoric periods (e.g., Pauketat 2013:23–24). In my focus on central Mexico (Figure 6.1), I first examine variability in the politics of religion along spatial and societal axes during the Aztec period, both for its own sake as well as for moving back and forth temporally to consider points of similarity and disjuncture in earlier archaeological contexts.

Religion and inequality in Aztec society

Aztec religion is perhaps the best known of the precolumbian Americas, because following the conquest of Mexico, the former imperial core became the capital of New Spain – a process that involved sustained efforts on the part of Spanish friars at both documenting and eradicating beliefs and practices (Léon-Portilla 1963; Tena 2012). Religious hybridity during the Colonial and early Republican periods in central Mexico are better documented still, and many researchers have demonstrated how rituals could be enacted to promote the power of the status quo or to challenge and mitigate power relations (Beezley et al. 1994; Burkhart 1989).

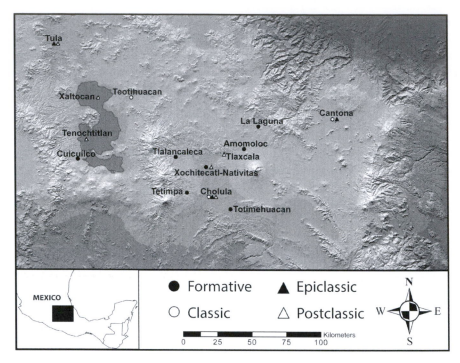

FIGURE 6.1   Central Mexico, depicting sites mentioned in the text and their major periods of occupation

Within archaeology, variability in Aztec religion along the axes of political strategy and socio-spatial context was most productively investigated by Brumfiel (2001, 2006, 2011). Her research illustrated the different goals and foci of practitioners of state religion operating within urban capitals, such as Tenochtitlan, and the religion of imperial subjects and commoners practiced in rural centers and households at Xaltocan and elsewhere (see also De Lucia 2014). Brumfiel problematized the study of Aztec religion by noting the prevailing focus on the official transcript of Mexica-Aztec state religion, and showing how elements such as sacrificial rites and martial and solar themes (both encapsulated in the imperial patron deity, Huitzilopochtli) were absent or minimized in hinterland, commoner, and domestic settings, where rituals were instead overwhelmingly oriented toward the agricultural cycle and human life cycle. Agricultural cycles and fertility themes were also central to the public rituals of urban state religion, but Brumfiel (2001:308) noted the dual structure of Middle to Late Postclassic (A.D. 1250–1519) religion allowed for shifts in foci depending on the historical contingencies of political and social hierarchies.

The social organization of the Aztecs was characterized by central dualisms that could create tensions or promote harmony when manipulated by leaders or challenged by others, and these dualisms were generated and mediated through religion (van Zantwijk 1985:94–95). One is exemplified in the dual structure of Tenochtitlan's Templo Mayor (Figure 6.2a), and other Postclassic twin temples called *huey teocalli* ("great god's house") in Nahuatl. At Tenochtitlan, this dual structure accommodated both the symbolism of an *Altepetl* ("Water Mountain") presided over by Tlaloc (associated with rain and fertility), and of *Coatepec* ("Serpent Mountain") presided over by Huitzilopochtli (associated with the sun, war, and the Mexica as an ethnic group) (López Austin and López Luján 2009; Matos Moctezuma 1988). This coupling presents an essential symbolic dualism between water and fire – one seen as so conflicted and irreconcilably opposed that it stood for war. Wright Carr (2012) details the paired concept in the two major languages of Postclassic central Mexico, Nahuatl and Otomí, and translates the Nahuatl version *atl tlachinolli* as "burning water." He traces iconography relating to this water-fire dualism to the earlier central Mexican state capitals of Tula and Teotihuacan. Wright Carr also identifies analogous terms in Otomí, such as *antehmabagi* ("the water of war"), and the pictographic coupling of water and fire signs for scenes of war in Otomi codices. The water-fire dualism was therefore pan-central Mexican at the time of the conquest and likely possesses significant time depth.

In addition to its bipartite division along lines of Tlaloc/Huitilopochtli and Altepetl/Coatepec, the juxtaposition of water and fire symbolism at the Templo Mayor is also seen in votive offerings featuring effigy jars depicting Tlaloc (Figure 6.2b) and sculptures depicting Xiuhtecutli (the Lord of Fire/the [solar] Year) (Figure 6.2c). In a climate that is semi-arid with highly seasonal precipitation, Tlaloc represents the ultimate public-goods deity, with a longstanding tradition of iconographic representation in central Mexico (Carballo 2007, 2012). Additional water symbolism on Tlaloc's half of the temple includes murals painted on the walls of the deity's shrine, sculptures of frogs and shells, a frontal frog altar, and buried offerings of greenstone beads placed within water jars (López Luján 2005). The solar- and fire-related deities of the Templo Mayor differ in that Xiuhtecutli (especially in his manifestation as Huehueteotl, the Old God) was also ancient to the central Mexican pantheon, whereas the solar patron deity Huitzilopochtli, and the symbolism of his half of the temple as Coatepec, connected cosmic history to the human history of the Mexica as an ethnic group who were newcomers to the political landscape. Whereas Tlaloc and Xiuhtecutli embodied relatively universalizing themes and fundamental tenets of central Mexican cosmology, Huitzilopochtli embodied the distinctiveness of the Mexica as a people, promoted especially by their ruling elite (van Zantwijk 1985:127–130).

Spectacles of violence involving human sacrifice at the Templo Mayor could certainly be considered part of a coercive political strategy (e.g., Kurtz 1978), and Aztec rulers participated in such rituals. Yet the basis of their authority derived not from their roles as divinities or even divine intermediaries; rather, it drew significantly on the evaluation of abilities by the noble councils who elected them, and offered several venues for the social promotion of lower nobles and even commoners (Blanton and Fargher 2008:246–248; van Zantwijk 1985:25–26, 178–179, 277–281). The contours of Aztec and other Postclassic central Mexican religion

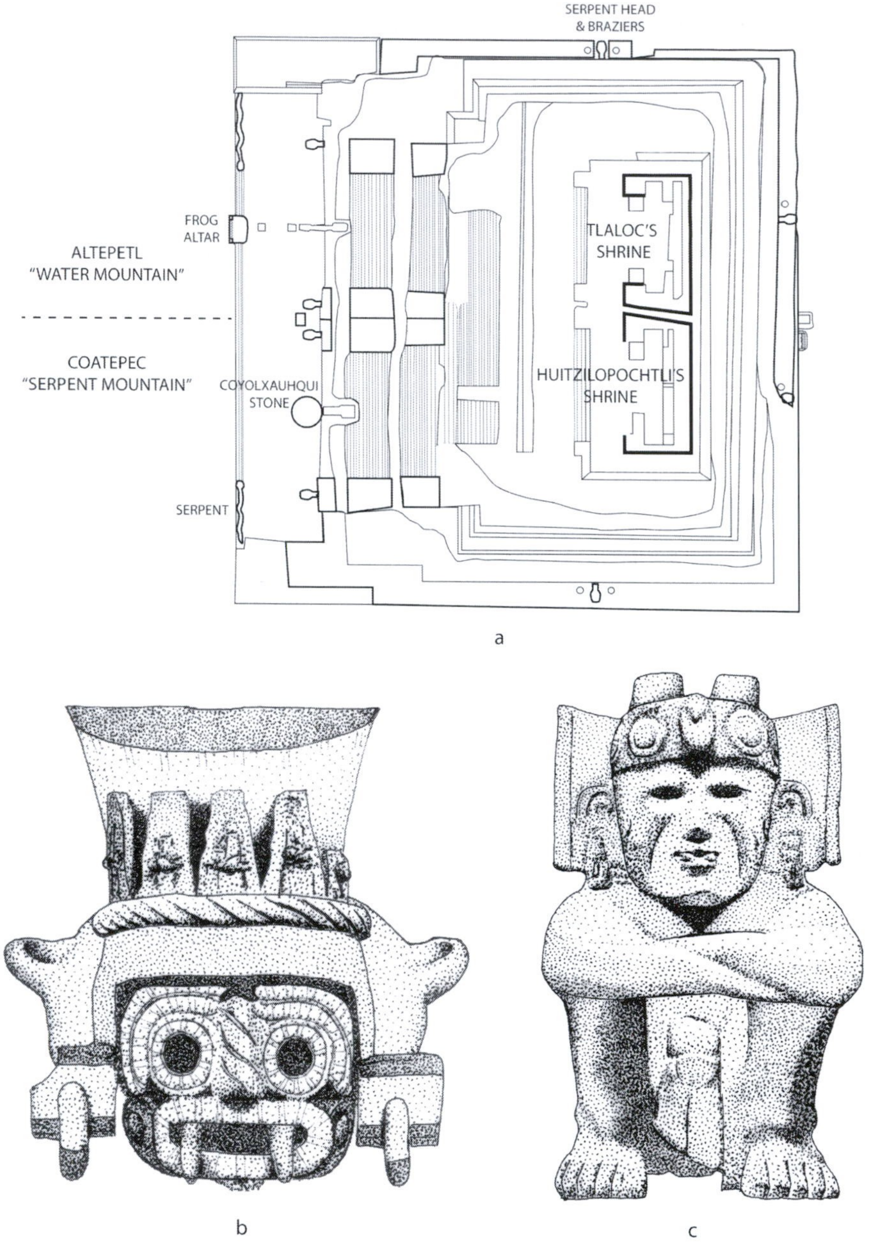

FIGURE 6.2 (a) The Templo Mayor at Tenochtitlan (based on López Luján 2005 and Matos 1988) and effigy depictions of (b) Tlaloc (based on Solís and Leyenaar 2002), and (c) Xiuhtecutli-Huehueteotl found in cache offerings within the temple (based on a photograph by Leonardo López Luján, used with permission)

away from the Templo Mayor presents a constellation of strategies and contexts for action, which span the axes of variability outlined earlier. For instance, the inhabitants of Tlaxcala, the major adversary of the empire within central Mexico, appear to have adopted a much more collective and volunteeristic state political strategy than the Mexica, which may have assisted the Tlaxcalteca in resisting imperial expansion (Fargher et al. 2010).

Brumfiel's attention to spatial setting and context further highlights the diversity of practices. Through an analysis of household ceramic motifs featuring calendrical and cosmogenic symbols, she noted that Aztec commoners used the 260-day ritual calendar (the *tonalpohualli*) for their own purposes prior to imperial expansion and its more politicized uses; they continued to use it distinctly from state religion during the empire; and certain native groups continue to use it to this day in manners disconnected from any centralized political and religious institutions (Brumfiel 2011). De Lucia (2014) also documents variability in ritual practices along spatial scales of household, compound, and community (private, semi-public, and public in the axis devised by Robin and Rothschild 2002), and the pre-imperial roots of other rituals such as the New Fire ceremony, which became coopted as an imperial spectacle of calendrical passage.

Elements of religion, such as calendar rituals, therefore present examples of enduring and resilient traditions, to which we could add rituals involving cosmogenic and fertility themes as part of the "hard nucleus" shared by Mesoamerican religions (Carrasco 2014:5; López Austin and López Luján 2009:19), but given a particular central Mexican expression in its materialized symbols and practices. The spatial expression and connections to power and inequality of such shared concepts were nonetheless variable within regions of central Mexico as well as over time. Consideration of earlier periods in the archaeological record removes us from the rich textual sources of the sixteenth century and contemporary groups such as the Nahua and Otomí. Attention to two variables is essential for bridging these temporal divides: (1) degrees of concordance between associated suites of material culture, considering both points of continuity and disjuncture (Robin 2013:70–81; Wylie 1985); and (2) pervasiveness of forms and use contexts of material culture, as a means of evaluating what key conceptual principles (*sensu* Marcus 2007), or cultural logic, they represent among communities considered at multiple scales of analysis.

Urbanization, inequality, and religion in Formative and Classic period central Mexico

If Aztec society represents a mature expression of pre-Columbian religion in central Mexico, with the substantial ethnohistoric and archaeological record permitting nuanced considerations of its variability through space and the hierarchy of power, the Formative period (1500 B.C.–A.D. 100) represents its much more nebulous coming-of-age. It is the period, however, when hierarchical relationships associated with initial urbanization became entrenched. There is archaeological evidence that a hereditary nobility developed at various urban centers of the period, and the political landscape was transformed through new urban-rural relations that established centers of power and tiered settlement hierarchies associated with these (Carballo 2016; Joyce 2009). Religion was central to all of these transformations. As urban centers and their leaders attracted people through ritual spectacles and the creation of widely shared, temporally enduring conceptualizations of deities, a sacred landscape, and the human actions appropriate to mediating these, important elements of a cultural logic of inclusion and exclusion, collectivity and inequality, became crystalized. Pervasive patterns of the first millennium B.C. established a macroregional template for later pulses of urbanism that included an east-west oriented temple-plaza (and occasionally ballcourt) arrangement, the widespread appearance of at least two major deities, and a symbolic grammar for ritual offerings. I will outline how these facets of central Mexican religion could be both inclusive and divisive when enacted within communities, and could serve as a source of variable identity between them.

Urbanization and inequality

Urbanization of the Formative and Classic periods was a macroregional phenomenon that resulted in a wide variety of settlement arrangements. During the Middle, Late, and Terminal Formative periods (ca. 800 B.C.–A.D. 100), settlements such as Cuicuilco, Tlalancaleca, and Xochitecatl emerged as the largest urban centers in central Mexico, with populations likely to have reached the high thousands to low tens of thousands (Pastrana and Ramírez 2012; Plunket and Uruñuela 2012; Serra Puche et al. 2001). These centers were then eclipsed in importance by a second pulse of urbanization occurring approximately 2,000 years ago that involved the rapid growth of Classic-period (ca. A.D. 100–600) cities such as Teotihuacan, Cholula, and Cantona, whose populations reached the tens of thousands to over a hundred thousand for Teotihuacan (Cowgill 2015; García Cook 2003; Uruñuela et al. 2009). Devastating volcanism appears to have played an important role in this subsequent wave of urbanization, resulting in migration and dramatic shifts in regional settlement toward Teotihuacan in the northern Basin of Mexico and toward Cholula in southern Puebla (Plunket and Uruñuela 2008).

Also part of this urbanizing landscape were smaller centers that could be classified as towns, villages of various sizes, and small hamlets. I refer to the first as having served urban functions on a regional scale and the second two as rural settlements. Collaborative investigations undertaken with colleagues show the site of La Laguna to have developed as a town of some 100 hectares in extent, with a chronology of occupation straddling the later Formative and transition to the Classic period (Borejsza and Carballo 2014; Carballo 2012). Other sites we have investigated in central Tlaxcala represent Formative villages and hamlets (Lesure et al. 2012). These investigations have revealed differential expressions of social status in the region, especially as seen in house construction and personal adornment (Carballo 2009; Carballo, Carballo, and Lesure 2014). The creation and regeneration of social asymmetry through larger, elevated residences and access to imported goods is seen elsewhere in Formative central Mexico at sites such as at Tetimpa (Plunket and Uruñuela 2012) and the Nativitas residential sector of Xochitecatl (Serra Puche and Lazcano Arce 2011). Domestic architecture and personal adornment represented material tropes for the expression of social identity and inequality.

Physical residences communicated and mediated social relations largely through what Rapoport (1988) classifies as mid-level meaning: nonverbal cues such as size, positioning, and architectural elaboration that convey divisions of status and identity in a built environment of houses. These cues constituted forms of indexical communication (*sensu* Blanton 1994), rather than canonical communication or high-level meaning that expressed cosmological principles, though the latter were part of domestic architecture of the period in instances such as the volcano shrines at Tetimpa, which indexed the sacred landscape and its "smoking mountain" Popocatepetl (Plunket and Uruñuela 2002, 2008). Indexical or mid-level messages were directed primarily to audiences somewhere intermediate in the spatial scale of interaction, such as semi-private or semi-public exchanges with other community members.

Personal adornment could be worn in the privacy of one's own home, but would have broader social impact in public venues, be they semi-private meals at home with guests, semi-public interactions at the scale of neighborhoods, or participation in public events. In the assemblages from Tlaxcala, we have noted a related decline in the frequency and elaborateness of decorations on ceramics over the first millennium B.C. coinciding with an increase in personal adornment and public ceremonial architecture (Carballo et al. 2014). This shift in materials and spaces likely captures the formalization of certain types of public ritual and community gathering associated with urbanization – venues that involved symbols and practices that created both solidarity and division.

Ceremonial architecture

Throughout precolumbian Mesoamerica, the pervasive form of public ceremonial architecture was the coupled temple and plaza, constructed from the earliest centers of the Formative period to Tenochtitlan on the eve of the conquest. This long-lived pairing would have encapsulated the dynamic tension of religious integration and division, as open plazas facilitated mutual visibility and more participatory rituals, while stepped pyramids spatially segregated religious specialists in possession of canonical knowledge from the assembled masses (see discussions in Bradley 1998; Moore 2005). Within these spaces, rituals with relatively more integrative themes and others with relatively more divisive themes could be undertaken in succession or simultaneously, each providing elements of a cultural logic for conceiving of, and acting toward, both community identity and social hierarchy.

Ceremonial architecture of La Laguna's Central and Eastern Plazas is known through various geophysical prospection techniques (Barba et al. 2009), and excavations that were realized in seven different areas of the site center (Carballo 2012).

Viewshed analyses that place a hypothetical spectator in the middle of the Central Plaza indicate that the space permitted mutual visibility of assembled spectators within the plaza and between these and individuals standing on top of the two major temples at the site (Carballo 2016:147). Also taking place at the level of the plaza were ballgames, which exemplify the entwined inclusive/divisive elements of public ritual, as people associate collectively as teams and antagonistically in their competition (Santley et al. 1991). La Laguna's I-shaped court and its configuration as a temple-plaza complex represent an early version of the layout of sacred space that became standard at Toltec and Aztec cities.

Consideration of a greater number of Formative centers illustrates the high level of standardization in the alignments of ceremonial precincts of the later Formative period. Through a compilation of these precincts, Anthony Aveni and I (Carballo and Aveni 2012) documented a dominant pattern in orientation consisting of a primary temple facing West/Northwest (Figure 6.3). If, as we propose, the orientation relates to solar observations from the temple to the western horizon, the cluster of azimuths would be most consistent with orientations calibrated for calendrical rituals early in the rainy season. Irrespective of the exact planning principle involved, the West/Northwest orientation proved enduring and continued in Classic and Postclassic cities, though heterogeneity is also observable and worthy of further investigation. The three major Classic period cities prioritized this orientation, but with a Teotihuacano emphasis on its central artery, the Street of the Dead (Cowgill 2015); a Choluteca emphasis on an acropolis-like pyramid platform, possessing multiple access-ways (Uruñuela et al. 2009); and a Cantoneco resistance to choosing any central place, instead creating dozens of temple-plaza compounds and 25 ballcourts (García Cook 2003), many with similarities to the layout of La Laguna's central precinct.

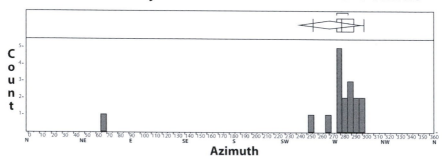

Orientation of Major Structures of Later Formative Centers

FIGURE 6.3   Distribution of azimuth orientations of temple-plaza groups at later Formative period (ca. 600 B.C.–100 A.D.) central Mexican ceremonial centers. Calculated based on the orientation of the frontal staircase of temple platforms following Carballo and Aveni (2012).

What do synchronic standardization and variability in ceremonial architecture mean? Or diachronic change or stasis? Gilman and Stone (2013:610) encapsulate the issue in a comparative evaluation of Southwestern kivas:

> Ritual is so powerful . . . because of both its communicative power and its ability to imbue space with meaning, thus transforming it from mere locale to socially important space with history and memory. [M]essages are either reinforced or transformed with each performance. Therefore, the variability evident in ritual structures within a region tells us a great deal about variability in the negotiation of relationships.

Within a broadly shared religious tradition, as we see in central Mexico, the similarities and variability in ceremonial precincts of the Formative and Classic periods provide means for identifying the different ways in which religion and politics intersected and what messages and social relationships were more enduring across space and time.

Deities and religious symbols

In addition to the broad convergences seen in ceremonial architecture, the appearance of recognizable deities in the archaeological record of Formative central Mexico signals a watershed in the emergence of its enduring religious tradition (Carballo 2007, 2012, 2015). A fundamental protagonist was the Storm God (Figure 6.4a), the direct precursor to Tlaloc, and the persistent style of globular effigy jar depicting his stylized likeness. These have been found cached in ceremonial centers from the early first millennium B.C. to the early Colonial period. Although Mesoamerican peoples shared certain conceptualizations of storm gods, the longstanding form, composite symbolism, and depositional contexts seen in central Mexico mark these as a specific, defining attribute in the religion of the macroregion. The deity appears to have been important to public ritual from its earliest appearances, continuing as perhaps the most important god in state religion at Teotihuacan (Manzanilla 2002:48) and as part of the dual structure of Tenochtitlan's Templo Mayor.

The Old God of Fire (Figure 6.4b), the direct precursor to Huehueteotl-Xiuhtecutli, also assumes a specific effigy form during the Formative period, but as a decidedly anthropomorphic brazier and with more mixed spatial contexts. The form is relatively consistent for over two millennia, yet morphs in its predominant use in more domestic settings (probably more evocative of the fire of the hearth) to its increased appearance in very public contexts of major pyramidal offerings (probably more evocative of volcanos and the solar year – and eventually losing his brazier as the Aztec deity Xiuhtecutli). One of the earliest clear depictions of the Old God of Fire was encountered in domestic refuse at the rural village of Amomoloc (ca. 800–700 B.C.), and throughout Tlaxcala-Puebla the form appears to have

FIGURE 6.4 Effigy vessels from La Laguna: (a) Storm God; (b) Old God of Fire

developed in household contexts to supplant an earlier zoomorphic effigy censer tradition (Lesure et al. 2012). The deity continues to be important in domestic rituals at Teotihuacan where, when found in secure context, Old God braziers are most frequently associated with the courtyards of apartment compounds (Manzanilla 2002).

Although the Old God was an important mediator of domestic concerns, the iconographic signs of fire/volcano (Langley 1986:252, sign 72) decorating many braziers from Teotihuacan suggest that the deity was also associated with fire of a more spectacular, potentially devastating kind. This public and monumental embodiment of fire – volcanic or cosmic fire – was likely conveyed by the very large Old God sculpture recently discovered within the summit of Teotihuacan's Sun Pyramid (Sarabia González 2013). This sculpture and a number of others found earlier at the Sun Pyramid express strong symbolism relating to fire (Fash et al. 2009), whereas the sculptural and offering complexes of the Moon Pyramid strongly index water (Sugiyama 2014; Sugiyama and López Luján 2007), another monumental instantiation of the water-fire dualism. A comparable but earlier Old God deposit comes from Tlalancaleca, where a large stone sculpture of the deity was reported by locals to have been encountered atop the tallest mound at the site. Based on the sculpture's lack of iconography seen on Classic period braziers, García Moll (1976) suggested the sculpture dates to later in the Formative period.

The examples of Storm God and Old God effigies in Figure 6.4 originated from Terminal Formative period contexts at La Laguna and express the water-fire dualism known from later periods. Fragments of such vessels from excavations throughout the site suggest that representations of both deities were venerated in domestic and public contexts. The density by excavation volume of Storm God vessel fragments found in ceremonial spaces (ranging from 0.03–0.21 pieces/ m^3 with a mean of $0.08/m^3$) at La Laguna was over twice the density found in domestic spaces (ranging from 0.02–0.05 pieces/m^3 with a mean of $0.035/m^3$). A mostly complete example likely originating from a ceremonial space is depicted in Figure 6.4a, which was found in a private collection in the town adjacent to the site but refit with a broken S-scroll ear motif that was excavated from a looter's trench bisecting an elevated platform (Structure 12M-1) to the east of the Eastern Plaza. Densities of Old God vessel fragments were, in turn, highest in an elite residential context and the mixed public/domestic contexts of the Eastern Plaza. An illustrative case of the latter is Structure 12M-3, for which multiple lines of evidence converge to indicate mixed uses, including domestic functions but also supra-household food storage and preparation activities that would have provided at least some of the consumables directed toward community rituals (Carballo et al. 2014). Examples of nearly complete Old God (Figure 6.4b) and Storm God vessels (the latter of the type in Figure 6.4a, but missing more parts) were found on the final floor of the structure, indicating the two deities and their water-fire symbolism were venerated in the same structure, but also likely as part of community rituals in the site center. The Storm God vessel was cached in a rectangular arrange-ment of stones and a pestle (*mano*) next to a granary, suggestive of a subsistence/ fertility symbolism known for later incarnations of the deity, but in a much hum-bler context.

Above all, the continuity between these Formative incarnations of the two deities and their appearance as part of the central water-fire dualism expressed by Tenochtitlan's Templo Mayor is remarkable. Yet variability in use across space and time is apparent and cannot be glossed over, particularly in the case of the Old God, who begins more in the domestic sphere, appears both in domestic and mon-umental contexts in early urban centers, and is transformed as a very public deity at the center of the world in the Aztec period. What might such spatial and temporal variability mean? Ethnographic and ethnohistoric data again provide possibilities for evaluation, and when drawn from both Nahua and Otomí communities, illus-trate trends more likely to be pan-central Mexican and not confined to one ethno-linguistic group. Among sixteenth-century Nahua, Xiuhtecutli was equated with the solar year, stellar fire, kingdoms, merchants, turquoise, and with the grass asso-ciated with New Fire ceremonies (Tena 2012:152; van Zantwijk 1985:136, 165). The related Old God, Huehueteotl, was equated with terrestrial fire, and through his female counterpart, Chantico, the domestic hearth. One manifestation of this Nahua fire god complex was Otonteucli ("Lord of the Otomis"), which demon-strates macroregional crossover in the conceptualization of the divinity. Further, contemporary Otomis refer to the deity as Padre Viejo (Old Father), and undertake pilgrimages to him that have strong directional symbolism (López Aguilar and Fournier García 2012), linking him to the broader cosmic order. The symbolic associations of the deity therefore possess a malleability that could be easily adapted for different uses along the private-public spatial spectrum and for differing strategies of either claiming solidarity or distinctiveness of a social group or aspect of the sacred, built environment such as a structure. Attention to the spatial contexts of ritual action is crucial for identifying such variability.

Ritual space

The program of excavations in public and domestic contexts at La Laguna permit spatial comparisons within this midsized community of the later Formative period and regional and temporal comparisons in central Mexico as a whole (Figure 6.5). A major contrast in the use of space at the center of La Laguna is signaled by the profound difference in total artifact densities between the Central and Eastern Plazas. Except for greenstone, artifact densities from the Central Plaza are generally the lowest at the site. The space was tellingly sparse in domestic artifacts, with the

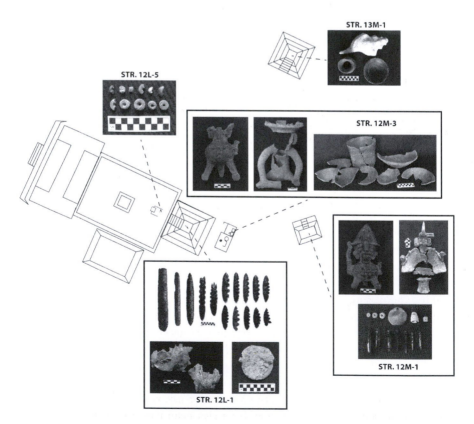

FIGURE 6.5 Ritual caches and deposits in La Laguna's central precinct

lowest densities at the site for food remains and stone tools, including the complete absence of grinding tools (Carballo et al. 2014:154–155). Densities from the Eastern Plaza contrast strongly in registering the highest in stone tools and having similar concentrations of food remains to contexts of a wholly domestic nature. The difference illustrates that the formally demarcated Central Plaza was kept clean as a locus for non-domestic activities, whereas the unbounded Eastern Plaza was used for varied activities, including intense craft production and food storage and preparation.

The highest concentrations of greenstone at La Laguna were registered for Structure 12L-5, a small altar in the eastern Central Plaza on its central axis in front of the site's major temple, Structure 12L-1. The plaza floor and contexts associated with this low altar combined represent less than 4 percent of project excavation volume but 40 percent of the greenstone. The scattered greenstone at the plaza level is consistent with the common Mesoamerican practice of the ritual sowing of a precious substance (Mock 1998). Among sixteenth-century Nahuas, greenstone was perceived as capable of attracting and expulsing moisture (Sahagún 1963:222–223). As was the case with the greenstone beads deposited in water jars at Tenochtitlan's Templo Mayor, those in La Laguna's Central Plaza likely also indexed water. However, individuals standing in La Laguna's Central Plaza would have been in direct view and close proximity to the ritual deposition of greenstone, which would not have been the case for the cache offerings deposited in the Templo Mayor. Even though the greenstone rituals in both settings would have emphasized matters of collective concern such as agricultural fertility, the temporal and scalar differences between a modest town such as La Laguna and an imperial capital such as Tenochtitlan point to fundamental differences in the openness and level of participation in certain public rituals.

The water and agricultural themes in public rituals at La Laguna are further supported by the densities of Storm God vessel fragments, which were highest at the site in the Central Plaza and on top of Structure 12L-1. Although neither of the two more complete effigies was found in these areas, they were deposited in the Eastern Plaza extending directly behind them, forming a contiguous central axis through the ritual precinct expressing water/fertility symbolism. Along this axis, on the upper floor of Structure 12L-1, excavations encountered two basin features that appear to be similar, but more modest counterparts of the megalithic stone basins found at three of the largest Formative period centers: Xochitecatl, Totimehuacan, and Tlalancaleca. In the case of the first two sites, the basins are associated with sculpture and relief carvings depicting frogs and thereby indexing aquatic themes. At Xochitecatl, Serra Puche and colleagues (2001) note that the basins are associated with sequential construction phases of the main pyramid and combine complementary lines of evidence in proposing they served for rituals relating to water and agricultural fertility.

The basins on the main temple at La Laguna are likewise associated with superimposed construction phases and may have also been used in water rituals. The basin within the final floor was terminated with the burial of a cache containing the

pelt of a large puma as part of a larger termination program that involved an elaborate second cache deposited at the back wall of the temple superstructure (Carballo
2012, 2014). The latter, an arrangement of 15 large obsidian knives and eccentrics
deposited in a composed scene with pyrite mirrors, contains formal and symbolic
similarities to the pyramidal offerings of Teotihuacan (Sugiyama and López Luján
2007), but again on a more modest scale. The martial themes expressed by the
obsidian bifaces and puma pelt are unlike any deposits seen elsewhere or previously
at La Laguna. The temporality and/or spatial context of the offering depart from
the more collective water and fertility themes. On a smaller and more subtle scale,
the deposits on top of Structure 12L-1 illustrate the potential exclusionary and
politicized elements of Formative religion.

Unequal social relations were also expressed and generated through domestic
ritual practices, as fine obsidian needles, commonly understood as bloodletters,
have been found exclusively in La Laguna's elite residential complex and central
ceremonial structures. Social distinction through domestic ritual is also conveyed
especially well through differential mortuary treatments at Tetimpa (Plunket and
Uruñuela 2012; Uruñuela and Plunket 2002). Yet in both cases, these differences
appear more gradated than those seen between rituals on the more urban and
public versus more rural and private poles of their spatial spectra. In that way, they
were also part of the more enduring suite of elements in central Mexican religion.

Conclusion

In elucidating the intersections of religion, urbanism, and the strategic thinking
that past peoples employed for negotiating hierarchies of status and power, the
particular cultural logics of belief systems represent a critical pivot for mediating
between more generalized models of human behavior and utility for applying to
specific cultural settings. Religion clearly offered venues for the integration of
larger populations and differentiation of them along spectra of urbanity, occupation, status, and power during instances of premodern urbanization across the
globe. Getting to the details of any sequence requires approaching particular systems of logic on their own terms to then examine the ways in which they defined
relationships, generated difference, and created collective knowledge and meaning.

Viewed diachronically, continuity is strong in many domains of religious symbols and practices in pre-Columbian central Mexico. Issues of broadest shared concern – including cosmogenesis, existential dualisms, and fertility cycles – fostered
group solidarity and have proved the most enduring over time, as they continue
to feature prominently in indigenous religion (Knab 2004; López Austin 1993;
Monaghan 2000). In contrast, group divisions based on lineage, status, and community saw much greater turnover. There is little evidence for the existence of
patron deities in Formative- or Classic-period central Mexico, which stands in
contrast to the Aztec period – when the Mexica assimilation of the patron gods
of conquered groups, which were placed in the *Coateocalli* ("Temple of Many
Gods" or "Temple of Unification"), served to grow the pantheon exponentially

(León-Portilla 1963:70–71; van Zantwijk 1985:112). In the case of the Classic-period Maya, divine kingship was legitimated based on the claim that kings possessed special communicative abilities that were channeled to patron deities (Baron 2014; Hutson et al., Chapter 8), but this was not the case in Aztec society; and for Classic-period Teotihuacan, we lack the textual detail that permits such insights. Based on the iconography of the city, if any patron deity existed for Teotihuacan, it would have likely been the Storm God or Feathered Serpent, yet both deities were venerated elsewhere in central Mexico and the individuals depicted in association with them are the formulaic sets of priests or warriors that give the city its corporate style, rather than any single ruler. The existence of patron deities in Formative-period central Mexico is even less likely, since depictions of the Storm God, Old God, and other possible deities are widespread geographically. Still, the more integrative dimensions of Formative religion would have provided possibilities for differentiation as well, particularly surrounding who was conducting public rituals related to water/fertility themes, water-fire duality, the calendar, and more militaristic rituals seen later in the occupation of La Laguna. These details are not emphasized through art, however, as they were during other periods of Mesoamerican history, and whether this represents fundamental differences in societal organization or sample bias remains an important issue to resolve.

Taken as a chronologically deep sequence, pre-Columbian religion in central Mexico exemplifies the differential participation and emphases along axes of politicization and socio-spatial context. This is best documented for the Aztecs where Brumfiel (2001, 2006), Tena (2012), and others illustrate the contrast between "official" religion involving more solar and militaristic themes, and overseen by nobles, priests, and elite warriors, and variable practices in more rural settings or among urban commoners. More rural and commoner religious practices of the Aztec world related to water and fertility, with the deepest roots in the symbolism and associated materials seen in many Formative public rituals. Change is nevertheless apparent as well. For instance, although the aquatic symbolism and caching practices associated with Formative temple basins are seen in later periods, it is interesting to note that basins as temple furnishings do not continue into the Classic. We also see evidence of more martial rituals during the Terminal Formative-period wave of urbanization that resulted in Classic-period cities, not only at these cities themselves, but also in smaller communities such as La Laguna. The divides between urban, state religions of the Classic period, and household or provincial religion, likely share elements of the divides that existed in Aztec society, but they require additional study across the settlement spectrum for understanding the diversity of religious thought and practice.

Acknowledgments

Research at La Laguna was funded by the National Science Foundation (BCS-0941278), National Geographic Society (CRE-8057–06 and CRE-8634–09), Foundation for the Advancement of Mesoamerican Studies, Inc. (#05018), and a

UCMEXUS/CONACYT Collaborative Grant (awarded jointly with Luis Barba). I thank Stacy Barber, Art Joyce, and other volume participants for their helpful comments. I am also grateful to the Consejo de Arqueología, Instituto Nacional de Antropología e Historia (INAH), and the de Haro Gonzalez family for permission to work at La Laguna.

References

Aldenderfer, Mark 2011 Envisioning a Pragmatic Approach to the Archaeology of Religion. In *Beyond Belief: The Archaeology of Ritual and Religion*, edited by Yorke M. Rowan, pp. 23–36. Archeological Papers of the American Anthropological Association, vol. 21. American Anthropological Association, Arlington,VA.

Barba, Luís, Jorge Blancas, Agustín Ortiz, and David Carballo 2009 Geophysical Prospection and Aerial Photography in La Laguna, Tlaxcala, Mexico. *Revue d'Archéométrie* 33: 17–20.

Baron, Joanne 2014 Metapragmatics in Archaeological Analysis: Interpreting Classic Maya Patron Deity Veneration. *Signs and Society* 2: 249–283.

Beezley, William H., Cheryl English Martin, and William E. French, eds. 1994 *Rituals of Rule, Rituals of Resistance: Public Celebrations and Popular Culture in Mexico*. Scholarly Resources, Inc., Wilmington.

Bell, Catherine 1992 *Ritual Theory, Ritual Practice*. Oxford University Press, Oxford.

———. 1997 *Ritual: Perspectives and Dimensions*. Oxford University Press, Oxford.

Blanton, Richard E. 1994 *Houses and Households: A Comparative Study*. Plenum Press, New York.

Blanton, Richard, and Lane Fargher 2008 *Collective Action in the Formation of Pre-Modern States*. Springer, New York.

Blanton, Richard E., Stephen A. Kowalewski, Gary M. Feinman, and Laura M. Finsten 1996 A Dual-Processual Theory for the Evolution of Mesoamerican Civilization. *Current Anthropology* 37: 1–14.

Borejsza, Aleksander, and David M. Carballo 2014 La Laguna: Overview of Site. In *Formative Lifeways in Central Tlaxcala, Volume 1: Excavations, Ceramics, and Chronology*, edited by Richard G. Lesure, pp. 83–88. Cotsen Institute of Archaeology Press, Los Angeles.

Bradley, Richard 1998 *The Significance of Monuments: On the Shaping of Human Experience in Neolithic and Bronze Age Europe*. Routledge, London.

Brumfiel, Elizabeth 2001 Aztecs Hearts and Minds: Religion and the State in the Aztec Empire. In *Empires: Perspectives from Archaeology and History*, edited by Susan E. Alcock, Terence N. D'Altroy, Kathleen D. Morrison, and Carla M. Sinopoli, pp. 283–310. Cambridge University Press, Cambridge.

———. 2006 Provincial Elites and the Limits of Dominant Ideology in the Aztec Empire. In *Intermediate Elites in Pre-Columbian States and Empires*, edited by Christina M. Elson and R. Alan Covey, pp. 166–174. University of Arizona Press, Tucson.

———. 2011 Technologies of Time: Calendrics and Commoners in Postclassic Mexico. *Ancient Mesoamerica* 22: 53–70.

Burkhart, Louise M. 1989 *The Slippery Earth: Nahua-Christian Moral Dialogue in Sixteenth-Century Mexico*. University of Arizona Press, Tucson.

Carballo, David M. 2007 Effigy Vessels, Religious Integration, and the Origins of the Central Mexican Pantheon. *Ancient Mesoamerica* 18: 53–67.

———. 2009 Household and Status in Formative Central Mexico: Domestic Structures, Assemblages, and Practices at La Laguna, Tlaxcala. *Latin American Antiquity* 20: 473–501.

————. 2012 Public Ritual and Urbanization in Central Mexico: Plaza and Temple Offerings From La Laguna, Tlaxcala. *Cambridge Archaeological Journal* 22: 329–352.

————. 2014 Obsidian Symbolism in a Temple Offering from La Laguna, Tlaxcala. In *Obsidian Reflections: The Symbolic Dimensions of Obsidian in Mesoamerica*, edited by Marc N. Levine and David M. Carballo, pp. 195–221. University Press of Colorado, Boulder.

————. 2016 *Urbanization and Religion in Ancient Central Mexico*. Oxford University Press, New York.

Carballo, David M., and Anthony F. Aveni 2012 Los vecinos formativos de Xochitécatl y la formalización religiosa. *Arqueología Mexicana* 117: 52–57.

Carballo, David M., Luis Barba, Agustín Ortíz, Jorge Blancas, Nicole Cingolani, Jorge Toledo Barrera, David Walton, Isabel Rodríguez López, and Lourdes Couoh 2014 Suprahousehold Consumption and Community Ritual at La Laguna, Mexico. *Antiquity* 87: 1–20.

Carballo, David M., Jennifer Carballo, and Richard G. Lesure 2014 Houses of Style: Consumption, Adornment, and Identity in Formative Tlaxcalan Households. *Ancient Mesoamerica* 25: 459–476.

Carrasco, Davíd 2014 *Religions of Mesoamerica*. 2nd ed. Waveland, Long Grove.

Cowgill, George L. 2015 *Ancient Teotihuacan: Early Urbanism in Central Mexico*. Cambridge University Press, Cambridge.

De Lucia, Kristen 2014 Everyday Practice and Ritual Space: the Organization of Domestic Ritual in Pre-Aztec Xaltocan, Mexico. *Cambridge Archaeological Journal* 24(3): 379–403.

Fargher, Lane F., Richard E. Blanton, and Verenice Y. Heredia Espinoza 2010 Egalitarian Ideology and Political Power in Prehispanic Central Mexico: The Case of Tlaxcallan. *Latin American Antiquity* 21: 227–251.

Fash, William L., Alexandre Tokovinine, and Barbara W. Fash 2009 The House of New Fire at Teotihuacan and Its Legacy in Mesoamerica. In *The Art of Urbanism: How Mesoamerican Kingdoms Represented Themselves in Architecture and Imagery*, edited by William L Fash and Leonardo López Luján, pp. 201–229. Dumbarton Oaks Trustees for Harvard University, Washington, DC.

Feinman, Gary M., and David M. Carballo 2017 Collaborative and Competitive Strategies in the Variability and Resiliency of Large-Scale Societies in Mesoamerica. *Economic Anthropology*, in press.

Fowles, Severin M. 2013 *An Archaeology of Doings: Secularism and the Study of Pueblo Religion*. School for Advanced Research Press, Santa Fe.

García Cook, Ángel 2003 Cantona: The City. In *Urbanism in Mesoamerica*, vol. 1, edited by William T. Sanders, Alba Guadalupe Mastache, and Robert H. Cobean, pp. 311–343. Instituto Nacional de Antropología e Historia, Mexico City, and Pennslavania State University, University Park.

García Moll, Roberto 1976 El Monumento 13 de Tlalancaleca, Puebla. *Boletín del INAH* 17: 47–50.

Gilman, Patricia A., and Tammy Stone 2013 The Role of Ritual Variability in Social Negotiations of Early Communities: Great Kiva Homogeneity and Heterogeneity in the Mogollon Regions of the North American Southwest. *American Antiquity* 78: 607–623.

Grimes, Ronald L. 2011 Ritual. *Material Religion* 7(1): 76–83.

————. 2014 *The Craft of Ritual Studies*. Oxford University Press, New York.

Handelman, Don. 1997 Rituals/Spectacles. *International Social Science Journal* 49(153): 387–399.

Handelman, Don, and Galina Lindquist, eds. 2004 *Ritual in Its Own Right: Exploring the Dynamics of Transformation*. Berghahn Books, New York.

Insoll, Timothy 2004 *Archaeology, Ritual, Religion*. Routledge, London.

Joyce, Arthur A. 2009 Theorizing Urbanism in Ancient Mesoamerica. *Ancient Mesoamerica* 20: 189–196.

Knab, Timothy J. 2004 *The Dialogue of Earth and Sky: Dreams, Souls, Curing, and the Modern Aztec Underworld*. University of Arizona Press, Tucson.

Kurtz, Donald V. 1978 The Legitimation of the Aztec State. In *The Early State*, edited by Henri J.M. Claessen and Peter Skalnik, pp. 169–189. Mouton, The Hague.

Langley, James C. 1986 *Symbolic Notation of Teotihuacan: Elements of Writing in a Mesoamerican Culture of the Classic Period*. British Archaeological Reports International Series 313. Archaeopress, Oxford.

León-Portilla, Miguel 1963 *Aztec Thought and Culture*. University of Oklahoma Press, Norman.

Lesure, Richard G., Jennifer Carballo, and David M. Carballo 2012 Changing Social Practices as Seen from Household Iconic Traditions: A Case Study From Formative Central Tlaxcala. In *Power and Identity in Archaeological Theory and Practice: Case Studies from Ancient Mesoamerica*, edited by Eleanor Harrison-Buck, pp. 21–38. University of Utah Press, Salt Lake City.

López Aguilar, Fernando, and Patricia Fournier García 2012 Peregrinaciones otomíes. Vínculos locales y regionales en el Valle del Mezquital. In *Peregrinaciones ayer y hoy: Arqueología y antropología de las religiones*, edited by Patricia Fournier, Carlos Mondragón, and Walburga Wiesheu, pp. 81–118. Colegio de México, Mexico City.

López Austin, Alfredo 1993 *The Myths of the Opossum: Pathways of Mesoamerican Mythology*. Translated by Bernard R. Ortiz de Montellano and Thelma Ortiz Montellano. University of New Mexico Press, Albuquerque.

López Austin, Alfredo, and Leonardo López Luján 2009 *Monte sagrado – Templo mayor: el cerro y la pirámide en la tradición religiosa mesoamericana*. Universidad Nacional Autónoma de México and Instituto Nacional de Antropología e Historia, Mexico City.

López Luján, Leonardo 2005 *The Offerings of the Templo Mayor of Tenochtitlan*. Revised ed. University of New Mexico Press, Albuquerque.

Manzanilla, Linda 2002 Living With the Ancestors and Offering to the Gods: Domestic Ritual at Teotihuacan. In *Domestic Ritual in Ancient Mesoamerica*, edited by Patricia Plunket, pp. 43–52. Cotsen Institute of Archaeology Press, Los Angeles.

Marcus, Joyce 2007 Rethinking Ritual. In *The Archaeology of Ritual*, edited by Evangelos Kyriakidis, pp. 43–76. Cotsen Institute of Archaeology Press, Los Angeles.

Matos Moctezuma, Eduardo 1988 *The Great Temple of the Aztecs: Treasures of Tenochtitlan*. Thames and Hudson, London.

McAnany, Patricia A. 2002 Rethinking the Great and Little Tradition Paradigm From the Perspective of Domestic Ritual. In *Domestic Ritual in Ancient Mesoamerica*, edited by Patricia Plunket, pp. 115–119. Cotsen Institute of Archaeology Press, Los Angeles.

Mock, Shirley Boteler, ed. 1998 *The Sowing and the Dawning: Termination, Dedication, and Transformation in the Archaeological and Ethnographic Record of Mesoamerica*. University of New Mexico Press, Albuquerque.

Monaghan, John D. 2000 Theology and History in the Study of Mesoamerican Religions. In *Ethnography*, edited by John D. Monaghan and Barbara Edmonson, pp. 24–49. Supplement to the Handbook of Middle American Indians, vol. 6, Victoria R. Bricker, general editor. University of Texas Press, Austin.

Moore, Jerry D. 2005 *Cultural Landscapes in the Ancient Andes: Archaeologies of Place*. University Press of Florida, Gainesville.

Pastrana, Alejandro, and Felipe Ramírez 2012 *Reinterpretando Cuicuilco*. Paper presented at the 77th Annual Meeting of the Society of American Archaeology, Memphis.

Pauketat, Timothy R. 2013 *An Archaeology of the Cosmos: Rethinking Agency and Religion in Ancient America*. Routledge, New York.

Peregrine, Peter 2012 Power and Legitimation: Political Strategies, Typology, and Cultural Evolution. In *The Comparative Archaeology of Complex Societies*, edited by Michael E. Smith, pp. 165–191. Cambridge University Press, Cambridge.

Plunket, Patricia, and Gabriela Uruñuela 2002 Shrines, Ancestors, and the Volcanic Landscape at Tetimpa, Puebla. In *Domestic Ritual in Ancient Mesoamerica*, edited by Patricia Plunket, pp. 31–42. Cotsen Institute of Archaeology Press, Los Angeles.

———. 2008 Mountain of Sustenance, Mountain of Destruction: The Prehispanic Experience with Popocatépetl Volcano. *Journal of Volcanology and Geothermal Research* 170: 111–120.

———. 2012. Where East Meets West: The Formative in Mexico's Central Highlands. *Journal of Archaeological Research* 20(1): 1–51.

Rapoport, Amos 1988 Levels of Meaning in the Built Environment. In *Cross-Cultural Perspectives in Nonverbal Communication*, edited by Fernando Poyatos, pp. 317–336. C.J. Hogrefe, Lewiston.

Redfield, Robert 1956 *Peasant Society and Culture*. University of Chicago Press, Chicago.

Renfrew, Colin 1994 The Archaeology of Religion. In *The Ancient Mind: Elements of Cognitive Archaeology*, edited by Colin Renfrew and Ezra B. W. Zubrow, pp. 47–54. Cambridge University Press, Cambridge.

Robin, Cynthia 2013 *Everyday Life Matters: Maya Farmers at Chan*. University Press of Florida, Gainesville.

Robin, Cynthia, and Nan A. Rothschild 2002 Archaeological Ethnographies: Social Dynamics of Outdoor Space. *Journal of Social Archaeology* 2: 159–172.

Sahagún, Bernardino de 1963 *Florentine Codex: General History of the Things of New Spain, Book 11, Earthly Things*. Translated and edited by Charles E. Dibble and Arthur J. O. Anderson. School of American Research and University of Utah, Santa Fe.

Santley, Robert S., Michael J. Berman, and Rani T. Alexander 1991 The Politicization of the Mesoamerican Ballgame and Its Implications for the Interpretation of the Distribution of Ballcourts in Central Mexico. In *The Mesoamerican Ballgame*, edited by Vernon L. Scarborough and David R. Wilcox, pp. 3–24. University of Arizona Press, Tucson.

Sarabia González, Alejandro 2013 *Proyecto Pirámide del Sol: Reporte de resultados de la temporada 2012*. Unpublished technical report on file at the Instituto Nacional de Antropología e Historia, Mexico City.

Serra Puche, Mari Carmen, and J. Carlos Lazcano Arce 2011 *Vida Cotidiana, Xochitécatl-Cacaxtla: Días, Años, Milenios*. Instituto de Investigaciones Antropológicas, Universidad Nacional Autónoma de México, México City.

Serra Puche, Mari Carmen, J. Carlos Lazcano Arce, and Liliana Torres Sanders 2001 Actividades rituales en Xochitécatl-Cacaxtla, Tlaxcala. *Arqueología* 25: 71–88.

Solís, Felipe, and Ted Leyenaar 2002 *Art Treasures of Ancient Mexico: Journey to the Land of the Gods*. Waanders Publishers, Lund Humphries, Amsterdam.

Sugiyama, Nawa 2014 *Animals and Sacred Mountains: How Ritualized Performances Materialized State Ideologies at Teotihuacan, Mexico*. Unpublished doctoral dissertation, Department of Anthropology, Harvard University.

Sugiyama, Saburo, and Leonardo López Luján 2007 Dedicatory Burial/Offering Complexes at the Moon Pyramid, Teotihuacan: A Preliminary Report of 1998-2004 Explorations. *Ancient Mesoamerica* 18: 127–146.

Tena, Rafael 2012 *La religión mexica*. 2nd ed. Instituto Nacional de Antropología e Historia, Mexico City.

Uruñuela, Gabriela, and Patricia Plunket 2002 Lineages and Ancestors: The Formative Mortuary Assemblages of Tetimpa, Puebla. In *Domestic Ritual in Ancient Mesoamerica*, edited by Patricia Plunket, pp. 21–30. Cotsen Institute of Archaeology Press, Los Angeles.

Uruñuela y Ladrón de Guevara, Gabriela, Patricia Plunket Nagoda, and Amparo Robles Salmerón 2009 Cholula: Art and Architecture of an Archetypal City. In *The Art of Urbanism: How Mesoamerican Kingdoms Represented Themselves in Architecture and Imagery*, edited by William L. Fash and Leonardo López Luján, pp. 135–171. Dumbarton Oaks Trustees for Harvard University, Washington, DC.

van Zantwijk, Rudolph 1985 *The Aztec Arrangement: The Social History of Pre-Spanish Mexico.* University of Oklahoma Press, Norman.

Wright Carr, and David Charles 2012 Teoatl tlachinolli: una metáfora marcial del centro de México. *Dimensión Antropológica* 19(55): 11–37.

Wylie, Alison 1985 The Reaction Against Analogy. In *Advances in Archaeological Method and Theory*, vol. 8, edited by Michael B. Schiffer, pp. 63–111. Academic Press, San Diego.

7

RELIGION IN A MATERIAL WORLD

Rosemary A. Joyce

Introduction

Religion, if not conflated with ritual or reduced to doctrine, must be understood as an articulation of belief with practice. In most archaeological settings, we can only infer belief from practice (including representational practices, such as production of images and texts). In this chapter, I will address religion – practices and beliefs – as implicated in political change in Formative Period Honduras (ca. 1600–400 B.C.). In line with recent ethnographic research, I will argue that the materiality of religious practice is both a productive site for recommitting to existing beliefs, and provides the only medium through which to transform beliefs, short of social crises such as colonization and forced conversion. By examining the pragmatic contexts in which media marked with representational imagery usually seen as indications of the spread of an ideology from the Gulf Coast of Mexico occur in Honduras, I will take steps to reconstitute a sense of religious practice as lived experience. Tacking back and forth between these "ritualized" contexts (in the sense defined by Catherine Bell; Bell 1992), and other pragmatic contexts normally viewed as reflecting political economy, I will address the question of how ritualized practices shaped the political economy, giving value to certain things, and created beliefs about the relations between humans and other-than-human agents that would be recognized as religious doctrine. While viewing these as recursive and permanently articulated, I will suggest that the nature of religion made it easier to promote social change through religious innovation than to institute political change and then retroactively sanction it.

Religion

For Clifford Geertz (1973:90), religion was a "cultural system," "a system of symbols" that could establish "powerful, pervasive, and long-lasting moods and motivations" by "formulating conceptions of a general order of existence." At first glance, his definition appears to entirely align religion with belief, a form of ideology that appears to have no roots in the pragmatic sphere at all. Religion was also capable of "clothing these moods and motivations with such an aura of factuality that . . . the moods and motivations seem uniquely realistic." Indeed, Geertz (1973:111) contrasts what he calls "the religious" with the "common-sensical, the scientific, and the aesthetic." He specifically describes common-sense as having:

> a mode of 'seeing' . . . a simple acceptance of the world, its objects, and its processes as being just what they seem to be . . . naive realism – and the pragmatic motive, the wish to act upon that world so as to bend it to one's practical purposes.
>
> *(Geertz 1973:111)*

This pragmatism, which takes the world at face value, he contrasts with "the aesthetic" that, following Suzanne Langer, he sees as absorbed in the surface of things "in themselves":

> the contemplation of sensory qualities without their usual meanings of 'here's that chair' . . . . The knowledge that what is before us has no practical significance in the world is what enables us to give attention to its appearance as such.
>
> *(Langer 1953:49)*

But the aesthetic, in the end, requires things in the world, what Geertz (1973:112) calls "quasi-objects," of which he instantiates four: "poems, dramas, sculptures, symphonies," forms that he argues dissociate themselves from "the solid world of common sense."

While he does not use the language of quasi-objects to identify the objectified (or as he says, concrete) embodiment of religion in ritual, it is clear that Geertz sees religion as gaining its power to persuade from its embodiment in similar things:

> It is in some sort of ceremonial form – even if that form be hardly more than the recitation of a myth, the consecration of an oracle, or the decoration of a grave – that the moods and motivations which sacred symbols induce . . . and the general conceptions of the order of existence which they formulate . . . meet and reinforce one another.
>
> *(Geertz 1973:112)*

With his insistence on language as the medium of performance and meaning as something conveyed in vehicles, Geertz seems an unpromising beginning point for an archaeological exploration of the way materialities are swept up in religion in practice. But occasionally, materialities slip into his text, unasked but clearly not unwelcome. Thus, we are invited to imagine the participant in ritual who "has just put off his Kachina mask," and are told that:

> what one 'learns' about the essential pattern of life from a sorcery rite and a commensal meal will have rather diverse effects on social and psychological [by which he means, personal] functioning.
>
> *(Geertz 1973:123)*

It is in this mode – where the participant in the commensal meal has just taken off her mask, has finished decorating the grave with objects that also are representational media, and starts to recite a myth – that we need to begin a consideration of religion as materially mediated practices that articulate belief and pragmatic actions, creating certain ways of being in the world.

Practice

In most archaeological settings, we can only infer belief from traces of materialized practice, including representational practices, such as production of images and texts, Geertz's peculiar category of quasi-object. It has become common in archaeology to rely on the framework of religious studies scholar Catherine Bell to move from the seemingly more abstract discussion of religion understood as a Geertzian system of symbols to a practice-based approach to ritual as the instantiation of religiously motivated action. Bell (1992:98) argued that the pragmatic outcome of ritual, "that which it does not see itself doing" is "the production of a 'ritualized body.'" A ritualized body has, as a result of its experience, embodied dispositions that are the product of and also the medium for reproduction of ritual experience. She offers the term *ritualization* for "a way of acting that is designed and orchestrated to distinguish and privilege that which is being done in comparison to other, usually more quotidian, activities" (Bell 1992:74).

Bell's invocation of pragmatics is echoed by archaeologists, including Mark Aldenderfer (2012), who proposes asking not what religion *is*, but what it *does*. The "pragmatic maxim" of Charles Sanders Peirce encourages us to "consider what effects, that might conceivably have practical bearings, we conceive the object of our conception to have. Then, our conception of these effects is the whole of our conception of the object" (Peirce 1878:286; cited in Lele 2006:54). The pragmatic effects of religion are often taken for granted in archaeological discussions, as, for example, serving the "function" of rationalizing the specific economic and political conditions at a place and time. But the call to think of what religion does pragmatically does not intend an answer in terms of function, but effects. Those effects, it turns out, take place not (solely) through belief, but through materialities that produce the effect of a ritualized body, ritualized spaces, and ritualized things.

Materiality

The materiality of religious practice is both a productive site for recommitting to existing beliefs, and also provides the only medium through which to transform beliefs, short of social crises such as colonization and forced conversion. (And even there, I would argue, what happens is a marked case of the continual re-negotiation of doxa – deeply held understandings of the world – as either recommitment to orthodoxy or creative innovation of heterodoxy.)

The editorial statement for *Material Religion*, a journal that began publishing in 2005, calling for "the study of religious images, objects, spaces, and material practices," argued that:

> religion is about the sensual effects of walking, eating, meditating, making pilgrimage, and performing even the most mundane of ritual acts . . . what people do with material things and places, and how these structure and color experience and one's sense of oneself and others.
>
> *(Material Religion 2005)*

This recalls Tim Insoll's (2004) advocacy of making religion a focal concept of archaeological investigation. He identifies the visibility of religion, the role of myth, ritual, temporality, religion's relation to identity, "belief/emotion/experience," and the status of "the numinous/the holy" as among the questions that any satisfactory discussion of religion needs to consider (Insoll 2004:148–150).

Insoll's arguments have often been taken as particularly intended for the expansion of archaeological study to world religions, where using an archaeology of ritual framework clearly impedes understanding. There is, however, a more general applicability of the shift he advocates within archaeology of ritual and religion, even when what is at issue is not the kind of globally extensive phenomenon, mediated by written texts and bodies of liturgists and theologians that distinguishes contemporary world religion. To illustrate that broader potential, I offer here an analysis of the archaeological traces of religion as practiced in Honduras before 400 B.C.

Honduras: religion, ritual, and material practice

A shift toward what Insoll calls for can benefit from the insights of scholars of religious studies. Catherine Bell described four key topics that she used to organize her teaching of "the social life of religion," including ritual but also symbol and myth, scripture and interpretation, and "types of religious communities dealing with change" (Bell 2007:179). Given an understanding of material traces as evidence of practice and engagement with materiality, I will demonstrate how we could use these aspects of religion's "social life" to understand political change in Formative Period Honduras (ca. 1600–400 B.C.).

The focus of my discussion is contexts from the site of Puerto Escondido (Figure 7.1), occupied continuously from before 1600 B.C. through at least 400–200 B.C. before a break in continuity of occupation in the specific locations under examination (Henderson and Joyce 1998, 2004, 2006; Joyce 2007a; Henderson et al. 2007; Joyce and Henderson 2001, 2007, 2009, 2017). Puerto Escondido was the site of a village today buried under extensive deposits representing later occupation; the excavated windows into this village site have given us glimpses of domestic living spaces, craft working areas for ceramics, shell ornament production, and the reduction of obsidian for tools, many probably used in secondary industries such as working bone and shell (Joyce et al. 2004; Luke et al. 2003). Our excavations also brought to light a range of less quotidian activities, including burial of objects and human remains in both domestic structures and larger earthen platforms, the construction and use of large burning features, and the use and disposal of small-scale and life-scale human images (Joyce 2003, 2004, 2011; Joyce and Henderson 2002, 2003, 2010).

I also include partly contemporary contexts from the site of Los Naranjos, previously dated from 700 B.C. to 400 B.C., but now, through my research with

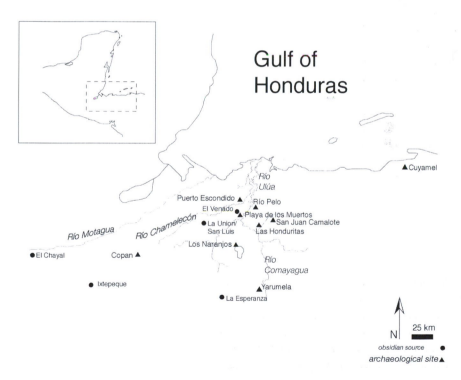

FIGURE 7.1   Map showing archaeological sites mentioned in Honduras. Illustration by Rosemary A. Joyce.

John Henderson, clearly demonstrated as having an in situ occupation from at least 1000 B.C. (Joyce and Henderson 2003, 2010; Morell-Hart et al. 2014; Tchakirides 2010; Tchakirides et al. 2006). The evidence of domestic activities at Los Naranjos is less extensive, due to limitations on excavations there, but includes a range of everyday provisioning activities. By 700 B.C., construction of large earthen platforms, selective burial of objects and human remains in those platforms, and installation of large-scale (life size) representation images of humans and zoomorphic beings is evident.

At both Los Naranjos and Puerto Escondido, the period between 1100 and 900 B.C. sees the use in domestic spaces of serving vessels marked with representational images (Figure 7.2), Geertzian "quasi-objects" suitable for analysis in terms of belief. Similar objects are found in other contemporary Honduran sites, although they are not uniformly present in such places. At Copan, they are found with primary burials in residential settings, and in the Caverns of Copan and

FIGURE 7.2 Sherds from Puerto Escondido showing complex incised motifs, dating to 1100–900 B.C. Photograph by Russell Sheptak, used with permission.

Cuyamel, with secondary ossuaries (Gordon 1898; Healy 1974; Longyear 1969; Viel and Cheek 1983).

Finally, I will add to the discussion the use, increasing dramatically in frequency after 900 B.C., of small-scale human and animal representations preserved as fired clay figurines (Joyce 2003, 2007b, 2008, 2014). At Playa de los Muertos, the type site for these figurines, excavators documented residential settings similar to those known from other contemporary villages, including subfloor burials. Some burials incorporated figurines along with a variety of serving vessels whose imagery is normally more schematic than earlier examples, but sometimes (especially on miniature vessels from graves) recapitulates the same imagery in full. Puerto Escondido yielded many examples of these figurines. They are rare and apparently imported to Los Naranjos in small numbers, likely from the area around Playa de los Muertos and Puerto Escondido, where many early sites are known only from such objects in museum collections. Examples are also found at the site of Las Honduritas, in the Oloman valley, where they were recovered with remains of an event that also featured the use and disposal of decorated serving vessels (Joyce et al. 2008). In the neighboring Cuyumapa valley, slightly later contexts adjacent to a Late Formative ballcourt produced examples of stylistically related but technologically distinct Rio Pelo style figurines, along with an assemblage of vessels dominated by bottles and incense burning forms (Fox 1994). At the Rio Pelo site itself, source of the largest known excavated sample of these later figurines, they accompanied faunal and ceramic evidence interpreted as remains of feasting around a tall earthen platform (Wonderley 1991).

My analysis begins with the pragmatic contexts in which what Geertz would call "quasi-objects," marked with representational imagery usually seen as indications of the spread of an ideology from the Gulf Coast of Mexico, that occur in Honduras. Tacking back and forth between these "ritualized" contexts (after Bell 1992) and other pragmatic contexts normally viewed as reflecting political economy, I address the question of how ritualized practices shaped the political economy, giving value to certain things, and created beliefs about the relations between humans and other-than-human agents that would be recognized as religious doctrine.

Ritual

We can recognize a series of ritualized practices in the records made of excavations at these early sites. At Puerto Escondido, the earliest such practices are the burial below residential floors of selected objects and materials that also had pragmatic uses (Figure 7.3). By removing a shell belt and groups of unworked obsidian nodules from their everyday circulation and use, burial ritualized these things. Following Bell's insight that ritual produces a ritualized embodied person, we might note that the burial of these things in domestic spaces produced the effect of stylizing certain everyday practices, wearing belts and knapping obsidian, as repetitions of past precedents. Initially, the stylized practices that we might thus suggest were

FIGURE 7.3 a   Objects buried in caches under house floor at Puerto Escondido, 1400–1100 B.C. (a) shell belt; (b) obsidian nodules. Photographs by Rosemary A. Joyce (a) and Russell Sheptak (b), used with permission.

ritualized include the production of obsidian tools from raw nodules; and whatever embodied performance (perhaps a dance) involved wearing the shell belt.

In time, burial below house floors was extended to encompass other things: pottery vessels and human remains. This is seen not only at Puerto Escondido, but also at Playa de los Muertos in the same region, and Copan far to the west. Since the original buried objects already indexed the presence of a human agent (who would wear the belt and work the obsidian nodules in pragmatic action), what is

FIGURE 7.3 b   (Continued)

new here is not the presence of traces of the human (in the form of bones) but the inclusion of pots. Consisting primarily of food-serving vessels, bottles, and bowls, shapes tested and found to have contained cacao-based foods (Henderson et al. 2007; Joyce and Henderson 2007), these pots extended the effect of ritualization to meals shared every day. With the inclusion of human skeletal remains in buried contexts, the ritualization of ornaments as worn, as parts of costume, was reinforced, iconically (through their placement on the body) referencing embodied performance in life.

Simultaneous with the apparent burgeoning number of such buried contexts, new forms of representations of human and animal bodies were produced, many themselves pierced as if to be worn as ornaments. At Las Honduritas and Puerto Escondido, large surfaces are covered by smashed serving vessels, the surfaces then buried, indexing the actual sharing of food and drink (Figure 7.4). The first known larger earthen platforms at these sites, and slightly later at Río Pelo as well, are preceded by such open-air ritualizations of pragmatic food sharing. At Puerto Escondido, the platform thus created became a site for burial of human skeletal remains. While there is no evidence to date of burial of similar remains of shared feasts at

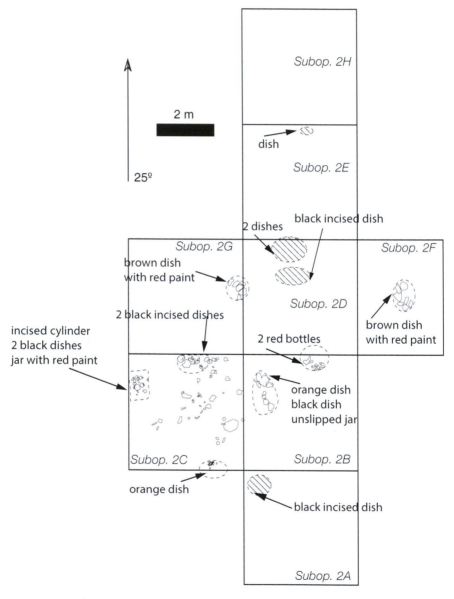

FIGURE 7.4   Plan of vessels smashed on a buried surface at Las Honduritas dating to ca. 1000 B.C. Illustration by Rosemary A. Joyce.

Los Naranjos, the contemporary construction of a large earthen platform created a space later used as a new kind of location for human burial.

This pragmatic segregation of some human burials within the settlement may have eclipsed an earlier practice of bringing the bones of the dead from the settlement out to caves in the mountains, witnessed at Copan and Cuyamel. While the ritual use of caves to deposit things, including pots and human bones, itself does not end abruptly, the majority of the pots reported in both of these locations can be identified as dating to 1100–900 B.C. Vessels included in cave ossuaries in far eastern Honduras, associated with accelerator mass spectrometry (AMS) dates on human remains that bracket the 1100–900 B.C. time frame, make innovative use of marble, ritualizing the pottery form by recreating it in stone (Brady et al. 2000).

At the same time that the ritualization of shared meals starts to be visible through the smashing and discard of pots and food remains on surfaces that are then buried, and as sites of ritual are made more visible through the construction of raised earthen platforms at some sites, fire begins to be incorporated in ritualization. At Puerto Escondido, the location of a surface covered with smashed serving vessels is a perishable building that is deliberately burned, the collapsed remains used to cover the pottery assemblage. In a second location at this site, an earthen terrace provided with stone steps faces a large stone hearth, dated to ca. 800 B.C. By 400–200 B.C., a large structure with a built-in bench in this second area of the site is surrounded by numerous, more expedient hearth features overlapping one another. Adjacent trash deposits in subterranean pits contained remains of fauna and highly decorated vessels indicative of shared feasting, as well as yielding many examples of figurines. We have tentatively identified the activities in this area as evidence of early use of sweat baths (Henderson and Joyce 2000). Multiple stone-built tombs in this section of the site included one that had been opened and refilled in antiquity, with a section of a life-size seated human figure deposited in the fill, along with a single intact figurine pendant.

The repertoire of ritualization in early Honduran villages, then, starts with burial of objects indexing and thus ritualizing pragmatic actions that we should regard as likely ritual performances of their own (discussed more on p. 160). Indexing human bodies is ultimately complemented by the inclusion of articulated human remains in buried deposits, often, if not always, iconically arrayed with ornaments that signal participation in other performances.

Contemporary with these residential-area burials, some sets of human remains are removed from the settlement to mountain caves, where they are no longer iconic of either the human form or particular persons, but rather merge with the bones of others. The community thus reprised may be likened to the community indexed at the same time by the inclusion of food-serving vessels in burials, both in the settlement and in cave ossuaries. With time, we see the ritualization of food sharing literally come to the surface, with some meals ending with the disposal of pots and other residues on residential surfaces, which are then buried above ground and often marked by elevated earthen platforms. These monuments to commensal ritual are subsequently selected for placement of human burials, unlike those under house floors in their apparent lack of included pottery vessels, which are deposited in some platforms, but as freestanding indexes of now-ritualized actions involved in shared meals.

With the construction of visible marks on the landscape of settlements in the form of raised earthen platforms, additional augmentation of the durability of spatial locales for action is seen: stone sculptures and columns or facing are added to both burials and platforms. Translation of ritual performance into more durable media is also seen in the production of stone versions of pottery vessels, and in the production of fired clay representations of ritual participants arrayed in costumes, ornaments, and elaborate hair treatments. Somewhat countering the emergence of a durable set of traces of ritualized action is the new use of burning as a ritual action, whether in purpose-built, durable stone hearths; in expedient, short-use hearths; or even in portable vessels constructed of fired clay.

In every case, what is ritualized is something that is also pragmatic: what is produced is a person who has internalized an embodied orientation toward the world. It is those embodied dispositions that are the "powerful, pervasive, and long-lasting moods and motivations" that Geertz identified as central to religion.

Scripture and interpretation

Over the course of the developments outlined above, a number of objects that participate in ritualization can be identified as both pragmatic things (bowls and bottles for serving food and beverages, clay pendants suspended from the body of participants) and "quasi-objects" of the kind that lend themselves to hermeneutic exegesis. It may seem unorthodox to identify carved ceramic bowls as scriptures. But this is precisely how we must approach these various things that, through conventionalized but still iconic markings, afford the potential for legibility today, as they would have in the past.

In writing about the earliest such things in Honduran contexts – ceramic vessels dating between 1100 and 900 B.C. – we should first identify what we think we see, and only once we have determined that proceed to discuss what frameworks and contexts these iconic quasi-objects might have had (Joyce and Henderson 2010). Most of the Honduran vessels have a variety of markings that seem to be abstract and geometric, a variety of brackets, star-shapes, and combinations of lines. The most identifiable images, also recognizable in the somewhat later (ca. 700 B.C.) stone sculptures of Los Naranjos and a few smaller ceramic vessels placed in graves at Playa de los Muertos at the same time, are apparent composites of animal features. Most common in Honduras are composite creatures with elements drawn from marine animals: shark teeth and fish fins (see Healy 1974:Figure 4E). With this realization, it is possible to identify many of the more abstract conventionalized motifs as commonly found on vessels with shark elements in other contemporary sites in a broad distribution reaching to Mexico. The second most common identifiable composite creature has a hand with four fingers and a thumb, a human-looking nose, and animal eyes and mouth. This set of features is also recognizable in that broader distribution.

If we treat these two images for the moment as a pair of scriptures, we can propose that they were interpreted through narratives that we do not have at our disposal. Commonly, archaeologists interpreting the widely distributed analogues of these two composites propose a single, shared, and fairly static "cosmology" in which they fit structurally, as elements related to the sea opposed to the land. Rather than take that step, following Bell (2007), we might want next to explicitly discuss what might have been specific, local narratives brought to bear on reading these things: the myths and symbols of Honduras, where these quasi-objects served in the first instance to ritualize pragmatic objects used in everyday food serving, making a meal a ceremonial feast.

Symbol and myth

The identification of the marine (shark) and terrestrial (caiman) icons as part of a Mesoamerica-wide cosmology presumes mythological traditions in which a sign relation was formed between known animals in the wider world, engaged with pragmatically, and concepts that would establish powerful motivations and moods in the people who used these things. The mythology underlying the presumed cosmology of "Olmec" imagery is one derived ultimately from early colonial Spanish texts aimed to re-interpret a variety of fragmentary insights into localized traditions. So the caiman is identified with (collapsed with) a variety of earth monsters based on reptilian or even amphibian models in the natural world (serpents, crocodilians, lizards, iguanas, frogs, toads, turtles). For whatever historical reasons, either in the episodes of Spanish colonization itself (the ceremonies participants in early conquest events personally witnessed may have been structured by the calendar, the place, and the localized groups involved), or in the history of development from the Formative period to the Late Postclassic, there is far less colonial discourse that can be directly related to the depictions of apparent monstrous fish whose central feature is always a shark-like tooth or teeth.

Thus, the schematic cosmological myths constructed and deployed by modern researchers tend to view the terrestrial monsters as "representing" the earth, as a powerful source of fertility, often embodied in vegetation, sometimes encompassed within an over-arching identification as "maize." The shark then comes to "represent" the surrounding ocean waters within which the earth was formed, as the late colonial Popol Vuh of the K'iche has it, when the feathered serpent was coiled in the waters. There are self-evident problems in using these philosophical tracts composed in part to reconcile Christian and local indigenous traditions as if they reflected a long-established singular way of looking at the world. But there is something even more serious to address here, which is how this kind of narrative-building treats our quasi-objects as symbols.

The earth monster represents the earth's surface iconically in these accounts. The earth is said to be understood as formed like a giant earth monster; specific imagery at sites like Chalcatzingo show caves as zoomorphic open mouths, and images from there and from the Gulf Coast of Mexico show plants sprouting from the back of these monsters. In terms of a Peircean semiotics, these images zoomorphise the terrestrial landscape, acting as icons for animate earth. The shark images, however, work differently. There are no apparent instances of the sea being zoomorphized as a marine monster. Instead, parts of marine creatures – especially those sharp parts represented by shark teeth, but also by sting ray spines and even, in the Templo Mayor of Tenochtitlan, in saw fish rostra – metonymically index the ocean waters. Symbolically, the earth monsters assert an identity with the local place; the marine monster brings a distant place into the locality. It is thus not particularly surprising that there are so many terrestrial zoomorphs, on so many models. While I find it facile to tell a myth from 3,000 years ago as if we were certain about it, I would suggest that each such myth was about the way the local place was centered in the animated landscape – not about a universal, or universalizing, creation.

The Honduran landscape so referenced varied dramatically between the different places where vessels were carved with these images (Joyce and Henderson 2010). If we do not want to simply say these are abstract designs with no local exegesis, then we have to begin with the proposition that the myths told about them were varied. Where caves in the hills near Copan existed, and were used for secondary deposition of ancestral bones, the earth mouth may well have been a critical image of the cave mouth as the actual opening to the land of ancestors. For people living in the extensive alluvial plains of the Ulúa river, the earth was not primarily the stony body with its cave mouth, but the earthy and penetrable source of fertility in the shape of plants. We might speculate that the pragmatic action of digging into the earth to ritualize objects was aligned with this understanding of the earth. In both the Honduran highlands and lowlands, the ocean was the edge of the land – but for people in the lowlands, it was an edge with which they could interact daily. Marine shells were worked from before 1300 B.C. at Puerto Escondido, and while we cannot be sure precisely how people in this area talked about the ocean, we can say that, unlike those in the highlands, for them it was a more present place. It was via the Caribbean that people in the Honduran lowlands most likely connected to others more distant from them, including residents of settlements in Belize, where the same kinds of inscription and interpretation of symbols and myths were taking place.

Religious communities dealing with change

The concept of a religious community, when applied to this early period, needs to be understood as a network of people that formed through the performance of specific ritualized actions facilitated by the participation in the community of assemblages of people, places, and things that created understandings of symbol and myth that could be interpreted from the inscribed media of the time. Starting with the material media of religion, moving to how they were employed in ritualized practices, and paying attention to when we can, and when we cannot, presume similar scriptural interpretation, we can follow the historical trajectory of religious action and finally arrive at some proposals about how this structured, and was structured by, pragmatic action we would recognize as "political." For this purpose, I take

political to mean dealing with the creation of relations of inequality in the ability
to formulate and carry out a course of action. Following the analysis of practices of
everyday life offered by Michel de Certeau (1984), I am as interested in the tactical
appropriation of structures by those we might think of as "less powerful" as I am
in the strategies of what de Certeau (1984:35–36) called "a subject with will and
power" itself. In Honduran history, we repeatedly see power constrained before it
succeeds in creating exaggerated levels of inequality. Understanding the Honduran
situation is, therefore, of particular importance in combatting the easy assumption
that inequality always increases in all societies over time.

Between 1400 and 1100 B.C. at Puerto Escondido, we can see ritualized actions
involving the use of marine shell performance costume and terrestrial stone involving at least the residents of two households, and quite likely of more. This is to say
that from this early period, the settlement hosted at least one religious community,
one that saw the interior of the earth as a ritualizing body accessed through digging
and burial, and saw the ocean as a source of material to be only slightly modified
in order to ritualize performance. The implication that obsidian nodules – derived
from the mountains surrounding the Ulúa valley, where they stand out as black
nuggets in white to orange, loosely consolidated volcanic ignimbrites (Joyce et al.
2004) – were reduced into usable flakes as ritualized performance on at least some
occasions, provides a unique image of this religious community. Whether there
were already stories in which the mountains, the fields, and the ocean were zoo-
morphised is impossible to know. What does seem clear is that the landscape was
seen as stratified, and color symbolism that would continue to be important later –
particularly the contrast of white and black – was already present. The religious
participants were co-residents of houses within a village where there was no apparent distinction in houses or household inventories, where relative wealth seems to
have been equally available to all.

During the period between 1100 and 900 B.C., different sectors within the
village of Puerto Escondido diverged in their participation in religious communities, and those where the religious communities participated most intensively in
new forms of ritualization also show differences in domestic inventories, with
greater diversity and more costly and exotic materials associated with houses of
what we might label the new, heterodox, religious community. It is important to
emphasize that the houses with evidence of participating in new religious practices, and those that had less evidence for such participation, were architecturally
indistinguishable: the degree of inequality may be less marked than the degree of
social difference involved.

The social differences evident in participation in the new heterodox religion
formed the basis for the exercise of political authority in two main ways. First, differential affiliation with new religious ideas allowed some community members to
change the ways they related to neighbors, now understood as others rather than
as co-participants in a single religious community. Second, the specific kinds of
claims authorized by religion allowed those engaged in the new religion to assert
critical relations to cosmic forces important to everyone's survival. Neither of these

moves would have been sufficient alone to allow the creation of inequality in the ability to formulate and carry out a course of action. Together, they facilitated the emergence of a small group of people who held themselves to be different than others in the community, and to have critical cosmological roles that benefitted others. An examination of the practices involved shows how this worked.

The new religious practice that is most obvious is the inscription of symbolic quasi-objects on pragmatic materials, specifically, at this time, limited to ceramic serving vessels and a few objects related to body ornamentation. While our excavations at Puerto Escondido did not encounter any burials of human remains, contemporary houses in the Copan village that also innovated new scriptures on serving vessels used these objects in both residential compound burials and secondary cave ossuaries. Rather than combine these two villages into a single "Honduran" religious community, I argue that what we are seeing is at least two religious communities, one at Copan in which ancestral caves are salient, and meals are shared directly with the newly dead; and another at Puerto Escondido, where meals are for the living, and the earth, if understood as zoomorphized, is not precisely the same as at Copan.

Some residents in each of these early Honduran villages were simultaneously participants in a religious community that extended across long distances, and only enlisted a few people or families in each village. This religious community likely spread not by missionaries from the Gulf Coast of Mexico, but by newly emergent exclusive social relations between families in villages already engaged with each other (Joyce and Henderson 2003, 2010). The prominence of burials as sites where shared meals were ritualized through scriptural media suggests that this network engaged local families in the kinds of social relations that make people part of mourning communities: marriage, fosterage of children, and all that goes with it (Joyce 2001, 2011). While archaeologists have a somewhat better potential to find the evidence of religious ceremonies associated with death (when they involve depositing the remains of a dead person), we can point to contexts like the feast residues left above ground at Puerto Escondido and Las Honduritas as possible indications of marking of other moments, such as birth, maturation, and marital alliance, in the life course of residents who formed kin across this network. While the number of examples is limited, it is worth noting that it is in these contexts of feast residues that the first examples of human representations, hollow ceramic figurines, are found in Honduras. All the examples registered have bodies rendered to suggest female sex, possibly placing the female life course as a focus of the wider religious network.

None of these figurines has been found in the burials under house floors, suggesting that residents who belonged to these two religious communities – the extensive network formed by kin ties among select families, and the localized community formed by sharing meals at the time of burial and possibly other events – negotiated different scriptures and deployed different myths in each context. While in this instance, the use of different objects allows us to see differences in practice that manifest differences in scripture and ritual, we should not assume that differences in scripture and ritual require use of different materials. The splitting of a scripture and myth in which some families were different than most of their neighbors, and a scripture and myth in which everyone in the village was related in similar ways to the earth and perhaps the ocean, could happen even through the use of quasi-objects whose symbolic inscriptions were the same, as different meanings could be created with what seem like the same images. Thus, a bottle marked with star motifs used in a commensal meal by residents of a particular house at Puerto Escondido could be read by the residents of the house as a sign of their connection to the extensive network that reached to the Gulf Coast of Mexico, forming a religious community in which these signs were part of the scripture of the caiman, while the same bottle and its contents deployed in the meal could be understood by the localized community as part of a scripture of shared substance appropriate to the commemoration of a dead family member.

By the period from 900–700 B.C., the interaction of participation in localized and extended religious communities facilitated the emergence of a marked group in some Honduran villages, notably Los Naranjos and Puerto Escondido, whose members participated in a different religious community than most of those in the village, and who asserted different rank, if not yet fully privileged economic status. At the same time, the participants in this extensive, cosmopolitan religious community also continued to participate in local religious practices, and so were able at one and the same time to belong to their villages and yet not be equated with other residents in those settlements.

Los Naranjos provides the best source of scripture for the extensive cosmopolitan religious community as Honduran families participated in it. The building of a monumental platform there, and its elaboration into a kind of built mountain at the center of a constructed landscape marked out with encircling ditches, provided a site used to bury individual humans, dressed in costumes, abstracted from the residential settings of everyday life and yet not merged into a single ancestral group as they would have been in the burial caves in the actual mountains.

It is noteworthy that the principal burial recovered in this location at Los Naranjos wears a costume identical to people buried in similar earthen platforms at contemporary Chiapa de Corzo and Chalcatzingo, Mexico, a costume laid out without a body in buried deposits at La Venta at the same time (Joyce 1999). Common to all the far-flung instances of this costume is the use of jade as the preferential material for ornaments. While jade has been taken for granted as naturally attractive symbolically, due to the wealth of meanings it has in much later periods, in the Honduran landscape, its use is a break with traditional color selection for ritual materials. At Puerto Escondido, jade mimics objects present in white shell and bone, or made out of black fired ceramic. Wearing green versions of ornaments others employed in more traditional materials (shell, bone, and fired clay) simultaneously tied participants in this religious community to the religious community of their own villages through the form of ornaments, and differentiated them from those local communities through the color of ornaments.

The monumental platforms at Los Naranjos were also accompanied by monumental stone sculpture (Joyce and Henderson 2002, 2003). The majority of the

pieces are anthropomorphic, a break with the previous traditions of iconic representation of composites of animal features, featured on one sculpture from the
site. Along with the fragment of large-scale stone sculpture preserved at Puerto
Escondido, the group of human figural stone sculpture at Los Naranjos can be
seen as evidence of participation in a broader religious community that extends to
Mexico – but with localized differences in themes.

Human imagery circulated much more widely in Honduras starting at this time
than it had previously, primarily in the form of small fired-clay figurines, but also
including medium-size jade or greenstone figures (Joyce 2003, 2007b, 2008). As
with the wearing of costumes in burial that indexed performances in living rituals,
but at the same time differentiated the buried person from the local and linked him
or her to the cosmopolitan, fired clay figurines (Figure 7.5) and the slightly larger

FIGURE 7.5 Figurine from Playa de los Muertos. National Museum of the American
Indian, Smithsonian Institution. Cat. No. 178373.000. (Photograph by
Russell Sheptak, used with permission).

stone figural sculpture (Figure 7.6) can be seen as bridging the two different religious communities in which a few families at Los Naranjos and Puerto Escondido were involved. The high numbers of fired clay figurines in these sites, compared to those elsewhere in contemporary Honduras, may partly be due to this intersection of scriptures of the human body that were local with others that were cosmopolitan, expressed in stone sculpture at both the monumental and smaller scale.

The cosmopolitan ritualized body inscribed in stone sculptures appears to have been less differentiated than the localized ritualized body commemorated in fired clay: the cosmopolitan body is that of an adult male, with little or no ornamentation. At the same time, these cosmopolitan ritualized bodies are the most distinctive in posture: one has a hand on the shoulder in a possible gesture of submission, a second crouches looking up, a third is seated cross-legged, and a fourth stands in a partly flexed position described as typical of shamanic transformation in Gulf Coast Mexico – a reading made somewhat relevant by the depiction on this ritualized body of skeletal elements visible on the surface of the flesh (Joyce and Henderson

FIGURE 7.6 Kneeling greenstone figure, found near La Lima, Cortés, Honduras. Photograph courtesy of Middle American Research Institute, Cat. No. H.1.2 40–3671, used with permission.

2002, 2003). The ritual performances indexed are those of specialists accessing powerful forces.

In contrast, the localized ritualized body is almost always either explicitly female, or unmarked as to sex; ranges in age from infant to elderly; adopts three repeated postures (seated cross-legged, standing with arms at side or raised to the head, perhaps dancing, or – rarely – lying down); and is provided with a plethora of details of hair; ear ornaments; neck, wrist, and ankle strands of beads; pendants; and belts, aprons, skirts and other textile garments (Joyce 2003, 2007b, 2014). The rituals implied are those of the life course of people in the villages.

We can view the increase in small-scale clay figural sculptures indexing the religious community of the life course of people of the villages as dialectically linked to the production of a smaller number of large-scale indexes of rituals of specialists in the cosmopolitan religious community introduced through a limited network. What we are witnessing is interpretable as religion confronting attempted formation of a claim to power and authority. Because these differences are made in the medium of ritualized bodies and their scriptural representations, we can suggest that the claims of power and authority here concerned differential access to the most basic resources of all: labor. Labor to build platforms claimed as a privileged site of burial by members of the more limited religious community; labor to produce life-size stone sculptures recording the embodied actions of those people; but above all, labor that produced the agricultural products on which everyone depended.

The history in Honduras is clear: the attempt to claim differential status by this limited religious community did not succeed in the end. Instead, after 300 B.C. we see a continuation and elaboration of the production of fired clay figurines, now a limited number of more stereotyped female images, seated and standing, including repeated examples of a feline skin apron. These occur in sites (Rio Pelo, San Juan Camalote) where commensality is the most visible ritualized practice, and where a novel use of ceramic vessels to burn materials hints at the conversion of some substances into scent, perhaps feeding the ancestors. The collective grouping of the dead under house compound floors continues, with ever less to differentiate some of the dead from others included in these residential group graves. Earthen platforms constructed in earlier periods remain standing at the edges of later settlements in which every person's house is raised on its own small platform, reclaiming whatever symbolic and mythic value the much larger platforms once advanced when built in only a few places. The use of green jade gives way to the working of whitish albitic jade and marble, reinstating the original colors of ritual performance prized in the earliest Honduran villages by religious communities that were local in their scriptural references (Hirth and Hirth 1993; Luke et al. 2003).

Conclusion

While viewing social practices and belief as structured recursively and permanently articulated, I suggest that the nature of religion made it easier to promote social change through religious innovation than to institute political change and then ret-roactively sanction it through religion. Participating socially in a cosmopolitan net-work that linked some families from Central Mexico to Honduras and El Salvador brought with it a role in a religious community with practices that at times were only subtly distinct from those already in place in local religious communities.

Some actors were involved in both the local religious community and the cos-mopolitan community, and these were the families and persons who began to strategically differentiate themselves from their local neighbors. But because they also (necessarily) had to be part of the local religious community, the practices they promoted were subject to interpretation within a local hermeneutic that pushed back against claims of personal authority due to privileged access to a powerful realm beyond reach of most people, instead promoting traditional connections to generational re-creation through rituals that included family ancestors.

The levels on which participation in religious communities can be monitored are the personal, the familial, and the settlement. From settlement to settlement, even across relatively short distances within Honduras, there is variability in how religious communities interacted with the earth, perhaps zoomorphized; and quite likely there are differences in the symbolic importance of the sea, even when it was indexed through iconically similar quasi-objects. There was quite likely always variability within these villages as well in the practices of religious communities, with different ancestral myths circulating in lines of connected families that might have owned them – and the right to embody them in material form – just as such rights are owned by families in the Northwest Coast, and persons in Melanesia (Lévi-Strauss 1999; Küchler 2002).

While we may not be able to disentangle the complexity in an early village as ethnographers in these areas have, we can make the assumption that there was as much variability in areas of similar scale in the distant past as in the recent past. If we understand our role as tracing things and their connections and dis-connections, rather than classifying them – for example, as ritual and religion, or ideology and cosmology – we should be able to develop thick descriptions, but ones that have the added advantage of explicitly including material forms as ritualized objects, interpreted scriptures, bundles of meaning, and locations of religious practice.

Acknowledgments

Research at Puerto Escondido and Los Naranjos was co-directed with John S. Henderson. Beyond the publications cited, this chapter builds on discussions in preparation for the 1995 symposium "Religion Popular y Religion del Estado," organized by the Instituto Hondureño de Antropología y Historia, held in Copan, Honduras, at which we were invited speakers. Without implying endorsement of the ideas presented here, I would like to acknowledge the importance of these discussions in developing my understanding.

References

Aldenderfer, Mark 2012 Envisioning a Pragmatic Approach to the Archaeology of Religion. In *Beyond Belief: The Archaeology of religion and Ritual*, edited by Yorke Rowan, pp. 23–36. Archeological Papers of the American Anthropological Association, vol. 21. American Anthropological Association, Arlington, VA.

Bell, Catherine 1992 *Ritual Theory, Ritual Practice*. Oxford University Press, Oxford.

————. 2007 Religion Through Ritual. In *Teaching Ritual*, edited by Catherine Bell, pp. 177–193. Oxford University Press, Oxford.

Brady, James E., Christopher Begley, John Fogarty, Donald J. Stierman, Barbara Luke, and Ann Scott 2000 Talgua Archaeological Project: A Preliminary Assessment. *Mexicon* 22(5): 111–118.

de Certeau, Michel 1984 *The Practice of Everyday Life*. Translated by Steven Rendall. University of California Press, Berkeley.

Fox, John G. 1994 *Putting the Heart Back in the Court: Ballcourts and Ritual Action in Mesoamerica*. Ph.D. dissertation, Department of Anthropology, Harvard University. University Microfilms, Ann Arbor.

Geertz, Clifford 1973 *Religion as a Cultural System*. *The Interpretation of Cultures*, pp. 87–125. Basic Books, New York.

Gordon, George Byron. 1898 Caverns of Copan, Honduras. *Peabody Museum Memoirs* 1(5). Peabody Museum of Archaeology and Ethnology, Harvard University, Cambridge.

Healy, Paul 1974 Cuyamel Caves: Preclassic Sites in Northeast Honduras. *American Antiquity* 39: 433–437.

Henderson, John S., and Rosemary A. Joyce 1998 Investigaciones Arqueológicas en Puerto Escondido: Definición del Formativo Temprano en el Valle Inferior del Río Ulúa. *Yaxkin* XVII: 5–35.

————. 2000 *Space and Society in the Lower Ulúa Valley, Honduras*. Paper presented at the 65th Annual Meeting of the Society for American Archaeology, Philadelphia.

————. 2004 Puerto Escondido: Exploraciones Preliminares del Formativo Temprano. In *Memoria del VII Seminario de Antropología de Honduras "Dr. George Hasemann"*, edited by Kevin Avalos, pp. 93–113. Instituto Hondureño de Antropología e Historia, Tegucigalpa.

————. 2006 Brewing Distinction: The Development of Cacao Beverages in Formative Mesoamerica. In *Chocolate in Mesoamerica: A Cultural History of Cacao*, edited by Cameron McNeil, pp. 140–153. University Press of Florida, Gainesville.

Henderson, John S., Rosemary A. Joyce, Gretchen R. Hall, W. Jeffrey Hurst, and Patrick E. McGovern 2007 Chemical and Archaeological Evidence for the Earliest Cacao Beverages. *Proceedings of the National Academy of Sciences* 104: 18937–18940.

Hirth, Kenneth G., and Susan Grant Hirth 1993 Ancient Currency: The Style and Use of Jade and Marble Carvings in Central Honduras. In *Precolumbian Jade: New Geological and Cultural Interpretations*, edited by Frederick W. Lange, pp. 173–190. University of Utah Press, Salt Lake City.

Insoll, Timothy 2004 *Archaeology, Ritual, Religion*. Routledge, London.

Joyce, Rosemary A. 1999 Social Dimensions of Pre-Classic Burials. In *Social Patterns in Pre-Classic Mesoamerica*, edited by David C. Grove and Rosemary A. Joyce, pp. 15–47. Dumbarton Oaks, Washington, DC.

————. 2001 Burying the Dead at Tlatilco: Social Memory and Social Identities. In *New Perspectives on Mortuary Analysis*, edited by Meredith Chesson, pp. 12–26. Archeological Papers of the American Anthropological Association, vol. 10. American Anthropological Association, Arlington, VA.

————. 2003 Making Something of Herself: Embodiment in Life and Death at Playa de los Muertos, Honduras. *Cambridge Archaeological Journal* 13: 248–261.

————. 2004 Unintended Consequences? Monumentality as a Novel Experience in Formative Mesoamerica. *Journal of Archaeological Method and Theory* 11: 5–29.

————. 2007a Building Houses: The Materialization of Lasting Identity in Formative Mesoamerica. In *The Durable House: House Society Models in Archaeology*, edited by Robin Beck, pp. 53–72. Center for Archaeological Investigations, Occasional Paper No. 35. Southern Illinois University, Carbondale.

————. 2007b Figurines, Meaning, and Meaning-Making in Early Mesoamerica. In *Material Beginnings: A Global Prehistory of Figurative Representation*, edited by Colin Renfrew and Iain Morley, pp. 107–116. McDonald Institute for Archaeological Research, Cambridge.

————. 2008 When the Flesh Is Solid But the Person Is Hollow Inside: Formal Variation in Hand-Modeled Figurines From Formative Mesoamerica. In *Past Bodies: Body-Centered Research in Archaeology*, edited by Dušan Borić and John Robb, pp. 37–45. Oxbow Books, Oxford.

————. 2011 In the Beginning: The Experience of Residential Burial in Prehispanic Honduras. In *Residential Burial: A Multiregional Exploration*, edited by Ron L. Adams and Stacie King, pp. 33–43. Archeological Papers of the American Anthropological Association, vol. 20. American Anthropological Association, Arlington,VA.

————. 2014 Ties That Bind: Cloth, Clothing, and Embodiment in Formative Honduras. In *Wearing Culture: Dress and Regalia in Early Mesoamerica and Central America*, edited by Heather Orr and Matthew Looper, pp. 61–78. University Press of Colorado, Boulder.

Joyce, Rosemary A., and John S. Henderson 2001 Beginnings of Village Life in Eastern Mesoamerica. *Latin American Antiquity* 12(1): 5–24.

————. 2002 La arqueología del periodo Formativo en Honduras: nuevos datos sobre el <<estilo olmeca>> en la zona maya. *Mayab* 15: 5–18.

————. 2003 Investigaciones recientes de la arqueología del periodo Formativo en Honduras: nuevos datos sobre el intercambio y cerámica pan-mesoamericana (o estilo "olmeca"). In *XVI Simposio de Investigaciones Arqueológicas en Guatemala, 2002*, edited by Juan Pedro Laporte, Barbara Arroyo, Hector Escobedo, and Hector Mejía, pp. 819–832. Museo Nacional de Arqueología y Etnología and Asociación Tikal, Guatemala.

————. 2007 From Feasting to Cuisine: Implications of Archaeological Research in an Early Honduran Village. *American Anthropologist* 109: 642–653.

————. 2009 Forming Mesoamerican Taste: Cacao Consumption in Formative Period Contexts. In *Pre-Columbian Foodways: Interdisciplinary Approaches to Food, Culture, and Markets in Ancient Mesoamerica*, edited by John E. Staller and Michael Carrasco. Springer, New York.

————. 2010 Being "Olmec" in Formative Honduras. *Ancient Mesoamerica* 21: 187–200.

————. 2017 "Olmec" Pottery in Honduras. In *The San Lorenzo Olmec and Their Neighbors: Material Manifestations*, edited by Jeffrey Blomster and David Cheetham, pp. 264–287. Cambridge University Press, Cambridge.

Joyce, Rosemary A., Julia A. Hendon, and Russell N. Sheptak 2008 Una nueva evaluación de Playa de los Muertos: Exploraciones en el Periodo Formativo Medio en Honduras. In *Ideología Política y Sociedad en el Periodo Formativo: Ensayos en homenaje al doctor David C. Grove*, edited by Ann Cyphers and Kenneth G. Hirth, pp. 283–310. Instituto de Investigaciones Antropológicas, Universidad Nacional Autonoma de Mexico, Mexico, DF.

Joyce, Rosemary A., M. Steven Shackley, Kenneth McCandless and Russell Sheptak 2004 Resultados preliminares de una investigación con EDXRF de obsidiana de Puerto

Escondido. In *Memoria del VII Seminario de Antropología de Honduras "Dr. George Hase-mann,"* edited by Kevin Avalos, pp. 115–129. Instituto Hondureño de Antropología e Historia, Tegucigalpa.

Küchler, Susanne 2002 *Malanggan: Art, Memory, and Sacrifice.* Berg, Oxford.

Langer, Susanne K. 1953 *Feeling and Form: A Theory of Art.* Scribner, New York.

Lele, Veerendra P. 2006 Material Habits, Identity, Semeiotic. *Journal of Social Archaeology* 6: 48–70.

Lévi-Strauss, Claude 1999 *The Way of the Masks.* Translated by Sylvia Modelski. University of British Columbia Press, Vancouver.

Longyear III, John M. 1969 The Problem of Olmec Influences in the Pottery of Western Honduras. *Proceedings of the 38th International Congress of Americanists* 1: 491–498. Stuttgart.

Luke, Christina, Rosemary A. Joyce, John S. Henderson, and Robert H. Tykot 2003 Marble Carving Traditions in Honduras: Formative Through Terminal Classic. In *ASMOSIA 6, Interdisciplinary Studies on Ancient Stone – Proceedings of the Sixth International Conference of the Association for the Study of Marble and Other Stones in Antiquity, Venice, June 15–18, 2000,* edited by Lorenzo Lazzarini, pp. 485–496. Bottega d'Erasmo, Padova.

Material Religion 2005 Editorial Statement. *Material Religion* 1: 4.

Morell-Hart, Shanti, Rosemary A. Joyce, and John S. Henderson 2014 Multi-Proxy Analysis of Plant Use at Formative Period Los Naranjos, Honduras. *Latin American Antiquity* 25: 65–81.

Peirce, Charles Sanders 1878 How to Make Our Ideas Clear. *Popular Science Monthly* 12: 286–302.

Tchakirides, Tiffany F. 2010 *Geophysical Investigations at Los Naranjos Honduras: Insights Into Early Mesoamerican Culture.* Unpublished PhD dissertation, Department of Earth and Atmospheric Sciences, Cornell University, Ithaca.

Tchakirides, Tiffany F., Larry D. Brown, John S. Henderson, and Kira Blaisdell-Sloan 2006 Integration, Correlation, and Interpretation of Geophysical and Archaeological Data at Los Naranjos, Honduras. *Symposium on the Application of Geophysics to Engineering and Environmental Problems* 2006: 1420–1429. Seattle.

Viel, René, and Charles Cheek 1983 Sepulturas. In *Introducción a la arqueología de Copán, Honduras,* vol. I, edited by Claude F. Baudez, pp. 551–609. SECTUR, Tegucigalpa.

Wonderley, Anthony 1991 Late Preclassic Sula Plain, Honduras: Regional Antecedents to Social Complexity and Interregional Convergence in Ceramic Style. In *Formation of Complex Society in Southeastern Mesoamerica,* edited by William Fowler, pp. 143–169. CRC Publications, Boca Raton.

8

POLITICAL ENGAGEMENT IN HOUSEHOLD RITUAL AMONG THE MAYA OF YUCATAN

Scott R. Hutson, Céline C. Lamb, and David Medina Arona

Introduction

The worldviews of many cultures across Mesoamerica, past and present, contain the monistic principle that a vital force or spirit inhabits a great variety of entities: mountains, animals, streams, forests, houses, clouds (Monaghan 2000). Ancient Maya worldviews were no exception (Houston 2013; Houston and Inomata 2009). This means that what a modern Western observer might see as opposites – animate vs. inanimate, sacred vs. profane – were not always opposed (Astor-Aguilera 2010:16–18). Furthermore, some entities maintain relationships of indebtedness with humans: one cannot take from the earth, for example, without giving back. According to Monaghan, these points have profound implications for the nature of daily life. In particular, work in forests, fields, and homes requires people to make regular offerings. Though we might conceive of these offerings as rituals, Mesoamericans merely perceive them as work, or production, making it difficult to separate ritual from the quotidian (cf. Bell 1992). Furthermore, "spiritual" beings are not necessarily seen as spiritual or exalted, but rather as common members of the community and regular participants in day-to-day activities. This Mesoamerican perspective accords with a more general view of religion endorsed by Insoll in his book *Archaeology, Ritual, and Religion*. Insoll (2004:Figure 2) maintains that analysts should not see religion as a domain of life alongside other domains such as economy, technology, or politics. Instead, Insoll perceives religion as so closely bound up with life that life/religion subsumes economies, technologies, politics, and the rest (see also Brück 1999; Lansing 1991; McAnany 2010). Of course, we should not overextend this approach since the centrality of religion varies across time and space (Fogelin 2007:60). Nevertheless, as we discuss below, this approach fits the Maya of Yucatan and entails two consequences of special importance to the theme of religion and political transformation. First, to the extent that everyone participates actively in the give and take of life, they also participate actively in religion and ritual. Second, ritual is power in the broadest sense: it constitutes actors and allows these actors to negotiate authority, access to resources, and community standing. Combining these two points underscores the notion that all people, from the humblest farmers to the most powerful lords, can play a role in politics through ritual practice.

We begin this chapter by presenting background about the ancient Maya and their ritual practices. In particular, we take pains to demonstrate the close articulation between ritual and politics and the degree to which religion permeates daily life. We then discuss the political impact of household ritual (see also Lucero 2003; Lohse 2007; Gonlin 2007; Robin 2003). Household rituals affect the succession of household leadership and also have a bearing on the constitution of authority at a variety of scales above the household. Specifically, we draw attention to two ritual practices that occur at many scales: ancestor worship and building dedication. We will argue that ancestor veneration at households from the Classic-period Maya site of Chunchucmil played a role in differentiating households and may have had the unintended consequence of stabilizing the power of centralized leaders. As for building dedication, we use data from sites within the Ucí polity to explore several ways in which rites performed by people of various social positions contribute to broader discourses about religion and power within those societies. In particular, this research explores two important dimensions of ritual politics: (1) engagement at multiple political levels, including those intermediate between households and kings; and (2) the role of independence in the perpetuation and transformation of ritual practice. As we discuss below, engagement refers to the concept that an audience's historically-grounded expectations of what counts as an appropriate performance constrain even the most powerful sponsors of such performances (Joyce et al. 2001). Independence refers to the fact that households located further away from political centers may have more leeway to develop alternative ritual practices (Joyce and Weller 2007).

Scholars of the ancient Maya find themselves in a privileged position when discussing ritual and religion. Following the heuristic that ritual refers to specific actions while religion refers to beliefs, myths, and orientations toward the world, both discursive and non-discursive, many archaeologists engage more directly with ritual since ritual practices often leave material traces that survive into the present (Fogelin 2007; Joyce 2011). At the same time, the act of interpreting the traces of ritual always gets us into religion as well, since we cannot interpret a material trace without using preconceived notions about meaning and belief (Insoll 2004; see also Hodder and Hutson 2003). Ritual and religion are also inseparable if we view religion as inherently lived, practiced, and experienced (A. Joyce, Chapter 1). Thanks to an abundance of deciphered hieroglyphic texts and an extremely rich corpus of art and iconography, Maya archaeologists can enter this hermeneutic spiral of interpretation well above ground level. We know quite a bit about ancient Maya myths and worldview, what the Maya attempted to accomplish with many of their rituals, and even how they experienced such rites (Houston et al. 2006; Schele and

Miller 1986; Stuart 2011). Thus, Mayanists often discuss both ritual and religion, and can move back and forth between them (e.g. Joyce 2011:186). All the while, following Monaghan, Astor Aguilera, and others, we ask the reader to recall that what an archaeologist calls ritual may have been perceived by the ancient Maya not as an exceptional or sacred act, but as a kind of work alongside other common forms of production.

Those committed to practice theory will recognize the point that religion and ritual are co-dependent. Religion, which cannot exist without the rituals that iterate it and substantiate it, informs ritual in the same moment that ritual practices can transform religion (Bell 1992). This leads to a final note about religion and ritual. Analogies to myths and rites documented among Maya speakers ethnohistorically and ethnographically often lend support to interpretations of ancient Maya material. This could be taken to imply a degree of conservatism in Maya religion at odds with the known fact that Maya religion underwent many transformations (e.g. Cecil and Pugh 2009). This apparent contradiction does not disqualify the use of analogy because historical anthropologists have shown that enduring, long-term structures of meaning can accommodate ruptures, inventions, and revisions (Hamann 2002; Sahlins 1996).

Maya religion and ritual

The Maya flourished in what is now Guatemala, Belize, eastern Mexico, and parts of Honduras and El Salvador (Figure 8.1), and continued to live with dignity despite colonialism and racism over the last 500 years. During the Classic period (A.D. 250–900), the institution of kingship reached its zenith, with hundreds of named rulers coming to our attention by means of lavish tombs and written texts chronicling their ancestry, accession to office, marriages, diplomatic visits, exploits in battle, and more (Martin and Grube 2008). Given that most kings and queens lacked standing armies and did not monopolize vital resources such as water, pottery, and stone tools (Clark 2003:52–54; Dunning et al. 2014; Fry 1979; Masson and Freidel 2012; Scarborough and Valdez 2009), much of their authority rested on their ability to convince others of the legitimacy of their status as leaders. Ritual and religion played an enormous role in these attempts to gain and maintain the loyalty of subjects. Many authors have argued that when leaders use ritual to acquire and bolster authority, they draw from religious understandings that are already widespread and intelligible among the people whose support they hope to win (Kertzer 1988; Kus and Raharijoana 2000; McAnany 1995). We therefore begin by discussing how religion stands at the core of some of the most basic and diverse aspects of life, and then later move to the ways in which centralized authorities used it.

Growing corn was at the center of ancient Maya life and continues to inform Maya identity in the present (Hervik 1999; Hostettler 2001). Both ancient and modern Maya understand maize to be the product of moral relationships between humans and the other-than-human entities with whom they reciprocated. Often

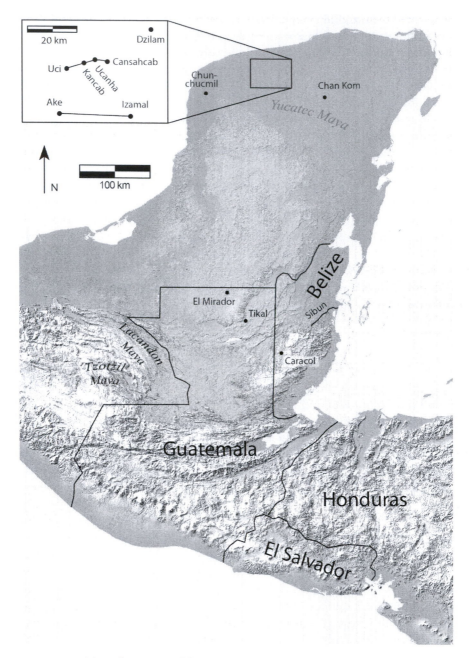

FIGURE 8.1   Map of a portion of the Maya area showing locations mentioned in the text

referred to by the Mayan word k'u or ch'u (pronunciation and spelling vary among specific Mayan languages), which has been glossed as holy, sacred, or divine, these entities consist of vital natural forces linked to things like water, earth, and sky, and can also be ancestors (Houston and Stuart 1996:291–292). The Maya often represented them anthropomorphically, and Mayanists often call them gods. The key element of the relationship between humans and gods is sacrifice. In their classic ethnography of the Yucatec Maya of Chan Kom (see Figure 8.1), Redfield and Villa Rojas (1962:127) state: "What man wins from nature, he takes from the gods." At many points in the agricultural cycle, successful farming (and all other activities which extract goods from the environment) depends on feeding the guardians of the farmed field – the milpa – and the forest out of which the milpa is carved. Neglecting this relationship results in sickness, injury, or a failed crop.

Thus, Maya subsistence economies involve a relationship of indebtedness with other-than-human beings (Hutson and Stanton 2007). Patricia McAnany (2010) expands on this point. From the perspective that the tendrils of ritual practice can wrap around any conceivable activity, McAnany (2010:13) follows Monaghan, Redfield, and others in seeing ritual as equivalent to work. Thus, offerings of shell placed within wetland fields during the Classic period in the Sibun River Valley, Belize, should not be seen as set apart from the hard labor of creating those fields (McAnany 2010:92). Beyond agriculture, ritual permeated other kinds of economic activity, such as weaving, potting, and knapping. Hruby (2007) uses the phrase "ritualized production" to refer to this seamless mesh of what we would call mundane steps, such as adding temper to clay, and what we would call sacred steps, such as offerings, chants, and fasting. Ethnographic and ethnohistorical accounts provide many examples of ritualized production (Clark 1989:305; Hruby 2007; McAnany 2010). The sacred steps in the production process serve not just to help ensure the successful execution of difficult tasks, such as firing a clay vessel or removing a critical flake, but to place the artisans in the proper balance with the universe, maintaining a dialogue with deities (McAnany 2010:214–215). Hruby's analysis of obsidian eccentrics from the Classic period suggests that ritualized production as seen in ethnographic and ethnohistorical sources had deep chronological roots.

Trash disposal provides another glimpse of this eliding of cosmology and everyday practice. Broken pottery carried strong cosmological meanings in many parts of Mesoamerica at the time of Spanish contact (Burkhart 1989; Hamann 2008). In the Maya area, Bishop Diego de Landa's sixteenth-century account of the indigenous new year ceremony shows that in some contexts, discarded pottery had symbolic power that caused people to avoid touching it (Tozzer 1941:151). Given that trash can carry religious freight, and given that religion shaped mundane activities such as farming and crafting, we used data from the site of Chunchucmil, Yucatan, to explore whether or not the seemingly mundane activity of discarding potsherds might have also been structured by sacred principles (Hutson and Stanton 2007). We found that the people of Chunchucmil preferred the west side of their houselot for dumping trash. This may relate to the fact that several Maya speakers see the west as a place of death and decay. West, *chik'in* in Yucatec Maya, is associated with the setting of the sun (Barrera Vazquez 1980), where the sun goes to die (Schele and Freidel 1990:66). Among the contemporary Tzotzil and Lacandon Maya of Chiapas, Mexico, west can symbolize death (Gossen 1974:33). Coggins (1980, 1988) has argued that the association of west with death also characterizes

Classic-period mortuary symbolism. Since Maya speakers from both before and after the Spanish conquest saw the west as a place of decay, throwing out rubbish to the west agrees with indigenous logic. Dumping trash to the west was explicable not only in terms of a seemingly abstract cosmology, but rather as part of the practical work of maintenance that contributes to the well-being of the houselot's inhabitants (Brück 1999:335). At the same time, cultural logics are flexible, not always followed, so there will always be exceptions to the pattern (Bourdieu 1990).

Beyond this example of discard, directional symbolism provides abundant examples of how the Maya blend ritual and daily practice. Returning to corn farming, the Maya of Yucatan grow corn in plots that are roughly square or rectangular (Hanks 1990:362; Redfield and Villa Rojas 1962:134). From a utilitarian standpoint, a rectangular shape allows for easier measurement of land to be cultivated. Yet to the Yucatec farmer, this shape is basic to the frame of reference in which he lives all aspects of his life (Hanks 1990). Quadripartition and a four-cornered world anchor Yucatecan cosmology and phenomenology. In Maya myths, the world itself was created as a four-cornered place, and in contemporary times, centering the self in a four-cornered world is also a prerequisite for proper life. Thus, when Yucatec farmers plant in four-cornered plots and make offerings to the four corners and the center, they do not simply appease the guardians of the milpa, they stand up a world in microcosm, a world in which the all-important relationships between human and deity become possible (Hanks 1990:378). In sum, the fact that the symbolic principles of the cardinal directions orient daily activities shows that a system of belief imbues quotidian work (Hodder and Hutson 2003).

Given how closely daily life intertwines with religion and ritual, it comes as no surprise that leadership among the ancient Maya could not exist apart from religion and ritual. Others have explored this point so thoroughly that we cannot do it justice in the short amount of space we have available. Several books flesh out the subject more richly than the capsule summary we provide below (Schele and Freidel 1990; Houston and Inomata 2009; Schele and Mathews 1998). Just as sacrifice was important in day-to-day work, sacrifice was critical to ancient leaders. Since the maize god sacrificed himself at the beginning of time in order to ensure human prosperity, Maya kings sacrificed their own blood to pay back this debt and help ensure a bounteous harvest for their polity (Schele and Miller 1986:176–182). Having made such sacrifices on behalf of their polity, rulers perhaps hoped that they would earn the trust of their supporters (see also Golden and Scherer 2013). Human sacrifice, usually of high-status prisoners captured on the battlefield, was the centerpiece of reenactments of creation mythology. Rulers orchestrated such reenactments in order to re-create an ordered world for their followers (Stuart 2003).

Royal rites involving god impersonation were not merely performances aimed at both human and other-than-human audiences. Portraits show leaders wearing masks of gods while accompanying glyphs contain what Houston and Stuart (1996:299) call an "impersonation phrase," which names a specific god and the specific lord or lady who takes the image of that god. In Postclassic Central Mexico, god masks are not just representations of the god but extensions of the god itself, thus making the god physically present at rites. The less well-understood instances of god-impersonation in the Maya area suggest, at least, that humans "shared in some manner the divinity of those gods" (Houston and Stuart 1996:299). Other royal rites summoned and communicated with ancestors, making them appear as visions in smoke rising from burning, blood-spattered paper (Schele and Miller 1986). Toward the end of the Classic period, rulers claimed ownership of gods and went as far as espousing a divine status for themselves. The title k'uhul ajaw – "holy ruler" – implies that the ruler claims the same qualities usually reserved for other-than-human entities (Houston and Stuart 1996:295). Since many of a ruler's subjects were dispersed across the countryside, one of the most important goals of ritual was simply to bring people together to materialize the polity as a community (Inomata 2006; Lucero 2003; Golden and Scherer 2013). Since most Maya rulers had little or no physical or economic control over their supporters, some have argued that theatrical performance of rituals was not just a formality, but rather the core of statehood itself (Demarest 1992).

If nothing else, this brief discussion of Maya ritual and religion should establish two points. First, ritual can imbue nearly any practice. Because of this, all sectors of Maya society participate actively in ritual. Archaeological evidence for this is well known (Borhegyi 1956; Leventhal 1983), and we provide more below. Second, ritual is politicized. Though we have only discussed royal politics thus far, the first point, that all people participate in ritual, implies that through ritual, all people have a voice in politics. This postulate ties into a growing chorus of voices that stress the different ways Maya commoners wielded power (Ashmore et al. 2004; Hutson 2013; Joyce and Hendon 2000; Lohse 2007; Lucero 2007; Robin 2002; Sheets 2000). Minimally, commoners are the audience for royal ritual, which means that commoners' understandings of appropriate ritual practice constrained royal performers (Joyce et al. 2001; Lucero 2003). Commoners responded to performances in a variety of ways, ranging from approval to rejection to apathy. Commoners could also vote with their feet by choosing to support a different faction within the polity or leave the polity altogether (Inomata 2004, 2006; Lucero 2007). The focus of the current chapter, however, is not how people received royal rituals at centers, but rather the ritual work that these people performed at a variety of scales. We begin with household contexts at the site of Chunchucmil.

Ancestor veneration and the politics of identity

In the Classic period, a variety of rituals took place in non-elite Maya households. In this section, we focus on ancestor veneration and the politics that go with it. Ancestor veneration comes in many forms, one of the clearest of which consists of burials with offerings beneath the floor of a building that becomes an ancestor shrine: a locale for later ceremonies and commemorations. Patricia McAnany (1995) has argued that later generations of household leaders stake their claims to the household's resources through rituals that venerate the ancestors. Such veneration demonstrates strong links to the ancestors and therefore legitimates the descendants' claims to the household's material and symbolic heritage (Hutson et al. 2004). As the vehicle through which people settle issues of household resource allocation, ancestor veneration becomes intensely political. In the example below from Chunchucmil, we argue that household ancestor shrines also entangled with politics beyond the household, namely in status competition between households and in relation to central authorities.

Chunchucmil reached its apogee in the fifth through seventh centuries A.D. with a population of perhaps 40,000 (Magnoni et al. 2012). The most common archaeological signature of households at Chunchucmil consists of an architectural compound with three or more platforms (usually ranging between 50 and 100 m^2) arrayed around a central patio covering over 100 m^2. The platforms supported residences, kitchens, shrines, and other kinds of buildings. Low stone walls encircle these compounds, forming houselots that usually contain 2,000 m^2 or more of unbuilt space for a variety of activities, such as gardening. In accord with a pattern noticed by archaeologists at other sites (Becker 1991; Kurjack 1974:75; Tourtellot 1983:41), platforms on the east side of the patio often supported shrines (Magnoni et al. 2012). Four eastern shrines were completely excavated at Chunchucmil. These excavations confirm that these buildings contained the burials of ancestors and served as spaces for household ritual.

The ancestor shrines at Chunchucmil resemble each other in that they consist of platforms that are higher and more square (as opposed to rectangular) relative to the other platforms in the compound. Despite these superficial resemblances, the four fully excavated structures, located in the Aak (S2E2-F), Lool (N2E2-N), Kaab' (S2E1-G), and Muuch (S2E2-C) houselots (Figure 8.2), are quite different. The ancestor shrine in the Muuch houselot consists of a solid platform possibly topped by a perishable superstructure. The front had a red-painted, modeled, stucco façade in association with sloped walls that flank a central stairway. The façade consists of a number of abstract design elements, including volutes and spirals. The ancestor shrine of the Lool houselot is a solid platform whose exterior contains a *talud tablero* façade (Ardren and Blackmore 2001): a base sloping inward toward the building topped by an overhanging tablero, which consists of a recessed panel bracketed above and below by protruding moldings. In the Aak houselot, the ancestor shrine underwent a series of modifications that produced three compartments on the south edge of the platform, each about 1 m^2. These compartments contained offerings such as complete serving vessels, jade and hematite mosaic pieces, grooved stones, and jade beads. Like the Aak ancestor shrine, the east structure of the Kaab' houselot had a complex construction history (Magnoni 2008). Unlike the Aak, Muuch, and Lool platforms, the ancestor shrine of the Kaab' group initially consisted of an impressive stone superstructure whose walls were 1.8 m thick, with unshaped boulders on the interior and nicely cut stones on the exterior. The superstructure initially contained a single room that was later subdivided.

Each of these ancestor shrines served as a unique ritual and social focus for its respective household. Building, using, and maintaining these structures would

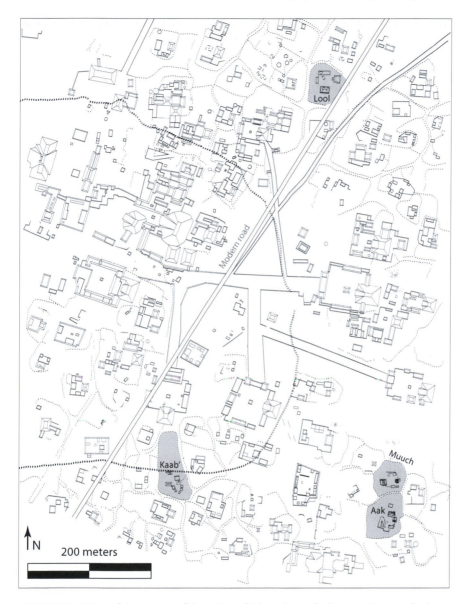

FIGURE 8.2   Map of the center of the ruins of Chunchucmil, showing in grey the location and plan of the four houselots discussed in the text

have created and reinforced an identity held in common among the multiple families living in each houselot (see also Blackmore 2011). Other features reinforce this group identity. For example, most houselots at Chunchucmil have a single food preparation area and a single patio. The low stone walls that encircle the houselots clearly delimit one household's realm from another. Sharing these spaces and activities promoted a life in common for the household, distinct from that of other households. Though the four groups might be seen as equivalent social units insofar as each group has evidence for consumption, production, transmission of wealth, and social reproduction (Ashmore and Wilk 1988), each group's ritual/ ceremonial focus differs strikingly from those of the other groups.

The uniqueness of each houselot's ancestor shrine emphasizes not only the fact that each group had a distinct identity, but also that each group consciously elaborated this identity for display. Ethnohistorical accounts of Postclassic residences in Yucatan suggest that visitors attended ceremonies within houselots (Tozzer 1941:85–86). Most striking about these residences is that the best stonework is in the front, exposed to visitors (Hutson 2010:142; see also Carmean et al. 2011). As several other authors have noted, Maya residential compounds were neither private nor merely domestic (Hendon 1997). Since houselots were points of encounter between people of different households, the ceremonies that took place at ancestor shrines were politicized in the sense that interactions between visiting and hosting households produced the kinds of mutual evaluations that establish social hierarchies among neighbors. Insofar as ancestral platforms were built as unique statements of identity – or even propositions of status – and residences were built in ways that put the best face forward (i.e., better stonework where visitors see it), these households worked to create built environments that would influence the tone of interaction with outsiders (Rapoport 1982).

In sum, inter-household politics imbued household rituals because hosts used the setting – a kind of home court advantage – to establish and/or reiterate diacritical differences between themselves and others (Hutson 2010). This underscores the point that Maya commoners were neither apolitical nor undifferentiated (Blackmore 2011; Gonlin 2007; Haviland 2014:66; Lohse 2007; Robin 2002).

Elsewhere, one of us (Hutson 2002) has argued that identity formation by means of household ritual in Mesoamerica cannot always be understood with reference to relations of power between central authorities and their subjects. We still agree with this, but would like to suggest that household rituals may indeed affect the nature of centralized authority. When households invest heavily in a ritual economy that differentiates one household from another, this may undercut the potential for building strong coalitions across households. In other words, an unintended consequence of these practices of differentiation is that commoners may have missed out on the opportunity to create a more formidable front in negotiating relations with Chunchucmil's centralized authorities. Along the lines of a divide-and-conquer strategy, Chunchucmil's central authorities may have benefitted from a populace whose attention was heavily invested in inter-household displays of status and identity but diverted away from the fundamental inequalities between themselves and elites. What Michael Kearney (1996:156) called a "subtle jujitsu" may be at play here: households move to get ahead of their peers, but their own momentum in this direction deflects them from a more deeply revolutionary politics. Most interesting here is that Chunchucmil's elites invested in the same ritual formations: patios with probable ancestor shrines on one side (usually the east side), though on a much larger scale. This fact of equivalencies in ritual up and down the social hierarchy helps frame new data from the Ucí-Cansahcab Regional Integration Project (UCRIP). Here as well, household ritual bears upon broader political relations.

Caching and scale of authority: offerings across the political spectrum

To what degree do household rituals and centralized rituals share some of the same content? What would such an overlap in content mean? Stephan de Borhegyi (1956:352) was one of the first to tackle these questions, arguing that in the highland Maya area, commoners and elites held "different and frequently opposing world views and mentalities" which, over a span of two millennia, "had little, if any, influence on the socio-religious structure of the other." Writing at the same time, Redfield (1956:72) took a different position, seeing the "little tradition" (akin to household ritual) and the "great tradition" (akin to centralized ritual) "ever flowing into and out of each other." More recently, archaeologists writing about the Maya lowlands have seen substantial overlap between the ritual practices of farmers and rulers. Interpreting this overlap requires historical context: did a particular ritual practice appear first in common household contexts or in the context of centralized authority, or perhaps in both contexts simultaneously? Data on caches suggest that offerings placed in buildings followed a different historical trajectory at different sites. For example, at Caracol, Belize, caches appear in elite contexts in the Late Preclassic but do not catch on elsewhere until the Classic period, where they eventually turn up in residences occupied by households of all statuses (Chase and Chase 1998:319). On the other hand, at Saturday Creek, Belize, and Tikal, Guatemala, people of various social positions deposited caches starting in the Middle Preclassic (Lucero 2003:531). Joyce and Barber (2015) have noticed similar variability in Formative Oaxaca. As status differentiation intensified in later periods, actors from all social levels continued to practice similar rites, though elite and eventually royal actors placed more exotic and more numerous goods in caches and expended more resources in the ceremonies of deposition (see also Becker 1993:49–50; McAnany 1995; Robin 2003:321–322). Lucero argues that leaders used such ceremonies to demonstrate solidarity with farmers while also legitimating unequal access to wealth and power. For these rites to have the intended effects, leaders had to make them intelligible to followers. Thus, followers exercise power because their expectations of a proper rite constrain leaders' performances (Inomata 2006). This stands as an example of engagement as defined by Joyce et al. (2001): an ever-evolving accommodation between followers' demands and leaders' desires shapes the public ceremonies sponsored by leaders.

Recent excavations along the Ucí-Cansahcab causeway, located in northern Yucatan, suggest a trajectory similar to that of Saturday Creek and Tikal, but add two dimensions to the discussion. First, by comparing caching rites performed in rural farmsteads with those performed in a local center, as opposed to rites performed in different contexts within the same local center, we have a better chance to assess the consequences of what Joyce and Weller (2007:147) call "independence." When people live further from political centers, they may not engage as often in state-sponsored ceremonies. Furthermore, authorities have few (or no) opportunities to monitor household rites. Under such conditions of partial independence, practices that diverge from those at centers may proliferate (see also Brumfiel 1996; Hutson 2002; Scott 1990). Second, many discussions of ritual politics create a dichotomy between elites and commoners. As Cynthia Robin (2003, 2004) has cogently argued, there is remarkable diversity among Classic Maya commoners, just as there is diversity among elites (Hammond 1991:264). In this section, we highlight only one aspect of this diversity: scale of authority. We measure scale of authority by the size of the network that an actor can call upon for support without having to reciprocate equally. As we discuss momentarily, we see five scales of authority in the vicinity of the Ucí-Cansahcab causeway, though there is some degree of conjecture at all levels. Our goal, however, is not to verify the precise structure of regional political hierarchies, but merely to emphasize that the voices that contribute to ritual discourse are more abundant and complex than the two customary voices of elite and commoner.

The Ucí-Cansahcab causeway extends 18 km, with Ucí at its western endpoint and Cansahcab at its eastern endpoint. Ucí is the largest site on the causeway, followed in size by Ucanha and Kancab (Hutson and Welch 2014; Maldonado 1995). Cansahcab was also important, but modern settlement has destroyed much of Cansahcab's architecture. Ucí and the other major ruins in the area, such as Aké and Dzilam, were likely vassals of the nearby regional capital Izamal (33 km southeast of Ucí), which contains one of the largest buildings ever constructed in the Maya area: a 17-m-high platform covering nearly 4 hectares, topped with a superstructure that climbs another 17 m. Izamal's leaders represented the highest scale of authority in the region, while the leaders of Ucí, Aké, and Dzilam represented the second level.

The Ucí-Cansahcab Regional Integration Project (UCRIP) has excavated several caches at Kancab and rural settlements west of it. Kancab peaked at the end of the Preclassic and the end of the Classic period. During each peak, the site consisted of approximately 100 extended family households, covering an area of slightly more than 1 km². During the Late Preclassic, the residents of Kancab built the bulk of a central plaza consisting of a basal platform, measuring about 5,600 m² and 2 m high, which supported two pyramids (Structures 1 and 6), each standing 5 m above the platform and measuring about 20 × 20 m (Figure 8.3). Though Kancab had only a fraction of Ucí's population, its central plaza indicates the presence of leaders able to mobilize a considerable labor force. Kancab's leaders, along with those of Ucanha and, presumably, Cansahcab, represent a third level of authority, subordinate to the leaders of Ucí, the premiere site along the causeway.

UCRIP excavations in the Kancab central plaza consist of six pits, covering 24 m². This sample is too small to reconstruct the detailed construction history of the plaza platform, but it suggests that the central and northeast parts of the

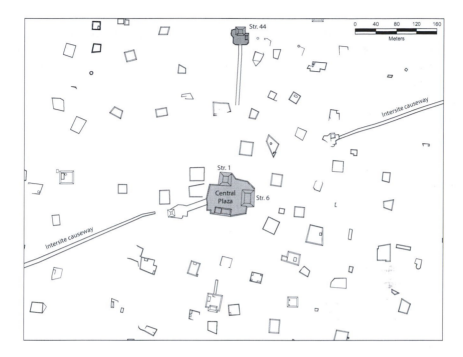

FIGURE 8.3   Map of the Kancab site core, showing in grey the architectural complexes discussed in the text

platform were constructed in the Middle Preclassic, whereas additional portions of the basal platform and the two pyramids on top of it were constructed in the Late Preclassic. A pit in the center of the basal platform recovered a complete Middle Preclassic Kin naranja vessel placed among the stone construction fill 15 cm above bedrock (Plank et al. 2014). Another cache was located 300 m to the north of the central plaza in the Structure 44 compound, the second largest at Kancab. Structure 44 consists of a basal platform covering 850 m² and rising 1.2 m above the natural ground surface. The platform supports major superstructures on the north and east sides. The north Superstructure (44a) is a pyramid rising 4.6 m above the top of the basal platform. A causeway connects to the south side of the platform and extends toward the central plaza. A test pit in the basal platform immediately to the south of Structure 44a documented three stages of construction. During the second stage of construction, which dates to the Late Preclassic, the builders placed a partially complete jar in the construction fill.

UCRIP has excavated caches in three platforms to the west of Kancab: N148, 38s14, and 42s2. All three platforms are located in a 3.4-km² mapping block that focused on the rural area between Ucí and Kancab (Figure 8.4; Lamb et al. 2014). N148 is located near the middle of a cluster of architectural compounds most likely occupied by households. This cluster, called Chunhuayum, is the subject of

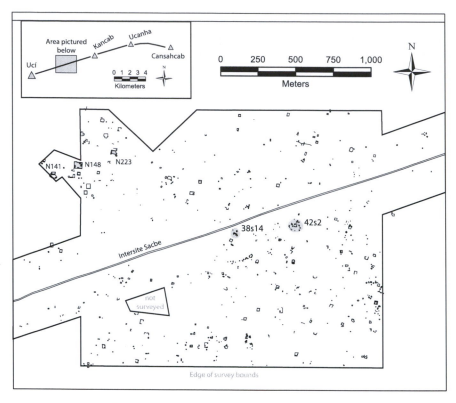

FIGURE 8.4 Map of a 3.4-km² polygon located in between Ucí and Kancab, showing in grey the architectural complexes discussed in the text

Celine Lamb's dissertation research. In addition to N148, UCRIP has excavated at two other platforms within this cluster: N141 and N223. Though ceramics from a variety of chronological periods came from these excavations, all three platforms have a strong occupation in the middle of the Classic period (Oxkintok Regional sphere). These data suggest N148 is at the core of a village.

The N148 platform, located at the northwest corner of the mapping block, is much larger than all other structures in the village and in the 3.4-km² mapping block as a whole. It measures about 55 m east/west by 40 m north/south (2,200 m²), though a historic period road damaged its southeast corner (Figure 8.5a). People from neighboring households probably helped build N148. The platform, whose average height is 0.6 m, reached its full size in the Middle Classic and supports eight clearly visible superstructures, the most distinctive being a square structure – N148a – on the east side, the top of which reaches a height of 3 m above the natural ground surface. Pottery from David Medina's block excavations of N148a shows Late Preclassic, Middle Classic, and Late Classic construction

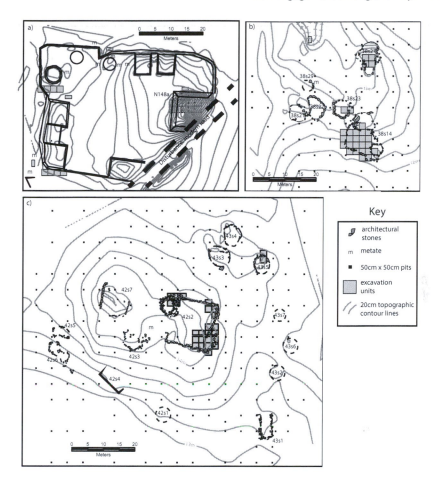

FIGURE 8.5   Maps of (a) the N148 compound; (b) the 38s14 compound; and (c) the 42s2 compound. All of the maps are shown at the same scale.

phases and proportions of bichrome, polychrome, and non-local ceramics that are higher than elsewhere in Chunhuayum. Excavations failed to locate human remains, suggesting that it was not an ancestor shrine, but the structure's relative height and placement on the east side of the group do support the interpretation that it served as a shrine of some kind (Kurjack 1974:75; Leventhal 1983). No other superstructures of such height exist in the 3.4-km^2 mapping area. Though artifacts from N148 suggest activities typical of a household (consumption, produc- tion, etc.), N148's large size and distinctive shrine suggest that from time to time, it hosted village-wide ceremonies. In sum, the heads of the N148 household were probably community leaders that served as intermediaries between their neighbors and authorities from Kancab or Ucí. They might have been able to call upon labor without having to reciprocate in kind. The residents of N148 stand as a fourth level of authority. To reiterate, Izamal, with the largest architecture in the northern Maya Lowlands (located 33 km away), represents the first level. Ucí, a fraction of the size of Izamal but seven times larger than Kancab (Hutson and Welch 2014), represents the second level. Kancab, a town with about a hundred households and mounds reaching 7 m above the natural ground surface, represents the third level.

Excavations of Structure 148a recovered a floor pertaining to a substructure constructed in the Late Preclassic. At the end of the Early Classic, N148's residents broke two holes in this floor and deposited a complete Hunabchen plate in one hole (Figure 8.6) and fragmented remains of three other vessels in the other, along with two beads. After these two deposits, the floor was buried by fill that supported a staircase to the top of the structure.

The residents of 38s14 and 42s2 are examples of the fifth scale of authority (Figures 8.4, 8.5b, 8.5c). Both 38s14 and 42s2 are megalithic platforms (38s14 covers 120 m² with a maximum height of 0.35 cm; 42s2 covers 190 m² with a maximum height of 0.7 m) surrounded by smaller structures (four in the case of 38s14, eleven in the case of 42s2). These architectural compounds are rural farm-steads. The households living here may have entered into labor exchanges with other households, but such exchanges would have been balanced, whereas the

FIGURE 8.6 Photo of the cache in Structure N148a, showing a hole in the plaster floor made in the middle of the Classic period to deposit a Hunabchen red tripod cajete. The floor and cajete were later covered with platform fill.

kinds of exchanges into which N148 and its neighbors entered were probably not balanced. Thus, 38s14 and 42s2 had the least amount of authority compared to Izamal, Ucí, Kancab, and N148. Excavations in 38s14 and 42s2 turned up a cache in each platform. In 38s14, the cache consisted of a single Saban jar placed above bedrock and covered by the fill of the platform. The platform had a single construction episode. Since we did not see any evidence of a pit dug into the platform, we presume the pot was placed in the platform during its construction. In 42s2, a polished greenstone axe and sherds from a Chancenote striated jar were placed in the construction fill of an eastern addition to the basal platform.

Caches like the ones described at Kancab, N148, 38s14, and 42s2 are not easy to interpret, as they could represent building dedications, building terminations, or other kinds of rites (Becker 1993; Chase and Chase 1998). However, the fact that most of them appear to have been deposited as part of construction episodes suggests that they represent building dedications. True to the monistic principle discussed in the introduction, both modern and ancient Maya consider the house as a living being (Gillespie 2000:136, Stuart 1998:395). Houses therefore require nourishment. Offerings of various types, but often of pots containing food, provide this nourishment and make the house an appropriate and safe place for habitation. Dedicatory caches placed into the ground can be seen more broadly as earth offerings: compensation to the gods for materials taken to build the structure, and food for the gods to renew life and continue the cycle of being (Becker 1993:67–68; Vogt 1998:21).

Though the sample of caches described above is small, we have found caches in every building where UCRIP has exposed at least 50 percent of the building's surface. Our finds suggest intriguing points for continued discussion. Caching rites at three different levels of authority – town center (Kancab), village head (N148), and modest households (38S14, 42S2) – share close similarities: the deposition of complete or nearly complete pots. This similarity in caches is important because it suggests that members of rural farmsteads, the leaders of a village, and the leaders of a local center (Kancab) each adhered to the same religious premises regarding building dedication. In other words, in relatively isolated locales such as rural villages and farmsteads, we do not see practices that clearly diverge from what leaders in centers are doing. Yet this does not imply that people at the bottom of the social hierarchy have accepted a dominant ideology (Lohse 2007). Rather than buying into a system of belief that benefits central authorities, people making offerings are working for their own well-being. They serve themselves in abiding by principles regarding the ontological status of buildings as social actors and the indebtedness between the building, its occupants, and other entities. Critically, the fact that people do this work in their own homes stands as an additional sign of their empowerment. Furthermore, when leaders with a greater scale of authority perform the kinds of rites that also take place in the homes of followers, these followers' knowledge of the rites positions them as actors who can judge whether or not a leader performs the rite properly. Thus, by performing rites independently of central authorities, people at N148, 38Ss14, and 42s2 may not have invented new rituals, but they did increase their leverage for engaging and constraining the practices and performances of more powerful leaders. UCRIP has not yet uncovered traces of performances at the next highest scale of authority, represented by the leaders of Ucí, located between 4 km and 8 km from the locales discussed above. There are likely to be variations in ritual performance at all scales, intimated already by the fact that not all building dedications uncovered thus far involved whole pots.

Conclusion

In this chapter, we have addressed two of the three themes also developed by other authors in this book: the role of religion in negotiating authority; and how indigenous, relational ontologies affect the politicization of religion/ritual (A. Joyce, Chapter 1). Regarding relational ontology, the monistic principle that we describe in the introduction holds that vital forces inhabit entities and locations with which ancient Maya people had regular contact. As a consequence, ritual behavior is not so easily circumscribed and tends to blend in with the other workaday tasks. True to this principle, the evidence for ancestor veneration at places like Chunchucmil and offerings found in a wide variety of buildings near Ucí imply that other-than-human entities were always close at hand in the ancient Maya world. Whereas it was once thought that ritual practice appeared in common Maya households only in the Postclassic, the data in this chapter once again show that people from a very broad cross-section of ancient Maya society took religion into their own hands well before the Postclassic (Leventhal 1983; Lucero 2003). If anything, household rites in the Ucí-Cansahcab area during the Postclassic period became less frequent: sherds from ceremonial censers are rarely found in Postclassic period residences.

Whereas the data from the Ucí-Cansahcab area lend themselves to vertical comparisons – e.g. differences and similarities in rites at various scales of authority – the comparisons of ancestor shrines at Chunchucmil focused more on differences between households of relatively similar power. Yet in both contexts – Chunchucmil and Ucí-Cansahcab – political life builds from religious practice. For Chunchucmil, we argued that ceremonies for ancestors played an important role both in the negotiation of power relations within the household and in establishing differences in symbolic capital between households. People performed ceremonies in order to send messages both within and beyond the houselot walls, making politics multi-scalar. We speculate that even though Chunchucmil's leaders may not have attended these neighborhood-scale rites, preoccupation with such rites and the broader project of identity creation at the level of the household may have taken attention away from unequal aspects of relations between household and state. In other words, the heavily localized politics of these rituals might have lessened the potential for transforming the broader political system.

The discussion of household ritual in the Ucí-Cansahcab area showed that caching within households with the most limited authority – rural farmsteads – was not very different from caching by actors with more clout. Despite this lack of differentiation, we argued that humble households were not duped by a dominant ideology. Rather, by conducting their own rites, they empowered themselves in two ways. First, they did the religious work necessary to make their lives safe and productive. Second, they gained the kind of familiarity with ritual labor that made them knowledgeable judges of the quality and appropriateness of ritual performances by leaders. In the Maya area, where ritual performance was a chief source of authority, such knowledge gave these farmers leverage in the engagements that reproduce and transform the status quo.

Acknowledgments

The UCRIP fieldwork discussed above was permitted by the Consejo de Arqueología, INAH, funded by NSF (BCS 1063667), and done with the help of Céline Lamb, Isabelle Martinez Muñiz, David Medina, Shannon Plank, Joe Stair, Daniel Vallejo-Cáliz, Iliana Ancona, and Millie Westmont.

References

Ardren, Traci, and Chelsea Blackmore 2001 Excavations at the Lool Group. In *Pakbeh Regional Economy Program: Report of the 2001 Field Season*, edited by Bruce Dahlin and Daniel Mazeau, pp. 69–73. Department of Sociology/Anthropology, Howard University, Washington, D.C.

Ashmore, Wendy, and Richard Wilk 1988 Household and Community in the Mesoamerican Past. In *Household and Community in the Mesoamerican Past*, edited by Richard Wilk and Wendy Ashmore, pp. 1–27. University of New Mexico Press, Albuquerque.

Ashmore, Wendy, Jason Yaeger, and Cynthia Robin 2004 Commoner Sense: Late and Terminal Classic Social Strategies in the Xunantunich Area. In *The Terminal Classic in the Maya Lowlands: Collapse, Transition and Transformation*, edited by Arthur A. Demarest, Prudence M. Rice, and Donald S. Rice, pp. 302–323. University Press of Colorado, Boulder.

Astor-Aguilera, Miguel A. 2010 *The Maya World of Communicating Objects: Quadripartite Crosses, Trees, and Stones.* University of New Mexico Press, Albuquerque.

Barrera Vazquez, Alfredo 1980 *Diccionario Maya Cordemex.* Ediciones Cordemex, Merida, Yucatan, Mexico.

Becker, Marshall 1991 Plaza Plans at Tikal, Guatemala and at other Lowland Maya Sites: Evidence for Patterns of Culture Change. *Cuadernos de Arquitectura Mesoamericana* 14: 11–26.

———. 1993 Earth Offering Among the Classic Period Lowland Maya: Burials and Caches as Ritual Deposits. In *Perspectivas Antropológicas en el Mundo Maya*, edited by Ma. Josefa Iglesias Ponce de León y Francesc Ligorred Perramon, pp. 45–74. Sociedad Española de Estudios Mayas, Madrid.

Bell, Catherine 1992 *Ritual: Perspectives and Dimensions.* Oxford University Press, Oxford.

Blackmore, Chelsea 2011 Ritual Among the Masses: Deconstructing Identity and Class in an Ancient Maya Neighborhood. *Latin American Antiquity* 22: 159–177.

Borhegyi, Stephan de 1956 The Development of Folk and Complex Cultures in the Southern Maya Area. *American Antiquity* 21: 343–356.

Bourdieu, Pierre 1990 *The Logic of Practice.* Translated by Richard Nice. Stanford University Press, Stanford.

Brück, Joanna 1999 Ritual and Rationality: Some Problems of Interpretation in European Prehistory. *European Journal of Archaeology* 2: 313–344.

Brumfiel, Elizabeth. M. 1996 Figurines and the Aztec State: Testing the Effectiveness of Ideological Domination. In *Gender and Archaeology*, edited by Rita P. Wright, pp. 143–166. University of Pennsylvania, Philadelphia.

Burkhart, Louise M. 1989 *The Slippery Earth: Nahua-Christian Moral Dialogue in Sixteenth Century Mexico*. University of Arizona Press, Tucson.

Carmean, Kelli, Patricia A. McAnany, and Jeremy A. Sabloff 2011 People Who Lived in Stone Houses: Local Knowledge and Social Difference in the Classic Maya Puuc Region. *Latin American Antiquity* 22: 143–158.

Cecil, Leslie, and Timothy Pugh, eds. 2009 *Maya Worldviews at Conquest*. University Press of Colorado, Boulder.

Chase, Diane Z., and Arlen F. Chase 1998 The Architectural Context of Caches, Burials and other Ritual Activities for the Classic Period Maya (as Reflected at Caracol, Belize). In *Function and Meaning in Classic Maya Architecture*, edited by Stephen D. Houston, pp. 299–332. Dumbarton Oaks, Washington, DC.

Clark, John E. 1989 Obsidian: The Primary Mesoamerican Sources. In *La obsidiana en Mesoamerica*, edited by Margarita Gaxiola and John E. Clark, pp. 299–319. Instituto Nacional de Antropología e Historia, Mexico.

———.2003 A Review of 20th Century Obsidian Studies. In *Mesoamerican Lithic Technology: Experimentation and Interpretation*, edited by Kenneth G. Hirth, pp. 15–54. University of Utah Press, Salt Lake City.

Coggins, Clemency Chase 1980 The Shape of Time: Some Political Implications of a Four-Part Figure. *American Antiquity* 45: 727–739.

———. 1988 Classic Maya metaphors of Death and Life. *Res* 16: 65–84.

Demarest, Arthur A. 1992 Ideology in Ancient Maya Cultural Evolution: The Dynamics of Galactic Polities. In *Ideology and PreColumbian Civilizations*, edited by Arthur A. Demarest and Geoffrey Conrad, pp. 135–158. School for Advanced Research Press, Santa Fe.

Dunning, Nicholas P., Eric Weaver, Michael P. Smyth, and David Ortegon Zapata 2014 Xcoch: Home of the Ancient Maya Rain Gods and Water Managers. In *The Archaeology of Yucatan*, edited by Travis Stanton, pp. 45–64. Archaeopress, Oxford.

Fogelin, Lars 2007 The Archaeology of Ritual. *Annual Review of Anthropology* 36: 55–71.

Fry, Robert 1979 The Economics of Pottery at Tikal, Guatemala: Models of Exchange for Serving Vessels. *American Antiquity* 44: 494–512.

Gillespie, Susan D. 2000 Maya 'Nested Houses': The Ritual Construction of Place. In *Beyond Kinship*, edited by Rosemary A. Joyce and Susan D. Gillespie, pp. 135–160. University of Pennsylvania Press, Philadelphia.

Golden, Charles, and Andrew Scherer 2013 Territory, Trust, Growth, and Collapse in Classic Period Maya Kingdoms. *Current Anthropology* 54: 397–435.

Gonlin, Nancy 2007 Ritual and Ideology Among Classic Maya Rural Commoners at Copán, Honduras. In *Commoner Ritual and Ideology in Ancient Mesoamerica*, edited by Nancy Gonlin and Jon C. Lohse, pp. 83–122. University Press of Colorado, Boulder.

Gossen, Gary 1974 *Chamulas in the World of the Sun*. Harvard University Press, Cambridge, MA.

Hamann, Byron 2002 The Social Life of Pre-Sunrise Things: Indigenous Mesoamerican Archaeology. *Current Anthropology* 43: 351–382.

———. 2008 Chronological Pollution: Potsherds, Mosques, and Broken Gods Before and After the Conquest of Mexico. *Current Anthropology* 49: 803–836.

Hammond, Norman 1991 Inside the Black Box: Defining Maya Polity. In *Classic Maya Political History*, edited by T. Patrick Culbert, pp. 253–84. Cambridge University Press, Cambridge.

Hanks, William 1990 *Referential Practice: Language and Lived Space Among the Maya*. University of Chicago Press, Chicago.

Haviland, William A. 2014 *Excavations in Residential areas of Tikal: Non-elite Groups without Shrines: Analysis and Conclusions*. Tikal Report No. 20B. University of Pennsylvania Museum of Archaeology and Anthropology, Philadelphia.

Hendon, Julia A. 1997 Women's Work, Women's Space, and Women's Status among the Classic Period Maya Elite of the Copan Valley, Honduras. In *Women in Prehistory: North America and Mesoamerica*, edited by Cheryl Claassen and Rosemary Joyce, pp. 33–46. University of Pennsylvania Press, Philadelphia.

Hervik, Peter 1999 *Mayan People Within and Beyond Boundaries*. Harwood Academic Publishers, Amsterdam.

Hodder, Ian, and Scott R. Hutson 2003 *Reading the Past*. 3rd ed. Cambridge University Press, Cambridge.

Hostettler, Ueli 2001 Milpa, Land and Identity: A Central Quintana Roo Mayan Community in Historical Perspective. In *Maya Survivalism*, edited by Ueli Hostettler and Matthew Restall, pp. 239–263. Verlag Anton Sauerwin, Markt Schwaben, Germany.

Houston, Stephen D. 2013 *The Life Within: Classic Maya and the Matter of Permanence*. Yale University Press, New Haven.

Houston, Stephen D., and Takeshi Inomata 2009 *The Classic Maya*. Cambridge University Press, Cambridge.

Houston, Stephen D., and David Stuart 1996 Of Gods, Glyphs, and Kings: Divinity and Rulership among the Classic Maya. *Antiquity* 70: 289–312.

Houston, Stephen D., David Stuart, and Karl Taube 2006 *The Memory of Bones: Body, Being and Experience Among the Classic Maya*. University of Texas Press, Austin.

Hruby, Zachary X. 2007 Ritualized Lithic Production at Piedras Negras, Guatemala. In *Rethinking Craft Specialization in Complex Societies: Archaeological Analyses of the Social Meaning of Production*, edited by Zachary X. Hruby and Rowan Flad, pp. 68–87. Archeological Papers of the American Anthropological Association, No. 17. American Anthropological Association, Arlington, VA.

Hutson, Scott R. 2002 Built Space and Bad Subjects: Domination and Resistance at Monte Albán, Oaxaca, Mexico. *Journal of Social Archaeology* 2(1): 53–80.

———. 2010 *Dwelling, Identity and the Maya: Relational Archaeology at Chunchucmil*. Altamira, Lanham, MD.

———. 2013 "Recap: Four Reasons for Relationality." In *Classic Maya Political Ecology: Resource Management, Class Histories, and Political Change in Northwestern Belize*, edited by Jon C. Lohse, pp. 211–25. Cotsen Institute for Archaeology, University of California, Los Angeles.

Hutson, Scott R., Aline Magnoni, and Travis Stanton 2004 House Rules? The Practice of Social Organization in Classic Period Chunchucmil, Yucatan, Mexico. *Ancient Mesoamerica* 15: 74–92.

Hutson, Scott R., and Travis W. Stanton 2007 Cultural Logic and Practical Reason: The Structure of Discard in Ancient Maya Houselots. *Cambridge Archaeological Journal* 17(1): 123–144.

Hutson, Scott R., and Jacob A. Welch 2014 Sacred Landscapes and Building Practices at Ucí and Kancab Yucatan, Mexico. *Ancient Mesoamerica* 25: 421–439.

Inomata, Takeshi 2004 The Spatial Mobility of Non-Elite Populations in Classic Maya Society and Its Political Implications. In *Ancient Maya Commoners*, edited by Jon C. Lohse and Fred J. Valdez, Jr., pp. 175–196. University of Texas Press, Austin.

———. 2006 Plazas, Performers and Spectators: Political Theaters of the Classic Maya. *Current Anthropology* 47: 805–842.

Insoll, Timothy 2004 *Archaeology, Ritual, Religion.* Routledge, New York.

Joyce, Arthur A., and Sarah B. Barber 2015 Ensoulment, Entrapment, and Political Centralization: A Comparative Study of Religion and Politics in Later Formative Oaxaca. *Current Anthropology* 56: 819–847.

Joyce, Arthur A., Laura A. Bustamante, and Marc N. Levine 2001 Commoner Power: A Case Study from the Classic Period Collapse on the Oaxaca Coast. *Journal of Archaeological Method and Theory* 8: 343–385.

Joyce, Arthur A., and Erin T. Weller 2007 Commoner Rituals, Resistance, and the Classic to Postclassic Transition in Ancient Mesoamerica. In *Commoner Ritual and Ideology in Ancient Mesoamerica*, edited by Nancy Gonlin and Jon C. Lohse, pp. 143–184. University Press of Colorado, Boulder.

Joyce, Rosemary A. 2011 What Should an Archaeology of Religion Look Like to a Blind Archaeologist? In *Beyond Belief: The Archaeology of Religion and Ritual*, edited by Yorke M. Rowan, pp. 180–188. Archeological Papers of the American Anthropological Association 21, Arlington, VA.

Joyce, Rosemary A., and Julia A. Hendon 2000 Heterarchy, History, and Material Reality: "communities" in Late Classic Honduras. In *The Archaeology of Communities*, edited by Marcello A. Canuto and Jason Yaeger, pp. 143–169. Routledge, New York.

Kearney, Michael 1996 *Reconceptualizing the Peasantry.* Westview, Boulder.

Kertzer, David 1988 *Ritual, Politics and Power.* Yale University Press, New Haven.

Kurjack, Edward B. 1974 *Prehistoric Lowland Maya Community and Social Organization: A Case Study at Dzibilchaltun, Yucatan, Mexico.* Middle American Research Institute 38. Middle American Research Institute, New Orleans.

Kus, Susan, and Victor Raharijoana 2000 House to Palace, Village to State: Scaling Up Architecture and Ideology. *American Anthropologist* 102: 98–113.

Lamb, Céline, Daniel Vallejo Cáliz, and Scott Hutson 2014 *Current Explorations of the Formative-Classic Maya Hinterlands of Ucí.* Paper presented at the 79th annual meeting of the Society for American Archaeology, Austin.

Lansing, Stephen 1991 *Priests and Programmers.* Princeton University Press, Princeton.

Leventhal, Richard M. 1983 Household Groups and Classic Maya Religion. In *Prehistoric Settlement Patterns: Essays in Honor of Gordon R. Willey*, edited by Evon Z. Vogt and Richaed M. Leventhal, pp. 55–76. Peabody Museum of Archaeology and Ethnology, Harvard University, Cambridge.

Lohse, Jon C. 2007 Commoner Ritual, Commoner Ideology: (Sub-)Alternate View of Social Complexity in Prehispanic Mesoamerica. In *Commoner Ritual and Ideology in Ancient Mesoamerica*, edited by Nancy Gonlin and Jon C. Lohse, pp. 1–32. University Press of Colorado, Boulder.

Lucero, Lisa J. 2003 The Politics of Ritual: The Emergence of Classic Maya Kings. *Current Anthropology* 44: 523–558.

———. 2007 Classic Maya Temples, Politics, and the Voice of the People. *Latin American Antiquity* 18: 407–428.

Magnoni, Aline 2008 *From City to Village: Landscape and Household Transformations at Classic Period Chunchucmil, Yucatán, Mexico.* PhD dissertation, Department of Anthropology, Tulane University.

Magnoni, Aline, Scott R. Hutson, and Bruce H. Dahlin 2012 Living in the City: Settlement Patterns and the Urban Experience at Classic Period Chunchucmil, Yucatan, Mexico. *Ancient Mesoamerica* 23: 313–343.

Maldonado, C. R. 1995 Los Sistemas de Caminos del Norte de Yucatan. In *Seis Ensayos sobre Antiguos Patrones de Asentamiento en el Area Maya*, edited by E. Vargas Pacheco, pp. 68–92. Universidad Nacional Autónoma de México, Instituto de Investigaciones Antropológicas, Mexico, DF.

Martin, Simon, and Nikolai Grube 2008 *Chronicles of the Maya Kings and Queens*. 2nd ed. Thames and Hudson, London.

Masson, Marilyn A., and David Freidel 2012 An Argument for Classic-era Maya Market Exchange. *Journal of Anthropological Archaeology* 31: 455–484.

McAnany, Patricia A. 1995 *Living With the Ancestors: Kinship and Kingship in Ancient Maya Society*. University of Texas Press, Austin.

———. 2010 *Ancestral Maya Economies in Archaeological Perspective*. Cambridge University Press, Cambridge.

Monaghan, John 2000 Theology and History in the Study of Mesoamerican Religions. In *Supplement to the Handbook of Middle American Indians Volume 6: Ethnology*, edited by John Monaghan, pp. 24–49. Handbook of Middle American Indians Supplement. University of Texas Press, Austin.

Plank, Shannon E., Ancona Aragon, and Isabelle Martinez Muniz 2014 *Two Thousand Years of Ceramics along the Ucí-Cansahcab Causeway*. Paper presented at the 79th annual meeting of the Society for American Archaeology, Austin.

Rapoport, Amos 1982 *The Meaning of the Built Environment: A Nonverbal Communication Approach*. Sage, Beverly Hills.

Redfield, Robert, and Alfonso Villa Rojas 1962 *Chan Kom: A Maya Village*. Carnegie Institute of Washington Publication No. 448. Carnegie Institute of Washington, Washington, DC.

Redfield, Robert 1956 *Peasant Society and Culture*. University of Chicago Press, Chicago.

Robin, Cynthia 2002 Outside of Houses: The Practices of Everyday Life at Chan Nòohol, Belize. *Journal of Social Archaeology* 2: 245–267.

———. 2003 New Directions in Classic Maya Household Archaeology. *Journal of Archaeological Research* 11: 307–356.

———. 2004 Social Diversity and Everyday Life Within Classic Maya Settlements. In *Mesoamerican Archaeology: Theory and Practice*, edited by Julia A. Hendon and Rosemary A. Joyce, pp. 148–168. Blackwell, Malden.

Sahlins, Marshall 1996 The Sadness of Sweetness: The Native Anthropology of Western Cosmology. *Current Anthropology* 37: 395.

Scarborough, Vernon L., and Fred Jr. Valdez 2009 An Alternative Order: The Dualistic Economies of the Ancient Maya. *Latin American Antiquity* 20: 207–227.

Schele, Linda, and David A. Freidel 1990 *A Forest of Kings: The Untold Story of the Ancient Maya*. William Morrow, New York.

Schele, Linda, and Peter Mathews 1998 *The Code of Kings*. Quill, New York.

Schele, Linda, and Mary E. Miller 1986 *The Blood of Kings*. George Braziller, New York.

Scott, James C. 1990 *Domination and the Arts of Resistance*. Yale University Press, New Haven.

Sheets, Payson 2000 Provisioning the Ceren Household. *Ancient Mesoamerica* 11: 217–230.

Stuart, David 1998 "The Fire Enters His House": Architecture and Ritual in Classic Maya Texts. In *Function and Meaning in Classic Maya Architecture*, edited by Stephen D. Houston, pp. 373–425. Dumbarton Oaks, Washington, DC.

———. 2003 La Ideología del Sacrificio entre los Mayas. *Arqueología Mexicana* 11(63): 24–29.

———. 2011 *The Order of Days: The Maya World and the Truth About 2012*. Random House, New York.

Tourtellot, Gair 1983 An Assessment of Classic Maya Household Composition. In *Prehispanic Settlement Patterns: Essays in Honor of Gordon R. Willey*, edited by Evon Vogt and Richard Leventhal, pp. 35–54. Peabody Museum of Archaeology and Ethnology, Harvard University, Cambridge.

Tozzer, Alfred M. 1941 *Landa's Relación de las Cosas de Yucatan: A Translation*. Papers of the Peabody Museum of American Archaeology and Ethnology, Harvard University, vol. XVII. Peabody Museum of American Archaeology and Ethnology, Cambridge.

Vogt, Evon Z. 1998 Zinacanteco Dedication and Termination Rituals. In *The Sowing and the Dawning: Termination, Dedication, and Transformation in the Archaeological and Ethnographic Record of Mesoamerica*, edited by Shirley B. Mock, pp. 21–30. University of New Mexico Press, Albuquerque.

9

RITUAL IS POWER?

Religion as a possible base of power for early political actors in ancient Peru

Matthew Piscitelli

Introduction

There is a comprehensive body of literature focused on the archaeology of religion and ritual and the role that they played in ancient societies (e.g., Fogelin 2007; Kyriakidis 2007; Insoll 2001, 2004, 2011). Some see religion as a subset of the dominant ideology and conceptualize it as a way for elites to acquire and to legitimate their power (e.g., Bloch 1991; DeMarrais et al. 1996; Demarest and Conrad 1992; Fox 1996; Kertzer 1988). Others view religion through the lens of practice theory and reject these elite-centered structural assumptions. Instead, they argue that religious ritual is a means for individuals or groups to negotiate, to resist, and to shape existing social structures according to differing and often contradictory interests (e.g., Bell 1992, 1997; Comaroff 1985; Humphrey and Laidlaw 1994). These dichotomous approaches are not mutually exclusive; rather, they simply represent different views of power relationships with one emphasizing a top-down perspective and the other assuming a bottom-up one. The specific theoretical approach of any particular study is often contextual and depends on whether one is studying elites, commoners, or interactions between the two.

Aldenderfer (2010:77) suggests that achieving a consensus on a single cross-cultural and cross-theoretical definition of religion is too difficult, if not impossible, to accomplish. Rather, he argues that archaeologists should focus "on what religion *does*" (emphasis in original). From his survey, it is apparent that religion offers a worldview, defines group membership/identity, provides social cohesion, and, conversely, serves as a means to undermine existing power relationships (Aldenderfer 2010:80–81). This multitude of functions reflects how religion can act as an "enabler" (Aldenderfer 2010:82) depending on the context and the particular social or political actors involved in its creation, practice, and manipulation.

During the Late Archaic Period (3000–1800 B.C.), dramatic cultural transformations took place in the Central Andes, including changes in subsistence practices and socio-political organization (Haas and Creamer 2004, 2006; Shady 2004, 2006; Shady and Leyva 2003). In an area of four adjoining river valleys known locally as the *Norte Chico* ("Little North"), archaeological surveys have identified at least 30 sites dating to the third millennium B.C. (Engel 1987; Creamer et al. 2007, 2013; Ruiz and Nelson 2007; Shady et al. 2001; Williams and Merino 1979; Zechenter 1988). Each site consists of large-scale ceremonial architecture such as monumental platform mounds and sunken circular plazas, yet little is known about how religion played a role in the emerging social complexity that occurred during this time.

Many scholars have argued that the monumentality of these ceremonial buildings is indicative of centralized leadership and decision-making (Feldman 1985; Haas and Creamer 2012; Haas et al. 2005; Pozorski and Pozorski 1987; Shady 2006). This reasoning reflects what Abrams (1989:53) refers to as the "energetic analysis of architecture." According to this theoretical framework, public architecture is an outcome of energy flows expressed in human labor and building materials. The scale and elaboration of the structure(s) is dictated by an assumed linkage between control over resources and the level of social complexity, whereby monumental ceremonial architecture is an indication of political centralization (Abrams 1989; Adams 1975). However, recent excavations at several Late Archaic sites are beginning to complicate this proposed relationship between resource management and social complexity.

Until recently, calculations of labor expenditure and building volume have been based on survey data, which portray the mounds and plazas as static elements of the landscape. Results from intensive excavations at sites such as Caral (Shady 2004, 2006; Shady and Leyva 2003), Cerro Lampay (Vega-Centeno 2007, 2010), among others (Benfer 2012; Benfer et al. 2007; Fuchs et al. 2006, 2009), reveal a degree of architectural complexity as evidenced by the various construction stages, remodeling events, and renovations. Thus, the mounds and plazas no longer communicate the monolithic statement of political power and centralization as we see them today, but they become these ever-evolving elements of the built landscape that may reflect a more dynamic socio-political environment in the past. In addition, at a more basic level, the "energetic analysis of architecture" assumes a relatively narrow, top-down perspective to social relations. By exploring the building *process*, however, the mounds and plazas become dynamic products of collective action among a multitude of political actors. It is then possible to examine construction as a form of ritual activity, particularly in the case of ceremonial architecture. Such an approach is similar to Hruby's (2007) notion of "ritualized production" in which seemingly mundane activities, such as building a wall or floor, are intertwined with what may be considered more religious ones, like caching or entombment (Onuki 1999; Vega-Centeno 2007; see also Hutson et al., Chapter 8). A more nuanced exploration of building process allows for a better understanding of the role of religion in ancient society by considering a broader variety of political actors who may or may not have similar interests.

This entanglement between ritual practice and construction echoes recent trends in the archaeology of religion. Some scholars view religion as something to be "lived and experienced" and thus inseparable from other domains of social life (Aldenderfer 2012; Hodder 2014; Joyce and Barber 2015; R. Joyce 2012; see also Alt and Pauketat, Chapter 3). This perspective avoids modernist ontologies and foregoes the dichotomy between belief and practice (Fogelin 2007). Such an approach is also conducive to an indigenous Andean worldview in which the natural landscape and its mountains, rocks, and springs are imbued with a certain spirituality or sacredness (Allen 2002; Bauer 1998). Subsequently, the ancient mounds and plazas can be viewed as dynamic components of the landscape and conceptualized as "living, metabolizing organism[s]" (Swenson, Chapter 10; see also A. Joyce, Chapter 1; Dillehay 2007). From this perspective, it becomes possible to simultaneously conceive of the Late Archaic ceremonial architecture of the *Norte Chico* region as a symbol of political centralization and a means for groups to negotiate and/or resist the power and authority of early rulers.

Beyond considerations of the ceremonial architecture, one must also consider what kinds of activities occurred within these structures. Concomitantly, it is necessary to take a much closer look at the architectural features that may yield information about religious rituals. While archaeologists routinely find evidence of re-plastering and re-painting of floors and walls in ceremonial structures at Late Archaic sites, little attention is paid to the actual surfaces of the floors and walls themselves (Haas and Creamer 2006:755). Such repeatedly re-surfaced floors and walls reflect the cyclical nature of ritual preparation and performance (Boivin 2000; Matthews et al. 1997). These construction events give these floors and walls "life-histories" (Tringham 1994, 1995) or "biographies" (Gosden and Marshall 1999; Kopytoff 1986) that can be explored to examine ceremonial performance and scheduling (see Swenson, Chapter 10) when investigated at appropriately fine scales of observation.

This chapter presents the results of archaeological fieldwork at the Late Archaic site of Huaricanga in the Fortaleza Valley of Peru. Intensive excavations have revealed a complicated series of walls, floors, and structures built within a small mound that has been designated Mound B2. The laboratory analyses and resultant data follow a multidisciplinary methodology to investigate a series of superimposed ceremonial contexts within this mound (Piscitelli 2013b, 2014). Pollen analysis, soil chemistry, and micromorphology allow for a more thorough treatment of religion and its role in the dramatic cultural transformations of the Late Archaic *Norte Chico* region. By going beyond integration/centralization to investigate the various ways in which religion may have affected prehistoric politics, this chapter provides new explanations for the density of religious activity (i.e. ceremonial architecture and performance) along the north central Peruvian coast during the Late Archaic Period.

Huaricanga

Huaricanga is a dual component site located 23 km from the Pacific coast in the Fortaleza Valley of Peru (Figure 9.1). The Pativilca-Huaraz highway runs through

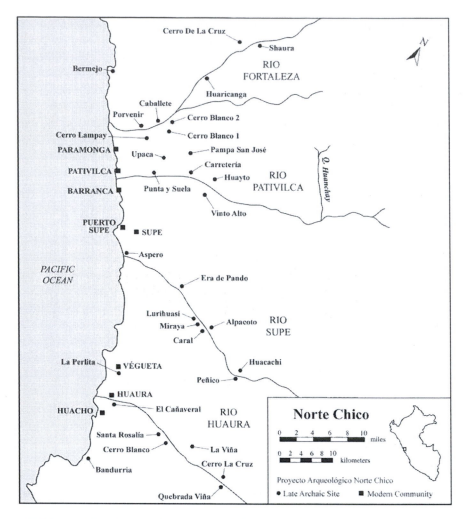

FIGURE 9.1 Map showing the location of Huaricanga along the north central coast of Peru in the Fortaleza Valley.

the main Late Archaic component of the site, which dates to between 3210 cal. B.C. and 2130 cal. B.C.[1] (Creamer et al. 2013:Tables 31–31b; Haas et al. 2013:Table SI 1). There is also a later Initial Period (1800-900 B.C.) component on the north side of the site. The Late Archaic architecture consists of six platform mounds and two, possibly three, sunken circular plazas. The Initial Period portion of the site, known as *El Castillo de Huaricanga*, is comprised of three platform mounds arranged in a U-shape (Authier 2012).

Approximately 20 m west of the Pativilca-Huaraz highway is a mound designated Mound B2, which measures 29 m by 29 m at its base and stands 3 m

FIGURE 9.2   General photo of Mound B2 taken prior to the 2012 season looking toward the north-northwest. Note the modern irrigation canal that cuts through the mound.

tall (Figure 9.2). Preliminary excavations in 2007 on the summit of Mound B2 revealed a 7 m by 8 m structure with a two-level plastered floor built atop an 8 m by 10 m structure that also has a plastered floor (see Operation VII in Ruiz and Haas 2007). These buildings were constructed on an approximately 1-m-thick layer of boulders that had been used to elevate the height of Mound B2. Below this large-scale construction fill are additional floors that became the focus of investigations carried out by the Huaricanga Archaeological Research Project (HARP) in 2012. The lack of residential features such as cooking hearths and domestic trash, the labor and material investment involved in constructing the permanent architectural features, and the proximity to the ceremonial core of the site distinguish the Mound B2 structures from household architecture at Huaricanga. These superimposed buildings offer an ideal laboratory to explore changing religious ritual and ceremonial architecture over time.

Evidence from Mound B2 at Huaricanga

A proposed construction sequence for Mound B2 is presented in Figure 9.3. The sequence consists of four phases and several sub-phases of construction (see Piscitelli 2014 for a more thorough description).

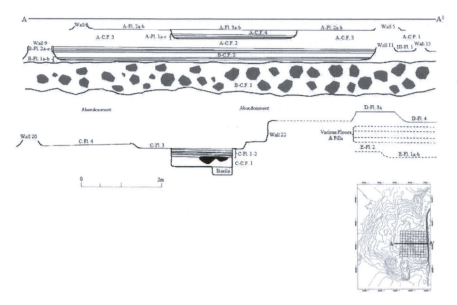

FIGURE 9.3 Cumulative profile of Mound B2 demonstrating the relative positions of the various structures and the spatial relationships between the architectural elements

Phase 1

Construction began in the area of Mound B2 around 3500 cal. B.C. when the ancient inhabitants built a two-level structure with plastered surfaces (Room E). The lower-level floor of Room E (E-Fl. 1a–b in Figure 9.3) consists of two layers, or what has been termed a "package" of floors (Piscitelli 2014). The first (lowermost) layer, or *falso piso*, consists of sediment that was applied and spread by hand and foot. Plant fibers were incorporated into the building material to strengthen the *falso piso*. This second layer in the floor package contains fewer plant fibers and has an overall smoother appearance. Observations made using a scanning electron microscope on a similar floor demonstrated the presence of cotton fibers in this formally prepared surface. These fibers were probably left by the brushes used to smooth the layer. Unlike the *falso piso*, no handprints or footprints were noted on these carefully constructed surfaces.

Two burn marks were noted on the surface of E-Fl. 1a. These features demonstrate that materials were burned directly on the floors, and the carbonized remains from the burning event were then swept up and deposited elsewhere. Micromorphological analysis revealed that the burning events reached a high temperature only possible through direct contact with fire. The lack of material debris on the floors suggests that the interior of the structure was carefully maintained.

Room E was eventually remodeled and a layer of construction fill (E-C.F. 1; not visible in Figure 9.3), principally consisting of fragmented shell, was used to cover the lower-level floor of the structure. Internal stratification in this fill deposit suggests that it was built in parts as if discrete units or perhaps basketfuls of material were added over time. E-C.F. 1 served as the foundation for another package of floors that transformed Room E from a two-level structure to a single-level one. The new *falso piso* and formally prepared plastered floor (E-Fl. 3a-b; not visible in Figure 9.3) also served as stages for additional burning events similar to those that occurred on the lower-level floor.

To the west of Room E is an additional superimposed series of elements that includes two plastered use surfaces, a construction fill, and another two-level structure. The gray color of the earliest floors (C-Fl. 1 and C-Fl. 2 in Figure 9.3) in this area is indicative of weathering, and the presence of hearths and the overall density of activity (depressions, stains, and burn marks) suggest that these floors were part of an outdoor patio or activity area. An abundance of fish bone was recovered from C-Fl. 1, C-Fl. 2, and an early construction fill (C-C.F. 1 in Figure 9.3), which indicates that small schooling fish and other slightly larger species were processed in that area. No radiocarbon dates were obtained from these floors, although architectural elements from the overlying two-level structure (Room C) date to between approximately 2500 and 2400 cal. B.C.

Room C contains two formally prepared plastered floors (C-Fl. 3 and C-Fl. 4) (Figure 9.4; also see Figure 9.3). Unlike the adjacent Room E, there are no *falso pisos*. In addition, there are no burn marks. However, there is a significant shift in the material culture found within Room C over time. Most of the specimens associated with C-Fl. 3 and C-Fl. 4 are plant fragments, while C-Fl. 1, C-Fl. 2, and C-C.F. 1 are primarily associated with bone specimens. This shift in the types of materials recovered may reflect a diachronic change in the activities that occurred in this area.

Phase 2

Room E was buried during the second construction phase on Mound B2 while Room C continued to function. Several layers of construction fill were deposited on top of the structure. The unique characteristics of each one of these fills indicate that each may have had a different origin. Phytolith and starch grain analyses revealed that clusters of burned rocks incorporated into the fills were used to prepare foodstuffs. Vega-Centeno (2007) documented similar features at Cerro Lampay that he interprets as leftovers from feasting events designed to recruit potential laborers. The quantity of burned rocks and possible comestibles makes such an interpretation unlikely. Instead, the foodstuffs may have been prepared as offerings to facilitate successful construction similar to *pagos* (literally "payments") practiced by modern shamans in the Central Andes to ensure positive outcomes in a variety of social contexts.

Room D is another two-level structure with plastered floors (Figure 9.5). These floors consist of both *falso pisos* and formally prepared plastered surfaces. The upper-level floor was built around the lower-level floor in order to create a sunken central area. Like Room E, burning events occurred on several of the floors.

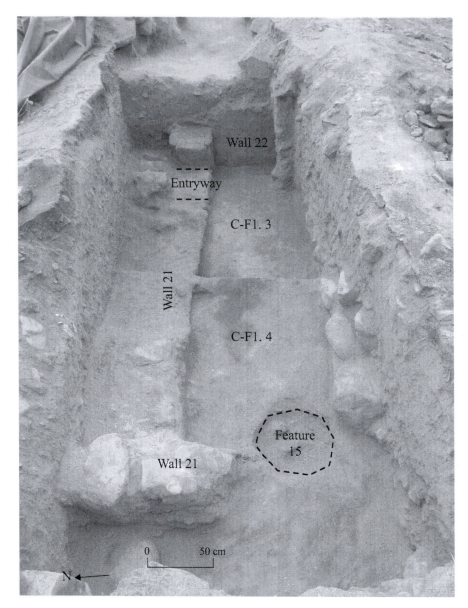

FIGURE 9.4 A photo of Room C with various architectural elements highlighted

Room D was eventually remodeled, but the two-level design was not altered. Instead, the width of the lower-level floor was changed twice during the use of the room. The first remodeling event involved narrowing the lower surface from 2.3 m (north-south) to 1.3 m (north-south), and the second reduced the sunken surface further so that it measured only 0.9 m wide (north-south). The earliest

FIGURE 9.5   Profile view of Room D taken from across the irrigation canal. The lines indicate the various versions of the structure as it underwent remodeling. Note the progressive reduction in the size of the lower space over time.

dates from Room D-1 indicate that construction may have begun between 3000 and 3100 cal. B.C., although the later manifestations of Room D (Room D-2 and Room D-3) date to between 2400 and 2300 cal. B.C. The discrepancy in radiocarbon dates may indicate that the proposed lower-level floor from Room D-1 (D-Fl. 1) was misinterpreted. However, the overlap in radiocarbon dates among contexts associated with Room D-2 and Room D-3 suggest generational remodeling.

Abandonment

Following the second phase of occupation, Mound B2 was abandoned for an unspecified period of time. Construction stopped and the inhabitants would occasionally deposit trash on the surface of the mound. A single radiocarbon date of 2520 cal. B.C. was obtained from this layer. While this date is earlier than the dates from the underlying Room D (Phase 2), plant fibers from fill contexts are more likely to represent older specimens (i.e., the "old wood" problem) than the annual plant fibers typically incorporated into floors. During this time, an abundance of material remains (relative to the other occupations) was deposited on Mound B2 and there is an increased presence of coprolites (human and dog). The continued deposition of trash suggests that despite the relative pause in construction activity, Mound B2 was still part of the collective memory of those who came to the site, and eventually the ancient inhabitants would return to the mound.

Phase 3

At the onset of the third construction phase, the builders drastically transformed the surface of Mound B2. A massive construction fill consisting of boulders was deposited to elevate the height of the mound and to level it for subsequent construction. During this occupation (Phase 3a), an 8 m (north-south) by 10 m (east-west) building called Room B was constructed (Figure 9.6). Room B exhibits a single-level design with entryways on the eastern and western sides of the structure. The interior floor consists of another package of surfaces (B-Fl. 1a–b in Figure 9.3).

A series of burning events took place in the western half of the first version of Room B. Pollen remains revealed that several species of domesticated crops, such as maize (*Zea mays*) and potato (*Solanum/Lycopersicon* sp.), as well as wild fruits, including guava (*Psidium guava*), were consumed/used/prepared. X-ray fluorescence (XRF) spectrometry confirms these results because elevated levels of potassium (K), which is often associated with wood ash and fire-related activities such as food processing (Entwistle et al. 1998; Middleton and Price 1996), were noted around the burn marks. To the east of Room B was another structure, but this building has been destroyed by modern irrigation canal and associated construction activity.

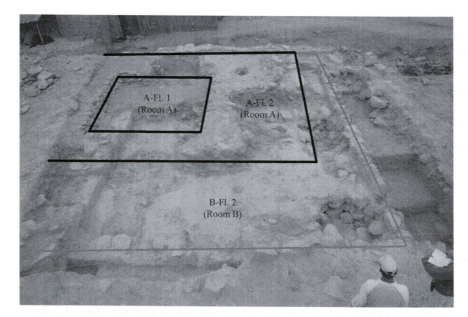

FIGURE 9.6   An image of Room A demonstrating its position relative to Room B

Room B was also remodeled during the third occupation period of Mound B2. A series of construction fills were deposited over the interior floor, which eventually served as the base for another package of surfaces. The dimensions of the entire structure remained the same and the entryways were still utilized. The nature of this new interior floor (B-Fl. 2a–c in Figure 9.3) was slightly different than its predecessor because an additional *falso piso* was added. Burning events continued to occur on this new set of floors although the focus of activity moved toward the center of the new version of Room B (Room B-2). There are indications on the burn marks of the materials having been arranged in a circular shape with an "X" in the center before the perishable remains were carbonized. Once again, the burned materials were swept up and deposited elsewhere. Radiocarbon dating of Room B and its associated features reveals that it was used between 2400 and 2300 cal. B.C.

Phase 4

During the final Late Archaic occupation on Mound B2, the entire surface was buried with several deposits of construction fill. These fills served as the foundation for another two-level structure called Room A (see Figure 9.6). Room A measures 7 m (north–south) by 8 m (east–west). The lower floor of Room A is approximately 3.5 m per side and consists of two *falso pisos* (A-Fl. 1b–c in Figure 9.3) and a formally prepared plastered floor (A-Fl. 1a in Figure 9.3). This lower level is surrounded on all sides by an elevated surface that is also a package of surfaces, albeit with only a single *falso piso* (A-Fl. 2a–b in Figure 9.3). The design of Room A with its centrally located sunken area recalls the layout of Room D, and burn marks in the middle of Room A on its lower-level floor indicate a continuation of the practice of burning events. Room A was eventually remodeled and, like Room E, the two-level structure became a single-level one. Construction fill (A-C.F. 4 in Figure 9.3) was deposited over the lower floor, and another *falso piso* (A-Fl. 3b in Figure 9.3) and formally prepared plastered surface (A-Fl. 3a in Figure 9.3) were built. Based on radiocarbon dates, Room A was used between 2400 and 2300 cal. B.C.

Discussion

The research conducted on Mound B2 at Huaricanga demonstrates a number of patterns in construction techniques, floor design, and activity performance throughout all the occupations. Cross-cultural ethnographic data (Artemova and Korotayev 2003; Winkelman 1990) and archaeological research (e.g., Chang 2005; Eliade 1964; Friedel 2008; Marcus and Flannery 2004; McAnany 1995) suggest that if political actors were using religious ritual as a source of power, then one would expect to see a gradual standardization of ceremonial practices and structures as individuals attempted to ascertain a degree of control over ideology. However, there is also considerable variation and certain idiosyncrasies that suggest a more complicated relationship between religion and political power during this early period in Andean prehistory.

Throughout the entire construction sequence, floors consist of a *falso piso* underlying a more formally prepared plastered layer – what is referred to here as a "package" of floors. Over multiple generations, there was a shared method for constructing floors that partly distinguishes these spaces from residential structures elsewhere at Huaricanga, which are characterized by packed earth floors made with coarse sediments and not with the elaborate treatment demonstrated on Mound B2 (Creamer et al. 2013:55). The consistency in floor construction practiced on Mound B2 may demonstrate a conservative tradition of building passed on from generation to generation.

There is also general preference for the construction of two-level structures during the occupation history of Mound B2. Four of the five rooms were dual-level buildings at some point during their life histories. However, the interior layouts of these two-level structures are not consistent. Only Room D and Room A exhibit centrally-located, sunken areas surrounded by upper-level floors. Room C, on the other hand, appears as though the entire western half of the room was elevated, and the same may hold true for the south side of Room E. The experimentation with the ground plan indicates that while there was some patterning in the architecture, there was still no consensus on the arrangement(s) of space over time.

The act of remodeling the various buildings on Mound B2 is another consistent diachronic pattern. In Room D, for example, the size of the lower-level floor was reduced in order to accommodate more private, face-to-face interactions. In the other instances, the purposes of the reconstruction are not as apparent. The transformations of Room E and Room A from two-level buildings to single-level ones, for example, may reflect stylistic preferences of those responsible for designing and/or building the structures. Alternatively, the function of the room may have changed. Such renovations to ritual spaces provided a venue for the performance of religious practices whereby participants could establish, manipulate, or reaffirm social relationships through ceremonial activity and/or construction (Dillehay 2004).

Despite the patterns noted above, there is variation in the overall layout of the surface of Mound B2 over time. During the earliest construction phases, there are several small structures and floors (Room E, Room C, and VI-Fl. 1) distributed across the entire mound surface. Following the abandonment period, these scattered, small buildings were replaced by a single large room that dominates the mound surface. The shift toward fewer, larger structures may suggest an increased investment in ceremonial architecture and/or increased centralization of activity performance. By focusing ceremonial activity within a single room, the ancient inhabitants may have been trying to better control who performed religious rituals. The diachronic changes in surface layout on Mound B2 may have also been related to the size and nature of the audience, participants, and/or the activities themselves.

In terms of the actual activities that took place within these structures, burning events occurred on almost all of the floors. Pollen analysis and XRF confirm that both domesticated and wild crops were placed directly onto the surfaces and burned. Slight differences in the colors of the burn marks and reddening/blackening on stone tools suggest that different types of materials (e.g., shell, bone, or stone) may have been used as well. Such activities are reminiscent of the ceremonies performed by contemporary shamans in the Central Andes who make offerings or *pagos* to placate local deities and to evoke positive outcomes (see description in Moore 2005:49–51). Burn areas were also documented by Vega-Centeno (2007, 2010) within ceremonial structures at the Late Archaic site of Cerro Lampay, also in the Fortaleza Valley. These two cases provide further evidence that such burned offerings were religious or ceremonial in nature. The exact locations of the burning events change over time and thus do not demonstrate any great degree of standardization. For example, the burn marks in Room B-1 are located on the western half of the floor near the entryway. Once Room B-2 was built, the location of the burning events changed and the center of the floor became the focus of activity. These shifting locations for activity performance may relate to the fact that the offerings were not made within permanent fire features like formally constructed hearths. Rather, the entire floor was an acceptable place for conducting these activities, and no specific rules determined where to make the offerings.

In addition to the burn marks, microscopic analysis such as pollen, micromorphology, and XRF revealed other traces of the activities that occurred within the structures on Mound B2. Microscopic bone, shell, and plant fragments embedded in several of the floors demonstrate that these materials were processed on the various surfaces. Furthermore, pollen analysis revealed the presence of certain plant species that are commonly used in traditional medicines. Thus, the structures may have been places of healing as well. However, many of these medicinal taxa are multi-functional and it is just as likely that they were used as dyes, fibers, or even fuel. Distinguishing between the possible uses is easiest when the plant variety serves a particularly unique function (e.g., hallucinogenic cacti). In most cases, though, it is not possible to determine the exact use. Synchronic variation in elemental enrichment also highlighted areas where food processing probably occurred. Indirect evidence of food processing is also manifested in the various grinding tools with starch grains and phytoliths that were recovered from secondary fill deposits as well as the burned rocks that were probably heated to prepare meals. These material traces of past activities are found throughout most of the proveniences in Mound B2. As previously mentioned, these food processing events may have served as offerings related to construction episodes.

Despite some variation in what occurred on the floors, there was a consistent effort over time to maintain clean surfaces. This cleanliness is also part of what characterizes the structures on Mound B2 as ceremonial architecture. Most of the broad observations were made using specimens from construction fills because these contexts provided more remains for analysis than the floors. The highly fragmented nature of both the shell and the bone remains indicate that these fills were extracted from nearby middens, but the exact origin of the building material is speculative. It seems logical, however, that such areas would have been located immediately around Mound B2. Despite having recovered shell, plant, and bone remains from various proveniences, only the lithics provide any significant diachronic patterning (across construction phases). Analysis of lithic material (see Piscitelli 2014:Appendix D) demonstrates a decrease in the number of stone tools and the diversity of tool types over time. These reductions may indicate that lithics were used less frequently or, alternatively, the variation in the types of activities was reduced, as is expected if behaviors became more restricted and formalized during later occupations.

The material culture from Mound B2 reflects the "local" character of the food and construction materials used by individuals who inhabited Huaricanga. Building materials were derived primarily from the areas surrounding the site. Micromorphological analysis of the sediments used to construct the floors and fills demonstrates that they are fluvial deposits from the nearby Fortaleza River. The incorporation of *yapana*, a form of naturally occurring clay found at the site, adds to the localness of the architecture and may reflect an attempt by the builders to identify themselves as locals. Many of the shell, plant, and bone taxa that were incorporated into fills and used in the various activities that occurred are also from the surrounding region. The faunal materials would have been acquired from the nearby coast that, at 25 km east, is only a day's walk away. Among these faunal remains are a variety of small schooling fish (sardines and anchovies) and other species (grunts, black drums, and gray mullets) that would have been caught using simple nets. The shellfish present include several varieties of mussels, clams, and chiton that would have been harvested from nearby sandy and rocky shorelines. Overall, the majority of the faunal taxa present are commonly found at other contemporary Late Archaic sites (see, e.g., Chu Barrera 2008; Creamer et al. 2013; Feldman 1985; Shady and Leyva 2003). In addition, most of the domesticated crops and wild fruits present in the botanical assemblage were grown locally. These plants would have been cultivated closer to the river floodplain, but within sight of the ceremonial architecture. The few non-local plant taxa such as quinoa (*Chenopodium/Amaranthus* sp.) and potato (*Solanum/Lycopersicon* sp.) would have been obtained from the highlands to the east of Huaricanga. Furthermore, there is a clear increase in the number of pollen grains from these two taxa over time that may indicate expanded contacts during later occupations.

These data from Mound B2 provide a nuanced look at how early political actors negotiated their social context through religious ritual. Situated at the foot of the principal mound at the site, the area around Mound B2 was likely under the purview of a specific community or some subset of a broader group that congregated at Huaricanga on a seasonal basis to participate in ceremonial activities. The series of small-scale ceremonial structures that were constructed served as meeting places for small congregations – such as community representatives or lineage heads – who performed burned offerings on the floors, perhaps in order to curry favor with deities or to adjudicate legal disputes. Across the occupations on Mound B2 there is variation in construction and certain aspects of activity performance. Burger and Salazar-Burger (1986) explain similar diversity in small-scale

ceremonial architecture from several highland Late Archaic sites by evoking different aspects of social organization (e.g., resource availability, responsibility, cargos).
It is possible that the structures on Mound B2 also reflect the ebbs and flows in
the socio-political and economic statuses of those responsible for maintaining and
using that area of Huaricanga. The idiosyncrasies may reflect factionalism within
the broader society or even maneuvering for political power. The evidence of
remodeling, whether the re-plastering of floors, sealing of entryways, or burial of
entire structures, may be interpreted as renewing rituals to reaffirm the associated
social contracts bound in the typical Andean exchange of labor for food. Dillehay (2004: 256), however, suggests that such remodeling events do not represent
buying into the existing social system, but are instead "deliberate pauses in ritual
action." The slight alterations to ceremonial architecture serve as a way for smaller
social units like households to slow the integrative process and to better negotiate
political centralization possibly reflected in the larger mounds elsewhere at the site.
Following Dillehay (2004), it is important to pay close attention to reflections of
the ritual calendar in the stratigraphy in order to glean the social tempo or rhythm
from cultural deposits. Such a fine-scale detail necessitates a more microscopic
approach that goes beyond what is normally extracted from just the walls and
floors.

Conclusion

As Haas and Creamer (2004, 2006, 2012) point out, the endogenous development
of these sites is remarkable for the size of the structures, the longevity of building
activity, and the relative standardization in design. Analyses of the Late Archaic
monumental architecture in the *Norte Chico* region predominately focus on the
motivations behind construction of such large-scale public structures (e.g., Haas
and Creamer 2012). Although recent data have confirmed the importance of agricultural products to the Late Archaic political economy (Haas et al. 2013), most
of the explanations for the associated cultural developments are best categorized as
"aggrandizer" models that privilege an economic base of power that, at best, posit a
complementary role for ideology (Roscoe 2008:78). Others have argued (Piscitelli
2013a; Roscoe 2008; Stanish and Haley 2005) that these models are good starting points given the available data that can only improve by incorporating a more
central role for ceremonial activity/religion as a means to promote cooperation and
collective action (see Carballo et al. 2012).

However, it is time to shift the focus from the question of "why?" to "why so
much?" Bell (1997:173) has used the term "ritual density" to help explain the une-
ven distribution of ritual practices throughout time and across space. Considering
the Late Archaic Central Andes as a whole, there are pockets of ceremonial architecture dotting the landscape, and then there is the *Norte Chico* region. Although
an area of only 1,800 km², there are 30 sites with plazas and mounds – some
measuring up to 300,000 m³ in volume. Large ceremonial centers with open plazas
spanning several hectares are situated just a 30-minute walk from one another.

Scholars working in the American Southwest have frequently made the connection between ceremonial architecture and social integration, particularly in times of stress (e.g., Lipe and Hegmon 1989). The dramatic cultural changes of the Late Archaic Period brought farmers and fishermen together – groups that operate on different celestial, and perhaps ritual, calendars. These disparate communities needed the fruits of each other's labor for survival, thus requiring ritually motivated staple finance to ensure social integration and to encourage the necessary interaction (Haas and Creamer 2004, 2006; Haas et al. 2005; cf. Stein 1994). However, the 1,800-year-long Late Archaic Period was not always a time of stress, but instead a time of relative stability. The excavation data from Mound B2 at Huaricanga as well as other Late Archaic sites in the *Norte Chico* region reveal a considerable amount of variation in ceremonial architecture and activity over that long period of time. That variation may reflect the efforts of local communities/factions to negotiate their socio-political status through religious expression. By serving as an outlet for resistance, religion may have facilitated the stability of the Late Archaic Period.

In addition, recent excavations along the coast of the *Norte Chico* region are revealing small-scale ceremonial buildings that challenge long-held tenets of Andean archaeology (Benfer 2012; Benfer et al. 2007; T. Pozorski and S. Pozorski 1996; Shady and Machacuay 2003 [2000]; Shady et al. 2003 [2000]). Traditionally we have drawn an etic distinction between the public, large-scale structures on the coast and the private, small-scale ceremonial chambers in the highlands (Donnan 1985; Moore 1996, 2005; Quilter 2014). Moreover, we conceptualize these architectural differences as reflections of alternative political strategies and power differentials. Aldenderfer (2005:13–14), for example, has argued that highland architecture represents "preludes to power" – material manifestations of political strategies that do not translate to the more persistent social formations evident on the coast. Continued investigations at coastal sites are revealing buildings that share many similarities to the architectural canons once thought to be unique to the highland regions of the Central Andes. Thus, the ceremonial landscape of the Late Archaic Period is not only dense, it is now more complicated, beckoning us to consider more nuanced understandings of the role of religion and religious ritual in the development of social complexity as well as how expressions of power and/ or political negotiation are manifested in architecture and activity performance.

The series of small-scale ceremonial architecture on Mound B2 at Huaricanga represents a fascinating and complex dataset. The juxtaposition of large-scale and small-scale buildings reveals the presence of multiple, contemporaneous venues for ceremonial performance. I suggest that ceremonial architecture in the Late Archaic *Norte Chico* region is more than an expression of political centralization and emergent leadership, but also an arena of political negotiation and more horizontally dispersed organizational structures. The communicative power of religious rituals, which are best reconstructed using a multidisciplinary approach, may have provided not only a base of power for early leaders, but also a source of leverage for different social units to negotiate that authority.

Acknowledgments

Funding for the 2012 excavations and analyses at Huaricanga was provided by the National Science Foundation (BCS-1249577), National Geographic Society, Curtiss T. & Mary G. Brennan Foundation, The Field Museum, University of Illinois at Chicago, The Vermont Community Foundation, as well as a successful crowdfunding campaign through Peerbackers. I would like to thank Jonathan Haas, Winifred Creamer, Sharlene Piscitelli, and Birgitta Piscitelli for their continued support. Lastly, this research would not have been possible without the help of Carmela Alarcón Ledesma, the community of Huaricanga, and all of the HARP team.

Note

1 All calibrated dates are weighted averages based on recalibrations made using CALIB 7.1 software and the SHCal13 calibration curve (Hogg et al. 2013). See Creamer et al. 2013:5 for how weighted averages are calculated.

References

Abrams, Eliot 1989 Architecture and Energy: An Evolutionary Perspective. In *Archaeological Method and Theory*, vol. 1, edited by Michael B. Schiffer, pp. 47–87. University of Arizona Press, Tucson.

Adams, Richard N. 1975 *Energy and Structure: A Theory of Social Power*. University of Texas Press, Austin.

Aldenderfer, Michael S. 2005 Preludes to Power in the Highland Late Preceramic Period. In *Foundations of Power in the Prehispanic Andes*, edited by Christina A. Conlee, Dennis Ogburn, and Kevin J. Vaughn, pp. 13–35. Archeological Papers of the American Anthropological Association, No. 14. American Anthropological Association, Arlington, VA.

——. 2010 Gimme That Old Time Religion: Rethinking the Role of Religion in the Emergence of Social Inequality. In *Pathways to Power*, edited by T. Douglas Price and Gary M. Feinman, pp. 77–94. Springer, New York.

Allen, Catherine J. 2002 *The Hold Life Has: Coca and Cultural Identity in an Andean Community*. Smithsonian Books, Washington, DC.

Artemova, Olga, and Andrey V. Korotayev 2003 Monopolization of Information and Female Status: A Cross-Cultural Test. *Cross-Cultural Research* 37(1): 81–96.

Authier, Martin 2012 *Monument, Memory, and Exchange at Huaricanga, Peru*. Paper presented at the 77th Annual Meeting of the Society for American Archaeology, Nashville.

Bauer, Brian S. 1998 *The Sacred Landscape of the Inca: the Cuzco Ceque System*. University of Texas Press, Austin.

Bell, Catherine 1992 *Ritual Theory, Ritual Practice*. Oxford University Press, Oxford.

——. 1997 *Ritual: Perspectives and Dimensions*. Oxford University Press, Oxford.

Benfer, Robert A. 2012 Monumental Architecture Arising from an Early Astronomical-Religious Complex in Perú, 220–1750 BC. In *Early New World Monumentality*, edited by Richard L. Burger and Robert M. Rosenswig, pp. 313–363. University Press of Florida, Gainesville.

Benfer, Robert A., Bernardino Ojeda, Neil A. Duncan, Larry R. Adkins, Hugo Ludeña, Miriam Vallejos, Victor Rojas, Andrés Ocas, Omar Ventocilla, and Gloria Villarreal

2007 La Tradición Religioso-Astronómica en Buena Vista. *Boletín de Arqueología PUCP* 11: 53–102.

Bloch, Maurice 1991 *Prey into Hunter: The Politics of Religious Experience*. Lewis Henry Morgan Lectures. Cambridge University Press, Cambridge.

Boivin, Nicole 2000 Life Rhythms and Floor Sequences: Excavating Time in Rural Rajasthan and Neolithic Catalhoyuk. *World Archaeology* 31: 367–388.

Burger, Richard, and Lucy Salazar-Burger 1986 Early Organizational Diversity in the Peruvian Highlands: Huaricoto and Kotosh. In *Andean Archaeology: Papers in Memory of Clifford Evans*, edited by Ramiro Matos, Solveig A. Turpin, and Herbert H. Eling, pp. 65–82. Monograph of the Institute of Archaeology, University of California, Los Angeles XXVII. Institute of Archaeology, University of California, Los Angeles.

Carballo, David M., Paul Roscoe, and Gary M. Feinman 2012 Cooperation and Collective Action in the Cultural Evolution of Complex Societies. *Journal of Archaeological Method and Theory* 21: 98–133.

Chang, Kwang-chih 2005 The Rise of Kings and the Formation of City-States. In *The Formation of Chinese Civilization: An Archaeological Perspective*, edited by Zhang Zhongpei, Xu Hung, and Wang Renxiang, pp. 125–140. Yale University Press, New Haven.

Chu Barrera, Alejandro 2008 *Bandurria: Arena, Mar y Humedal en el Surgimiento de la Civilización Andina*. Instituto Nacional de Cultura, Lima.

Comaroff, Jean 1985 *Body of Power, Spirit of Resistance: The Culture and History of a South African People*. University of Chicago Press, Chicago.

Creamer, Winifred, Alvaro Ruiz, and Jonathan Haas 2007 *Archaeological Investigation of Late Archaic Sites (3000–1800 B.C.) in the Pativilca Valley, Peru*. Fieldiana 40. Field Museum of Natural History, Chicago.

Creamer, Winifred, Alvaro Ruiz, Manuel F. Perales, and Jonathan Haas 2013 *The Fortaleza Valley, Peru: Archaeological Investigation of Late Archaic Sites (3000–1800 BC)*. Fieldiana 44. Field Museum of Natural History, Chicago.

Demarest, Arthur A., and Geoffrey W. Conrad, eds. 1992 *Ideology and Pre-Columbian Civilizations*. School for Advanced Research Press, Santa Fe.

DeMarrais, Elizabeth, Luis J. Castillo, and Timothy Earle 1996 Ideology, Materialization, and Power Strategies. *Current Anthropology* 37: 15–31.

Dillehay, Tom. D. 2004 Social Landscape and Ritual Pause. *Journal of Spatial Archaeology* 4: 239–268.

———. 2007 *Monuments, Empires, and Resistance: The Araucanian Polity and Ritual Narratives*. Cambridge University Press, Cambridge.

Donnan, Christopher, ed. 1985 *Early Ceremonial Architecture in the Andes*. Dumbarton Oaks, Washington, DC.

Eliade, Mircea 1964 *Shamanism: Archaic Techniques of Ecstasy*. Bollingen Series 76. Princeton University Press, Princeton.

Engel, Frédéric 1987 *De las Begonias al Maíz: Vida y Producción en le Perú Antiquo*. Ediagraria, Universidad Agraria La Molina, Lima.

Entwistle, Jane A., Peter W. Abrahams, and Robert. A. Dodgshon 1998 Multi-Element Analysis of Soils From Scottish Historical Sites: Interpreting Land-Use History From the Physical and Geochemical Analysis of Soil. *Journal of Archaeological Science* 25: 53–68.

Feldman, Robert A. 1985 Preceramic Corporate Architecture: Evidence for the Development of Non-Egalitarian Social Systems in Peru. In *Early Ceremonial Architecture in the Andes*, edited by Christopher B. Donnan, pp. 71–92. Dumbarton Oaks Research Library and Collection, Washington, DC.

Fogelin, Lars 2007 The Archaeology of Religious Ritual. *Annual Review of Anthropology* 36: 55–71.

Fox, John G. 1996 Playing with Power: Ballcourts and Political Ritual in Southern Mesoamerica. *Current Anthropology* 37: 483–509.

Friedel, David 2008 Maya Divine Kingship. In *Religion and Power: Divine Kingship in the Ancient World and Beyond*, edited by Nicole Brisch, pp. 191–206. The Oriental Institute of the University of Chicago, Chicago.

Fuchs, Peter R., Renate Patzschke, Claudia Schmitz, German Yenque, and Jesús Briceño 2006 Investigaciones Arqueológicas en el Sitio de Sechín Bajo, Casma. *Boletín de Arqueología PUCP* 10: 111–135.

———. 2009 Del Arcaico Tardío al Formativo Temprano: Las Investigaciones en Sechín Bajo, Valle de Casma. *Boletín de Arqueología PUCP* 13: 55–86.

Gosden, Chris, and Yvonne Marshall 1999 The Cultural Biography of Objects. *World Archaeology* 31: 169–178.

Haas, Jonathan, and Winifred Creamer 2004 Cultural Transformations in the Central Andean Late Archaic. In *Andean Archaeology*, edited by Helaine Silverman, pp. 35–50. Blackwell Publishing, Oxford, UK.

———. 2006 Crucible of Andean Civilization: The Peruvian Coast from 3000 to 1800 BC. *Current Anthropology* 47: 745–775.

———. 2012 Why Do People Build Monuments? Late Archaic Platform Mounds in the Norte Chico. In *Early New World Monumentality*, edited by Richard L. Burger and Robert M. Rosenswig, pp. 289–312. University Press of Florida, Gainesville.

Haas, Jonathan, Winifred Creamer, Luis H. Mesia, David Goldstein, Karl Reinhard, and Cindy V. Rodriguez 2013 Evidence for maize (*Zea mays*) in the Late Archaic (3000–1800 B.C.) in the Norte Chico region of Peru. *Proceedings of the National Academy of Sciences* 110: 4945–4949.

Haas, Jonathan, Winifred Creamer, and Alvaro Ruiz 2005 Power and the Emergence of Complex Societies in the Peruvian Preceramic. In *Foundations of Power in the Ancient Andes*, edited by Kevin J. Vaughn, Dennis Ogburn, and Christina Conlee, pp. 37–52. Archeological Papers of the American Anthropological Association, No. 14. American Anthropological Association, Arlington, VA.

Hodder, Ian, ed. 2014 *Religion at Work in a Neolithic Society: Vital Matters*. Cambridge University Press, Cambridge.

Hogg, Alan G., Quan Hua, Paul G. Blackwell, Mu Niu, Caitlin E. Buck, Thomas P. Guilderson, Timothy J. Heaton, Jonathan G. Palmer, Paula J. Reimer, Ron W. Reimer, Christian S. M. Turney, and Susan R. H. Zimmerman 2013 SHCal13 Southern Hemisphere Calibration, 0–50,000 Years Cal BP. *Radiocarbon* 55: 1889–1903.

Hruby, Zachary X. 2007 Ritualized Lithic Production at Piedras Negras, Guatemala. In *Rethinking Craft Specialization in Complex Societies: Archaeological Analyses of the Social Meaning of Production*, edited by Zachary X. Hruby and Rowan Flad, pp. 68–87. Archeological Papers of the American Anthropological Association, No. 17. American Anthropological Association, Arlington, VA.

Humphrey, Caroline, and James Laidlaw 1994 *The Archetypal Actions of Ritual: A Theory of Ritual Illustrated by the Jain Rite of Worship*. Oxford University Press, Oxford.

Insoll, Timothy 2004 *Archaeology, Ritual and Religion*. Routledge, London.

Insoll, Timothy, ed. 2001 *Archaeology and World Religions*. Routledge, London.

———. 2011 *The Oxford Handbook of the Archaeology of Ritual and Religion*. Oxford University Press, Oxford.

Joyce, Arthur A., and Sarah. B. Barber 2015 Ensoulment, Entrapment, and Political Centralization: A Comparative Study of Religion and Politics in Later Formative Oaxaca. *Current Anthropology* 52: 819–847.

Joyce, Rosemary 2012 What Should an Archaeology of Religion Look Like to a Blind Archaeologist? In *Beyond Belief: The Archaeology of Religion and Ritual*, edited by Yorke

M. Rowan, pp. 180–188. Archeological Papers of the American Anthropological Association, No. 21. American Anthropological Association, Arlington, VA.

Kertzer, David I. 1988 *Ritual, Politics, and Power*. Yale University Press, New Haven.

Kopytoff, Igor 1986 The Cultural Biography of Things: Commoditization as Process. In *The Social Life of Things: Commodities in Cultural Perspective*, edited by Arjun Appadurai, pp. 64–91. Cambridge University Press, Cambridge.

Kyriakidis, Evangelos, ed. 2007 *The Archaeology of Ritual*. Cotsen Institute of Archaeology, Los Angeles.

Lipe, William D., and Michelle Hegmon 1989 Historical and Analytical Perspectives on Architecture and Social Integration in the Prehistoric Pueblos. In *The Architecture of Social Integration in Prehistoric Pueblos*, edited by William D. Lipe and Michelle Hegmon, pp. 15–34. Occasional Papers, No. 1. Crow Canyon Archaeological Center, Cortez.

Marcus, Joyce, and Kent V. Flannery 2004 The Coevolution of Ritual and Society: New 14C Dates From Ancient Mexico. *Proceedings of the National Academy of Sciences* 101: 18257–18261.

Matthews, W., C. A. I. French, T. Lawrence, D. F. Cutler and M. K. Jones 1997 Microstratigraphic Traces of Site Formation Processes and Human Activities. *World Archaeology* 29: 281–308.

McAnany, Patricia A. 1995 *Living With the Ancestors: Kinship and Kingship in Ancient Maya Society*. University of Texas Press, Austin.

Middleton, William D., and T. Douglas Price 1996 Identification of Activity Areas by Multi-Element Characterization of Sediments from Modern and Archaeological House Floors Using Inductively Couples Plasma-Atomic Emission Spectroscopy. *Journal of Archaeological Science* 23: 673–687.

Moore, Jerry D. 1996 *Architecture and Power in the Ancient Andes: The Archaeology of Public Buildings*. Cambridge University Press, Cambridge.

———. 2005 *Cultural Landscapes in the Ancient Andes: Archaeologies of Place*. University Press of Florida, Gainesville.

Onuki, Yoshio 1999 El Periodo Arcaico en Huanuco y el Concepto del Arcaico. *Boletin de Arqueología PUCP* 3: 325–333.

Piscitelli, Matthew 2013a *Economy, Ritual, and Power in the Late Archaic Norte Chico*. Paper presented at 2013 Second City Anthropology Conference University of Illinois, Chicago, IL.

———. 2013b *A Brand New Toolbox: Using Modern Science to Reconstruct Ancient Ritual in Peru*. Paper presented at the 41st Annual Midwest Conference of Andean and Amazonian Archaeology and Ethnohistory. Dekalb, IL.

———. 2014 *Ritual Is Power? Late Archaic Small-Scale Ceremonial Architecture in the Central Andes*. Ph.D. dissertation, Department of Anthropology, University of Illinois, Chicago.

Pozorski, Shelia, and Thomas Pozorski 1987 *Early Settlements and Subsistence in the Casma Valley, Peru*. University of Iowa Press, Iowa City.

Pozorski, Thomas, and Sheila Pozorski 1996 Ventilated Hearth Structures in the Casma Valley, Peru. *Latin American Antiquity* 7: 341–353.

Quilter, Jeffrey 2014 *The Ancient Central Andes*. Routledge, London.

Roscoe, Paul 2008 Catastrophe and the Emergence of Political Complexity: A Social Anthropological Model. In *El Niño Catastrophe, and Culture Change in Ancient America*, edited by Daniel H. Sandweiss and Jeffrey Quilter, pp. 77–100. Dumbarton Oaks Research Library and Collection, Washington, DC.

Ruiz, Alvaro, and Kit Nelson 2007 *Proyecto de Investigación Arqueológica en el Valle de Huaura, Costa Norcentral del Perú, Lima – Perú*. Informe Final submitted to the Instituto Nacional de Cultura, Lima.

Ruiz, Alvaro, and Jonathan Haas 2007 *Informe: Excavacions en Huaricanga, Valle de Fortaleza, Perú*. Informe Final submitted to the Instituto Nacional de Cultura, Lima.

Shady, Ruth 2004 *Caral: La Ciudad del Fuego Sagrado (The City of Sacred Fire)*. Translated by M. Dalton. Interbank, Lima.

———. 2006 America's First City? The Case of Late Archaic Caral. In *Andean Archaeology III: North and South*, edited by William H. Isbell and Helaine Silverman, pp. 28–66. Kluwer Academic/Plenum Publishers, New York.

Shady, Ruth, Jonathan Haas, and Winifred Creamer 2001 Dating Caral, a Preceramic Site in the Supe Valley on the Central Coast of Peru. *Science* 292: 723–726.

Shady, Ruth, and Carlos Leyva, eds. 2003 *La Ciudad Sagrada de Caral-Supe: Los Orígenes de la Civilización Andina y la Formación del Estado Prístino en el Antiguo Perú*. Instituto Nacional de Cultura, Lima.

Shady, Ruth, and Marco Machacuay 2003 [2000] El Altar del Fuego Sagrado del Templo Mayor de la Cuidad Sagrada de Caral-Supe. In *La Ciudad Sagrada del Caral-Supe: Los Orígenes de la Civilización Andina y la Formación del Estado Pristino en el Antiguo Perú*, edited by Ruth Shady and Carlos Leyva, pp. 169–186. Instituto Nacional de Cultura, Lima.

Shady, Ruth, Marco Machacuay, and Sonia López 2003 [2000] Recuperando la Historia del Altar del Fuego Sagrado. *Boletín del Museo de Arqueología y Antropología, UNMSM* 3(4): 2–19.

Stanish, Charles, and Kevin J. Haley 2005 Power, Fairness, and Architecture: Modeling Early Chiefdom Development in the Central Andes. In *Foundations of Power in the Prehispanic Andes*, edited by Kevin J. Vaughn, Dennis Ogburn, and Christina A. Conlee, pp. 53–70. Archeological Papers of the American Anthropological Association, No. 14. American Anthropological Association, Arlington,VA.

Stein, Gil 1994 Economy, Ritual, and Power in 'Ubaid Mesopotamia. In *Chiefdoms and Early States in the Near East: The Organizational Dynamics of Complexity*, edited by Gil Stein and Mitchell S. Rothman, pp. 35–46. Monographs in World Archaeology, No. 18. Prehistory Press, Madison.

Swenson, Edward 2007 Adaptive Strategies or Ideological Innovations? Interpreting Sociopolitical Developments in the Jequetepeque Valley of Peru During the Late Moche Period. *Journal of Anthropological Archaeology* 26: 1–30.

———. 2008 Competitive Feasting, Religious Pluralism and Decentralized Power in the Late Moche Period. In *Andean Archaeology III: North and South*, edited by William H. Isbell and Helaine Silverman, pp. 112–142. Springer, New York.

Tringham, Ruth 1994 Engendered Places in Prehistory. *Gender, Place and Culture* 1: 169–203.

———. 1995 Archaeological Houses, Households, Housework, and the Home. In *The Home: Words, Interpretations, Meanings, and Environments*, edited by David N. Benjamin, David Stea, and Eje Arén, pp. 79–107. Avebury, Aldershot.

Vega-Centeno, Rafael 2007 Construction, Labor Organization, and Feasting during the Late Archaic Period in the Central Andes. *Journal of Anthropological Archaeology* 26: 150–171.

———. 2010 Cerro Lampay: Architectural Design and Human Interaction in the North Central Coast of Peru. *Latin American Antiquity* 21: 115–146.

Williams, Carlos, and Manuel Merino 1979 *Inventario, Catastro y Delimitación del Patrimonio Arqueológico del Valle de Supe*. Instituto Nacional de Cultura, Lima.

Winkelman, Michael J. 1990 Shamans and Other "Magico-Religious" Healers: A Cross-Cultural Study of Their Origins, Nature, and Social Transformations. *Ethos* 18: 308–352.

Zechenter, Elzbieta M. 1988 *Subsistence Strategies in the Supe Valley of the Peruvian Central Coast during the Complex Preceramic and Initial Periods*. Ph.D. dissertation, Department of Anthropology, University of California, Los Angeles.

10

TIMING IS EVERYTHING

Religion and the regulation of temporalities in precolumbian Peru

Edward Swenson

Introduction

Anthropologists have argued that elites endeavoured to regulate the "motion of people's daily activities," their everyday temporal rhythms, by controlling calendars, monumental evocations of social memory, and the timing of seasonal festivals (Assmann 2006; Gosden 1994:126; Hassig 2001; Munn 1992; Nilsson 1920; Rice 2008). Therefore, precolumbian religions did much more than ideologically legitimize political authority, and archaeologists should be attentive to how religious spectacles differently regulated the temporalities of social practice beyond the immediate staging of specific ceremonial events. In this vein, archaeologists have recently refined methods to intrepret how place-making actively created political subjects and set the parameters for the contestation of social inequalities (Bowser and Zedeño 2009; Casey 1997; Pauketat 2013; Smith 2003; Swenson 2012a). Place-making, as defined here, refers to the complex process by which built environments were constructed, maintained, perceived, lived, and imagined (Lefebvre 1991; Swenson 2012a; 2015). The term foregrounds landscape not as a static backdrop to social action but as integral to the inculcation of habitual rhythms and to the ideological construction of everything from personhood and community to being and cosmology. An often profoundly religious undertaking, place-making is thus implicated in the creation of very different material, temporal, and political worlds (see A. Joyce, Chapter 1). At the same time, the social production of place is inseparable from *material* constructions and experience of time (Gosden 1994:34; Lefebvre 2004). A comparison of the Roman liturgical calendar with the onerous Aztec festival round reveals that the temporal regulation of *emplaced* ritual and economic practices was central to the materialization of both ideological programs and everyday dispositions (Clendinnen 1991; Scullard 1981). However, the social dependencies and cultural sensibilities they engendered were as historically distinct as the built environments of Rome's Capitoline Hill and Tenochtitlan's Templo Mayor (Swenson 2013a).

In this chapter, I examine how time was materialized in place and politically regulated through elaborate dedication and termination rituals at the Moche ceremonial center of Huaca Colorada in the Jequetepeque Valley of northern Peru. Archaeological signatures of commemorative rites and ritualized time-reckoning will then be compared to temporally recurrent activities at the site as reflected in midden deposits and household reoccupations. The analysis will demonstrate that archaeologists have much to gain in comparing quotidian "taskscapes" as preserved archaeologically with symbolically charged landscapes of public ceremonialism and social memory (see Gosden 1994:89–90; Ingold 2000; Mills and Walker 2008; Olivier 2011; Van Dyke and Alcock 2003; Swenson 2012a). Determining how transformations in one domain related to either stability or change in the other should improve interpretations of the political reach of past religious institutions. Indeed, political revolutions are often directly related to changes in temporal cycles and ideological constructions of time (Cobb and King 2005; Lefebvre 2004:53–57). Therefore, a comparison of both the explicitly historical and temporal aspects of past landscapes complements the larger theoretical objectives of this volume, for it permits a more nuanced approximation of the structuring effects of precolumbian religions than would traditional Durkheimian and Marxian models that reduce religion to instruments of integration, legitimization, or mystification (see A. Joyce, Chapter 1). Ultimately, an investigation of differences in the frequency, scheduling, and duration of interconnected fields of action proves critical for interpreting religious constructions of time, history, and identity in past societies (Bradley 2002; González-Ruibal 2014; Murray 1999; Olivier 2004).

To prove this point, my case study will focus on a comparison of the Moche occupation of Huaca Colorada with the Early Lambayeque presence at the site. The transition from the Late Moche (A.D. 650–800) to the Early Lambayeque Period (A.D. 800–920) was marked by abrupt changes in ritualism and monumental construction at Huaca Colorada. Nevertheless, periodic and elaborate feasts were continually orchestrated at Huaca Colorada as evidenced by a succession of distinct but recurring feasting deposits and associated kitchen contexts dating to both the Moche and Transitional/Early Lambayeque Periods. Despite continuities in the temporalities of feasting practices, notable disjunctures in official time-reckoning and related ritual observances characterized the final occupation of the center. In fact, the disappearance of the Moche stylistic tradition has been described as a "crisis" and "collapse," and the inception of the subsequent Lambayeque era has been interpreted as a "revitalization movement" spurred in part by environmental perturbations (Bernuy 2008; Castillo 2001; Jennings 2008; Rucabado 2008; Rucabado and Castillo 2003; Shimada 1995). However, the analysis reveals that the effects of religious and ideological reformation, as expressed in changes in ceramic iconography, alterations in sacrificial ritual, and the suspension of architectural renovation, appear to have been superficial; macro-scale political and religious disruptions minimally altered quotidian lifeways, temporal regimes, and practical dispositions in Early Lambayeque Huaca Colorada.

Ritual in the making of history and the construction of time

Archaeologists have recently explored the complexity of historical process as under-written by different durations, rhythms, and ideologies of time (Bailey 2007; Bintliff 1991; Bradley 1991; Gonzalez-Ruibal 2014; Gosden 1994; Knapp 1992; Lucas 2005). In their endeavor to move "beyond chronology" and linear, event-based his-toriographies, these scholars have drawn inspiration from theories that recognize an analytical distinction between "temporality" and "historicity." The temporal refers to issues of duration, continuity, and repetition, while historicity pertains to change and conscious time-reckoning. As Kubler notes (1976:72): "Without change there is no history; without regularity there is no time. Time and history are related as rule and variation: time is the regular setting for the vagaries of history" (see Ingold 2000:194). In this framework, temporality is identified with McTaggart's A series, Ingold's taskscape, and time construed as "social," "experienced," "substantive," "habitual," and "subjective." Indeed, as archaeological research has demonstrated, habitual, iterative practices have played an integral role in structuring the archaeo-logical record (Ingold 2000; Lucas 2005; Olsen 2010; Mills and Walker 2008). On the other hand, historicity is commonly equated with McTaggart's B series, succession, and time understood as "abstract," "measured," "public," "narrated," and "monumental" (see Gosden 1994:124–126; Herzfeld 1991:6–10; Ingold 2000; Lucas 2005; Munn 1992:98; Roddick 2013). In fact, a plethora of dichotomies have been devised that discuss time as either explicitly marked (history, memory, myth) or as habitually internalized and reproduced in social practice (see Febvre 1947:471; Gell 1992; González-Ruibal 2014:27; Gosden 1994; Rice 2008:276).

To provide one specific example, Connerton (1989) makes the distinction between commemorative rites of history making ("inscription") and the more unconscious, doxic rhythms of what he calls incorporative practices of a routinized nature. Commemorative rituals conjure up and explicitly materialize the past as a conscious construct, and rites of this kind often performatively re-enact past his-torical and mythic events, including, most notably, cosmogonic narratives. It is in precisely such ceremonies that history, identity, and community are ideologically negotiated (Assmann 2006). Nevertheless, it is important to keep in mind that tem-poralized practices, whether dictated by astronomical, meteorological, or various traditions of social time, entailed both unconscious and conscious behavior, and it would be wrong to ascribe the temporal strictly to the realm of everyday activ-ity and the historical or eventful to the domain of ritual, myth, and ideology (as Durkheim would have it) (Bradley 1991; Connerton 1989; McGlade 1999:141–147; Olsen 2010:124–125). Indeed, the scheduling of quotidian practices was often intermeshed with ritualized spectacles of history and place making, and they no doubt inculcated culturally specific understandings of time's passage (Gosden 1994:125). Routinized practices, irrespective of their degree of synchronization with codified "public time," can also sow the seeds of environmental, economic, and ideological change (Bailey 2007; Munn 1992:102). In a similar manner, material objects and landscapes defy the successive timescales of conventional historiography. The physical persistence of the past in the present and the efficacy of buildings and accumulated artifacts to direct future action reveal that social time is dynamic and "pluritemporal," one of diverse retentions, protentions, and discontinuities (see Bradley 2002; Dawdy 2010; Gosden 1994; González-Ruibal 2014; Morley 2007; Olivier 2011). At the same time, the historical register should not be equated simply with transformation, agency, the dialectic of structure and event, or rigid ideologies specifying the linear relationship of past, present, and future (Hill 1988). As González-Ruibal notes (2014:18): "there are other possible histories [other than change] – "histories of continuity, of the very long term, histories of slow rhythms and ancient remnants."

Trouillot's distinction between "historicity I" and "historicity II" constitutes a more nuanced version of the abovementioned dichotomy. The former signifies the "materiality of the socio-historical process," while the second term refers to the "sociopolitical management" of this material process entailing its ordering, sequencing, narration, or silencing (Trouillot 1995). The concept of historicity II acknowledges considerable cultural diversity in the selective political making of history but also recognizes that the naturalization of social rhythms could be the direct outcome of historiographic projects.

In light of the above discussion, the temporal and historical defy rigid dichotomies; instead, archaeologists should be attentive to the degree in which they differently interpenetrated in past cultures. For instance, in his "rhythmanalysis" of the effects of capitalism on social life, Lefebvre (2004:6) set out to prove that "biological rhythms of sleep, hunger, thirst, walking, excretion" have been largely determined by the commodification of time underwriting the scheduling of the workweek in capitalist societies. He also argues that the temporalities of the Mediterranean world diverged significantly from North Atlantic Europe due to differences in ecology, social mores, rate of industrialization, and religion. In the end, Lefebvre contends that Mediterranean cultures better resisted the sublimation of their temporal *habitus* and circadian rhythms to the mechanized time-regimes of capitalism. Of course, much has been written on how the growing popularity of the mechanical clock, coinciding with economic changes of the early modern period in Europe, led to increased bodily discipline and to the tighter regulation of intimate routines (Thompson 1967). However, this was a process that met fierce resistance as indicated by the tenacious maintenance of irregular feast days and the popularity of "Saint Mondays" (Thompson 1967).

In pre-modern societies, ritual performance and religious doctrine occupied center stage in the crafting of historical consciousness and ideologies of time – Trouillot's "historicity II" understood as the "sociopolitical management" of time and historical process (Palmié 2013; Pauketat 2013). As Assmann notes (2006:34–35):

> Formerly, sacred time was more strictly regulated by hours, minutes, and seconds than the profane order of time. . . . And a lot earlier still, the order of time was exclusively religious in nature. In Egypt the measurement of time was reserved exclusively for priests; clocks were cult instruments. It was religious rites and not everyday life that called for the precise measurement of time.

Maya kings have also been described as embodiments of time and rulers of its passage. Rice (2008:276) notes that time and power were inextricably intertwined in Mesoamerica, and she argues that "an ideology based on time and its reckoning" constituted one of the most "important means of accumulating and exercising power." Of course, anthropologists have long argued that past religious and political institutions were founded on the effective calculation of time involving the synchronization of auspicious actions, taboos, and normative social practice with astronomically or ritually reckoned time-measurement (Aveni 1989; Pauketat 2013). The history of the Sabbath and the seven-day week provides a particularly fascinating example of the profoundly political and religious construction of a now largely taken-for-granted temporal unit. Sunday was legally decreed the Christian day of rest for a number of reasons, including Constantine's attempts to placate both Christian and Pagan factions and early Christian initiatives to differentiate themselves from traditional Judaism (see Salzman 2004).

In fact, in pre-modern cultures, divisions of time transcending the day (weeks, months, years, etc.) were largely calculated by a calendar of religious feasts (Assmann 2006:39–40; Nilsson 1920:336). It would thus stand to reason that the degree to which calendars regulated activities (as opposed to activities regulating the calendar) would correlate with the degree to which political structures permeated everyday tempos and activities (Sjørslev 2013). Assmann (2006) also notes that in pre-literate societies, the propagation of social memory relied heavily on direct participation in festivals, a participation that commonly entailed visits to aesthetically charged public spaces. These places of assembly and celebration could have been experienced as *other* spaces and times – "heterochronies" and "heterotopias" at once generative of history but removed from the flow of ordinary time (Foucault 1986; Swenson 2012a). However, large-scale ceremonies often demanded months of preparation, and the mobilization of considerable labor and economic resources. Therefore, the orchestration of large-scale feasts and related rites of historical commemoration underwrote veritable "ritual economies" and dictated the scheduling of extended periods of production, exchange, and consumption (Inomata and Coben 2006; McAnany and Wells 2008). In other words, "historically amplified" events could play a decisive role in structuring temporal routines outside the ritual frame. Indeed, the evanescent, peak periods of public ceremonies could create a powerful sense of anticipation that motivated more prosaic tasks defining protracted intervals of "mundane" life. The creation of such anticipation was no doubt essential for the manufacture of desires and dispositions critical for the construction of past political subjects.

The centrality of festive time in the development of official calendars indicates that ritual constituted an essential instrument of "ancient historiography." In fact, many theories have been proposed that postulate the unique temporal framework of ritual performance as distinct from everyday practice (Bradley 1991; Rappaport 1992). Certainly, the cherished trope of liminality denotes a suspension or alteration in space-time, and anthropologists have explored how time can slow down, accelerate, or become inverted in particular ritual performances. To be sure, cosmographic rites have long fascinated anthropologists who have debated their potential to orchestrate an "eternal return" to a primeval moment of creation – where time and space are repeatedly created anew (Eliade 1954). A number of social scientists have shown that ritual performance is integral to the making of time (Leach 1961; Rappaport 1992). Although ritual can create a place and time "out of time" (i.e., an escape from temporal routines), its chronometric faculty is evident in its punctilious ability to delineate stages, phases, and series (Rappaport 1992:6–10). Ritual observances can thus intensify the spatial and temporal grasp of the "eventful." Indeed, the material reframing of action underwriting the ritual process often sets apart recognized "events" (initiations, pilgrimages, festivals, etc.) from the stream of everyday practice (Leach 1961; Morley 2007). At the same time, the heighted aesthetic of the ritual process is realized in part through an intensified or altered rhythmic structure entailing the formal synchronization and sequencing of prescribed actions (hence the common association of ceremonialism with music and dance) (Sjørslev 2013:100–101). As Lefebvre notes (2004:87), ritual is more self-consciously and aesthetically rhythmic than repetitive.

Finally, ritual plays a key role in "timework," for it commonly functions to precipitate or prevent *change* (Flaherty 2011). Whether a foundation sacrifice to animate a dwelling, a rite of intensification to ward off environmental perturbations, or an initiation to transform a girl into a woman, different rituals either reinforce or alter the relational orders of self, society, and cosmos (Descola 2013:37; see A. Joyce, Chapter 1). Action is ritualized to more effectively dissolve, strengthen, or realign social, temporal, and material relationships. As an instrumental act – to initiate, fertilize, hex, divine, etc. – ritual is thus essential to the creation, maintenance, and (re)appropriation of time itself. As a corollary, ritualized action can serve as a powerful vehicle for political change (see Alt and Pauketat, Chapter 3; Barber, Chapter 5; Hutson et al., Chapter 8; A. Joyce, Chapter 1). The faculty of ritual to recalibrate relational networks further explains its appeal to anthropologists interested in ceremony as a locus of historical discourse (Palmié 2013). Indeed, the past (mythic charters, ancestral time), present (immanence of other-than-human powers, experience of *communitas*), and future (divination, cyclical renewals) are more easily conceptualized in the mediated form of ritual performance. By extension, ritualized place-making and the object world played as critical a role in the material mediatization of time and history as did texts, oral histories, or the changing of the seasons and the movement of the stars. As argued by many of the contributors to this volume, "authority" in pre-modern societies is thus irreducible to (religious) ideologies of legitimation and integration. Instead, the parameters for political action were set by the landscapes, things, and temporal cycles of historically specific social and material worlds.

In his landmark work, *Silencing the Past*, Trouillot concedes that historians can only realistically interpret this mediated "historicity II," and that "historicity I" can never be objectively reconstructed (Trouillot 1995; and see Palmié 2013:238). However, archaeological attention to how time was materialized in past landscapes can permit an approximation of how the "media of history" may have molded experiences of time while contributing to social change. Indeed, Ingold (2000) famously claimed that archaeologists are ideally positioned to interpret the periodicities of routinized practices, including seasonal occupation of sites or regularized depositions in formal middens. In fact, I argue that archaeologists are well equipped to examine how the temporalities of quotidian life either complemented or contradicted explicit politico-religious strategies wielded to naturalize people's place in time and history. In line with the above theoretical discussion, the following analysis will examine how the ritualized management of time (historicity II) conditioned the temporalities of practice at the Middle Horizon site of Huaca Colorada (A.D. 650–900).

Rituals of time and history at the Late Moche "Chronotope" of Huaca Colorada

The ceremonial center of Huaca Colorada is the largest Late Moche settlement in the dunated southern bank of the Jequetepeque Valley, and it played an important role in the political and religious history of the region. It occupies an area of approximately 20 hectares and is dominated by an elongated platform built on a modified and stationary sand dune. This principal mound measures 390 m × 140 m and rises 20 m at its central highest point. It is comprised of three sectors which delimit Huaca Colorada's principal ceremonial and residential areas (Figure 10.1) (Swenson 2012a, 2015; Swenson and Warner 2012). The elaborate adobe constructions dominating the central prominence of the pyramid (Sector B) points to the presence of high-status individuals who likely presided over a largely autonomous polity that ascribed to Moche religious and political values (Swenson 2012b; Swenson and Warner 2012). The recovery of copper ornaments, tools, and production detritus in domestic constructions indicates that metallurgy constituted an important pursuit of the settlement's inhabitants (Swenson and Warner 2012). Most evidence of production derives from the non-elite sectors (Sectors A and C), and peripatetic artisans appear to have visited the huaca during specific seasons under the patronage of the site's leaders. In fact, excavations in the extensive domestic zones revealed that communities resided in the settlement seasonally and episodically, visiting Huaca Colorada during great fairs or established feast-days in order to fulfill tribute obligations and partake in religious festivals. The monumental core of the huaca is also surrounded by thick feasting middens containing food remains

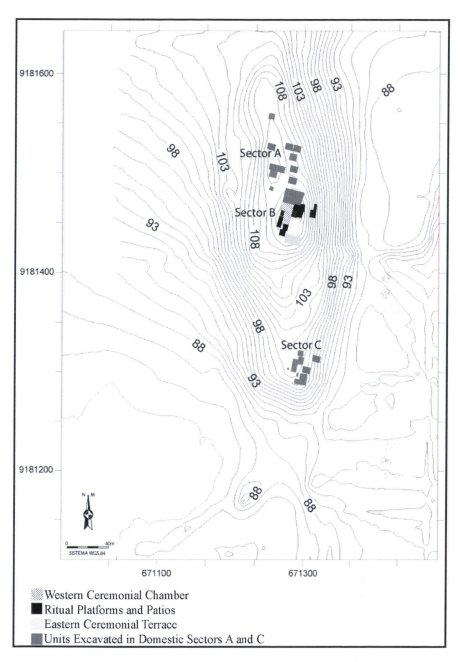

FIGURE 10.1 Plan of Huaca Colorada indicating the location of feasting middens, ceremonial architecture, and the two main residential sectors of the center

and fine serving vessels (Swenson et al. 2013). Exotic imported pottery, some Wari but predominantly highland Cajamarca tableware, were recovered in statistically high concentrations from these dumps, and it is evident that elites staged exclusive "diacritical feasts" to showcase their authority and religious pre-eminence. In contrast, Late Moche finelines predominate in the lower and expansive domestic areas beyond the central and elevated ceremonial zone, and patron-client feasts forged political and economic dependencies between high-status officials and the larger community of transient artisans and pilgrims (Dietler 2001; Lynch 2013; Swenson and Warner 2012). Excavations in both the lower residential areas and higher ceremonial sector show that communities gathered from throughout the valley and perhaps farther afield to partake in feasts entailing the consumption of prodigious quantities of corn beer, shellfish, and dog and llama meat.

It deserves mention that a significant number of ceremonial centers proliferated in Jequetepeque during the Late Moche Period, including San José de Moro, the seat of the famous priestess cult located in the Chaman drainage 25 km to the north (Castillo 2001, 2010; Swenson 2012b). Rural population also increased significantly in Jequetepeque during the early years of the Middle Horizon, and a number of sites with ceremonial architecture were built throughout the region (Castillo 2010; Dillehay 2001; Dillehay et al. 2009; Swenson 2006). Many of the Late Moche settlements were fortified, but Huaca Colorada and San José de Moro are anomalous for their open location and lack of fortifications (Castillo 2001, 2010). Archaeologists have interpreted the settlement data and the redundant irrigation networks of the valley as reflecting a high degree of political decentralization (see Castillo 2010; Dillehay 2001; Dillehay and Kolata 2004; Swenson 2006). However, the number of different settlement types and evidence for ephemeral occupation also point to seasonal transhumance (Swenson et al. 2013; Swenson and Warner 2012: 322–324).

Huaca Colorada was constructed to stage specific kinds of ceremonies unique to the region, as is indicated by the site's exceptional layout, location, and artifactual associations. Moreover, excavation in the central ceremonial sector of the site reveals that quotidian taskscapes, which included food preparation, craft production, weaving, waste-management, and llama breeding among other activities, were most likely synchronized with the scheduling of dramatic religious spectacles. Most notably, cyclical rites of architectural renovation distinguished Huaca Colorada's monumental core; ritual platforms, chambers, and corridors were regularly terminated and ritually re-dedicated in concert with the sacrifice of young women, animals, and copper objects (Swenson 2012a, 2015; Swenson and Warner 2012) (Figure 10.2). The sacrificial nature of reconstruction is exemplified by the sequential decommissioning of six distinct ceremonial platforms. These altar-like constructions were painstakingly sealed under hard floors or buried under thick deposits of clean sand.

The succession of renovations, corresponding with the sacrifice of human victims, likely served to ensure rebirth and the continuation of life – central themes of Moche political theology (Bawden1996; Swenson 2013b). Human and animal sacrifices accompanied the renovation of six ceremonial platforms, and an additional female sacrifice was discovered incorporated in construction fill associated with incremental reductions of the main chamber prior to its termination (Figure 10.3). Indeed, time was enlivened and somatically renewed in the sacrificial

FIGURE 10.2   Photographs of an astronomical gnomon and a human sacrificial victim and copper offering associated with a ritually terminated platform at Huaca Colorada. The lower register illustrates examples of such platforms.

reconstructions of the site's monumental nucleus. Thus, in engineering the consubstantiation of people, copper offerings, and "vibrant" architecture, Huaca Colorada acted as a monumental chronotope, emanating a specific temporality centered on gestation, growth, death, and regeneration (Swenson 2015). The superimposition of informal graffiti at Huaca Colorada also projects an ethos of evanescence, with the complexion of the plaster walls forever changing, like the ceaselessly transforming human body (Swenson 2012a). The figures express movement and transience, while their hurried applications are equally expressive of the momentary passage of the artists themselves – pilgrims or religious tourists wishing to memorialize their evocative encounters with the edifice. The palimpsest of shifting floors, sand fill, human offerings, and superimposed platforms further suggest that Huaca Colorada was celebrated for its kinaesthetic force and was perhaps perceived as a living, metabolizing organism (Swenson 2015; see A. Joyce, Chapter 1).

Therefore, the ceremonial sector of the huaca appears to have been in a constant state of renovation, and it is evident that there was a religious expectation to ritually terminate and re-dedicate altars, rooms, and platforms, as dictated by a religious calendar or festival round. Comparable architectural practices have been documented at other centers, including Huacas de Moche, Cao Viejo, and Dos Cabezas (Donnan 2007; Franco et al. 2010; Uceda 2010), and the sacrificial termination of

FIGURE 10.3   A sacrificed female incorporated in the construction fill at Huaca Colorada (top). A plan drawing and photograph illustrating incremental reductions documented for the main ceremonial precinct (bottom).

space appears to have been as widespread in the Moche world as it was elsewhere in the Americas (see Mock 1998). As mentioned above, the largest ceremonial chamber at Huaca Colorada was regularly and incrementally reduced in size (at least in five sequences) (see Swenson 2015; Figure 10.3). The periodic diminution of the central chamber was most likely expressive of the distinctive religious meanings and temporalizing functions of the monument.

In light of the evidence, Huaca Colorada is productively interpreted as a monumental time piece, a medium for charting and controlling the passage of time through the materialization of temporal cycles. The calendrical and temporal significance of the huaca finds parallels in the cosmographic layout of many other precolumbian centers (Aveni 2002; Pauketat 2013; Sugiyama 2005). Therefore, the huaca served as both a "sign in history" and "sign of history" as theorized by Parmentier (1987). Signs in history refer to "value-laden objects implicated in social strategies that focus attention on specific historical processes," while signs of history are those that directly reify and objectify the past (an understanding implied in the etymology of our word monument) (cited in Preucel 2010:86). The discovery of features that served astronomical functions at Huaca Colorada further points to the importance of ritualized time-reckoning at the center. For instance, a pentagonal gnomon (1.42 m long × 1.18 m wide and 18 cm high) made of pointed adobes was discovered in the northeast zone of the monumental sector (see Figure 10.2). The pointed corners of the apparatus align with different peaks of neighboring mountain ranges to the east and north of the huaca, while the central point aligns with the sunrise on the winter solstice (June 21). The peculiar shape of the installation, forming multiple lines of sight with prominent features of the surrounding topography, suggests that it functioned in rituals related to astronomy, time-reckoning, and communion with sacred landscapes.

Major junctions in the production and festive cycle appear to have coincided with the literal sacrifice and renovation (rebirth) of sacred space at Huaca Colorada. In this regard, the sacrifice of buildings and people rendered physically real the dialectical movement of time peculiar to the Moche. Huaca Colorada's monumental core was literally charged with life and time's recursive flows. Similar to the religious objectives of human sacrifice, ritualized architectural construction appears to have been envisioned as a tool of social *engineering*, an attempt to control people, their lifecycles, and the unfolding of time itself. Indeed, time and society were given a concrete and manipulable form in the cyclical reconstructions of the site's monumental nucleus. The dedication and termination rites at Huaca Colorada demonstrate that the Moche made explicit their understanding that "time and space are integral to each other" and that in the "lived world, spatial and temporal dimensions cannot be disentangled," a point that has long fascinated philosophers of time (see Munn 1992:94–95).

Huaca Colorada's ceremonial architecture was thus grounded in an aesthetic of violence linked to a particular conception of temporality understood as animate and inherently material. In other words, sacrifice seems to have activated the movement of time itself (see Read 1998; Uceda 2010:152). This living, materialization of time has been documented in other Amerindian societies, especially in Meso-american civilizations, where time was perceived as an animate bundle to be carried (Hassig 2001; Rice 2008; Read 1998). In fact, the creative "movement" of space–time was realized through the bundling together of heterogeneous sacrificial offerings at Huaca Colorada (see Fowles 2013:154–164, Pauketat 2013 and Zedeño 2008 for a discussion of ritual bundles as catalysts of generative process in Amerindian religions).

In many Amerindian societies, cosmogonic origins and the space-time of violent creation served as the ultimate measure and referent of historical process (Hamann 2002). Such archetypical acts of cosmogonic "place-making" also appear to have underwritten ideologies of space, temporality, and history at Huaca Colorada. However, notions of "eternal returns" or primoridal time should not be relegated to the realm of timeless myth, the purview of "cold societies," for mythical time also emphasizes "moments of rupture, of a change of temporality, as much as of continuities" (Harris 1995:16). In this regard, rites pivoting on pain, the disfiguring of bodies, and the sacrificial extinction of life physically instantiate, in the most dramatic fashion, changes in time and being (Read 1998; Scarry 1985). Ritual homicide consummates an irreversible subject re-formation, wherein human bodies are objectified as conduits of time's *physical* passage (Swenson 2013b). For Nietzsche, memories are powerfully made through pain and sacrifice (Assmann 2006:5). The periodic ritual renovations of the monumental chamber at Huaca Colorada, vitalized by the sacrifice of young women, animals, and copper implements, similarly served to emplace memory and regulate the movement of an animated time. In this sense, the ritually renovated precinct of Huaca Colorada could be productively interpreted as a "chronotope," as theorized by Bahktin. A chronotope designates

> points in the geography of a community where time and space intersect and fuse. Time takes on flesh and becomes visible for human contemplation; likewise, space becomes charged and responsive to the movements of time and history and the enduring character of a people. . . . Chronotopes thus stand as monuments to the community itself, as symbols of it, as forces operating to shape its members' images of themselves.
>
> *(Bakhtin 1981:7)*

As a direct materialization of Moche conceptions of history, and as a place animated by the sacrificial incorporation of young women, the multiple rebuilding phases encapsulated the metamorphic and even procreative power of Huaca Colorada's ceremonial architecture.

The distinctive rituals of time-reckoning at Moche Huaca Colorada are best interpreted in relationship to the archaeological signatures of more quotidian temporal rhythms at the settlement. The shifting and overlapping floor constructions identified throughout the site's expansive domestic zones suggests that the bulk of Huaca Colorada's population only inhabited the settlement seasonally or periodically (Swenson and Warner 2012). In fact, during the Late Moche Period, the Jequetepeque Valley as a whole was distinguished by the regular internal movement of people, and a certain value was placed on circulation and impermanent domesticity (Dillehay 2001; Swenson and Warner 2012; Swenson 2012b). The priestess center of San José de Moro, the headquarters of the dominant polity in the north valley, is largely devoid of domestic contexts (unlike Huaca Colorada), and people congregated here in large numbers only at specific and shorter moments in time to participate in grand funerary and feasting rites (Castillo 2010). Therefore, the transient occupations and pulsating social landscape of Jequetepeque was dictated in part by the scheduling of religious festivals at a number of ceremonial sites in the valley. It remains to be determined whether the region was distinguished by a "competition between calendars" or by a more centralized and integrated festival round (Swenson 2012b).

In any event, it seems likely that rituals of sacrifice and architectural renovation coordinated the comings and goings of large gatherings that partook in large-scale feasting events at Huaca Colorada. The ephemeral and superimposed domestic occupations of the two residential areas anchored a number of activities, including cooking, floor resurfacing, camelid rearing, metallurgy, spinning, weaving, ceramic production, short-term storage, domestic ritual, and, of course, feasting. However, these contexts are surprisingly devoid of fishing and farming implements common at other Late Moche sites in the Valley (Dillehay et al. 2009). This conspicuous absence lends further support to the argument that communities visited the huaca for short, stipulated periods, and that time spent there was defined by set tasks that largely supported the ritual economy of the ceremonial core. Therefore, the rites of "time-making" and historical commemoration orchestrated at Huaca Colorada clearly structured more encompassing temporalities at the site. The lack of primary production tools also suggests that the huaca was experienced as a heterotopic landscape – an *other* space and time of exceptional ritualism and intense introspection on both Moche mythology and local history (Foucault 1986; Swenson 2012a). However, it was clearly a place that conditioned the rhythms of life both within and outside the settlement (Swenson 2012a). In fact, the tradition of participating in periodic feasts outlived the chronometric function of the huaca at the end of the Late Moche Period.

Changing histories and perduring temporalities at Huaca Colorada

In 2012, we discovered a portion of a large feasting midden amassed just to the north of the perimeter wall of the main ceremonial precinct of the site (Swenson et al. 2013) (see Figure 10.1). The upper midden layers dated to the Transitional and Early Lambayeque Period (A.D. 800–900) and contained Early Sicán (Lambayeque) Blackwares, musical instruments, and fine Cajamarca feasting bowls (Figure 10.4). Both relative chronological indicators and recent radiometric assays confirm that Lambayeque Period midden deposits directly overlay Moche feasting

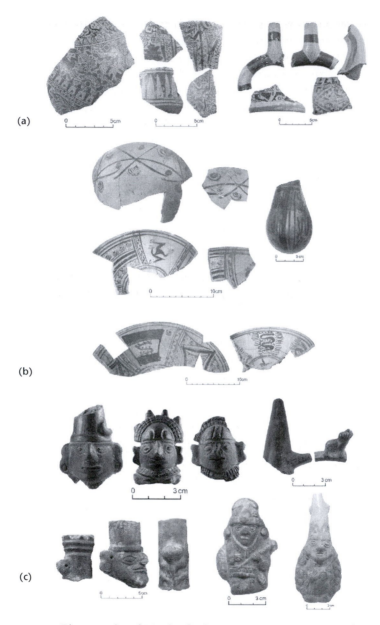

FIGURE 10.4   Photographs of Moche fineline ceramics (a), Cajamarca bowls (b), and Sicán reduced wares and musical instruments (c) recovered from the feasting middens at Huaca Colorada

and kitchen remains. Although Moche fineline ceramics and certain utilitarian cooking vessels disappeared in the most recent strata, periodic and elaborate feasts continued to be orchestrated at Huaca Colorada, as evidenced by this succession of superimposed feasting deposits and associated kitchen contexts dating to the Early

Lambayeque Period. Moreover, recent research conducted in 2014 identified both ephemeral and more permanent domestic constructions dating to this post-Moche phase in the south end of the northern domestic area (Sector A). This domestic zone was located just to the north of the Transitional midden, and they were clearly contemporaneous. This later residential sector was considerably smaller than the Moche occupation, but it shows that communities persisted in peregrinating to the huaca to drink corn beer, eat llama meat, and consume food from elaborate Cajamarca bowls – an iconic ceramic vessel that remained popular following the collapse of the Moche religious complex (Figure 10.4).

It is especially significant that despite the continuity of the feasting round, the recurrent renovation of ceremonial architecture, coinciding with the sacrifice of women and animals, ceased with the close of the Moche Period (Swenson et al. 2013). In addition, this development was marked by the disappearance of Moche fineline ceramics at the site, an important religious medium that celebrated Moche myths and divinities, including the famed priestess of San José de Moro (see Figure 10.4). Therefore, the scheduling of ritualized feasting at Huaca Colorada – now possibly directed by lower-status inhabitants – endured into the Transitional Period despite the cessation of the presumed chronometric faculties of the ceremonial zone. In other words, the demise of Moche ceremonialism and rituals of historical reckoning at the site seems to have had little effect on the periodicities of feasting rites and transient, seasonal occupation at the center. Despite the decreased size of the post-Moche occupation, the feasts were equally rich and elaborate as the preceding phase (Swenson et al. 2013).

In fact, the later celebrants seem to have viewed the massive garbage dumps as material signifiers of past festivals, conspicuous consumption, and public ceremonies, events which likely created strong and enduring attachments to the site. The Lambayeque feasting deposits are distinctive in that kitchens dating to this period were constructed directly on Lambayeque and Moche garbage heaps. These communal kitchens were associated with grinding stones, impressive hearths to boil chicha, storage vessels, and both formally and informally prepared use-surfaces (Figure 10.5). Mounded feasting garbage was possibly read as metaphors of prosperity and hospitality, and the re-establishment of kitchens within older rubbish piles could have been deemed an auspicious practice that effectively tapped the power of past feasts and emotionally charged celebrations (Fowler 2011:143; Van Dyke 2003). Therefore, it is intriguing that the most extensive and substantial post-Moche occupation discovered at the site relates to later kitchens and middens north of the façade wall, and not to the restoration of ritual constructions in the ceremonial district just to the south (see Figure 10.5). In other words, the later inhabitants of the center appear to have been more impressed by the great feasting deposits than the ceremonial architecture of Sector B. It is revealing, then, that the "marks of repetition" (Olivier 2004:210) so dramatically and violently materialized in the ritual zone of the Moche Period are only legible in the domain of kitchen construction and waste management during the subsequent phase.

In fact, formalized rites dating to the Lambayeque Period appear to have been displaced to the south end of Sector A in direct proximity to the mountain of

FIGURE 10.5   Early Lambayeque *Chicha* hearths, cooking pots, and midden debris found superimposed on earlier Moche kitchens in the southern end of Sector A. The fineline sherd of the priestess boat was recovered from a Moche-phase kitchen floor.

garbage and associated kitchens. Small-scale rituals may also have been orchestrated on the final and highest Moche altar overlooking the midden in the northeast sector of the site. A few Lambayeque Blackware sherds were recovered intermixed with Moche finelines in an abandonment layer above the platform in question. However, it is evident that this altar was never rebuilt or modified in this terminal phase. Hence, the data suggest that the temporalities of feasting continued at Huaca Colorada despite significant changes in religious iconography, ideologies of history, and the monumental regulation of social activities.

The possible contradiction between the cessation of sacrificial ritual and the survival of the feasting calendar at Huaca Colorada will no doubt prove critical for interpreting religious and political transformations marking the transition between the Moche and Lambayeque Periods in the Jequetepeque region. In any event, the evidence strongly suggests that the huaca's distinctive feasting calendar propagated an ethos of anticipation and participation that engendered a powerful and enduring sense of community that long outlived the fall of the Moche religious complex.

The evidence complicates interpretations that the disappearance of the Moche style represented an abrupt break caused by social upheaval, Wari incursions, environmental perturbations, and religious crisis (Bernuy 2008; Castillo 2001; Jennings 2008; Rucabado 2008; Rucabado and Castillo 2003; Shimada 1995). Castillo and Uceda note (2008:725):

> Of all things Mochica, religion was the one thing most dramatically transformed, as it was probably – more than anything else – associated with ways the Mochicas had ruled the land. We do not agree with the idea that the Mochicas simply melted down into the Chimú and Lambayeque, or that we can recognize them in their heirs. Rather the Mochicas – as a system, as a way to control the land and give sense to society, as an explanation for the universe – collapsed and disappeared.

The changes at Huaca Colorada would not necessarily contradict this statement, and it is significant that sacrifice, ritualized architectural renovation, and elite funerary ritual disappeared suddenly at the onset of the Early Lambayeque Period, only to remerge transformed during the Middle Lambayeque (Sicán) Period (Shimada 2014). In fact, large-scale projects of ritualized place-making are conspicuously lacking during the Early Lambayeque Period (Shimada 2014:22). This contrasts with the recorded innovations in technology and ceramic production defining this transitional phase. However, it is becoming increasingly apparent that the transition between the Moche and Lambayeque Periods varied remarkably throughout the North Coast and even within particular river valleys. At San José de Moro, communal burials appear for the first time in the Transitional Period (a possible highland influence), while large-scale mortuary feasts were discontinued (Rucabado 2008). Nevertheless, large-scale festivals continued at Huaca Colorada for quite some time. Moreover, the interment of high-status women distinguished the mortuary traditions of both Moche- and Transitional-era burials at San José de Moro (Bernuy 2008; Castillo 2006). In the Lambayeque and La Leche regions, archaeologists have recently argued that lower-status communities continued to adhere to Moche religious and cultural values well into the Lambayeque era, coexisting with populations that embraced the prevailing Sicán religion (Klaus et al. 2010; Shimada et al. 2005). The excavations at Huaca Colorada also would indicate that religious collapse only accurately describes the experiences of specific elite communities and political institutions. Certain values and ways of life identified with Moche religion may have persisted for a century or more among a large substratum of the community.

In the end, the data strongly suggest that the cessation of Moche political order did not immediately affect domestic economies, gender relations, attachments to place, or experiences of time in the southern Jequetepeque valley of Peru. Metallurgy, ceramic production, spinning, weaving, and the large-scale processing of camelid and shellfish continued with little alteration into the Lambayque Period, and pilgrims still visited the revered center without their farming or fishing implements. Therefore, the prescriptions of an emerging Lambayeque-political theology cannot be correlated with a totalizing way of life, nor did they engender a uniform process of ethnogenesis. Of course, the corollary to this statement is that the Moche-inspired religious feasts at Huaca Colorada inculcated a rhythm of practice that was extremely difficult to eradicate.

Conclusion

Anthropological research has shown that ideological innovations, often related to social upheaval or environmental perturbations, have disrupted longstanding dispositions, leading to new material realities and naturalizing novel experiences of time and place (Comaroff and Comaroff 1991). However, in some instances, new religious movements may have had little success in altering embodied temporal routines or everyday perceptions of the world, as seems to have been the case with the initial spread of Lambayeque religion in Jequetepeque at the end of the Moche era. Ironically, this iconoclastic political theology is believed to have arisen in reaction to the widespread rejection of Moche religious values (Shimada 1995). In the end, an important objective of the Huaca Colorada case study is to show that archaeological analysis of shifts in the periodicities of practice – as relates to continuity or change in the religious regulation of time – offers a much stronger basis from which to interpret sociopolitical transformations than do studies relying simply on alterations in ceramic styles, ceremonial architecture, and religious iconography (Barrett 2004; Roddick 2013).

In fact, the case study further demonstrates that much is lost when archaeologists investigate religious landscapes simply through the lens of "historical change." As González-Ruibal (2014:28–33) has chided, the anthropological privileging of history as transformation betrays Neoliberal and modernist sensibilities, and he argues that the deep temporalities of certain practices and things (say, millennial traditions of grinding corn with *batanes*) can tell us a great deal about the resiliency of particular structures of practice (see also Joyce 2009:43–44, 50–51). These practices were often the prerogative of women and subalterns, and González-Ruibal (2014) remarks that they should be interpreted as modes of timework as equally significant as revitalization or messianic movements. It is telling, for instance, that despite rather abrupt changes in elite religious iconography and fine ceramics, an array of cooking pots used to prepare feasting foods continued to be made in Jequetepeque well into the Chimú Period. The same holds for the beautiful Cajamarca bowls imported from the highlands, a class of vessel that transcended any narrow association with Moche political theology. To conclude, archaeologists have much to gain in examining the temporalities of distinct but often overlapping fields of action. Investigations of this kind can reveal how past religions, economic systems, or social movements variably structured the everyday realities and experiences of ancient communities.

Acknowledgments

I wish to express my sincere gratitude to the Wenner-Gren Foundation for Anthropological Research, National Geographic, the Social Sciences and Humanities Research Council of Canada, The Canadian Foundation for Innovation, and the University of Toronto for their generous financial support of my research at Huaca Colorada. In addition, I extend my profound thanks to my co-directors John Warner, Jorge Chiguala, and Francisco Seoane for their many years of friendship and support.

References

Assmann, Jan 2006 *Religion and Cultural Memory*. Stanford University Press, Stanford.

Aveni, Anthony 1989 *Empires of Time: Calendars, Clocks, and Cultures*. University Press of Colorado, Boulder.

———. 2002 *Empires of Time: Calendars, Clocks and Cultures*, Revised Edition. University Press of Colorado, Boulder.

Bailey, Groff 2007 Time Perspectives, Palimpsests, and the Archaeology of Time. *Journal of Anthropological Archaeology* 26: 198–223.

Bakhtin, Mikhail 1981 *The Dialogic Imagination: Four Essays by M. Bakhtin*. Edited by Michael Holquist. Translated by Carly Emerson and Michael Holquist. University of Texas Press, Austin.

Barrett, John C. 2004 Temporality and the Study of Prehistory. In *Time and Temporality in the Ancient World*, edited by Ralph M. Rosen, pp. 11–27. University of Pennsylvania Museum of Archaeology and Anthropology, Philadelphia.

Bawden, Garth 1996 *The Moche*. Blackwell, Malden.

Bernuy Quiroga, J. 2008 El Periodo Lambayeque en San José de Moro: patrones funerarios y naturaleza de la ocupación. In *Arqueología Mochica: Nuevos Enfoques*, edited by Luis Jaime Castillo, Hélène Bernier, Greg Lockard, and Julio Rucabado, pp. 53–66. Fondo Editorial Pontificia Universidad Católica del Perú, Lima.

Bintliff, John 1991 *The Annales School and Archaeology*. New York University Press, New York.

Bradley, Richard 1991 Ritual, Time, and History. *World Archaeology* 23: 209–219.

———. 2002 *The Past in Prehistoric Societies*. Routledge, New York.

Bowser, Brenda J., and María Nieves Zedeño, eds. 2009 *The Archaeology of Meaningful Places*. University of Utah Press, Salt Lake City.

Casey, Edward S. 1997 *The Fate of Place: A Philosophical History*. University of California Press, Berkeley.

Castillo, Luis Jaime 2001 The last of the Mochicas. In *Moche Art and Archaeology in Ancient Peru*, edited by Joanne Pillsbury, pp. 307–332. National Gallery of Art and Yale University Press, New Haven.

Castillo, Luis Jaime 2006 Five Sacred Priestesses From San José de Moro: Elite Women Funerary Rituals on Peru's Northern Coast. *Arkeos: Revista Electrónica de Arqueología*. PUCP, Lima.

———. 2010 Moche Politics in the Jequetepeque Valley: A Case for political Opportunism. In *New Perspectives in Moche Political Organization*, edited by Jeffrey Quilter and Luis Jaime Castillo, pp. 1–24. Dumbarton Oaks, Washington, DC.

Castillo, Luis Jaime, and Santiago Uceda 2008 The Mochicas. In *Handbook of South American Archaeology*, edited by Helaine Silverman and William H. Isbell, pp. 707–729. Springer, New York.

Clendinnen, Inga 1991 *Aztecs: An Interpretation*. Cambridge University Press, Cambridge.

Cobb, Charles R., and Adam King 2005 Re-Inventing Mississippian Tradition at Etowah, Georgia. *Journal of Archaeological Theory and Method* 12: 167–192.

Comaroff, Jean and John Comaroff 1991 *Of Revelation and Revolution: Christianity, Colonialism, and Consciousness in South Africa*, vol. 1. University of Chicago Press, Chicago.

Connerton, Paul 1989 *How Societies Remember*. Cambridge University Press, Cambridge.

Dawdy, Shannon L. 2010 Clockpunk Anthropology and the Ruins of Modernity. *Current Anthropology* 51: 761–793.

Descola Phillipe 2013 Presence, Attachment, Origin: Ontologies of Incarnates. In *A Companion to the Anthropology of Religion*, edited by Michael Lambek and Janice Boddy, pp. 35–49. Wiley-Blackwell, Malden, MA.

Dietler Michael 2001 Theorizing the Feast: Rituals of Consumption, Commensal Politics, and Power in African Contexts. In *Feasts: Archaeological and Ethnographic Perspectives on Food, Politics, and Power*, edited by Michael Dietler and Brian Hayden, pp. 65–114. Smithsonian, Washington, DC.

Dillehay, Tom D. 2001 Town and Country in Late Moche Times: A View From Two Northern Valleys. In *Moche Art and Archaeology in Ancient Peru*, edited by Joanne Pillsbury, pp. 259–284. National Gallery of Art and Yale University Press, New Haven.

Dillehay, Tom D., and Alan L. Kolata 2004 Long-Term Human Response to Uncertain Environmental Conditions in the Andes. *Proceedings of the National Academy of Sciences* 101: 4325–30.

Dillehay, Tom D., Alan L. Kolata, and Edward Swenson 2009 *Paisajes Culturales en el Valle del Jequetepeque: Los Yacimientos Arqueológicos*. Ediciones Sian, Lima.

Donnan, Christopher B. 2007 *Moche Tombs at Dos Cabezas*. Costin Institute of Archaeology Press, Los Angeles.

Eliade, Mircea 1954 *The Myth of the Eternal Return*. Translated by William R. Trask. Princeton University Press, Princeton.

Febvre, Lucien 1947 *La Problème de L'Incroyance au XVI Siècle*. Albin Michel, Paris.

Flaherty, Michael G. 2011 *The Textures of Time: Agency and Temporal Experience*. Temple University Press, Philadelphia.

Fowler, Chris 2011 Personhood and the Body. In *The Oxford Handbook of the Archaeology of Ritual and Religion*, edited by Timothy Insoll, pp. 133–150. Oxford University Press, Oxford.

Fowles, Severin M. 2013 *An Archaeology of Doings: Secularism and the Study of Pueblo Religion*. SAR Press, Santa Fe.

Foucault, Michel 1986 Of Other Spaces. *Diacritics* 16: 22–27.

Franco, Régulo, César Gálvez, and Segundo Vásquez 2010 Moche Power and Ideology at the El Brujo Complex and in the Chicama Valley. In *New Perspectives on Moche Political Organization*, edited by Jeffrey Quilter and Luis Jaime Castillo, pp. 110–131, Dumbarton Oaks, Washington, DC.

Gell, Alfred 1992 *The Anthropology of Time: Cultural Constructions of Temporal Maps and Rhythms*. Berg, Oxford.

González-Ruibal, Alfredo 2014 *An Archaeology of Resistance: Materiality and Time in an African Borderland*. Rowman and Littlefield, New York.

Gosden, Christopher 1994 *Social Being and Time*. Blackwell, Malden.

Hamann, Byron 2002 The Social Life of Pre-Sunrise Things: Indigenous Mesoamerican Archaeology. *Current Anthropology* 43: 351–82.

Harris, Oliva 1995 The Coming of the White People: Reflections on the Mythologisation of History in Latin America. *Bulletin of Latin American Research* 14(1): 9–21.

Hassig, Ross 2001 *Time, History, and Belief in Aztec and Colonial Mexico*. University of Texas Press, Austin.

Herzfeld, Michael 1991 *Place in History: Social and Monumental Time in a Cretan Town*. Princeton University Press, Princeton.

Hill, Jonathon D., ed. 1988 *Rethinking History and Myth: Indigenous South American Perspectives on the Past*, University of Illinois Press, Urbana.

Ingold, Timothy 2000 *The Perception of the Environment: Essays in Livelihood, Dwelling, and Skill*. Routledge, New York.

Inomata, Takeshi, and Larry S. Coben 2006 *Archaeology of Performance: Theaters of Power, Community, and Politics*. Altamira Press, Lanham.

Jennings, Justin 2008 Catastrophe, Revitalization, and Religious Change on the Prehispanic North Coast of Peru. *Cambridge Archaeological Journal* 18: 177–194.

Joyce, Arthur 2009 The Main Plaza of Monte Albán: A Life History of Place. In *The Archaeology of Meaningful Places*, edited by Brenda J. Bowser and María Nieves Zedeño, pp. 33–52. University of Utah Press, Salt Lake City.

Klaus, Haagen, Jorge Centurión, and Manuel Curo 2010 Bioarchaeology of Human Sacrifice: Violence, Identity, and the Evolution of Ritual Killing at Cerro Cerrillos, Peru. *Antiquity* 84: 1102–1122.

Knapp, A. Bernard, ed. 1992 *Archaeology, Annales, and Ethnohistory*. Cambridge University Press, Cambridge.

Kubler, George 1976 *The Shape of Time: Remarks on the History of Things*. Yale University Press, New Haven.

Leach, Edmund 1961 *Rethinking Anthropology*. Althone, London.

Lefebvre, Henri 1991 *The Production of Space*. Blackwell, Malden.

Lefebvre, Henri 2004 *Rhythmanalysis: Space, Time, and Everyday Life*. Bloomsbury, London.

Lucas, Gavin 2005 *The Archaeology of Time*. Routledge, London.

Lynch, Sally 2013 *A Ceramic Based Analysis of Feasting and Power at the Moche Site of Huaca Colorada*. Master's thesis, Department of Anthropology, University of Toronto, Toronto.

McAnany, Patricia, and E. Christian Wells 2008 Toward a Theory of Ritual Economy. *Research in Economic Anthropology* 27: 1–16.

McGlade, James 1999 The Times of History: Archaeology, Narrative, and Non-linear Causality. In *Time and Archaeology*, edited by Tim Murray, pp. 139–163. Routledge, London.

Mills, Barbara J., and William H. Walker, eds. 2008 *Memory Work: Archaeologies of Material Practice*. School for Advanced Research Press, Santa Fe.

Mock, Shirley B., ed. 1998 *The Sowing and the Dawning. Termination, Dedication, and Transformation in the Archaeological and Ethnographic Record of Mesoamerica*. University of New Mexico Press, Albuquerque.

Morley, Iain 2007 Time, Cycles and Ritual Process. In *Cult in Context: Reconsidering Ritual in Archaeology*, edited by David A. Barrowclough and Caroline Malone, pp. 205–209. Oxbow, Oxford.

Munn, Nancy 1992 The Cultural Anthropology of Time: A Critical Essay. *Annual Review of Anthropology* 21: 93–123.

Murray, Tim, ed. 1999 *Time and Archaeology*, Routledge, New York.

Nilsson, Martin P. 1920 *Primitive Time-Reckoning*, C.W.K. Gleerup, Lund.

Olivier, Laurent 2004 The Past of the Present: Archaeological Memory and Time. *Archaeological Dialogues* 10: 204–213.

Olivier, Laurent 2011 *The Dark Abyss of Time: Archaeology and Social Memory*. Altamira, Lanham.

Olsen, Bjørnar 2010 *In Defense of Things: Archaeology and the Ontology of Objects*. Altamira, Lanham.

Palmié, Stephan 2013 Historicist Knowledge and its Condition of Impossibility. In *The Social Life of Spirits* edited by Ruy Blaines and Diana Espírito Santo, pp. 218–263. University of Chicago Press, Chicago.

Pauketat, Timothy 2013 *An Archaeology of the Cosmos: Rethinking Agency and Religion in Ancient America*. New York, Routledge.

Parmentier, Richard J. 1987 *The Sacred Remains: Myth, History, and Polity in Belau*. University of Chicago Press, Chicago.

Preucel, Richard W. 2010 *Archaeological Semiotics*. Wiley-Blackwell, Malden, MA

Rappaport, Roy A. 1992 Ritual, Time, Eternity. *Zygon* 27(1): 5–30.

Read, Kay 1998 *Time and Sacrifice in the Aztec Cosmos*. Indiana University Press, Bloomington.

Rice, Prudence 2008 Time, Power and the Maya. *Latin American Antiquity* 19: 257–298.

Roddick, Andrew 2013 Temporalities of the Formative Period Taraco Peninsula, Bolivia. *Journal of Social Archaeology* 13: 287–309.

Rucabado Yong, Julio 2008 Practicas funerarias de elite en San José de Moro durante la Fase Transicional Temprana: el caso de la tumba colectiva M-U615. In *Arqueología Mochica: Nuevos Enfoques*, edited by Luis Jaime Castillo, Hélène Bernier, Greg Lockard, and Julio Rucabado, pp. 359–380. Fondo Editorial Pontificia Universidad Católica del Perú, Lima.

Rucabado, Julio, and Luis Jaime Castillo 2003 'El Periodo Transicional en San José de Moro. In *Moche Hacia el Final del Milenio, Tomo I*, edited by Santiago Uceda and Elías Mujica, pp. 15–42. Universidad Nacional de Trujillo y Fondo Editorial de la Pontificia Universidad Católica del Perú, Lima and Trujillo.

Salzman, Michele R. 2004 Pagan and Christian Notions of the Week in the 4th Century CE Western Roman Empire. In *Time and Temporality in the Ancient World*, edited by Ralph M. Rosen, pp. 185–212. University of Pennsylvania Museum of Archaeology and Anthropology, Philadelphia.

Scarry, Elaine 1985 *The Body in Pain: The Making and Unmaking of the World*. Oxford University Press, Oxford.

Scullard, Howard Hayes 1981 *Festivals and Ceremonies of the Roman Republic*. Cornell University Press, Ithaca.

Shimada, Izumi 1995 *Cultura Sican: Dios, Riqueza y Poder en la Costa Norte del Perú*. Fundación del Banco Continental, Lima.

———. 2014 *Detrás de la máscara de oro: la cultura Sicán*. In *Cultura Sicán: Esplendor de la Costa Norte*, edited by Izumi Simada, pp. 15–92. Fondo Editorial del Congreso del Perú, Lima.

Shimada, Izumi, Kenichi Shinoda, Steve Bourget, Walter Alva, and Santiago Uceda 2005 mtDNA Analysis of Muchik and Sicán Populations of Prehispanic Peru. In *Biomolecular Archaeology: Genetic Approaches to the Past*, edited by David M. Reed, pp. 61–92. Center for Archaeological Investigations, Occasional Paper 32. Southern Illinois University Press, Carbondale.

Sjørslev, Inger 2013 Boredom, Rhythm, and the Temporality of Ritual: Recurring Fieldwork in the Brazilian Candomblé. *Social Analysis* 57(1): 95–109.

Smith, Adam T. 2003 *The Political Landscape: Constellations of Authority in Early Complex Societies*. University of California Press, Berkeley.

Sugiyama, Saburo 2005 *Human Sacrifice, Militarism, and Rulership: Materialization of State Ideology at the Feathered Serpent Pyramid, Teotihuacan*. Cambridge University Press, Cambridge.

Swenson, Edward 2006 Competitive feasting, Religious Pluralism, and Decentralized Power in the Late Moche Period. In *Andean Archaeology III: North and South*, edited by William H. Isbell and Helaine Silverman pp. 112–142. Springer, New York.

———. 2012a Moche Ceremonial Architecture as Third Space: the Politics of Place-Making in Ancient Peru. *Journal of Social Archaeology* 12: 3–28.

———. 2012b Warfare, Gender, and Sacrifice in Jequetepeque Peru. *Latin American Antiquity* 23: 167–193.

———. 2013a Interpreting the Political Landscape of Early State Religions. In *A Companion to the Anthropology of Religion*, edited by Michael Lambek and Janice Boddy, pp. 471–88. Wiley-Blackwell, Malden, MA.

———. 2013b Dramas of the Dialectic: Sacrifice and Power in Ancient Polities. In *Violence and Civilization*, edited by Rod Campbell, pp. 28–60, Joukowsky Institute Publication 4. Oxbow Press, Oxford.

———. 2015 The Materialities of Place-making in the Ancient Andes: a Critical Appraisal of the Ontological Turn in Archaeological Interpretation. *Journal of Archaeological Method and Theory* 22: 667–712.

Swenson, Edward, Jorge Chiguala, and John Warner 2013 *Technical Report: Proyecto de Investigación Arqueológica Jatanca- Huaca Colorada 2012, Valle de Jequetepeque*. Ministerio de Cultura, Lima.

Swenson, Edward, and John Warner 2012 Crucibles of Power: Forging Copper and Forging Subjects at the Moche Ceremonial Center of Huaca Colorada, Peru. *Journal of Anthropological Archaeology* 31: 314–333.

Thompson, E.P. 1967 Time, Work-Discipline, and Industrial Capitalism. In *Essays in Social History*, edited by Michael W. Flinn and T. Christopher Smout, pp. 56–97. Claredon, Oxford.

Trouillot, Michel R. 1995 *Silencing the Past: Power and the Production of History*. Beacon Press, Boston.

Uceda, Santiago 2010 Theocracy and Secularism: Relationship Between the Temple and Urban Nucleus and Political Change at the Huacas de Moche. In *New Perspectives on Moche Political Organization*, edited by Jeffrey Quilter and Luis Jaime Castillo, pp. 132–158. Dumbarton Oaks, Washington, DC.

Van Dyke Ruth M. 2003 Memory and the Construction of Chacoan Society. In *Archaeologies of Memory*, edited by Ruth M. Van Dyke and Susan E. Alcock, pp. 180–200. Blackwell, Malden.

Van Dyke, Ruth M., and Susan E. Alcock, eds. 2003 *Archaeologies of Memory*. Blackwell, Malden.

Zedeño, María Nieves 2008 Bundled Worlds: The Roles and Interactions of Complex Objects From the North American Plains. *Journal of Archaeological Method and Theory* 15: 362–78.

11

FROM LANDSCAPE TO ONTOLOGY IN AMAZONIA

The Llanos de Mojos as a middle ground

John H. Walker

Introduction

This chapter begins in a tangle of geographic questions: Why was so much labor invested in the landscape over thousands of years in the Llanos de Mojos, in south-western Amazonia (Figure 11.1)? Why are so many raised fields and other earthworks found here, and does this make Mojos fundamentally different from other places in the Andes and the Amazon? Do these extensive anthropogenic landscapes mean that Mojos was not truly "Amazonian"? Finally, how are the variations in earthwork patterns related to the societies that created them?

Anthropogenic landscapes have proven to be widespread across South America and the Americas (Walker 2012; Denevan 2001; Doolittle 2000). Raised fields are a particularly visible kind of wetland landscape modification, but perhaps as more information accumulates, similar anthropogenic landscapes across Amazonia and the Americas will prove more commonplace. Since the early 1960s, evidence of raised fields and other earthworks continues to emerge in satellite imagery, increasing the estimates of their number and extent by orders of magnitude (Denevan 1966; Walker 2008). However, until we have more information about other parts of the Americas and the Amazon Basin, Mojeño earthworks remain a distinguishing feature of the region.

One influential approach begins with an evaluation of the Amazonian environment. A focus on the environment at a continental scale has long been part of the definition of archaeology in the Amazon Basin (Meggers 1971, 1994). This chapter starts from a different set of theoretical assumptions, and empirical evidence showing that complex societies in the Amazon were based in larger populations, built earthworks, and modified environments. The agricultural landscapes of the Llanos de Mojos in eastern Bolivia form a persuasive example of long-term human modification of the environment (Denevan 2001; Erickson 2008; Walker 2008).

FIGURE 11.1 Location of West Central Mojos within the Llanos de Mojos, the Madeira River Basin, and South America

Raised fields and other anthropogenic landscapes are found throughout lowland South America, but the examples from Mojos cover thousands of square kilometers and represent a monumental investment of labor. Raised field farming in Mojos was an established way of life that lasted for thousands of years and involved tens or hundreds of thousands of people. The diversity of agricultural earthworks over such a large space and time indicates that a strictly environmental interpretation is insufficient.

A second alternative is that Mojos earthworks are associated with the migration of agriculturalists across the continent. Two influential discussions of the long-term history of the Arawak diaspora both emphasize the role of Arawak speakers, although they disagree in many respects about that role (Hornborg 2005; Heckenberger 2002, 2005). Arawak speakers are identified with intensive agriculture and key aspects of political organization. Other language groups, both other language families (Panoan or Tupian, for example), and the large number of language isolates found throughout the basin, and in Mojos in particular, are not important factors in these models. While earthworks are associated with Arawak speakers in many places, nowhere do they reach the extent or variety that they do in Mojos. The migration of Arawak speakers is certainly related to the long-term history of Mojos, but it does not by itself constitute an explanation. Precolumbian inhabitants included Arawak speakers, but Mojos' defining factor is extreme and sustained linguistic diversity.

This chapter cultivates a third answer using a concept of ontology developed by Philippe Descola (2013). Ontology, the ways in which groups of people define and then categorize phenomena, is an abstract phenomenon, but it has visible effects in the archaeological record. An ontological perspective is different from a focus on religion because within a community, ontology describes those ideas that allow people to act in the world, more fundamental than religious ideas. In precolumbian America, an idea of religion as a discrete category within social structure, or as an indigenous cultural category, seems to be less useful (Fowles 2013).

In addition to providing a better fit than "religion" for Amazonian cases, "ontology" provides a useful perspective on the connection between anthropogenic landscape and agriculture. An ontological perspective on an agricultural landscape moves analysis out of a well-worn loop of thinking about agricultural intensification. How an agricultural landscape is assembled from plants, animals, people, and landscapes is a visible application of foundational ideas about how people and things are assembled into social worlds. The test of ontology lies in the strength of its connections to the archaeological record. As part of a central argument, Descola's (2013:384–385) *Beyond Nature and Culture* develops an ontological explanation for why Amazonians never domesticated animals. A similar argument was also proposed independently by Peter Stahl (2014). Both authors, incorporating the Amazonian perspectivism of Viveiros de Castro, developed similar interpretations to explain why Amazonians did not domesticate animals, as in other parts of the world.

Viveiros de Castro proposes that Amazonian thought about relationships between people and animals can be explained as a combination of different perspectives (Viveiros de Castro 1998, 2014). When a human hunter walks through the forest, he sees a jaguar as an animal, and another human as a human. But when a jaguar walks through the forest, he sees a jaguar as a human, and the human as an animal. The difference between the jaguar and the human hunter is not one of essence, but of perspective. Some communities use this ontology to relate to many kinds of animals as social beings, which affects how humans behave toward animals. Crucially, when the Achuar interact with infant animals in a social or kinship model, including women who nurse the orphaned babies of hunted animals, this makes the consumption of those animals impossible.

Descola and Stahl independently used this idea to explain a paradox in Amazonia (Descola 2013; Stahl 2014). Amazonian peoples have social relations with all kinds of plants and animals, from the combination of parts of different plants to create powerful hallucinogens, to the tuning of manioc varieties to meet local soil, rainfall, and pest conditions. With this depth and complexity of local environmental knowledge, it is surprising that Amazonians did not domesticate animals (excepting muscovy ducks). As a faunal analyst, Stahl disposes of the supposed lack of suitable animal species, and both he and Descola arrive at ontology as an explanation for Amazonian (non)domestication. If such a fundamental, long-term aspect of economic life is part of an ontological difference, then perhaps other agricultural differences can be similarly explored. Raised fields might be part of such a significant difference in agriculture.

The principal difference between Mojos and the rest of the Amazon is the combination of unexceeded linguistic diversity with the density and variety of agricultural earthworks. As documented by Denevan (2001), raised fields and other agricultural earthworks are found throughout the South American lowlands, but Mojos is unique in terms of total area and variety. Descola's ontological distinctions and Viveiros de Castro's perspectivism can be used to interpret the long-term history of population, agriculture, and intensification in Mojos.

This chapter takes a landscape perspective, meaning that there are no conditions independent of the landscape which made raised fields emerge in Mojos but not in neighboring regions. No prime mover by itself explains the geography and history of landscapes in Mojos, because they themselves are part of this causality. Historical and geographic contingency are related to the "temporality of the landscape" (Ingold 1993; see also Swenson, Chapter 10), and landscapes are the specific contexts in which these differences develop. The combination of Descola's and Stahl's independent analyses suggests that if ontological differences can explain the lack of animal domestication, they can also help explain differences in anthropogenic landscapes.

From perspective to ontology

Descola (2013:56) outlines a new anthropological project from this understanding that the distinction between nature and culture is specific to Western thought and anthropology. He classifies this distinction as an example of "naturalist" ontology. If naturalism is only one of several alternatives found in the ethnographic record, then anthropology starts over with a new subject matter: not the variety of human societies or cultures, defined in opposition to the natural world, but the different ways that people build collectives out of both humans and non-humans. Descola uses the contrast between "naturalism" and "animism" as a starting point for analysis, illustrating how animist ontology includes a wide and complex web of social relationships between humans, animals, plants, and other entities. Naturalist ontology, by contrast, is predicated on a strict division between humans and non-humans, with social relations confined within the category of humans. In this formulation, naturalism loses its universal potency, becoming one of four historical patterns.

Moving on to redefine animism, Descola (2013:11) entertains the notion that Amazonian societies are the result of an environment in which an unsurpassed number of distinct species of plants and animals are found in the forests, while never appearing in dense groups without the intervention of human societies. Descola (2013:13) then dismisses this argument by drawing out the similar animist ontology of circumpolar groups, whose environment is quite different in this sense.

Perhaps ontological differences align with specific groups of people, through language. In this way, we could connect some distinctive ontology to Arawak speakers in Amazonia, and perhaps another, distinct animist ontology to other language families. However, the examples used to define this animist category include the Jivaroan-speaking Achuar, the Tukanoan-speaking Desana, and the Arawak-speaking Campa. There is no reason to suspect that ontologies align exclusively with Arawak speakers, or any other language family.

Ontologies are not mutually exclusive categories into which individual humans or human societies fall. Just as a biological scientist might maintain a strict conceptual boundary between humans and animals, and then go home to treat his or her dog as a member of the family, so multiple ontologies comfortably coexist within individuals, families, societies, or other kinds of collectives.

In the precolumbian Amazon, communities were in contact with one another over many generations, over many millennia. Perhaps the difference between landscape domesticators and non-landscape domesticators in South America is associated with ontological difference, rather than with language. Or more pointedly, perhaps the geographic distinction between the Altiplano and Mojos is not as significant as such differences, with two of the largest concentrations of landscape capital in the Americas located within a few hundred kilometers of each other, one in the highlands on the shores of Lake Titicaca, and the other in the lowlands of the Llanos de Mojos.

The domestication of animals is an example of ontological differences between animism, as exemplified by Amazonian societies, and naturalism, which underlies twenty-first century industrial agriculture and global markets. This difference could play out in other kinds of relationships that are associated with communal tasks that connect agriculture and religious ritual. The interplay of daily practice and ritual is usefully analyzed in such cases as the organization of irrigation in Bali (Lansing 1991) or the relationship of religious ritual to the forest in highland Vietnam (Condominas 1977). Fowles (2010) also makes a strong case against the utility of religion as a distinct category in archaeological thought, tracing the history and use of the term. This is a strong critique of religion as a category for archaeology in general, and landscape archaeology in particular, particularly when a most striking alternative set of analytical terms is emerging from Amazonia, the closest source of ethnographic analogy for Mojos.

Archaeological evidence from the Llanos de Mojos provides unusual access to a domesticated landscape. A domesticated landscape is one where communal tasks produce material correlates that are experienced and used by descendants (Ingold 1993; Walker 2011). Some tasks involved intentional investments of labor in the landscape, reflecting an instrumental understanding of soil and water, and improving conditions for cultivation. We now turn to landscape domestication in Mojos in greater detail.

Precolumbian landscapes in Mojos

At the regional scale, diversity in Mojos landscapes was and is spatially discrete (Denevan 1966; Erickson 2006; Walker 2008). Different landscapes were connected to different kinds of daily routines (Figure 11.2). The landscapes reflect differences in how people, fire, water, animals, and fish moved across the landscape. The diversity of how Mojos communities created and experienced their landscape through daily routine was patterned in that it can be divided into seven areas, four to the west and three to the east of the Mamoré River. For at least three areas,

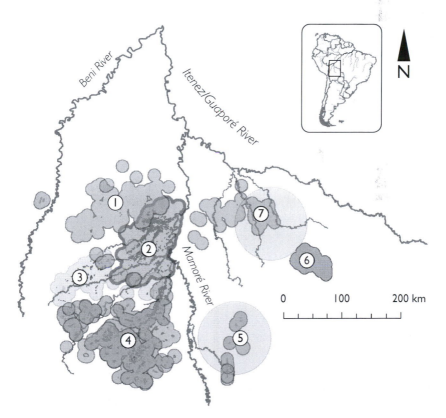

FIGURE 11.2 Variation in types of earthworks across the Llanos de Mojos: 1. Ditched fields, 2. Large Raised fields, 3. Mound fields, 4. Raised fields and causeways, 5. Large mounds and causeways, 6. Baures hydraulic complex, 7. Ring ditches and ditched fields.

clear evidence suggests that the landscapes were occupied over more than 1,000 (in some places 2,000) years. Some differences between the landscapes are profound, such as the presence or absence of agricultural fields or mounds, or the density of the investment of labor in the landscape.

Different landscape patterns suggest that different combinations and schedules of community activities were required in order to construct and maintain those landscapes. This also implies that different kinds of community activities were made possible by those landscapes. The analogy is not perfect between anthropogenic landscapes and architecture or built environment, but landscapes affect people as buildings do. Seven different types of landscape architecture were practiced over the last 2,000 years in Mojos. Consequently, the ontologies of people traveling and working there on a daily basis had distinctive effects on those seven landscapes, and were affected by them differently.

East of the Mamoré River (and south of the Guaporé/Itenez), Mojos communities built three landscapes. The first and perhaps best known is the landscape of large mounds and causeways in the southeast, associated with the modern city of Trinidad, identified with the Arawak- speaking Mojo, first excavated by Nordenskiöld (1913) early in the twentieth century, and recently by Heiko Prümers and his colleagues (Prümers 2004, 2012). Next, to the north and east, is the Baures Hydraulic Complex, described by Erickson, and consisting of large forest islands with ring ditches, causeways, and fishweirs (Erickson 2000). Moving to the north and west is a large area with ring ditches and ditched fields (Erickson 2010; Prümers 2014; Prümers et al. 2006). Ditched fields continue to the north across a large area, although in this third landscape they are not well known at all.

Continuing across the Mamoré River to the west, ditched fields are found across a large area around and to the north of the large lakes of Mojos. As they are east of the Mamoré, these fields are not well known. Moving to the south, the next landscape is that of large raised fields, around and near the Iruyañez, Omi, Yacuma, and Rapulo Rivers in west central Mojos (Walker 2004, 2011). Upriver from this area, to the south and west, is an area of mound fields, another landscape that is not well known. Finally, in the south is the best known area of earthworks, with causeways, raised fields, and mounds, associated with San Ignacio de Moxos (Erickson 1995, 1980).

Accompanying the evidence of landscape diversity are clues about diversity in ceramics. Jaimes Betancourt (2012) has produced a sequence based on excavations at Loma Salvatierra in the southeast, which is the new benchmark for the region. Vessel forms like grater plates are found in this sequence as well as along the Apere River to the west of the Mamoré, but are not found along the Iruyañez River in the north. Such differences in vessel forms suggest differences in basic patterns of cooking and serving food and drink. Another difference from ceramics is the presence of ceramic figurines along the Apere but not along the Iruyañez. These figurines, with coffee bean eyes and representations of female genitalia, may be associated with larger patterns outside of Mojos.

Precolumbian burial treatment is spatially patterned as well. Prümers has excavated several patterns of inhumation burial in the southeast and northeast of Mojos, and the southeast also is characterized by urn burial (Nordenskiöld 1913; Prümers 2004). Urn burials have also been found along the Apere River, but neither urn burials nor inhumations have emerged from west central Mojos. Although we do not have enough information to interpret these patterns across Mojos, the differences across the region are suggestive of considerable diversity in three significant domains, in addition to the landscape: ceramic forms associated with cooking and serving food and drink, associated with curation of the human body, and associated with abstract concepts of the female body. As a whole, the archaeological evidence shows patterned diversity across the region.

The archaeological record of landscape continues to produce more evidence of anthropogenic landscapes, and of more modification within each landscape. In 1966 and 2001, Denevan (1966:90, 2001:246) characterized raised fields in the west central part of Mojos as having perhaps 5,000 field platforms. In fieldwork since the mid-1990s, and as more satellite images have become easier to use, that estimate has changed (Walker 2004, 2008). Today, we have mapped more than 30,000 raised fields of that type in west central Mojos, and the final number will be closer to 40,000. Similar increases will likely emerge in other areas within Mojos (and nearby regions).

These landscapes appear to have been long-inhabited. Excavations in west central Mojos document a long chronology for occupation and use of raised fields (Walker 2000, 2004, 2017). Raised fields are difficult to date, but radiocarbon dates are taken from excavations in the forest islands in direct spatial association with fields. Excavation does not suggest a small population, building raised fields for a single use and then abandoning them. I argue that farmers living in networks of settlement both along and far from the rivers better fits the survey and radiocarbon data (Walker 2004, 2017). Pollen and phytolith evidence also suggests a longer-term tenure for raised fields, because the environmental record is stable from about 400 CE until 1400 CE (Whitney et al. 2014).

These long-inhabited, diverse landscapes have implications for how people thought about nature and culture, or how they organized the landscape in which they lived. The first source of analogy for interpretation of raised field builders, maintainers, farmers, and users comes from the groups that were living on these landscapes in the seventeenth and eighteenth centuries.

Ethnohistoric and linguistic evidence

Ethnographic and ethnohistoric evidence (mostly from the 1700s) provides details that illustrate the picture of diversity taken from archaeological landscapes. Arawak speakers were well known to Jesuit missionaries, but the chronicles also describe diversity in culture and language, including four linguistically isolated groups, as well as many other, less well-documented groups. It is unlikely that the regional pattern of distinct landscapes depends on Arawak societies in isolation from these other language groups.

The Handbook of South American Indians remains a good starting point for review, although other scholars have developed ethnohistoric research here (Block 1994; Van Valen 2013). The following summary is drawn from Metraúx's (1942) compilation. The *Mojo* (both Ignaciano and Trinitario) and *Baure* are Arawak speakers, well represented in the ethnohistoric record (Eder 1985). They spun cotton and wore *tipoys* (tunics), lived in villages with chiefs, had a complex religious life, and were thereby recognized by the Jesuit missionaries as "civilized." Jesuit sources often lump Arawak groups together, although they mention the distinctive palisaded villages of the Baure.

The *Movima* are described as excellent farmers (Figure 11.3), living along the Yacuma River, which connects both the area of large raised fields and the area of mound fields, stretching for more than 200 km to the west of the Mamoré River. The *Cayuvava* are described as fierce and dangerous, although the mission

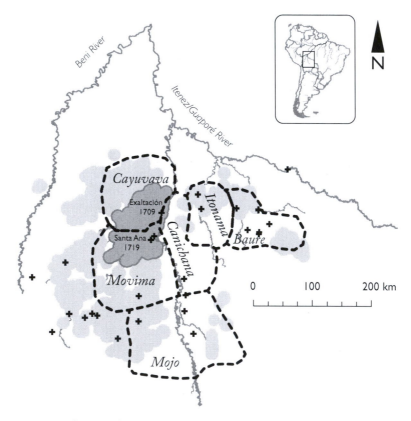

FIGURE 11.3 Distribution of different language groups in the Llanos de Mojos, as originally reconstructed by William Denevan (1966: Figure 3) with respect to anthropogenic landscapes

outpost established among this group at Exaltación would later become the capital of Mojos. The Cayuvava had large villages and a chief ruling over them, as well as a permanent temple housing a sacred fire and ritual sacrifice. At contact in 1698, they lived in a region characterized by large raised fields. The *Canichana* are much less well described, although they are said to have causewayed villages, another trait associated with Arawak speakers. The *Itonama* are described as famous weavers, as well as maize farmers.

Because the Jesuits were much concerned with it, religious organization is described from the few ethnohistorical sources that describe the Mojo, Baure, and other groups. The Mojo had religious specialists and are said to have worshipped particular, named divine beings. Arawak religious practices are known more generally both from the ethnohistoric record in the region, and from the literature of Arawak ethnography and ethnohistory around the Amazon basin. Arawak speakers are described as inscribing historical events on the landscape, in the form of rivers, caves, and other landscape features (Hornborg 2005; Hill and Hornborg 2011; Hill and Santos-Granero 2002).

In both Heckenberger's and Hornborg's discussions of Amazonian cultural history, Arawak speakers are connected to a set of agricultural practices and political or economic characteristics, and religious life is less often described (Heckenberger 2002; Hornborg 2005). Arawak music and ritual musical instruments have been described from across the Amazon, and sacred flutes are associated both with gender relations, political organization, and architectural forms (Neihardt 2011). The Mojo and Baure are described as having flutes, as well as a jaguar cult (Metraux 1942).

Although sacrifice is a significant part of religious practice in the Andes and in Mesoamerica, in Mojos it appears to have been less important. The Inca and the Aztecs are strong examples of analogism, and Descola (2013:207–221) uses descriptions of Mesoamerican sacrifice as illustrations for this distinctive ontology. This kind of relationship between people and the divine does not make sense in an Amazonian, animist ontology. Mojos examples include an ethnohistoric example of sacrifice, an account of Cayuvava religious ritual, taking place in a public building where a permanent fire was maintained, and where sacrifices were carried out, of rhea, deer, and rabbit (a term which conceivably could refer to a variety of rodents as well) (Zapata 1906). These ethnohistoric accounts provide only fragmentary evidence, but they suggest a diversity of religious practices, and perhaps of ontological perspectives.

Recent linguistic work has placed the languages of Mojos in a much stronger comparative context (Haude 2006). The linguistic isolates Movima, Cayuvava, Canichana, and Itonama have been confirmed to be unrelated to any other extant languages. Mojos is part of the Guaporé-Mamoré linguistic area, with as great a linguistic diversity as any place in the world. Mojeño languages were part of a group of languages that were in contact over the long term, as indicated by similarities in grammatical attributes (Epps 2009; Michael and Epps 2015). In a manner distinctive to Amazonia, such linguistic areas are not characterized by code switching or borrowing, as is the case among similar areas in other parts of the world. Although Amazonians often speak several languages, and have many opportunities to "mix" languages in these ways, they apparently do not do so. Instead, similarities across languages can be seen in distinctive shared grammatical features that they each exhibit. Perhaps Amazonian multilingual situations reflect a different kind of linguistic identity. If this assessment holds, then Mojeños spoke a group of distinct languages, in contact for thousands of years, each of which maintained their independence while being in contact with the others.

The combination of archaeological, ethnohistoric, and linguistic evidence suggests that precolumbian Mojos was characterized by persistent diversity in language, burial practice, ritual practice, landscape, economy, political structure, body decoration, music, sedentism, and diet. Many of these abstracted attributes vary spatially: language, burial practice, landscape, economy, and diet, for example. For landscape, chronology suggests at least 1,500 years of distinct, patterned anthropogenic landscapes. For language, at least 2,000 years of sustained interaction between languages is possible. The overall picture is one of potential for ontological diversity over a long period of time: six major languages; complex economies that involve fishing, farming, and hunting; and contact with outside groups and areas. This diversity was associated with diversity in landscape patterns. If animist ontology changes how people live in relation with plants and animals, and other humans, then this landscape patterning could be related to ontological difference.

Toward precolumbian Mojeño ontologies

Pattern in the west central Mojos landscape is conspicuous in a more intimate way. At the smallest scale, the boundaries that created forest islands and raised field platforms provide insight into Mojeño ontology, through the communal tasks that correspond to them, and through the plants, animals, and people that were contained within and crossed those boundaries. Much like architecture (another aspect of the built environment), landscape is in a recursive relationship with behavior, because in some cases the behavior that the landscape affords is the same behavior that helps create and maintain the landscape (Rapoport 1990). The spatial pattern of raised fields and forest islands in west central Mojos shows that while the landscape encouraged investment of labor in particular places, those places were not particularly close to one another (Figure 11.4). The pattern suggests that in many cases, Mojeños traveled kilometers to fields or other inhabited islands. Although major rivers would have facilitated longer journeys, not all islands and fields are close to rivers.

Sedentism is the most important difference between the Amazonian societies known through ethnohistoric and ethnographic research, and Mojeño societies that built raised fields. Modern Amazonian peoples live in permanent settlements, but many communities trek throughout the year. The forest islands and raised fields that form the landscape record in Mojos suggest that precolumbian Mojeños were sedentary in ways less common since contact. Sedentism is a strategy

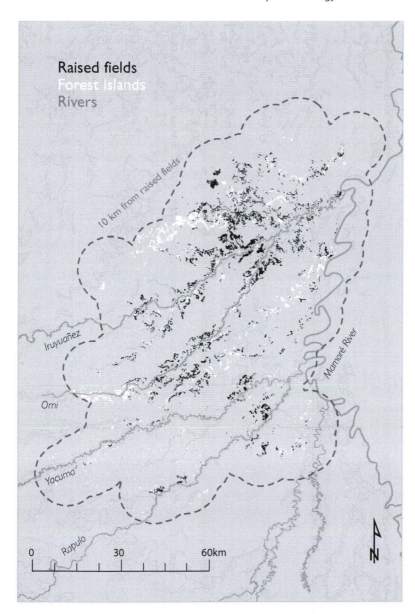

FIGURE 11.4 The distribution of neighborhoods of raised fields, forest islands, and rivers in west central Mojos

that communities adapt and abandon as part of their relations with other groups of people. This can be seen in eastern Bolivia, in the relationship between the Siriono of Holmberg's studies in the 1940s, and of Stearman's studies in the 1980s (Holmberg 1969; Stearman 1987). In the course of a generation, the same community went from trekking to sedentary life, in response to changes in political and economic context. Similar discussions of politically motivated sedentism, migration, and nomadism are central to influential models of montane Southeast Asia over the long term (Scott 2009). The patterned landscape of west central Mojos suggests that shifts to a non-sedentary lifestyle would be easy for communities to make. If the political situation on the larger rivers became unsustainable, raised fields far from the river would make viable either a trekking life or settlement far from the river. This kind of shift could have been routine, and variation in political organization could have been part of a seasonal cycle.

Another way to accommodate variation is to arrange it hierarchically. It is not clear that Mojeño landscapes were particularly compatible with hierarchy. We do not have strong evidence for hierarchy in burial treatment, or a site hierarchy, or a hierarchy of raised fields. Some fields and forest islands are bigger, but their arrangements do not correspond to a settlement hierarchy. The landscape does facilitate flexibility of cultivation, and the use of many different crops. It favors diversity, and connection along the principal rivers. Mojos is a crossroads at a large scale, because it lies between the Andes, the Gran Chaco, and the Amazon, and it is crossed by major rivers, but at a medium scale it is harder to travel, making a potential refuge.

Hornborg (2005) highlights the importance of Arawak speakers (and this network of rivers) to the integration of societies into a pan-Amazonian world. Because river systems enable the movement of people and ideas across thousands of kilometers, they make a good focus for examining the evidence for such a system. If raised fields represent investment of community work in the landscape, in specific locations, then it is notable that in west central Mojos, half of the mapped raised field platforms are found more than 2 km from any navigable river. Only about 20 percent of the field platforms are within 2 km of a river. At the least, this is equivocal evidence that the raised field landscape is oriented around the river system. Many fields are, but many are not. Similar numbers of forest islands are found near rivers, while many are found far from rivers.

Mojos landscapes correspond to communities of people who lived for many generations in a context of high diversity. It is possible that Mojeños organized variation without hierarchy. Crumley's (1979, 1994) concept of heterarchy presented the idea that variation could be organized into several hierarchies simultaneously, or that people could move between hierarchies with little difficulty. Another organizational option is rotation, in which different elements assume different positions within a hierarchy over time. In these ways hierarchy exists, but does not fossilize, as particular people and places shift and rotate through that hierarchy over time, so that the material remains are more ambiguous.

If Mojeño ontologies were associated with diversity in economy, language, and culture, seemingly without establishing permanent hierarchies, this did not create an agrarian utopia. Inequality on the basis of age, gender, and status could have been expressed in the economy and in language, even if it did not lead to the stratification of settlements or the creation of permanent classes. Ethnohistoric evidence makes it clear that precolumbian societies were not utopias: that kinship, captive slavery, and interactions between language groups can be both stable and deeply unequal, part of the construction of economies based on inequality (Santos-Granero 2010). Historical changes could also structure and restructure differences between gender roles. Mojeño agriculture undoubtedly included inequality between different segments of society, perhaps between genders or between the people who built and those who farmed the fields. Landscapes of raised field agriculture were the products and the producers of specific historical contexts, not utopian models.

Mojeños divided the world into farmland and not-farmland, as evidenced by their construction of raised fields, which have clear boundaries separating one kind of place from another. They also lived in forest islands, which divided the world between small areas of dry forest and large expanses of savanna. These divisions do not correspond to the naturalist division between culture and nature. But the record of landscape archaeology confirms that precolumbian Mojeños created these divisions, many times over, and we may assume that these differences arose from, and reinforced, their systems of thought.

Transspecies communities

When Mojeños built raised fields, tended useful trees, or raised a forest island, they invested labor in the landscape, making those places more useful for generations to come. The anthropogenic landscape creates affordances for later generations, and movements of people and community tasks follow patterns that we can identify on the landscape. Forest islands and raised fields both define some places in opposition to others. A feature of Mojeño ontology expressed through landscape is that lines were drawn between inside and outside. From these distinctions, we can try to understand what goes inside and outside these bounded landscape features. Ring ditches and raised fields are the permanent correlates of ontological categories.

The landscape in west central Mojos includes hydrological processes, the rainfall cycle, artificial fire regimes, earthwork construction, and other processes which are usually sorted into "natural" and "cultural" categories. Precolumbian Mojeños classified and organized the landscape in order to undertake communal tasks. The archaeological record suggests they attached meaning to two categories of landscape features: raised fields and forest islands (Figures 11.5, 11.6). Each are used by and create what can be called transspecies communities: combinations of refugee animals, economically useful plants, and humans in forest islands, and ants, termites, and worms, crop plants, pest animals, and humans in raised fields. We can suggest that precolumbians saw these landscape features as distinct categories because they created them with clear, physical boundaries. They cannot have failed to recognize these features as relevant to the transspecies communities that inhabited them. In the case of raised fields, these communities are related to domestication, although not perhaps exactly as in other agricultural examples from outside Amazonia. As Scott outlines the term, "we might term the assemblage of domesticates

FIGURE 11.5 Several large raised field platforms, as seen in the dry season of 1997, north of the Iruyañez River, in west central Mojos. These fields are roughly 20 meters wide, and up to 1,100 meters long.

FIGURE 11.6 A forest island, as seen in the dry season of 1997, along the Florida creek, east of the Omi River, in west central Mojos. More than 75 percent of forest islands in west central Mojos show evidence of human habitation on the surface. About 2,000 forest islands can be found within 10 km of large raised fields.

the 'late-Neolithic multispecies resettlement camp'" (Scott 2012:206). Different kinds of agriculture might be associated with different ontologies.

A key distinction in agricultural ontology is the difference between positive, direct action, which characterizes Western agriculture, and negative, indirect action which characterizes agricultures based in other ontologies. The difference is nicely illustrated by the powerful religious image (Descola 2013; Haudricourt 1962) of a European or Middle Eastern shepherd boy, who intervenes to save the sheep from the wolf, and who selectively breeds some wooly, docile sheep but not others. This relationship is contrasted with the boy who watches the water buffalo in southeast Asia. When the tiger comes, the water buffalo protect the boy, rather than the reverse. This difference is a paradigmatic example of ontological difference. In a related way, different landscapes could come from different understandings of the relationship between humans, plants, and animals. Analogies for the interpretation of these landscape elements should begin from indigenous categories first, and second from the theoretical expectations of economics or agricultural theory. Raised fields are better imagined on Amazonian terms than as units of alienable land used to produce commodities for a market.

The problem with analyzing Mojos communities as though they were made up only of humans is that they were likely also made up of plants and animals, spirits, mounds, and fields. A raised field has a clear boundary, but many plants and animals came or were brought across that boundary. We know about several kinds of plants that were cultivated on raised fields, including sweet potato (*Ipomoea batata*), New World taro (*Xanthosoma sp.*), maize (*Zea mays*), achiote (*Bixa orellana*), and hierba mate (*Ilex sp.*) (Erickson 1995; Whitney et al. 2014). Inga or ice-cream bean, a tree crop, was grown and used, perhaps outside of raised fields. The raised field in particular shows how Mojeños define things and place them into categories. In other words, a raised field, particularly in conjunction with paleoethnobotanical or faunal data, is an example of precolumbian Mojeño ontology in action. By seeing what is included in the field and what is excluded, we catch a glimpse into how Mojeños categorized the worlds of plants and animals, fire, water, and soil.

According to Kohn (among others), an Achuar gardener has a sophisticated knowledge of plant characteristics and the uses of plants (Kohn 2013). Her agricultural knowledge crosses non-Achuar categories of "social" and "not-social." Her manioc plants are as much her children as her human children. The family must be carefully managed, because although plant children provide food for the human, they are dangerous, and manioc plants will suck the blood of babies and children, if they can.

Descola's interpretation of Arawak agricultural terminology provides another starting point: "The terminological pair *aramu* and *ikiamia* thus in no way covers an opposition between the domesticated and wild. Rather, it applies to the contrast between plants that are cultivated by humans and those that are cultivated by spirits" (Descola 2013:39). If raised fields are where plants were planted by humans, then we must be aware of how indigenous categories might change the use of the field, and affect our archaeological study of the record of agriculture that it represents.

Similarly, forest islands are landscape elements where we have recovered the best evidence of habitation over several generations, and in some areas hundreds of generations (Balée and Erickson 2006; Balee 2013). They are botanically significant because their elevation makes them good locations for plants that cannot tolerate flooding. Forest islands held and created meaning for Mojeños as places that were inhabited by the living, and in some cases as burial grounds that were inhabited by ancestors as well. Forest islands could have been the location of intensive gardens, where labor and attention allowed the "experimental" cultivation and domestication of many different plants. Because of their elevation, they also would have been well suited for the management of forests, including palm forests (Smith 2015). Plants and animals share the places that humans constructed, maintained, abandoned, and reused. For example, communities of useful plants persist on forest islands through different kinds of human habitation. Prey animals migrate into a house during the wet season, because the flooding makes that island the only safe place. Forest islands are crucial intersections where plants and humans come together, both in the present day and in the historical and even the mythical past. Many forest islands, both in west central Mojos and throughout Mojos, have earthen mounds inside their boundaries. Elsewhere in South America, such constructions are part of traditions of indigenous placemaking that include social relations between human persons and mounds (Dillehay 2007).

The patterned habitation of forest islands and raised fields suggests a set of problems that codetermined political and economic relations. Relationships between ethnic or language groups and the landscape could be mediated by land tenure or other relations to place. If some communities held claim on islands or fields, then how those claims were negotiated and renegotiated with each generation was a problem that had to be solved by any ecology of ideas (Bateson 1972) based in an ontology of people, plants, and places. Mojeño ontology answers a set of questions: what is a plant, what is an animal, and what is a human? It then describes how these entities are organized into different categories. People, animals, and plants were related to each other through time in particular forest islands and raised fields. These are the primary two landscape elements for west central Mojos, but at least six other landscapes are present in Mojos, and still more are being studied across Amazonia (Rostain 2013; Schaan 2011).

Within a naturalist ontology, it is possible to have a Cartesian "god's eye view" of the landscape, and this is how archaeologists often think, using tools like maps, computers, and Geographic Information Systems (GIS) (Ingold 2000:209–218). But from within an Amazonian ontology, it is not possible to describe spatial and social relations without placing oneself on the map. The point of talking about landscape is to recite history, to figure out how to behave, and to keep track of obligations – for example, obligations about cohabitation, agricultural labor, or where one is welcome to go. Precolumbian Mojeños helped create landscape elements, organizing variation in persistent ways, but it is unlikely that they saw themselves as outside observers, abstracted from those places, looking on them from above. Perhaps Descola's strongest argument is that such a point of view is distinctive to a naturalist, Western ontology that developed in the 1600s in a newly connected Europe.

Conclusion

Accounts that temper the perfection of ecological models with the messiness and contingency of history are healthier and more robust. Fowles (2013) argues that because an institution mediates or addresses a conflict, it does not imply that it resolves it. Another way of thinking about this is that a landscape is historically contingent, much like the institutions of intergroup relations that made up the "middle ground" discussed by Richard White (1991) in the context of the Great Lakes in the seventeenth and eighteenth centuries. Moiety organization or the "middle ground" doesn't resolve differences between two groups, or even facilitate accurate communication, but it outlines the parameters of a self-perpetuating relationship.

Mojos landscapes and their corresponding ways of life or taskscapes (Ingold 1993) were such places, perhaps over and over again, between Tupian peoples such as the Siriono; language isolates like the Movima, Cayuvava, Canichana, and Itonama; Arawak peoples such as the Mojo and Baure; and then the Jesuits and the rubber barons. Such middle grounds are created at points in space and time, but when as a result they create landscapes, they channel future community tasks. Just as connections were created in the Upper Midwest and on the Great Lakes of North America between Algonquians, Iroquoians, European-based empires, and the American republic, or a new society was created in Mojos between the Jesuit missionaries and a range of savanna groups, a middle ground was created in precolumbian Mojos between communities with different languages, economies, and political structures. This middle ground did not resolve the differences between linguistic isolates, Arawaks, and Tupians, or between farmers, fishers, and hunters, but it did create stable settings for interactions that sometimes lasted for centuries.

A landscape is necessarily a palimpsest produced by the compromises that were agreed on over a long period of time. A longer-lasting compromise will necessarily be better represented in the landscape to a greater extent than one of shorter tenure. Those that created more durable infrastructure will be better represented than those that did not. A landscape does not represent a utopia but a compromise, a realpolitik, a mess, and the accompanying taskscape is a "middle ground."

Amazonian societies include a wide diversity of language, and the ethnographic record includes many "dialectical" societies, and groups organized around moieties. These social forms may be particularly successful middle grounds that helped very different groups of people exist in compromises that persisted through several generations. Students of Amazonian societies have long debated whether Amazonian societies might be inoculated against the state and other centralized political middle grounds (Lévi-Strauss 1944; Clastres 1977). Perhaps Mojos landscapes represent a constellation of successful, non-state compromises.

Mojeños did not divide the world into "nature" and "culture," but they could not have failed to recognize their own intentional actions building fields and elevating forest islands. They sorted the world into things that live in raised fields and those that do not, and things that live on forest islands and those that do not. Spatial context was part of the construction and use of ontological categories. When new communities of people moved into the landscape, these new facts must have been reconciled with the past, as it was already inscribed. As a new group integrates with the landscape, relations with the current inhabitants are established. How can they help to make places and move from being interlopers to being established? How do outsiders become insiders? If Mojeños of many languages coexisted over a hundred generations, it suggests that they solved these problems repeatedly. The mosaic of seven distinct landscape patterns suggests that these processes of integration lent stability to specific patterns of placemaking, earthwork construction, and forest island use. History settled into patterns, some of which are still visible today.

Mojos communities were not perfectly adapted to the environment, they didn't construct perfect niches for themselves, and they didn't terraform the entire savanna. They did inhabit the entire savanna and forest for many generations, and in doing so they built middle grounds that afforded compromise between communities of Arawaks and Movima, of humans and non-humans, and of plants and animals. It requires the creation of new middle grounds for us to learn this longer story, and become a part of it.

Acknowledgments

I would like to thank the Museo Yacuma in Santa Ana del Yacuma; the Unidad de Arqueología y Museos in La Paz, Bolivia; and the people of Yacuma Province, Beni, Bolivia, for hospitality over many years. The analysis presented here also represents research supported by the National Science Foundation, the University of Central Florida, the Brennan Foundation, and many others.

References

Balée, William L. 2013 *Cultural Forests of the Amazon: A Historical Ecology of People and Their Landscapes.* University of Alabama Press, Tuscaloosa.

Balée, William L., and Clark L. Erickson 2006 *Time and Complexity in Historical Ecology: Studies in the Neotropical Lowlands.* Columbia University Press, New York.

Bateson, Gregory 1972 *Steps to an Ecology of Mind.* Ballantine Press, New York.

Block, David 1994 *Mission Culture on the Upper Amazon: Native Tradition, Jesuit Enterprise and Secular Policy in Moxos, 1660–1880.* University of Nebraska Press, Lincoln.

Clastres, Pierre 1977 *Society Against the State.* Translated by Robert Hurley and Abe Stein. Blackwell, Oxford.

Condominas, Georges 1977 *We Have Eaten the Forest: The Story of a Montagnard Village in the Central Highlands of Vietnam.* Farrar Straus & Giroux, New York.

Crumley, Carole L. 1979 Three Locational Models: An Epistemological Assessment for Anthropology and Archaeology. In *Advances in Archaeological Method and Theory* Volume 2, edited by Michael Schiffer, pp. 141–173, Academic Press, Orlando.

Crumley, Carole L., ed. 1994 *Historical Ecology: Cultural Knowledge and Changing Landscapes*. School of American Research Advanced Seminar Series xiv. School for Advanced Research Press, Sante Fe.

Denevan, William M. 1966 *The Aboriginal Cultural Geography of the Llanos de Mojos of Bolivia*. Ibero-Americana 48. University of California Press, Berkeley.

———. 2001 *Cultivated landscapes of native Amazonia and the Andes*. Oxford University Press, Oxford.

Descola, Philippe 2013 *Beyond Nature and Culture*. University of Chicago Press, Chicago.

Dillehay, Tom D. 2007 *Monuments, Empires, and Resistance: The Araucanian Polity and Ritual Narratives*. Cambridge studies in archaeology. Cambridge University Press, Cambridge.

Doolittle, William Emery 2000 *Cultivated landscapes of native North America*. Oxford University Press, Oxford.

Eder, Francisco Xavier 1985 *Breve descripción de las Reducciones de Moxos*. Translated by Josep María Barnadas. Historia Boliviana, Cochabamba.

Epps, Patience 2009 Language Classification, Language Contact, and Amazonian Prehistory. *Language and Linguistics Compass* 3: 581–606.

Erickson, Clark L. 1980 Sistemas agrícolas prehispánicos en los Llanos de Mojos. *América Indígena* 40: 731–755.

———. 1995 Archaeological Methods for the Study of Ancient Landscapes of the Llanos de Mojos in the Bolivian Amazon. In *Archaeology in the Lowland American Tropics: Current Analytical Methods and Applications*, edited by Peter W. Stahl, pp. 66–95. Cambridge University Press, Cambridge.

———. 2000 An Artificial Landscape-Scale Fishery in the Bolivian Amazon. *Nature* 408(6809): 190–193.

———. 2006 *The Domesticated Landscapes of the Bolivian Amazon,* edited by William Balée and Clark Erickson, pp. 235–278. Columbia University Press, New York.

———. 2008 Amazonia: The Historical Ecology of a Domesticated Landscape. In *The Handbook of South American Archaeology*, edited by Helaine Silverman and William H. Isbell, pp. 157–183. Springer, New York.

———. 2010 The Transformation of Environment into Landscape: The Historical Ecology of Monumental Earthwork Construction in the Bolivian Amazon. *Diversity* 2: 618–652.

Fowles, Severin 2010 The Southwest School of Landscape Archaeology. *Annual Review of Anthropology* 39: 453–468.

———. 2013 *An Archaeology of Doings: Secularism and the Study of Pueblo Religion*. School for Advanced Research Press, Santa Fe.

Haude, Katharina 2006 *A Grammar of Movima*. Radboud Universiteit, Nijmegen.

Haudricourt, André G. 1962 Domestication des animaux, culture des plantes et traitement d'autrui. *L'Homme* 2: 40–50.

Heckenberger, Michael 2002 Rethinking the Arawakan Diaspora: Hierarchy, Regionality, and the Amazonian Formative. In *Comparative Arawakan Histories: Rethinking Language Family and Culture Area in Amazonia*, edited by Jonathan D. Hill and Fernando Santos-Granero, pp. 99–122. University of Illinois Press, Urbana.

———. 2005 *The Ecology of Power: Culture, Place, and Personhood in the Southern Amazon, AD 1000–2000*. Routledge Press, New York.

Hill, Jonathan David, and Alf Hornborg 2011 *Ethnicity in Ancient Amazonia: Reconstructing Past Identities From Archaeology, Linguistics, and Ethnohistory*. University Press of Colorado, Boulder.

Hill, Jonathan D., and Fernando Santos-Granero 2002 *Comparative Arawakan Histories: Rethinking Language Family and Culture Area in Amazonia.* University of Illinois Press, Urbana.

Holmberg, Allan R. 1969 *Nomads of the Long Bow: The Siriono of Eastern Bolivia.* Natural History Press, New York.

Hornborg, Alf 2005 Ethnogenesis, Regional Integration, and Ecology in Prehistoric Amazonia: Toward a System Perspective. *Current Anthropology* 46: 589–620.

Ingold, Tim 1993 The Temporality of the Landscape. *World Archaeology* 25: 152–174.

———. 2000 *The Perception of the Environment: Essays on Livelihood, Dwelling and Skill.* Routledge, New York.

Jaimes Betancourt, Carla 2012 *La Ceramica de la Loma Salvatierra.* DAI, La Paz.

Kohn, Eduardo 2013 *How Forests Think: Toward an Anthropology Beyond the Human.* University of California Press, Berkeley.

Lansing, J. Stephen 1991 *Priests and Programmers: Technologies of Power in the Engineered Landscape of Bali.* Princeton University Press, Princeton.

Lévi-Strauss, Claude 1944 The Social and Psychological Aspect of Chieftainship in a Primitive Tribe: the Nambikuara of Northwestern Mato Grosso. *Transactions of the New York Academy of Sciences* 7(1 Series II): 16–32.

Meggers, Betty J. 1971 *Amazonia: Man and Culture in a Counterfeit Paradise.* Aldine, Chicago.

———. 1994 Archeological Evidence for the Impact of Mega-Nino Events on Amazonia During the Past Two Millennia. *Climatic Change* 28: 321–338.

Metraux, Alfred 1942 *Native Tribes of Eastern Bolivia and Western Matto Grosso.* Bureau of American Ethnology Bulletin 134. BAE, Washington, DC.

Michael, Lev David, and Patience Epps 2015 The Areal Linguistics of Amazonia. In *The Handbook of Areal Linguistics*, pp. 934–963. University of California Press, Berkeley.

Neihardt, John G. 2011 *Burst of Breath: Indigenous Ritual Wind Instruments in Lowland South America.* University of Nebraska Press, Lincoln.

Nordenskiöld, Erland 1913 Urnengraber und mounds im Bolivianischen Flachlande. *Baessler Archiv* 3: 205–255.

Prümers, Heiko 2004 Hügel umgeben von" schönen Monstern": Ausgrabungen in der Loma Mendoza (Bolivien). *Expeditionen in vergessene Welten* 25: 47–78.

———. 2012 ¿"Charlatanocracia" en Mojos? investigaciones arqueológicas en la Loma Salvatierra, Beni, Bolivia. *Boletín de arqueología PUCP* 11: 103–116.

———. 2014 Sitios prehispánicos con zanjas en Bella Vista, Provincia Iténez, Bolivia. In *Amazonía: Memorias de las Conferencias Magistrales del 3er Encuentro Internacional de Arqueología Amazónica*, edited by Stéphen Rostain, pp. 73–89. IFEA, FLACSO, Quito.

Prümers, Heiko, Carla Jaimes Betancourt, and Ruden Plaza Martínez 2006 Algunas tumbas prehispánicas de Bella Vista, Prov. Iténez, Bolivia. *Zeitschrift für Archäologie Au\s sereuropäischer Kulturen* 1: 251–284.

Rapoport, Amos 1990 *The Meaning of the Built Environment: A Nonverbal Communication Approach.* University of Arizona Press, Tucson.

Rostain, Stéphen 2013 *Islands in the Rainforest: Landscape Management in Pre-Columbian Amazonia.* Translated by Michelle Eliott. Left Coast Press, Walnut Creek, California.

Santos-Granero, Fernando 2010 *Vital Enemies: Slavery, Predation, and the Amerindian Political Economy of Life.* University of Texas Press, Austin.

Schaan, Denise P. 2011 *Sacred Geographies of Ancient Amazonia: Historical Ecology of Social Complexity.* Left Coast Press, Inc, Walnut Creek, California.

Scott, James C. 2009 *The Art of Not Being Governed: An Anarchist History of Upland Southeast Asia.* Yale University Press, New Haven, CT.

———. 2012 Four Domestications: Fire, Plants, Animals, and . . . Us. *The Tanner Lectures on Human Values* 31: 185–227. University of Utah Press, Salt Lake City.

Smith, Nigel 2015 *Palms and People in the Amazon.* Springer, New York.

Stahl, Peter W. 2014 Perspectival Ontology and Animal Non-Domestication in the Amazon Basin. In *Antes de Orellana: Actas del 3er Encuentro Internacional de Arqueología Amazónica,* edited by Stéphen Rostain, pp. 221–232. IFEA, FLACSO, Quito.

Stearman, Allyn M. 1987 *No Longer Nomads: The Sirionó Revisited.* Hamilton Press, Lanham, MD.

Van Valen, Gary 2013 *Indigenous Agency in the Amazon: The Mojos in Liberal and Rubber-Boom Bolivia, 1842–1932.* University of Arizona Press, Tucson.

Viveiros de Castro, Eduardo 1998 Cosmological deixis and Amerindian perspectivism. *Journal of the Royal Anthropological Institute* 4: 469–488.

———. 2014 *Cannibal Metaphysics: For a Post-Structural Anthropology.* Translated by Peter Skafish. Univocal, Minneapolis.

Walker, John H. 2000 Raised Field Abandonment in the Upper Amazon. *Culture & Agriculture* 22(2): 27–31.

———. 2004 *Agricultural Change in the Bolivian Amazon.* Memoirs in Latin American Archaeology 13. Department of Anthropology, Pittsburgh.

———. 2008 The llanos de Mojos. In *The Handbook of South American Archaeology,* edited by Helaine Silverman and William H Isbell, pp. 927–939. Springer, New York.

———. 2011 Social Implications From Agricultural Taskscapes in the Southwestern Amazon. *Latin American Antiquity* 22: 275–295.

———. 2012 Recent Landscape Archaeology in South America. *Journal of Archaeological Research* 20: 309–355.

———. 2017 *Island, River, and Field.* Archaeologies of Landscape in the Americas, No. 4. University of New Mexico Press, Albuquerque.

White, Richard 1991 *The Middle Ground: Indians, Empires, and Republics in the Great Lakes Region, 1650–1815.* Cambridge studies in North American Indian history. Cambridge University Press, Cambridge.

Whitney, Bronwen S., Ruth Dickau, Francis E. Mayle, John H. Walker, J. Daniel Soto, and José Iriarte 2014 Pre-Columbian Raised-Field Agriculture and Land Use in the Bolivian Amazon. *The Holocene* 24: 231–241.

Zapata, Agustín 1906 Carta del Padre Agustín Zapata al Padre Joseph Buendia, en la que da noticias del Paititi. In *Juicio de Limites Entre el Perú y Bolivia,* edited by Victor M. Maurtua, pp. 24–28. Imprenta de Henrich y Compania, Barcelona.

12

THE MULTIVALENT MOLLUSK

Spondylus, ritual, and politics
in the prehispanic Andes

Jerry D. Moore

Introduction

Over the last two decades, studies of material culture have engaged an increasingly complex body of theoretical debates dubbed "the ontological turn." These debates have oscillated around two poles of argument, as Pedersen (2012) has suggested, between "the study of, or reflection on, the question of what there is – what are the fundamental entities or kinds of stuff that exist?" and the idea of the "radical alterity of certain societies" in that they do not have "different socially constructed viewpoints on the same (natural world), but in their living in actually different worlds." These debates have intersected with another set of theoretical questions regarding human subjects, material objects, and their respective capacities for agency (e.g., Alberti 2014; Descola 2013; Gell 1998; Gosden 2005; Ingold 2010, 2012; Miller 2005). Discussing Maya ontology and ritual, Hutson et al. (p. 165, this volume) note that categories that "a modern Western observer might keep separate – animate and inanimate, sacred and profane – remain undivided" among the Maya. Similarly, anthropologists have argued that such theoretical concerns are congruent with traditional worldviews in South America, which attribute vital force and agency to phenomena that are considered "inanimate" in Western thinking. For example, Allen (1998:20) observes that Andean ethnographers must make a "simple but fundamental mental shift and accept the premise that all material things (including things we normally call inanimate) are potentially active agents in human affairs" and although not every object is constantly treated as a subject, "There are ritually prescribed times and places at which human beings communicate with these nonhuman entities in order to maintain a harmonious relationship with them." Among various Amazonian societies, cosmologies linking landscape, "natural" phenomena, plants and animals, and humans are widespread (e.g., Descola 2013; Viveiros de Castro 1998, 2004, 2007; Weiss 1975).

Similarly, Andean archaeologists have argued that artifacts, constructions, and landscape features were enmeshed in pre-Contact ontologies (e.g., Alberti and Bray 2009; Bray 2012; Angelo 2014; Lau 2010). Bray (2012) has documented evidence for ritual commensalism with sacred landforms or *wakas*. Further, Bray (2009:362) has argued that Inca miniature figurines were "powerful or power objects imbued with the ability and agency to serve as proxies for, or agents of the State," a perspective requiring the admission of "the possibilities of alternative ontologies or states of being beyond that of the dichotomized categories of subject/object." Bray (2009) glosses the Quechua concept of *camaquen* as "thinking with things," derived from *camay*, denoting a constellation of concepts including "to make," "to animate," or "to give form and force." Taylor (1974:236) discussed cognates such as *camaquenc*, "a transmissible vital force," observing that "The Andean animated world evoked a broader horizon than its Western equivalent: anything that has a function or purpose is animated in order for its function or purpose to be realized: fields, mountains, and stones – as well as men." Finally, Salomon (1991:16) defines *camay* as connoting "the energizing of extant matter . . . a continuous act that works upon a being as long as it exists."

In light of these theoretical debates and ontological turns, I attempt to understand a very distinctive mollusk. Over four millennia of prehistory, the shells of the genus *Spondylus* were desired, depicted, and deployed in prehispanic Andean societies of vastly different scales and organization (Figure 12.1). Two species were used in prehistoric South America – *Spondylus princeps* and *Spondylus calcifer*, respectively known as the thorny oyster and the spiny rock scallop. *Spondylus* shells were used in surprisingly diverse contexts and settings – as artifacts, raw materials, and icons[1] – including by people living long distances from the mollusks' natural habitat.

In the following, I discuss the multiple settings in which *Spondylus* were engaged with and implicated in ritual contexts with political and other valences in Andean

FIGURE 12.1   *Spondylus princeps.* Photo by the author.

South America. An attempt to decode "*the*" meaning of *Spondylus* is misguided, because the archaeological evidence indicates that *Spondylus* was irreducible to a single quality or property. Rather, *Spondylus* exemplify what Keane (2003:414) calls "bundling" in which "the sensuous qualities of objects . . . bundled together in any object will shift in their relative value, utility, and relevance across contexts" (see also Alt and Pauketat, Chapter 3; Pauketat 2013:34–36). *Spondylus* were not thought of as *objects* manipulated by human *subjects* but rather something akin to Ingold's (2012:436) concept of a *thing* as "a gathering of materials in movement – a particular knotting together of the matter-flow – and to witness a thing is to join with the processes of its ongoing formation," a concept strikingly similar to the Quechua *camay*. Following from this, "the thing has the character not of an externally bounded entity, . . . but of a knot whose constituent threads, far from being contained within it, trail beyond, only to become caught with other threads in other knots" (Ingold 2010:4). Finally, the histories of things are influenced not only by ontologies but also by political, ideological, or technological factors (Hutson et al., Chapter 8; Swenson 2015).

The following reviews the uses of *Spondylus* in Andean societies of dramatically different scales and socio-political organizations, and discusses the varying biographies of *Spondylus* "things" in the prehispanic Andes. First, I briefly discuss the biology, habitats, and distribution of *S. princeps* and *S. calcifer*. Second, I summarize the archaeological contexts in which *Spondylus* have been found in the Andes – whether as an artifact, raw material, or icon – with a particular attention to ritual and political uses. Third, I argue that *Spondylus* had several sets of associations – used in construction rituals, incorporated into elite garments, affiliated with acts of transitions – as well as with rituals focused on water, hydraulic systems, and agricultural fertility. I suggest that the heightened significance of *Spondylus* in water rituals and agricultural rites was linked to challenges faced by complex political systems dependent on irrigation systems during centuries marked by extreme environmental fluctuations. These societies attempted to ensure the continued flow of water with rituals involving *Spondylus*, a particularly pressing concern after circa A.D. 300 and continuing until the arrival of the Spaniards, when such rites were classified as idolatrous.

Spondylus: biology, distribution, and archaeological assumptions

With more than sixty species, *Spondylus* are widely distributed in warm oceans and their shells were prized by ancient and traditional societies from northern Europe to Melanesia (e.g., Chapman et al. 2011; Ifantidis and Nikolaidou 2011; Malinowski 1922). A distinctive feature of this molluscan family is their shell's exterior spines, creating a complex surface attracting epibionts that inhabit and camouflage the mollusk (Feifarek 1987; Lamprell 1987; Mackensen et al. 2012). *Spondylus princeps* and *Spondylus calcifer* live in the eastern Pacific Ocean, in the warm waters between the Gulf of California and Punta Sal, Peru, their southern limit determined by the cold Peruvian or Humboldt Current (Keen 1971:96). It is often asserted that the Gulf of Guayaquil was the southern limit of its habitat (e.g., Paulsen 1974), but in fact *Spondylus* are found approximately 110 kilometers south of the Gulf of Guayaquil, where *Spondylus calcifer* occurs in sufficient densities (three to four individuals per square meter at depths of 10–12 meters) that artisans collect the shells today (Carter 2008:118–119). Recent intensified collection of *Spondylus* has significantly reduced populations. For example, in the year 2000, divers from three or four boats along the coast of Esmeraldas, Ecuador, had an average daily catch of 300 *Spondylus*; in April 2010, surveys of six 100-square-meter survey areas that previously supported *Spondylus* failed to find *a single individual* (Mackensen et al. 2011:115; Mackensen et al 2012). In light of these data, it is amazing that these mollusks were collected with varying levels of intensity over several millennia of Andean prehistory.

Numerous scholars have discussed the significance of *Spondylus* in the prehispanic Andes (Bauer 2007; Blower 1995; Carter 2008, 2011; Cordy-Collins 1990, 2001; Eeckhout 2004; Glowacki and Malpass 2003; Gorriti Manchego 2000; Hocquenghem 2010; Mackey and Pillsbury 2013; Marcos 1977–78; Martin 2009; Moore and Vílchez, 2016; Murra 1975; Paulsen 1974; Pillsbury 1996; Velázquez et al. 2006). The acquisition and use of *Spondylus* shells were activities deeply enmeshed in Andean ritual and politics as practiced by a wide variety of social groups ranging from small villages to vast empires. For example, Cordy-Collins (2001:36) has written:

> My long-term study of *Spondylus* shells in pre-Hispanic Peru has revealed a clear pattern: from the beginning of the Initial Period (ca. 1800 B.C. [sic]) through the end of the Late Horizon (ca. A.D. 1530), Peru's ancient cultures consistently allocated the thorny oyster to four specific ends. They presented it whole or in part in petitions to the gods, interred it as elite mortuary offerings, worked it into jewelry and ornaments for their nobility, and infused its image into all high-status media, including ceramics, textiles, and metal. It is widely associated with sacrifice, in part, surely, because of its reddish color, and also because of its significance as a sacred substance.

In fact, *Spondylus* was used earlier and in elite *and* non-elite contexts. First, *Spondylus* was imported to the central coast of Peru by at least 2600–2000 B.C. as indicated by whole valves and finished beads at Caral in the Supe Valley (Shady Solis 2006:53). Second, while it has long been assumed that the presence of *Spondylus* at sites in Peru and further south indicated the existence of prehispanic trade with coastal Ecuador (Cordy-Collins 1990:396), it is now clear that *Spondylus* also could be obtained in far northern Peru (Carter 2008, 2011). Third, although it has been argued that *Spondylus* exchange peaked with the Inca Empire, in fact significant quantities were obtained much earlier by the Moche (circa A.D. 300–700), Middle Sicán/Lambayeque (A.D. 900–1100), and Chimú (A.D. 900–1470) societies. Fourth, *Spondylus* did not necessarily require specialist divers (Cordy-Collins

1990:397; Paulsen 1974). In fact, the mollusks live at shallower depths, either intertidally or below 3 meters (Carter 2011:63). Although mollusks are difficult to pry off their rocky substrate, specialized divers would only be necessary when *Spondylus* were over-fished.

Finally, *Spondylus* were used in contexts, purposes, and meanings in addition to those of divine offerings, elite burial goods or ornaments, or raw materials for high-status crafts and objects. As Carter (2011:64) writes, recent data "highlight the great variability of *Spondylus* consumption by Prehispanic South Americans through time and space." I discuss these variations as the values, associations, and potentialities of *Spondylus* were variously emphasized and engaged with in different social, ritual, and political contexts.

Spondylus: artifact, raw material, and icon

Spondylus were used in prehispanic South America in three different, but not mutually exclusive ways – as artifact, icon, and raw material – and these overlapping associations characterize some of the oldest known examples of their use (see Table 12.1). For example, the valves themselves were used as offerings and grave goods with no or little modifications, converted into a range of objects such as beads, figurines, and decorative elements incorporated into other objects (e.g., as inlay on wooden objects), or iconographically depicted in a wide array of media. The following discussion considers these different uses separately, but this is simply an organizational strategy probably unrecognizable to the people who used, modified, and depicted *Spondylus*.

Whole shells as artifacts

Unmodified *Spondylus* valves were offered in various rituals. They were commonly used as offerings in construction rituals, either initiating building or ceremonially burying a construction, such as at the Valdivia site of Real Alto, where Marcos (1988:188) describes the placement of a *Spondylus princeps* shell on a ramp associated with the Phase III (circa 2700–2600 B.C.) construction of the Charnel House. Some 700 kilometers to the south in Peru's Nepeña Valley, *Spondylus* were in dedicatory offerings at the Initial Period site of Punkuri, where Julio Tello found a spectacular tomb containing a decapitated woman interred with an engraved Strombus trumpet, food offerings, and a pair of *Spondylus* shells (Burger 1992:89; Falcón et al. 2005). *Spondylus* were used in construction rituals in domestic architecture. At La Vega in southern Ecuador, Guffroy (2004:55–57, 82–83) uncovered an offering associated with a small dwelling that consisted of a whole *Spondylus* and two small worked and drilled pieces of jadeite, all radiocarbon-dated to 2900 ± 60 BP or 1216–893 cal. B.C. (two sigmas). The placement of the *Spondylus* offering under foundation stones of a small rectangular dwelling "may correspond to ritual practices linked with the construction phase" (Guffroy 2004:57, translation mine). A similar offering associated with domestic construction rituals was uncovered at El

TABLE 12.1 Selected *Spondylus* forms and associations in the prehispanic Andes

	Site	Date	Context of Find	Distance from Source (km, straight line)	Sociopolitical Organization	Possible Associations	Objects	Reference
Spondylus as Artifact (valves)	Punkuri	ca. 3000–1800 BC	sculpture on monument	670	regional polity?	dedicatory offering		Burger 1992; Falcón et al. 2005
	Caral	ca. 2600–2000 BC		890	regional polity?			Shady Solis 2006
	La Vega	1216–893 cal BC	residence	160	village	construction offering		Guffroy 2004
	Real Alto	2700–2600 BC	ramp on public architecture	5	large village	construction offering		Marcos 1988
	Achallán	ca. 900–100 BC	albarrada	3	village	construction and/or hydraulic		Stothert 1995, 2003
	El Porvenir	ca. 800–500 BC	residence	15	hamlet	construction offering		Moore 2010a
	Salango	600–100 BC	ceremonial platform	1	village	construction offer in post holes and post-construction ritual offerings		Lunniss 2008
	Sicán	AD 950–1050	temples on monumental mounds	300	regional polity	post-construction ritual offering		Shimada et al. 2004
	Sicán	AD 950–1050	elite burial	300	regional polity	funeral offering		Shimada et al. 2004
	Chan Chan-barrio	ca. AD 900–1470	residence	530	commoner barrio	"dedicatory offering"		Topic 1982
	Pedregal	ca. AD 1100–1300	residence	450	rural village	remodeling or abandonment		Cutright 2013

(Continued)

TABLE 12.1 (Continued)

	Site	Date	Context of Find	Distance from Source (km, straight line)	Sociopolitical Organization	Possible Associations	Objects	Reference
	Sipán	ca. AD 350–550/600	royal burial	380	regional polity	funeral offering		Alva and Donnan 1993
	Manchan	ca. AD 1300–1470	intentional burial in fardo	720	empire/provincial center	dedicatory offering		personal observation, 1982
	Central Andes	AD 1500–1800	various		various	dedicatory offering, hydraulic		Arriaga 1999 [1620]; Cobo 1990 [1653]
	Magdalena de Chao	post-1578	domestic	510	Colonial reducción	remodeling or abandonment		Van Valkenburgh and Quilter 2008
Spondylus as Raw Material	La Galgada	2232–895 cal BC	staircase on mound	620	regional center	dedicatory offering	beads	Grieder et al. 1988
	Cerro Nario	ca. 1400–1000 BC	workshop	80	village	unknown	figurines, beads, pendants	Blower 1995
	Caylán	800–1 cal BC	workshop	670	regional center	workshop	preforms, beads	Chicoine and Rojas 2013
	Salango	600–100 BC	ceremonial platform	5	village	construction offer in post holes and post-construction ritual offerings	"tusk-shaped pendant" and beads	Lunniss 2008

Site	Date	Context	Count	Polity	Function	Material	Reference
La Florida	AD 100–450	shaft tombs	180		funeral offerings in shaft tombs	beads	Doyon 1988, 2002; later dates between AD 600–680 and AD 1500 are given by Molestina Zaldumbide (2006) for the shaft tombs
Sipán	ca. AD 350–550/600	royal burial	380	regional polity	funeral offering	beads in pectorals	Alva and Donnan 1993
San José de Moro	AD 550–650/700	elite burial (infant)	430	regional center	jewelry	beads in form of ulluchuas	McClelland 2008
Pampa Grande		workshop	370	regional center		pendants, plaques	Shimada 1994
Sicán	AD 950–1050				post-construction ritual offering	beads with human sacrifice	Shimada et al 2004
La Viña	AD 1450–1530	burial of craftworker	300	unknown	burial offerings; craftworker's tools	raw materials, figurines, beads	Shimada 2010
Las Avispas, Chan Chan	ca. AD 900–1400	burial platform	530	empire/capital	funeral offering	powder	Pozorski 1979
"Ñamlap legend"	unknown	oral tradition	340	regional polity?	transition	powder	Donnan 1990
Taller Conchales	AD 1450–1530	workshop	5	empire/provincial center	workshop	worked valves, pendants, figurines, inlays	Moore and Vilchez 2016

(Continued)

TABLE 12.1 (Continued)

	Site	Date	Context of Find	Distance from Source (km, straight line)	Sociopolitical Organization	Possible Associations	Objects	Reference
	Cerro Llullilaco	AD 1430–1520	high elevation capacocha offerings	2700	empire/regional	mountain veneration	figurines	Wilson et al 2007; Reinhard and Ceruti 2010
	Central Andes	AD 1500–1800	various	n/a	village	dedicatory offering, hydraulic	"mullu"	Murra 1975
	Rimac	post-contact	"huaca"	1020	unknown	unknown	beads	Polia 2012 [1620]
	Sequia Vieja	cal AD 1426–1497	unknown	3100	regional center		beads	Taboada and Farberman 2014:16
Spondylus as Icon	Santa Ana-La Florida	ca. 2900–2100 BC	burial	190	village	shamanic transformation	stirrup-spout vessel	Valdez 2008
	Chavin de Huantar	ca. 1500–500 BC	stelae in ceremonial architecture	750	pilgrimage center	processions, agriculture, hydraulic		Burger 1992; Rick 2005
	Cupisnique ceramics		mold-made ceramics	n/a				Jones 2010
	Moche V	ca. AD 600–900	mold-made ceramics	n/a				Shimada 1994:239; also "A rare Moche V stirrup-spout bottle" Museo de la Nación, Lima

Lambayeque/ Sicán	AD 900–1100	mold-made ceramics	n/a	regional polity		For example, Museo Larco Item MLO18763
Lambayeque/ Sicán	AD 900–1100	silver kero	n/a	regional polity	hydraulic, agriculture, fertility, childbirth	Mackey and Pillsbury 2013
Chimú		silver kero	n/a	empire	elite procession, zoomorphic warriors	personal observation; Denver Museum of Art
Chimú	AD 900–1470	mold-made ceramics				
Chimú	AD 900–1470	wall reliefs	530	empire/capital	transition?	Pillsbury 1996

Porvenir in far northern Peru. The offering consisted of a whole *Spondylus*, an unidentified gastropod, and a necklace of greenstone beads in between the two mollusks (Figure 12.2). This was placed at the base of a fill layer before a rectangular wattle and daub dwelling was constructed; based on stratigraphic associations with absolute dates, this offering was made at circa 800–500 B.C. (Moore 2010a:157).

Offerings of *Spondylus* in commoner dwellings were made several millennia later at Chimú sites on the coast of Peru. In his excavations in the commoner barrio at the Chimú capital of Chan Chan, in the Moche Valley, Topic (1982) uncovered six whole *Spondylus* shells in a used olla and placed in a pit under two interior walls. "The nature of the materials and the location of the pit," Topic (1982:158) observed, "suggest a dedicatory offering." In the small farming village of Pedregal, located in the Jequetepeque Valley, Cutright (2013:8-9) has identified household ritual during the Chimú Empire's presence in the region, when *Spondylus* valves were incorporated into domestic rituals, usually with specific phases in house construction, closing rituals, or as "post abandonment offerings."

Spondylus shells were offered in other contexts. At Santa Rosa in the Tumbes Valley, stone cairns post-dating A.D. 1400–1470 contained partial secondary burials with offerings of *Spondylus* valves (Moore 2010b:543). At the Chimú provincial center of Manchan, an assemblage of thirty whole *Spondylus* – the valves wrapped securely together with bulrush cords – were wrapped with cloth as if they were a mummy bundle and buried (Carol Mackey, personal communication, 1983).

FIGURE 12.2   El Porvenir Mound II; offerings of *Spondylus*, conch, and beads

Among the staggeringly beautiful objects interred with the Moche-period Lord of Sipán, whole *Spondylus* valves were some of the first items placed in the elaborate funerary sequence associated with this ancient ruler (Alva and Donnan 1993:59).

Another use of *Spondylus* as an offering comes from a Late Formative (circa 1300–300 B.C.), rainfall catch-basin or *albarrada* at Achallán on the Santa Elena Peninsula, Ecuador, that contained an offering of three large *Spondylus* valves (Stothert 1995, 2003). Stothert (2003:364) writes, "The Achallán offering testifies to an early community ritual of propitiation. This ceremonial context demonstrates the association of water catchment, rainfall, and spondylus shell with the ancient belief that the successful functioning of the *albarrada* could be magically ensured."

The meanings associated with these different offerings of *Spondylus* were not identical, but rather comprised a bundle of commonly and recurrently associated symbolic valences: the distinctive sacrality of the *Spondylus*, its association with building rituals, burials, and with water rites, and its availability to elites *and* non-elites in various contexts in Andean prehistory.

Raw material for artifacts

Spondylus was used as a raw material, worked into a wide array of artifacts: pendants, beads, inlays in other composite artifacts, and figurines (Moore and Vílchez 2016). This process involved complex interactions in which craftworkers assessed and realized the inherent qualities of individual shells. The most nuanced insights into these interactions derive from 2011 excavations at the Inca provincial center of Cabeza de Vaca, located in the Department of Tumbes, that focused on an extensive *Spondylus* workshop (Moore and Vílchez, 2016; Vílchez and Rodriguez 2012). Excavations at the Taller Conchales recovered whole valves, finished objects, and production debris totaling 110,196 artifacts and weighing 51,824 grams. This rich material record indicated that craft specialists carefully assessed the properties of each shell – especially examining its thickness and whether it was pockmarked by the borings of epibonts that once lived among its spines – and only then began the process of converting shells into beads, geometric inlays, pendants, and figurines. Among these figurines were depictions of maize kernels, beans, squash seeds, ceramic vessels (ollas, tinajas), marine birds, fish, and a miniature *Spondylus* shell made from *Spondylus* (Figures 12.3, 12.4).

It is unclear when the *Spondylus* objects first were made in the Andes, but there is clear evidence for importing and working *Spondylus* at Cerro Narrio sometime after 1400 B.C. (Collier and Murra 1943:69, Plate 49; for a discussion of chronology, see Bruhns 2003). Blower (1995:88) has studied a number of *Spondylus* objects from Cerro Narrio and identified distinctive figurines, 1 to 9 centimeters long, anthropomorphs with "chubby cheeks and baby-faced appearance" whose slug-like bodies were carved from the curving edge of *Spondylus* shells. In addition, Cerro Narrio collections had "complete *Spondylus* shells without spines, square and round *cuentas, chaquiras*, pendants, collars [necklaces], earspools and highly polished rim fragments that might have been a form of currency" (Blower 1995:89). At

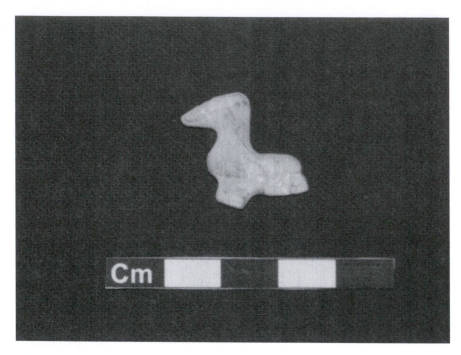

FIGURE 12.3 Figure from the Taller Conchales

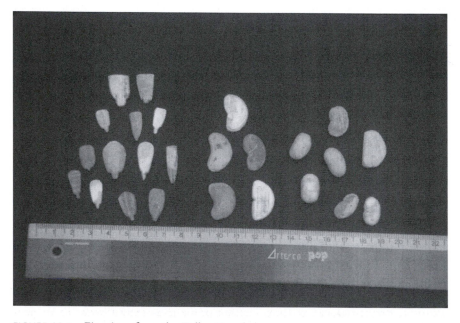

FIGURE 12.4 Figurines from the Taller Conchales

approximately the same time, *Spondylus* disk ornaments sewn onto a cotton textile were placed as a dedicatory offering under a staircase on the North Mound of La Galgada, located on a tributary of the Santa River in the Central Andes of Peru (Grieder et al. 1988). A radiocarbon sample from the textile resulted in a date of 3320 ± 270 BP or 1910–1220 cal. B.C. (one sigma).

By at least 1500–1400 B.C., *Spondylus* were modified into ornaments and other objects at workshops located at some distances from the warm waters of the mollusk's coastal habitat. Although *Spondylus* was used as a raw material over subsequent centuries, a significant increase in production and consumption occurred after A.D. 300. Examining the production of shell beads along the coast of Ecuador, Carter (2011:75) argues, "During . . . 100 BC–AD 700, *Spondylus* consumption increased dramatically. The most significant consumption was in the form of tiny shell beads." Among the most spectacular examples were the seventeen pectorals made from thousands of minute beads from *Spondylus* and other shells interred with the Lord of Sipán. Carter (2008:143) notes,

> *Spondylus* consumption increases dramatically with the development of Moche culture on the North Coast of Peru and Huari . . . culture in the Peruvian highlands. Although originally it was thought that the Moche used little *Spondylus* . . ., it is now clear that they were the first Peruvian group to use it on a wide scale.

In fact, other Andean societies obtained vast quantities of *Spondylus* beads, figurines, and other objects. At the highland Ecuador site of La Florida, Doyon (1988, 2002) excavated a half-dozen shaft tombs dating to circa A.D. 100–450, and retrieved some 674,643 *Spondylus* beads. Although Carter (2011) has suggested that bead production diminished after A.D. 1100 as demand for figurines and geometric appliqués from *Spondylus* increased, Spanish colonial accounts suggest that *Spondylus* beads remained highly desired; a 1612 Jesuit account of the sacking of a single huaca near Lima recovered some fourteen *cargas* of beads – approximately 193 kilograms of an estimated 3.5 million beads from that one shrine alone (Polia 2012: 220).

A final artifact made from *Spondylus* was powder. The legendary ruler Ñamlap, who sailed from the north to establish a dynasty in the Lambayeque Valley, was accompanied by a retinue of queen, concubines, nobles, and courtiers – including one "Fonga Side, Preparer of the Way (he scattered seashell dust where his lord was about to walk)" (quoted in Donnan 1990:243–244). Cordy-Collins (1990:412–414) argues that "Fonga Side" referred to a court office charged with obtaining *Spondylus* for North Coast polities. The use of ground *Spondylus* was documented by Pozorski's excavations of the Las Avispas burial platform at the Chimú capital, Chan Chan, where a stone-lined bin contained crushed *Spondylus* (Pozorski 1979:384). The unknown author of the circa 1559 *Relación de los Adoratorios y Huacas del Cusco* describes the various shrines affiliated with the ceque system and lists the offerings appropriate to each, including ground *Spondylus* shell (Julien 2008:578). This final class of *Spondylus* artifacts bolsters the inference that the transformation of shells into inlays, beads, figurines, and even powder probably was not considered to be of a passive conversion of brute material, but an engaged metamorphosis of the inherent properties of this mollusk.

Spondylus *as icon*

Spondylus were portrayed in a number of media – ceramics, fine textiles, metal objects, sculptures, and architectural reliefs – and this occurred very early in Andean prehistory. One of the earliest known examples is a stirrup-spout vessel from the site of Santa Ana-La Florida in southeastern Ecuador, which is dated to circa 2900–2100 B.C., showing a human emerging from a *Spondylus* shell (Valdez 2008). Valdez (2008:882) has suggested that the vessel depicts a "shaman . . . evoked in the act of transformation" as two versions of a human face – one side jovial, the other side severe – emerge from the opened valves of a *Spondylus*, "the effigy of a particular and important member of that [i.e., Santa Ana-La Florida] society." Later depictions of *Spondylus* are well-known from Chavín de Huántar, where supernaturals hold the distinctive shell and *Spondylus* were depicted on the Tello Obelisk near the mouth of Cayman A (Lathrap 1977).

Spondylus are portrayed three-dimensionally in mold-made stirrup spout vessels associated with Cupisnique ceramics (Jones 2010), and on later Moche, Lambayeque/Sicán, and Chimú pottery. Oddly enough, *Spondylus* were rarely shown on Moche fine-line painted pottery or in other iconographic displays, despite being used extensively as an offering and raw material (Cordy-Collins 2001; Christopher Donnan, personal communication, 2015). *Spondylus* were represented in other media, such as on adobe reliefs on the walls of elite architecture at the Chimú capital of Chan Chan (Pillsbury 1996) and fine textiles (e.g., Harvard Peabody Museum 46–77–30/10386A; Cordy-Collins 1990).

Mackey and Pillsbury (2013) have conducted a detailed analysis of a Lambayeque/Sicán silver beaker (*kero*), a masterpiece that displays three narratives executed in *repoussé* (Denver Art Museum 1969.302). Characterized as "one of the most complex compositions in ancient Andean art" (Mackey and Pillsbury 2013:115), the *kero* (15.2 by 13.9 centimeters in diameter) illustrates the presentation of high-valued objects – including trophy heads, llamas, deer, and *Spondylus* shells – to a divine being. The recipient of these objects is a female supernatural with clawed hands and feet who wears a Lambayeque-style mask, a headdress whose tassels end in serpents' heads, and a dress with a net motif, a figure similar to a late Moche icon known as "the Priestess" (Mackey and Pillsbury 2013:126–128). In other registers on the *kero*, similar figures are shown with legs splayed and knees drawn up, as if in childbirth. These females are associated with other elements, including a curving flow of water filled with fish and frogs, crabs and catfish (Mackey and Pillsbury 2013:129). The uppermost register of the *kero* contains a band of supernaturals: six major figures associated with the sea, and six major figures associated with the land.

The terrestrial beings are depicted with land animals and plants – maize, manioc, and some form of leguminous pod – and the marine supernaturals are shown with reed boats, paddles, sea birds, divers, and *Spondylus* valves. The complex imagery of the Denver beaker, Mackey and Pillsbury (2013:138) write,

> is perhaps in part a cosmological map, depicting a realm of divinities at the top and a watery substratum at the bottom, which together frame an abundant terrestrial region. . . . The striking figures with knees drawn up in the water channel are associated with *Spondylus*, suggesting the intriguing possibility that they are drawing water to plants. . . . The water channel is one of the dominant motifs on the beaker, and it reminds us of the importance of the circulation of water in Andean life, in both ritual and political ways.

Similar associations between *Spondylus* and fertility appear on another kero held by the Denver Art Museum (Figure 12.5), a silver Chimú beaker (Frederick and Jan Meyer Collection 1969.303).[2] Standing 17.8 centimeters tall and 19.1 centimeters in diameter, the Chimú kero has three zones of figures on its side. The uppermost band depicts a line of zoomorphic warriors (possibly deer warriors) wearing elaborate headdress and marching with clubs above a sinuous wave. The lowest zone frontally depicts elites with impressive headdresses. Some of the elites hold keros, and they are flanked by a complex array of retainers, a possible litter, and depictions of sea lions and other animals. In the middle sector of this kero, there is a band of circular zones, some containing front-facing nobles, others tree-like elements flanked by zoomorphs (possibly foxes), who are in turn surrounded by dozens of motifs depicting *Spondylus* valves (personal observation, June 27, 2014).

Summary

A rich body of archaeological data documents the significance of *Spondylus* to a wide range of prehispanic Andean societies. Whether used as an artifact, employed as raw material, or depicted as an icon, there are diverse but recurrent indications of the importance of *Spondylus* for Andean societies of varying scales and cultural traditions. Table 12.1 summarizes data on the various uses, contexts, and objects in which and for which *Spondylus* was used over the about four millennia of prehistory as well as into the Colonial Era. This is not a complete inventory of all known occurrences, but a sample of known cases. Of course, some data are problematic: chronological controls may be imprecise, information on "sociopolitical organization" is often very approximate, and "distance from source" is simply a straight line between archaeological site and nearest *Spondylus* habitat measured on Google Earth, which underestimates actual travel distance.

Yet, these data point to some intriguing and counter-intuitive inferences about *Spondylus*. For example, one might expect that the earliest uses would be in places close to the mollusks' natural habitat, but that seems incorrect: *Spondylus* was used in the fourth and third millennia B.C. at sites near *Spondylus* habitats (Real Alto)

FIGURE 12.5 Chimú kero, Lambayeque. "Beaker with Ceremonies and Scorpion Deity," circa A.D. 800–1470. Denver Art Museum Collection: Gift of Frederick R. Mayer, 1969.303. Photography © Denver Art Museum, used with permission.

and at sites nearly 670–900 kilometers distant (Punkuri, Caral). Another proposition: one might expect that one class of *Spondylus* use – for example, the use of the whole valve as an offering – would precede its uses as an icon or as a material transformed into other objects, but that seems incorrect: by the third millennium B.C., *Spondylus* appears as an artifact, a raw material, *and* an icon. These two counter-intuitive patterns may indicate that even earlier uses of *Spondylus* may have been widespread in the Andes. Further, one might think that *Spondylus* would be an exotic item restricted to "elite" contexts, unavailable to non-elites, but – again – that is incorrect: *Spondylus* valves were used in construction offerings in non-elite dwellings at sites in southern Ecuador and northern Peru (La Vega, El Porvenir) at circa 1200–500 B.C., and in the commoner barrio at Chan Chan (A.D. 900–1470) and the rural village of Pedregal (A.D. 1100–1300).

To repeat, it seems that *Spondylus* exemplify Keane's (2003: 414) idea of "bundling" in which the varied meanings and values "shift in their relative value, utility, and relevance across contexts." Nevertheless, those meanings are not randomly assigned but form a polythetic set. The shells were recurrently engaged with specific settings – construction rites for domestic and public architecture, post-construction pit offerings, burial goods, processions/transitions, mountain veneration, childbirth, fertility, agriculture, and water.

A final observation: significant efforts were invested in obtaining, transporting, modifying, burying, and depicting *Spondylus* shells – efforts coordinated by Andean societies of different size, scales, and sociopolitical organizations (for a similar discussion, see Hutson et al., Chapter 8). If Santa Ana-La Florida was a small hamlet of twelve to fifteen families (Valdez 2008), its Valdivia III contemporary, Real Alto, was a 600–1,100 person community, possibly a simple chiefdom (Zeidler 2008). When *Spondylus* shells were buried at offerings at the small hamlet of six house mounds at El Porvenir circa 800–500 B.C. (Moore 2010a), *Spondylus* also were being depicted on carved stelae at Chavín de Huántar, a ceremonial center with wide influence over the Central Andes between circa 1500 and 500 B.C. (Burger 1992; Rick 2005). If, as Carter (2011) has suggested, there was a major increase in demand for *Spondylus* after 100 B.C. through A.D. 700, perhaps this correlates with the repeated emergence of complex polities on the North Coast of Peru; but even there, the nature of those political organizations ranged from regional polities (Northern Mochica), multi-valley states (Southern Moche, Sicán-Lambayeque), and empires (Chimú). And finally, if the most widespread distribution of *Spondylus* occurred in late prehistory under the Inca Empire, it was accompanied by embedded sets of rituals and symbolic associations that survived the onslaughts of extirpation well into the Colonial Era. These examples range from communities of less than 100 people to prehispanic empires with populations in excess of 14 million. *Spondylus* was desired and respected by all of them. The obvious question is "Why?"

In the following section, I explore one of the persistent valences "bundled" into *Spondylus*, its association with water and agriculture. As should be clear from above, this is not the only meaning imbricated into Andean ritual and political ceremonies associated with *Spondylus*, but it was a particularly important and well-documented valence that was extremely important for complex societies dependent on irrigation agriculture.

Spondylus: hydraulic associations

Spondylus were frequently portrayed in Andean iconography and deployed in ritual practice in association with water and, by extension, agricultural fertility (Blower 1995:34–36; Carrión Cachot 1955). *Spondylus* were incorporated into various Andean water rituals, whether they were cyclical rituals or scarcity rituals (Rösing 1995). Hydraulic associations are clearly documented in Colonial accounts of the Inca and other Andean peoples. The government official Polo de Ondegardo (1916:39, translation mine) stated, "they sacrifice or make offerings of sea shells called *Mollo*. And they offer them to the fountains and springs, saying that the shells are the daughters of the sea, the mother of all waters." These shell objects were so deeply implicated in Inca religion and thus idolatry, the extirpator Father Jose de la Arriaga (1999 [1621]:174, translation mine) instructed that Catholic priests ensure that "no Indian, male or female, will have *mullu*." The seventeenth-century priest and chronicler Bernabé Cobo (1990 [1653]:117) observed:

> These Indians were also accustomed to sacrifice seashells, especially when they made offering to the springs. They said this was a very appropriate sacrifice because the springs are the daughters of the sea, which is the mother of the waters. . . . This sacrifice was offered to the above mentioned springs after the planting was done so that the springs would not dry up that year and so that these springs would flow with abundance and irrigate their sown fields as had happened in past years.

A related association may be at work at Chavín de Huántar. Not only did the Tello Obelisk convey a relationship about water and fertility, but this association with water was bolstered by the extensive systems of drains and canals within the ceremonial complex at Chavín de Huántar:

> The evident importance of water in ritual practice at Chavín may thus be deduced from the water-bearing channels within the temple complex as well as inferred from the broader Andean cultural context, in which water was commonly of great religious and ceremonial significance. Elaborate ritual manipulation of water is well documented in sites spanning the geography and chronology of the Central Andes. . . . In the pre-Hispanic Andes generally, the manipulation of water was apparently a significant religious act and its control a powerful statement of ritual power.
>
> *(Contreras and Keefer 2009:614)*

Apparently, there were recurrent associations between *Spondylus*, water, and agricultural fertility among various Andean societies. These associations may account for the significant increase in *Spondylus* production after A.D. 300 and its subsequent high demand by complex Andean societies (Carter 2008, 2011). A number of paleoclimate studies indicate Late Holocene variations in the intensity of El Niño/Southern Oscillation events, droughts, and other water-related phenomena. For example, paleoenvironmental studies at the Urpi Kocha Lagoon at Pachacamac documented particularly unsettled water conditions, including El Niño flooding and tsunamis, at A.D. 436–651 and at A.D. 995–1008 (Winsborough et al. 2012). Despite these environmental and related catastrophes, as Eeckhout (2013:151) observes, "At Pachacamac, it seems that periods of crisis – be they environmental, social, political or other – constituted opportunities for adaptation and modification rather than merely resulting in the collapse of seemingly obsolete beliefs, images and architectural conventions." On the southern coast of Peru, Goldstein and Magilligan (2011) have identified agrarian societies' responses to extended droughts and catastrophic El Niño floods in the

Late Holocene, with major well-dated El Niño events at A.D. 690 and 1607, the extensive Miraflores Flood at A.D. 1330 (Keefer et al. 2003), and additional flood events at 50–100 year intervals, with increasing intensity between A.D. 1300 and 1600 (Magilligan and Goldstein 2001; Goldstein and Magilligan 2011:155). In the Casma Valley, the A.D. 1330 flooding event has been identified in geological studies (Wells 1990) as well as in changes in molluscan assemblages associated with a Chimú site, Quebrada Santa Cristina, where state-supported workers lived as they built extensive drained fields in the aftermath of El Niño inundations (Moore 1991).

Such environmental variations were exacerbated by increased demand for arable lands. In the Moche Valley, Billman (2002) has documented prehistoric expansions of farmland and irrigation systems. As marginal land was brought into cultivation, the number of years with inadequate water substantially increased: by the Late Intermediate Period (circa A.D. 900–1470), there were water shortfalls twenty-five of every forty years. The occurrence of multiple periods of extended drought that occasioned different settlement strategies in the Jequetepeque Valley, as discussed by Dillehay and Kolata (2004), is also associated with the increased demand for *Spondylus* by North Coast societies.

Andean societies were simultaneously engaged in water projects at the pragmatic and symbolic domains, and offerings of *Spondylus* were not the only form of hydraulic ritual. Bray (2013) has documented the variety of constructions – canals, fountains, reservoirs, and other hydraulic features – associated with water rituals in the Inca Empire. She observes,

> The Inca, like their ancestors, were clearly masters of hydraulic engineering. Their virtuosity in the harnessing and manipulation of natural flows was built upon the technical savoir faire of generations of Andean peoples. What they may have surpassed their predecessors in was the co-option of the symbolic significance of water for their own imperial ends.
>
> *(Bray 2013:185)*

Gose (1993:509) points out,

> Under the Inkas, the administration of water was probably more developed as ritual than it was at a purely utilitarian level. Yet the evidence . . . does not support the idea that Andean hydraulic ritual was a purely expressive practice. On the contrary, those who developed this elaborate ritual complex undoubtedly thought it was a practical way to manage a scarce resource. But like all judgments of utility, this one was mediated by a specific cultural understanding of the world.

Simply put, water was power and powerful, and ensuring and channeling its flow was a preoccupation of the Incas and their predecessors, a preoccupation also engaged with in the ritual use and political significances of *Spondylus*.

Conclusion

W. J. T. Mitchell (2004:127) has observed,

> there can be no history of images without some notion of what is abiding about them. The question is not whether images 'come alive' or not, but where, how, and what kind of life they take on, and how people respond to that life.

This issue is of central significance to understanding the importance of *Spondylus* in the political and ritual practices of Andean societies. A detailed comparison identified some of the variations in their uses and meanings. Whether used as artifacts themselves, transformed and realized as artifacts ranging from beads to figurines, or iconographically depicted in multiple media, *Spondylus* had recurrent significances to Andean peoples from at least 2600 B.C. until well into the Colonial Era (Figure 12.6). Irreducible to a single meaning or function, *Spondylus* were deployed in multiple settings – construction rituals in monumental and domestic architecture, elite garments, funerary and propitiary offerings, and water and fertility rites – and thus exhibited varied, but not infinitely varied, valences.

One of those sets of meanings – their importance in water and fertility rituals – gained prominence as more complex polities emerged in the Central Andes between circa A.D. 300 and 1400. These sociopolitical developments intersected with *Spondylus* acquisition and use in two fundamental manners. First, these more complex societies had greater political capacity for organizing the acquisition of *Spondylus*. These increasing organizational capacities are indicated by the greater

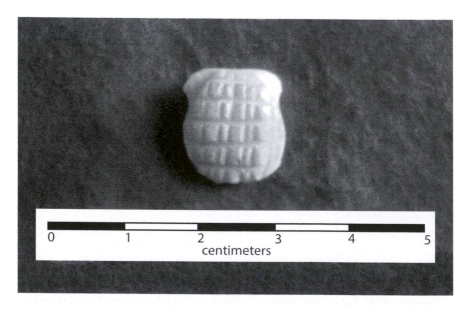

FIGURE 12.6 *Spondylus* figurine from the Taller Conchales

quantities of imported shells, the broader distribution of *Spondylus* in elite and non-elite settings, the wider geographic distribution of shells at great distances from their natural habitats, and efforts made to directly control production such as that exhibited by the Inca Empire in their establishment of the state-sponsored *Spondylus* workshop at their provincial center in Tumbes. Conversely, one set of meanings associated with *Spondylus* – its significance in water and agricultural rituals – became prominent as these complex polities expanded their agrarian base during centuries marked by environmental fluctuations, characterized by extended droughts, periodic floods, and tsunamis. To reiterate, the increased significance of *Spondylus* for Central Andean polities cannot be reduced to a simplistic environmental explanation, but neither can it be extracted from the real worlds that Andean peoples encountered and created. In those worlds, *Spondylus* had a particular bundle of meanings that shifted or became prominent in the varied political and ritual contexts in which they were engaged, multivalent associations of a beautiful and meaningful mollusk.

Notes

1 I use these terms in their colloquial meanings: *artifact* referring to how a *Spondylus* shell is used, *raw material* denoting its transformation into other classes of objects, and *icon* to denote its depiction in other media.
2 Pillsbury and Mackey have also studied the Chimú kero and have a more detailed discussion in preparation (Joanne Pillsbury, personal communication 2014).

References Cited

Alberti, Benjamin 2014 Archaeology, Risk, and the Alter-Politics of Materiality. *Fieldsights – Theorizing the Contemporary, Cultural Anthropology Online*, www.culanth.org/fieldsights/476-archaeology-risk-and-the-alter-politics-of-materiality, accessed January 13, 2014.

Alberti, Benjamin, and Tamara Bray 2009 Animating Archaeology: Of Subjects, Objects, and Alternative Ontologies. *Cambridge Archaeological Journal* 19: 337–343.

Allen, Catherine 1998 When Utensils Revolt: Mind, Matter, and Modes of Being in the Pre-Columbian Andes. *RES: Anthropology and Aesthetics* 33: 18–27.

Alva Alva, Walter, and Christopher Donnan 1993 *Royal Tombs of Sipán*. Fowler Museum of Cultural History, University of California, Los Angeles.

Angelo, Dante 2014 Assembling Ritual, the Burden of the Everyday: An Exercise in Relational Ontology in Quebrada Humahuaca, Argentina. *World Archaeology* 46: 270–277.

Arriaga, Padre José de 1999 [1621] *La extirpación de la idolatría en el Piru*. Centro Bartolomé de las Casas, Cuzco.

Bauer, Daniel 2007 The Reinvention of Tradition: An Ethnographic Study of *Spondylus* Use in Coastal Ecuador. *Journal of Anthropological Research* 63: 33–50.

Billman, Brian R. 2002 Irrigation and the Origins of the Southern Moche State on the North Coast of Peru. *Latin American Antiquity* 13: 371–400.

Blower, David 1995 *The Quest for Mullu: Concepts, Trade and the Archaeological Distribution of Spondylus in the Andes*. Master's thesis, Department of Anthropology, Trent University, Ontario.

Bray, Tamara 2009 An Archaeological Perspective on the Andean Concept of *camaquen*: Thinking Through Late Pre-Columbian Ofrendas and Huacas. *Cambridge Archaeological Journal* 19: 357–366.

————. 2012 Ritual Commensality Between Human and Non-Human Persons: Investigating Native Ontologies in the Late Pre-Columbian Andean World. In *Between Feasts and Daily Meals: Toward an Archaeology of Commensal Spaces*, edited by Susan Pollock, pp. 197–212. eTopoi: Journal of Ancient Studies, Special Volume 2, Berlin.

————. 2013 Water, Ritual and Power in the Inca Empire. *Latin American Antiquity* 24: 164–190.

Bruhns, Karen 2003 Social and Cultural Development in the Ecuadorian Highlands and Eastern Lowlands During the Formative. In *The Archaeology of Formative Ecuador*, edited by J. Scott Raymond and Richard Burger, pp. 125–74. Dumbarton Oaks, Washington, DC.

Burger, Richard L. 1992 *Chavín and the Origins of Andean Civilization*. Thames and Hudson, New York.

Carrión Cachot, Rebeca 1955 El culto al agua en el Antiguo Perú: la paccha elemento cultural pan-andino. *Revista del Museo Nacional de Antropología y Arqueología* 2(2): 50–140.

Carter, Benjamin 2008 *Technology, Society, and Change: Shell Artifact Production Among the Manteño (AD 800–1532) of Coastal Ecuador*. Ph.D. dissertation, Department of Anthropology, Washington University, St. Louis.

————. 2011 *Spondylus* in South American prehistory. In *Spondylus in Prehistory: New Data and Approaches – Contributions to the Archaeology of Shell Technologies*, edited by Fotis Ifantidis and Marianna Nikolaidou, pp. 63–89. British Archaeological Reports, International Series 2216. Archaeopress, Oxford.

Chapman, John, Bisserka Gaydarska, Evangelia Skafida, and Stella Souvatzi 2011 Personhood and the Life Cycle of *Spondylus* Rings: An Example From Neolithic Greece. In *Spondylus in Prehistory: New Data and Approaches – Contributions to the Archaeology of Shell Technologies*, edited by Fotis Ifantidis and Marianna Nikolaidou, pp. 139–160. British Archaeological Reports, International Series 2216. Archaeopress, Oxford.

Chicoine, David, and Carol Rojas 2013 Shellfish Resources and Maritime Economy at Caylán, Coastal Ancash, Peru. *The Journal of Island and Coastal Archaeology* 8: 336–360.

Cobo, Bernabé 1990 [1653] *Inca Religion and Customs*. Translated and edited by R. Hamilton. University of Texas Press, Austin.

Collier, Donald, and John Murra 1943 *Survey and Excavations in Southern Ecuador*. Anthropological Series, vol. 35. Field Museum of Natural History, Chicago.

Contreras, Daniel, and David Keefer 2009 Implications of the Fluvial History of the Wacheqsa River for Hydrologic Engineering and Water Use at Chavín de Huántar, Peru. *Geoarchaeology* 24: 589–618.

Cordy-Collins, Alana 1990 Fonga Sigde, Shell Purveyor to the Chimú Kings. In *The Northern Dynasties: Kingship and Statecraft in Chimor*, edited by Michael Moseley and Alana Cordy-Collins, pp. 393–417. Dumbarton Oaks, Washington, DC.

————. 2001 Blood and the Moon Priestesses: *Spondylus* shells in Moche Ceremony. In *Ritual Sacrifice in Ancient Peru*, edited by Elizabeth Benson and Anita Cook, pp. 35–53. University of Texas Press, Austin.

Cutright, Robyn 2013 Household *ofrendas* and Community Feasts: Ritual at a Late Intermediate Period Village in the Jequetepeque Valley, Peru. *Ñawpa Pacha* 33(1): 1–21

Descola, Phillipe 2013 *Beyond Nature and Culture*. Translated by Janet Lloyd. University of Chicago Press, Chicago.

Donnan, Christopher 1990 An Assessment of the Validity of the Naymlap Dynasty. In *The Northern Dynasties: Kingship and Statecraft in Chimor*, edited by Michael Moseley and Alana Cordy-Collins, pp. 243–274. Dumbarton Oaks, Washington, DC.

Doyon, Leon 1988 Tumbas de la nobleza en La Florida. In *Quito antes de Benalcazar*, edited by I. Cruz Cevalos, pp. 51–66. El Centro Cultural Artes, Quito.

———. 2002 Conduits of ancestry: Interpretation of the geography, geology, and seasonality of North Andean shaft tombs. In *The Space and Place of Death,* edited by Helaine Silverman and David Small, pp. 79–95. Archaeological Papers of the American Anthropological Association, vol. 11. American Anthropological Association, Arlington, VA.

Eeckhout, Peter 2004 Relatos míticos y prácticas rituales en Pachacamac. *Bulletin de l'Institut Français d'Études Andines* 33(1): 1–54.

———. 2013 Change and Permanency on the Coast of Ancient Peru: The Religious Site of Pachacamac. *World Archaeology* 45: 137–160.

Falcón Huayta, Victor, Milano Trejo Huayta, and Rosa Martínez Navarro 2005 La huayl-laquepa de Punkurí Costa Nor-Central del Perú. *Anales del Museo de América* 13: 53–74.

Feifarek, Brian P. 1987 Spines and epibionts as antipredator defenses in the thorny oyster *Spondylus* americanus Hermann. *Journal of Experimental Marine Biology and Ecology* 105: 39–56.

Gell, Arthur 1998 *Art and Agency: An Anthropological Theory.* Clarendon Press, Oxford.

Glowacki, Mary, and Michael Malpass 2003 Water, Huacas, and Ancestor Worship: Traces of a Sacred Wari Landscape. *Latin American Antiquity* 14: 431–448.

Goldstein, Paul, and Francis J. Magilligan 2011 Hazard, Risk and Agrarian Adaptations in a Hyperarid Watershed: El Niño Floods, Streambank Erosion, and the Cultural Bounds of Vulnerability in the Andean Middle Horizon." *Catena* 85: 155–167.

Gorriti Manchego, Manuel 2000 Moluscos marinos: Spondylus, Strombus y Conus, su significado en las sociedades andinas. *Boletín del Museo de Arqueología y Antropología de la Universidad Nacional Mayor de San Marcos* 3(11): 10–21.

Gosden, Chris 2005 What Do Objects Want? *Journal of Archaeological Method and Theory* 12: 193–211.

Gose, Peter 1993 Segmentary State Formation and the Ritual Control of Water Under the Incas. *Comparative Studies in Society and History* 35: 480–514.

Grieder, Terrence, Alberto Bueno Mendoza, Claude Earle Smith, and Robert M. Malina 1988 *La Galgada, Peru: A Preceramic Culture in Transition.* University of Texas Press, Austin.

Guffroy, Jean 2004 *Catamayo Precolombino: Investigaciones Arqueológicas en la provincia de Loja (Ecuador).* Travaux de l'Institut Fracais, tomo 164. IRD Editions, Paris.

Hocquenghem, Ann Marie 2010 El *Spondylus princeps* y la edad de bronce en los Andes centrales: Las rutas de intercambios. In *Producción de Bienes Ornamentales y Votivos de la América Antigua,* edited by Emiliano Melgar Tísoc, Reyna Solís Ciriaco, and Ernesto González Licón, pp. 34–49. Syllaba Press, Deale.

Ifantidis, Fotis and Marianna Nikolaidou, eds. 2011 *Spondylus in Prehistory:New Data and Approaches—Contributions to the Archaeology of Shell Technologies* British Archaeological Reports, International Series 2216. Archaeopress, Oxford.

Ingold, Tim 2010 Bringing Things to Life: Creative Entanglements in a World of Materials. *Realities.* Working Paper No. 15. University of Manchester Morgan Centre for Research into Everyday Lives, Manchester.

———. 2012 Toward an Ecology of Materials. *Annual Review of Anthropology* 41: 427–442.

Jones, Kimberly 2010 *Cupisnique Culture: The Development of Ideology in the Ancient Andes.* Unpublished Ph.D. dissertation, Department of Anthropology, University of Texas, Austin.

Julien, Catherine 2008 Relación de los Adoratorios y Huacas del Cusco – Relación de los Ceques (ca. 1559). In *Guide to Documentary Sources in Andean Studies, 1530–1900,* vol. 2, edited by Joanne Pillsbury, pp. 578–580. University of Oklahoma Press, Norman.

Keefer, David K., Michael E. Moseley, and Susan D. Defrance 2003 A 38,000-Year Record of Floods and Debris Flows in the Ilo Region of Southern Peru and Its Relation to El Niño Events and Great Earthquakes. *Palaeogeography, Palaeoclimatology, Palaeoecology* 194: 41–77.

Keen, Angeline M. 1971 *Seashells of Tropical West America*. Stanford University Press, Stanford.

Keane, Webb 2003 Semiotics and the Social Analysis of Material Things. *Language & Communication* 23: 409–425.

Lamprell, Kevin 1987 *Spondylus: Spiny Oysters Shells of the World*. E.J. Brill, Leiden.

Lathrap, Donald W. 1977 Our Father the Cayman, Our Mother the Gourd: Spinden Revisited, or a Unitary Model for the Emergence of Agriculture in the New World. In *Origins of Agriculture*, edited by Charles A. Reed, pp. 713–751. Mouton Publishers, The Hague.

Lau, George 2010 The Work of Surfaces: Object Worlds and Techniques of Enhancement in the Ancient Andes. *Journal of Material Culture* 15: 259–286.

Lunniss, Richard 2008 Where the Land and the Ocean Meet: The Engoroy Phase Ceremonial Site at Salango, Ecuador, 600–100BC. In *Pre-Columbian Landscapes of Creation and Origin*, edited by John Staller, pp. 203–248. Springer, New York.

Mackensen, Annika, Thomas Brey, and Stanislaus Sonnenholzner 2011 The Fate of *Spondylus* Stocks (Bivalvia: Spondylidae) in Ecuador: Is Recovery Likely? *Journal of Shellfish Research* 30: 115–121.

Mackensen, Annika, Thomas Brey, Christian Bock, and Soledad Luna 2012 *Spondylus crassisquama* Lamarck, 1819 as a Microecosystem and the Effects of Associated Macrofauna on Its Shell Integrity: Isles of Biodiversity or Sleeping With the Enemy? *Marine Biodiversity* 42: 443–451.

Mackey, Carol, and Joanne Pillsbury 2013 Cosmology and Ritual on a Lambayeque Beaker. In *Pre-Columbian Art and Archaeology: Essays in Honor of Frederick R. Mayer*, edited by Margaret Young Sanchez, pp. 115–141. Denver Art Museum, Denver.

Malinowski, Bronislaw 1922 *Argonauts of the Western Pacific*. Dutton, New York.

Magilligan, Francis, and Paul Goldstein. 2001 El Niño Floods and Culture Change: A Late Holocene Flood History for the Rio Moquegua, Southern Peru. *Geology* 29: 431–434.

Marcos, Jorge 1977–1978 Cruising to Acapulco and Back With the Thorny Oyster Set: A Model for a Lineal Exchange System. *Journal of the Steward Anthropological Society* 9(1–2): 99–132.

———. 1988 *Real Alto: La historia de un centro ceremonial Valdivia. Primera parte*. Biblioteca Ecuatoriana de Arqueología 4. Corporación Editora Nacional, Quito.

Martin, Alexander 2009 *The Domestic Mode of Production and the Development of Sociopolitical Complexity: Evidence from the Spondylus Industry of Coastal Ecuador*. Unpublished Ph.D. dissertation, Department of Anthropology, University of Pittsburgh, Pittsburgh.

McClelland, Donna 2008 Ulluchu – An Elusive Fruit. In *The Art and Archaeology of the Moche: An Ancient Andean Society of the Peruvian North Coast*, edited by Steve Bourget and Kimberly L. Jones, pp. 43–65. University of Texas Press, Austin.

Miller, Daniel 2005 Materiality: An Introduction. In *Materiality*, edited by Daniel Miller, pp. 1–50. Duke University Press, Durham.

Mitchell, W. J. T. 2004 *What Do Pictures Want? The Lives and Loves of Images*. University of Chicago Press, Chicago.

Molestina Zaldumbide, María del Carmen 2006 El pensamiento simbólico de los habitantes de La Florida (Quito-Ecuador). *Bulletin de l'Institut Français d'Etudes Andines* 35: 377–395.

Moore, Jerry 1991 Cultural Responses to Environmental Catastrophes: Post-El Niño Subsistence on the Prehistoric North Coast of Peru. *Latin American Antiquity* 2: 27–47.

————. 2010a Architecture, Settlement, and Formative Developments in the Equatorial Andes: New Discoveries in the Department of Tumbes, Peru. *Latin American Antiquity* 21: 147–172.

————. 2010b Making a Huaca: Memory and Praxis in Prehispanic Far Northern Peru. *Journal of Social Archaeology* 10: 531–555.

Moore, Jerry, and Carol Mackey 2008 The Chimú. In *The Handbook of South American Archaeology*, edited by Helaine Silverman and William Isbell, pp. 783–807. Springer, New York.

Moore, Jerry, and Carolina María Vílchez 2016 Techné and the Thorny Oyster: *Spondylus* Craft Production and the Inca Empire at Taller Conchales, Cabeza de Vaca, Tumbes, Peru. In *Making Value, Making Meaning: Techné in the Pre-Columbian World*, edited by Cathy Costin, pp. 221–252. Dumbarton Oaks, Washington DC.

Murra, John 1975 El trafico de mullu en la costa del Pacifico. In *Formaciones Económicas y Políticas Del Mundo Andino*, pp. 255–268. Instituto de Estudios Peruanos, Lima.

Paulsen, Allison 1974 The Thorny Oyster and the Voice of God: *Spondylus* and *Strombus* in Andean Prehistory. *American Antiquity* 39: 597–607.

Pauketat, Timothy 2013 *An Archaeology of the Cosmos: Rethinking Agency and Religion in Ancient America*. Routledge, London.

Pedersen, Morten Axel 2012 Common Nonsense: A Review of Certain Recent Reviews of the "Ontological Turn." *Anthropology of the Century*, Issue 5. Electronic document, http://aotcpress.com/archive/issue-5/, accessed March 19, 2015.

Pillsbury, Joanne 1996 The Thorny Oyster and the Origins of Empire: Implications of Recently Uncovered *Spondylus* Imagery From Chan-Chan, Peru. *Latin American Antiquity* 8: 313–340.

Polia Meconi, Mario 2012 Siete cartas inéditas del Archivo Romano de la Compañia de Jesús (1611–1613): huacas, mitos y ritos andinos. *Anthropologica*, 14: 209–259.

Polo de Ondegardo, Juan 1916 [1585] Los errores y supersticiones de los indios, sacados del tratado y averiguación que hizo el licenciado Polo [1585]. In *Colección de libros y documentos referentes a la historia del Perú por Horacio Arteaga*, vol. 111, pp. 207–223. Imprenta y Libería Sanmarti Ca., Lima.

Pozorski, Thomas 1979 The Las Avispas Burial Platform at Chan Chan, Peru. *Annals of the Carneige Museum* 48: 119–137.

Reinhard, Johan, and María C. Ceruti 2010 *Inca Rituals and Sacred Mountains: A Study of the World's Highest Archaeological Sites*. Los Angeles: Cotsen Institute of Archaeology Press, Los Angeles.

Rick, John 2005 The Evolution of Authority and Power at Chavín de Huántar, Peru. In *Power and Authority in the Prehispanic Andes*, edited by Christina Conlee, Dennis Ogburn, and Kevin Vaughn, pp. 71–89. Archeological Papers of the American Anthropological Association, vol. 14. American Anthropological Association, Arlington, VA.

Rösing, Ina 1995 *Paraman Purina* – Going for Rain – "mute anthropology" Versus "speaking anthropology": Lessons From an Andean Collective Scarcity Ritual in the Quechua-Speaking Kallawaya and Aymara-Speaking Altiplano Region (Andes, Bolivia). *Anthropos* 90: 69–88.

Salomon, Frank 1991 Introductory Essay: The Huarochiri Manuscript. In *The Huarochiri Manuscript: A Testament of Ancient and Colonial Andean Religion*, edited and translated by Frank Salomon and George Urioste, pp. 1–38. University of Texas Press, Austin.

Shady Solís, Ruth 2006 America's First City? The Case of Late Archaic Caral. In *Andean Archaeology III*, edited by William Isbell and Helaine Silverman, pp. 28–66. Springer, New York.

Shimada, Izumi 1994 *Pampa Grande and the Mochica Cultura*. University of Texas Press, Austin.

————. 2010 *Shell Artifact Manufacturing: Insight From a Late Horizon Shellworker's Tool Kit*. Paper presented at the 75th Annual Meeting of the Society for American Archaeology, Sacramento.

Shimada, Izumi, Crystal Barker Schaaf, Lonnie G. Thompson, and Ellen Mosley-Thompson 1991 Cultural Impacts of Severe Droughts in the Prehistoric Andes: Application of a 1,500-Year Ice Core Precipitation Record. *World Archaeology* 22: 247–270.

Shimada, Izumi, Kenichi Shinoda, Julie Farnum, Robert Corruccini, and Hirokatsu Watanabe 2004 An Integrated Analysis of Pre-Hispanic Mortuary Practices: A Middle Sicán Case Study 1. *Current Anthropology* 45: 369–402.

Stothert, Karen 1995 Las albarradas tradicionales y el manejo de aguas en la Península de Santa Elena. *Miscelánea Antropológica Ecuatoriana* 8: 131–160.

————. 2003 Expression of Ideology in the Formative Period of Ecuador. In *Archaeology of Formative Ecuador*, edited by J. Scott Raymond and Richard Burger, pp. 337–421. Dumbarton Oaks, Washington, DC.

Swenson, Edward 2015 The Materialities of Place Making in the Ancient Andes: A Critical Appraisal of the Ontological Turn in Archaeological Interpretation. *Journal of Archaeological Method and Theory* 22: 677–712.

Taboada, Constanza, and Judith Farberman 2014 Asentamientos prehispánicos y pueblos de indios coloniales sobre el río Salado (Santiago del Estero, Argentina): miradas dialogadas entre la arqueología y la historia. *Revista de Arqueología Histórica Argentina y Latinoamericana* 8(1): 7–44.

Taylor Gerald 1974 *Camay, Camac* et *Camasca* dans le manuscrit quechua de Huarochiri. *Journal de la Société des Américanistes* 63: 231–244.

Topic, John 1982 Lower Class Social and Economic Organization at Chan Chan. In *Chan Chan: Andean Desert City*, edited by Michael E. Moseley and Kent C. Day, pp. 145–176. School of American Research and University of New Mexico Press, Albuquerque.

Valdez, Francisco 2008 Inter-zonal Relationships in Ecuador. In *Handbook of South American Archaeology*, edited by Helaine Silverman and William Isbell, pp. 865–888. Springer, New York.

Vanvalkenburgh, Nathaniel Parker, and Jeffrey Quilter 2008 *Continuity and Transformation in Indigenous Households During the Colonial Period: Recent Insights From Magdalena de Cao Viejo, Peru*. Paper presented at the 73rd Annual Meeting of the Society for American Archaeology, Vancouver.

Velázquez, A., Castro E., Melgar Tísoc, and A. M. Hocquenghem 2006 Análisis de las huellas de manufactura del material malacológico de Tumbes, Perú. *Bulletin de l'Institut Français d'Études Andines* 35: 21–35.

Vílchez Carrasco, Carolina, and Fanny Rodríguez, eds. 2012 *Informe Final: Proyecto de Investigación Arqueológica y Puesta en Uso Social Cabeza de Vaca: Excavación en el Taller Malacológico*. Submitted to the Programa Qhapaq Ñan, Tumbes.

Vivieros de Castro, Eduardo 1998 Cosmological Deixis and Amerindian Perspectivism. *The Journal of the Royal Anthropological Institute* 4: 469–488.

————. 2004 The Transformation of Objects Into Subjects in Amerindian Ontologies. *Common Knowledge* 10: 463–484.

————. 2007 The Crystal Forest: Notes on the Ontology of Amazonian Spirits. *Inner Asia* 9: 153–172.

Weiss, Gerard 1975 Campa Cosmology: The World of a Forest Tribe in South America. *Anthropological Papers of the American Museum of Natural History* 52: 217–588.

Wells, Lisa 1990 Holocene History of the El Niño Phenomenon as Recorded in Flood Sediments of Northern Coastal Peru. *Geology* 18: 1134–1137.

Wilson, Andrew S., Timothy Taylor, Maria Constanza Ceruti, Jose Antonio Chavez, Johan Reinhard, Vaughan Grimes, Wolfram Meier-Augenstein, Larry Cartmell, Ben Stern, Michael P. Richards, Michael Worobey, Ian Barnes, and M. Thomas P. Gilbert 2007 Stable Isotope and DNA Evidence for Ritual Sequences in Inca Child Sacrifice. *Proceedings of the Natural Academy of Sciences* 104: 16456–16461.

Winsborough, Barbara M., Izumi Shimada, Lee A. Newsom, John G. Jones, and Rafael A. Segura 2012 Paleoenvironmental Catastrophies on the Peruvian Coast Revealed in Lagoon Sediment Cores From Pachacamac. *Journal of Archaeological Science* 39: 602–614.

Zeidler, James 2008 The Ecuadorian Formative. In *The Handbook of South American Archaeology*, edited by Helaine Silverman and William Isbell, pp. 459–488. Springer, New York.

13

POWER AT THE CROSSROADS OF POLITICS AND RELIGION

A commentary

María Nieves Zedeño

Introduction

Through a careful examination of the archaeological record of religious practices among diverse Amerindian societies, volume contributors deftly demonstrate that religion is fundamental to the fabric of political life. Editors Art Joyce and Sarah Barber have challenged these scholars with breaking away from long-standing intellectual traditions that regard ancient religions as phenomena existing apart from the grind of daily practice – a "superstructure" so-to-speak, whose main purpose is to furnish people with overarching, integrative principles that can then be manipulated by leaders to achieve order and compliance. In response, contributors variously address three main themes that are grounded in contemporary social theory (A. Joyce, Chapter 1): (1) the role of religion in the constitution of political formations, e.g., authority, negotiation, contestation, and resistance, as well as in political and social transformations; (2) the importance of accounting for Amerindian ontologies in religious practice, for example, in the emergence of complex social relationships among people, objects, places, and other-than-human entities; and (3) the role of objects in the development of religious covenants, social networks, entanglements, or meshworks (as mediators or witnesses), and in the transfer of religious idioms (through things such as symbols, quasi-scriptures, quali-signs, or index objects) that, in turn, may have an effect on political formations.

This volume not only succeeds at demonstrating the extraordinary diversity of religious practice and its potential for generating political mobility, but also breaks down the socio-evolutionary notion that religious institutions are nodes of political power that belong in societies with institutionalized inequality. Having devoted most of my career to the examination of hunter-gatherer landscapes that are embedded in holistic understandings of religion and daily life, I find that these chapters and these themes crosscut all forms of societal organization. To drive home this point, my comments about the main themes discussed by contributors are thus augmented with observations about religion and politics among Plains mobile bison hunters, notably the Blackfoot.

Essence and experience

At the heart of this volume lies an inquiry on the nature of religion and its place in the constitution and manipulation of the human condition. Carballo (Chapter 6) and R. Joyce (Chapter 7) variously characterize religion as a communicative system of knowledge that combines thought and action and articulates belief and practice to define and redefine relationships among people and between people, nature, and the cosmos. Communication may be achieved through the "bundling" of principles and practice that together, as Rodning (Chapter 4) notes, materialize as overt religious symbols that can be acknowledged by peoples of different backgrounds. Germane to a discussion of religion as materially mediated political practice are questions regarding the nature of religious knowledge and how it positions people vis-a-vis the cosmos: what it is, where it originates, how it is acquired, how it engages the tangible and the intangible in ritual objects and practices, and when/how/why it changes. To delve into the constitution of religious knowledge, contributors appeal to discussions of Amerindian ontologies to which archaeologists have partial access through objects and features and, in many cases, through ethnohistory and ethnography.

Alt and Pauketat (Chapter 3; Pauketat 2013) note that religion touches on the deepest, most profound of human recognitions: the existence of otherness around us, and the ability to tap into that otherness to improve our lives and our futures. Native religious knowledge first and foremost derives from this recognition of being in the world with others: from daily observation and experience of powerful phenomena; from entanglement with things, persons, and forces that populate the cosmos; and from the realization that people may selectively engage these elements to influence the outcome of their decisions and actions (A. Joyce, Chapter 1; Barber, Chapter 5). Rodning (Chapter 4) points out that the mystical world of Amerindians, and the Cherokee in particular, was indeed centered over such interactions, the significance of which transcended time and continue, to some extent, to inform institutions and human experiences today (Zedeño and Scheiber 2015).

Oral traditions and practices provide abundant evidence that the consecration of nature was initiated by events in which individuals or communities experienced first-hand the non-human entities inhabiting it and the cosmos (e.g., Fowles 2013; Harrod 2000; Pauketat 2013; Rodning 2015). Through sustained socialization with these powerful but increasingly familiar "others" (whether it is a unique object, such as the *Spondylus* shell [Moore, Chapter 12], a set of tangible and intangible things inside a Cahokian shrine [Alt and Pauketat, Chapter 3], an ensouled building [Joyce and Barber 2015; Piscitelli, Chapter 9; Rodning, Chapter 4], or a mountain [Zedeño and Scheiber 2015]), people learned how to order and manipulate them materially to achieve a desired effect. This is not to say that humans are the only actors, or that objects are mere representations of powerful elements of the cosmos; on the contrary, the success of religious ritual necessitates that a reciprocal relationship, a compact or covenant, be first established between humans and "others" (A. Joyce, Chapter 1).

In these social covenants, a certain order or scheme for action is acknowledged, and the rules and regulations of reciprocity are laid out. Covenants carry within them ancient myths, words, songs, body language, natural elements, cardinal directions, technologies, colors, objects, and places that materialize the past in the present, making it relevant to all participants by maintaining a dialogue with deities and reinforcing the world's order. The reciprocity of the covenants not only transforms spirits into community members and hence political entities, as Hutson et al. (Chapter 8) observe, but further involves a dialogue between leaders and followers, where leaders promote existential security among followers whilst followers accept or reject the role of leaders as cosmic intermediaries. Covenants, Rodning (Chapter 4) explains, are also the road to achieve, maintain, and restore balance in the world.

Walker (Chapter 11) questions the validity of "religion" as a category that explains human-nature interactions and uses instead "ontology (ies)" to characterize these interactions and to explain the formation of domesticated landscapes in Amazonia. While ontology is central to the understanding of Amerindian religion, as A. Joyce (Chapter 1) notes, it alone is insufficient to explain the millenary persistence of human-nature relationships, or the order they impart upon the landscape. I, along with many other contributors (Alt and Pauketat, Chapter 3; Barber, Chapter 5; Gruner, Chapter 2; Pauketat 2013; Moore, Chapter 12; Piscitelli, Chapter 9; Rodning, Chapter 4; Zedeño 2008, 2009, 2013), apply instead the concept of "bundling" (Keane 2003) to capture as broadly as possible the nature of particular covenants. Bundles encompass not only notions of being in the world (ontology), but also forms of knowledge acquisition (epistemology), and schemes that order human knowledge and arbiter daily practice and politically motivated action (systematics).

The process of "bundling" provides a clear path to understanding the metaphysical world of Amerindian societies and their covenants. Bundling and its signature material manifestation, a distinctive and polythetic set of objects and places, is the ultimate act of metaphysical discernment, where people, influenced by specific experiences with the cosmos, combine tangible and intangible things that commemorate or recreate such experiences, and in doing so they create a new covenant wherein people, places, forces, and things interact with one another during religious performances. Shrines (Alt and Pauketat, Chapter 3), burial platforms associated with feasting (R. Joyce, Chapter 7), ballcourts (Barber, Chapter 5), or ensouled buildings (Joyce and Barber 2015; Rodning, Chapter 4) are good illustrations of the bundling process. Bundles, too, may materialize at a larger scale, involving mound and townhouse complexes (Rodning, Chapter 4), raised fields and causeways (Walker, Chapter 11), or even permanent bison hunting facilities (Zedeño et al. 2014).

Bundling requires that people step aside from life's daily (and often mindless) entanglements and use their ordering schemes to identify particular forces, objects, and practices which, when deployed in formal and exacting ways, may successfully bring about a desired effect. Through repetitive ritual, bundles set the rhythms and routines that organize the social body much as calendars do (Swenson, Chapter 10) and help people plan for the future (e.g., Alt and Pauketat, Chapter 3). Among the Blackfoot, for example, rituals associated with the oldest and most important bundles (Beaver and Pipe bundles) not only captured the most essential cosmic principles and entities, but were also intimately tied to the seasons of the year and, most importantly, to the rhythms of communal bison hunting (Zedeño 2013). These bundles continue to represent ancient covenants and mark seasonal ritual obligations among contemporary communities, even though communal hunting has not taken place since the late 1800s.

Thus religion, as defined and understood in this volume, emerges from past and present experience, and through experience it evolves. Not surprisingly, religion has a causal role in the development of political formations and transformations, as Alt and Pauketat (Chapter 3) and A. Joyce (Chapter 1) observe.

Dynamics of religious practice

Arthur Joyce notes in the introduction to this volume (Chapter 1) that the traditional archaeological view of religion as belief, and thus materially unknowable, prevented the understanding of the connections between thought and practice. Yet, the archaeological record of the Americas abundantly shows how, through the actual transfer of covenants and their material expressions, religion as materially mediated practice is reproduced in politically charged contexts. While it is not always clearly manifest in the archaeological record, religious practice can be a vehicle for political inequality, particularly at times of critical economic transition, such as the development of sedentary agriculturalists along the Pacific Coast in southwest Mexico (Barber, Chapter 5). This is also clear in Hutson et al.'s (Chapter 8) discussion of Maya ontology and ritual in the context of political legitimization and longevity of the ruling lineages. Likewise, Edward Swenson's (Chapter 10) analysis of the temporality of religion, its cyclical nature, and the differentially regulated rhythms of practice it creates beyond the immediate state of specific ceremonial events, offers viable explanations for how religion endures and why it is so difficult to eradicate at the grassroots. Gruner's (Chapter 2) discussion of the resilience of the Chacoan Great House is yet another example of cultural logic that transcended its original founders and continued on, along founder kin and clan lines, outside Chaco Canyon.

Central to the development of enduring relationships between pervasive religious principles and actual practices is ritual performance and its palpable success. In Hutson et al.'s case study (Chapter 8), as in many other instances, performance was at the core of statehood and what held together people across the Maya world. Without success, the religious principles that leaders utilized to legitimize their kinship systems and justify their position in society would collapse. Similarly, Rodning (Chapter 4) highlights the intricate connections among Cherokee sacred formulas, fire, and ritual performance in balancing society and the cosmos, most notably evident in the war-peace duality of their organization. In his discussion of religion and the state in the Central Valley of Mexico, Carballo (Chapter 6) also notes that there is always a tension between transformation and stasis, but when the hardiest of religious principles must be translated into multiple contexts and enacted by culturally or ethnically heterogeneous communities, change is inescapable.

Innovation in successful religions is generally quantifiable by the additions or deletions of certain elements of an enduring covenant; generally, these elements correlate with the historical trajectories of participants in the covenant. To paraphrase Rosemary Joyce, the practice of religion involves a continual renegotiation of *doxa* (socially unquestioned truths), a recommitment to orthodoxy or innovation of heterodoxy. A participant's successful vision or even a memorable encounter with a non-human person may introduce quantifiable change in the order and rhythm of ritual practice without altering its essential principles. Contemporary Blackfoot religious leaders, for example, acknowledge that their most important religious institution (the *Okan* Medicine Lodge or "Sun Dance") is a composite of knowledge, ritual sequences, and complex objects that accrued or shed components through the passage of time. Among the Blackfoot, the powers of certain bundles were combined in complex activities and ceremonies that addressed broader religious issues and practical needs, such as sacred tobacco planting and communal bison hunting (Zedeño 2013). Some bundles (and their covenants) aged and were replaced or decommissioned as life's situations and demands changed (Pard 2015).

External influences also produced quantifiable innovation; just as Mississippians recognized (and often fought) the spiritual power of the Christian cross and the church bell (Thomas 2016), the Blackfoot incorporated the power of horses, rosary ("Padre") beads, brass bells, and commercial dyes into their oldest and most sacred bundles (Scriver 1990). Some additions likely required covenant adjustments without necessarily changing the *doxa* and purpose of the bundles; others were transformative. The shattering effect of the smallpox pandemic of 1780–1782 across the Plains, for instance, fostered a search for new forms of "medicine" among Blackfoot religious leaders, who then founded the Horn Society, a mystical and highly exclusive institution of considerable political and economic influence (McHugh 2014). This society was incorporated into the logic and rhythm of older religious and social institutions and continues to thrive today.

Oral traditions and archaeology furnish multiple examples of the transformative effect of interactions with powerful natural forces on political systems. A drought, a flood, an earthquake, an eclipse, or a volcanic eruption (as, for example, in Central Mexico; Carballo, Chapter 6) could alter the demographic, religious, and political makeup of communities just as individual interactions with the supernatural through visions and encounters could transform an average person into a medicine man or a political leader. Among Plains Indians, for example, certain corporate

institutions that exerted social and political control over communities in fact originated from visions where individuals acquired religious rights, liturgies, instruc-
tions, taboos, and protections from particular spirits (Wissler 1916).

Innovation notwithstanding, there is an element of timelessness in religious
practice; one need only delve into material forms of religious expression found
in archaic sites or even in Paleoindian sites (e.g., mounds, animal effigies, caches,
use of red paint) to realize just how old the animistic foundation of Amerindian
religions really is, and how it came to domesticate the landscape (e.g., Rodning,
Chapter 4; Walker, Chapter 11). There are cases (e.g., the Mandan, Bowers
2004) where successful rituals have been reproduced for so long that practitioners
don't even know what the sacred words and songs mean any more – they just
know that as long as they reproduce them, things will work just fine. Because of
the formal, exacting nature of the liturgical order, one would expect successful
religions to endure without much qualitative change, if it were not for the fact,
profusely illustrated in this volume, that religion itself is a source of social change
as it generates, through practice, opportunities for power acquisition and social
inequality.

The pragmatic and results-oriented quality of religious practice necessitates that
its principles be tested during each and every religious ritual, and then confirmed,
questioned, and sometimes, rejected in whole or in part (e.g., Alt and Pauketat,
Chapter 3; R. Joyce, Chapter 7; Piscitelli, Chapter 9). When religion is imagined
as residing at the crossroads of timeless essence and everyday experience, its relevance to the rise, persistence, or demise of political formations becomes clear, as
it is both a source of, and a road to, power.

The religious community

Contributors demonstrate that individuals or communities can manipulate the
ways in which religion is experienced, maintained, or changed through the abduc-
tion of overt material symbols and esoteric knowledge or through the delimitation
of levels of participation in certain rituals, all for political gain. To unpack the relationship between religion and politics, it is useful to think, as R. Joyce does, about
the structure of the "religious community" or "collectivity" (Barber, Chapter 5)
as a departing point for political action. Contrary to religious studies that generally
regard leaders and followers as two monolithic categories, religious communities
imagined by volume contributors are truly "communities of practice" or "a kind
of community created over time by the sustained pursuit of a shared enterprise"
(Wenger 1998:45). Such communities could in turn represent traditional social
groupings, including household, kin, lineage, clan, moiety, linguistic family, ethnic group, and class; they could be defined simply by differential access to esoteric
knowledge and levels of participation in religious networks, or both. The potential
for religious plurality thus existed in societies structured as interconnected communities of practice (A. Joyce, Chapter 1); within and between these communities, religious principles and practices were maintained, contested, or reproduced,

generally outliving the original practicing members or "founders," as Gruner's (Chapter 2) Chacoan Great House illustrates, but nonetheless limiting participation to religious specialists who segregated others from the *inner sanctum*.

With sustained pursuit of the religious enterprise, cycles of practice developed by religious communities became naturalized, and the most successful rituals and ritual contexts endured over generations and beyond the political milieu within which they were conceived, as Swenson (Chaprer 10) envisions happened at Huaca Colorada during and after the Moche influence. The persistence of the domesticated landscape in Llanos de Mojos irrespective of Amazonian ethnic and linguistic diversity, too, may be imagined as evidence of broadly naturalized cycles of practice (Walker, Chapter 11). At Coweeta Creek, stability came from the intergenerational building and rebuilding of mounds and townhouses according to principles received at the time of creation and knowledge acquired through mystical experience and passed on in the form of sacred formulas and written texts. Inside the townhouses, maintaining the everlasting fire "from day to day, from year to year, and from one generation to another" (Rodning, p. 90, this volume) not only anchored the religious community in place, but also lent it balance and the possibility of renewal in the annual ritual cycle.

Membership in a religious community of practice was crucial to the development of a sense of legitimacy, identity, and belonging. Conservative communities, such as those small-scale Peruvian Late Archaic communities discussed by Piscitelli (Chapter 9), were resilient and tended to develop strategies of resistance and negotiation that benefited them. These local, grassroots communities kept the pace of change by lending would-be leaders a firm, familiar ground from which relations of power could be developed and justified while at the same time keeping certain ritual knowledge domains (in this case, architectural technology) beyond the reach of the broader socio-polity. In contrast, other religious communities of practice could involve networks of participants across group boundaries, as was the case in Central Mexico (Carballo, Chapter 6), Honduras (R. Joyce, Chapter 7), Amazonia (Walker, Chapter 11), and the Mississippian world (Alt and Pauketat, Chapter 3; Rodning, Chapter 4). Southwestern archaeologists once interpreted such networks of religious practice as "cults" (Adams 1991; Crown 1994). The most salient example of cults in North America is the Ghost Dance Religion of 1890, which spread from the Nevada prophet *Wovoka* across the Plains. This cult could be categorized as a cosmopolitan network that united disparate polities and cultural traditions in the pursuit of one goal (the disappearance of the Whites and restoration of precolumbian life), and connected one another through the sharing of a bundle of principles, practices, objects, and places (e.g., Carroll et al. 2004).

In many instances, individuals participated in more than one religious community, adopting innovations or challenging deeply set cannons as they expanded their world of mystical experience – the incorporation of Christian symbols and objects into Amerindian rituals is a case in point. This kind of multiscalar participation in religious communities also created fertile ground for inequality and political transformation. Membership in a cosmopolitan network of religious practice could bring about economic and social advantages and political clout to an individual or a household that surpassed the benefits obtained by belonging solely to a local, more conservative community (R. Joyce, Chapter 7). At the very least, religion promoted horizontal difference and social and political mobility among communities who distinguished themselves by their material and ritual practices associated with a religious body that limited participation to certain standards. This form of inequality, examined by R. Joyce in Honduras (Chapter 7) and by Barber in southwest Mexico (Chapter 5), is more subtle and constrained than that found in Central Mexico (Carballo, Chapter 6) and Central America (Hutson et al., Chapter 8), where religious communities *were* political communities with a deeply embedded cultural logic of social inequality, and whose leaders held divine power over the life and death of their subjects.

Nonetheless, the development of local and regional networks of people who shared ritual practices but excluded others are signs of emergent exclusive social relations and ranking systems that paved the road to centralized political power and economic inequality (Alt and Pauketat, Chapter 3). The leaders of Mississippian polities discussed by Rodning (Chapter 4), for example, shared religious symbols and practices (from mounds to shell gorgets) that allowed them not only to acknowledge each other's political power, but also to find weaknesses in their rivals that they could exploit for the benefit of the ruling class and without active involvement of their followers. Moreover, successful religious communities could engage the help of the "spirit folk" – yet another kind of community – in times of great need, as was the case during a battle between the Cherokee and their powerful enemies (Rodning, Chapter 4).

Successful leaders knew how to walk the fine line between old and new religious principles and practices. Carballo (Chapter 6) notes that at times of political transition, such as the move toward institutionalized inequality within a polity, would-be rulers faced the conundrum of simultaneously projecting similarity and difference. In Late Formative times in Central Mexico, this was achieved in two connected ways: one, by manipulating older religious systems that served the public and reproduced horizontal relationships; and two, by using elements of a shared cultural logic to establish new, exclusive institutions that created difference and vertical division within communities. Likewise, there are many elements of Late Archaic and Woodland religion embedded in Mississippian communities of practice that facilitated the incorporation of new overarching political leadership and forms of social inequality by local and immigrant groups of heterogeneous backgrounds (Alt and Pauketat, Chapter 3). From the perspective of the Chacoan Great House, Gruner (Chapter 2) further argues that communities that were once peripheral to founders of certain religious movements in time co-opted the principles of these movements and became agents of their continuity, with or without some innovation.

Building common religious ground had the added benefit of being able to extract labor from community members, as would be the case in the construction of vast agricultural features (e.g., Walker, Chapter 11) and public buildings (e.g., Barber, Chapter 5; Carballo, Chapter 6; R. Joyce, Chapter 7; Piscitelli, Chapter 9; Rodning, Chapter 4), even if laborers did not directly benefit from the fruits of their labor. Emergent sociopolitical complexity may be, in certain cases, a response to the need for control over expanding labor pools and their products (e.g., Arnold 1996). Among the Blackfoot, the rise of a kind of religious community represented by esoteric societies of exclusive and expensive membership is closely associated with the need to manage expansive communal bison hunting and long-distance trade in the Late Prehistoric Period (CE 1000–1700) (Zedeño et al 2014). These were corporate institutions composed of religious leaders and people from different bands and in various stages of initiation. Although society liturgies were centered in ancient religious principles and practices known to everyone (e.g., contained in the Beaver and Pipe bundles), rights to specific liturgical sequences and sacred objects were privileged and expensive to obtain (Duvall 1904–1911; McClintock 1999; Wissler and Duvall 1912). Ostensibly, corporate institutions maintained order and promoted religious continuity and reciprocity. However, these societies also abducted techno-ritual knowledge specific to the communal bison hunt that was not accessible to all members of the hunting bands. Rights to esoteric knowledge thus generated divisions between the "knowing" religious elite and the average hunters. Such divisions were made explicit in every hunting event and other social activities.

Generally, religious and political power, along with social prestige, could be amassed by Blackfoot individuals of both sexes through visions, warfare, esoteric society memberships, and acquisition of supernatural power and powerful objects and symbols (Ewers 1955, 1958). This system held tensions between prestigious individuals and corporate institutions in check. Yet, the economic opportunism brought about by participation in the historic fur trade fostered individual wealth accumulation and concomitant political clout that surpassed that which could be amassed through membership in an esoteric society alone (Nugent 1993). A wealthy man could acquire many wives and captives and support a large household, thus having ready access to the labor required to process quantities of bison meat and hides for trade. The spoils of this labor could, in turn, be used to acquire religious rights, thus furnishing successful hunters and traders an opportunity for upward social and political mobility (Zedeño 2017).

In short, identifying a religious community as a community of practice united primarily by shared essence and experience furnishes a liberating tool for the search of social and historical junctures at which politics and religion harmonize or collide (Swenson, Chapter 10, this volume).

Contexts of practice

Volume contributors break ground around the fundamental dimensions of contexts of religious practice. Just as religious practice encompasses a range of spaces and temporalities, from private to theatrical and from quotidian and cyclical to life-changing, contexts of practice vary in scale from a household shrine and altar to a pyramid and ballcourt, a lake or a mountain range, or an entire raised field; and from ephemeral to millenary. Yet, there are a few things that all religious contexts have in common that deserve further comment. R. Joyce (Chapter 7) states that religious communities manipulate contexts of practice through the selection and placement of objects as well as their deposition to create powerful configurations [bundles!] and long-lasting pervasive moods and motivations. She illustrates this point with a discussion of the placement of human burials in caves, the use of fire to consecrate or seal ritual deposits, and the construction of earthen platforms for burial and feasting in Honduras.

Along similar lines, Swenson (p. 223, this volume) discusses how religious practice creates a "heterotopic landscape": a highly charged, "different space and time of exceptional ritual and intense introspection." In this liminal space-time, people engage in partnerships with tangible things and intangible forces to make transformations possible (Barber, Chapter 5; Moore, Chapter 12). Here, natural forces such as fire and water (e.g., Alt and Pauketat, Chapter 3; Carballo, Chapter 6; R. Joyce, Chapter 7; Rodning, Chapter 4) as well as other entities (not the least of which are individuals' spirit helpers) manifest themselves to people, and come to enact or commemorate a given covenant. Heterotopic landscapes can be segregated from everyday activity or fully integrated into the rhythms of social life; they are "living organisms" (Piscitelli, Chapter 9) that participate in the social dynamics of the community. Such landscapes can take hold of places with liminal qualities afforded by their natural characteristics (e.g., elevation, orientation, unique geology), by the inherent properties of the objects they contain (e.g., *Spondylus* shell, Moore, Chapter 12; red paint, Zedeño 2009), or by purposeful human action (e.g., building construction and ensoulment [Joyce and Barber 2015; Piscitelli, Chapter 9; Rodning, Chapter 4], inscription through rock art [Ruuska 2015]).

Swenson, like Barber, A. Joyce, and R. Joyce, suggests that the key to harmonizing religion and politics lies in the manipulation and regulation of the heterotopic landscape. In Piscitelli's (Chapter 9) examination of early public architecture in the Central Andes, for example, it is evident that the processes of architectural creation, dwelling, and abandonment involved individual and community labor as much as leadership; these are processes of time-space-matter transformation: people from all walks of life both reiterate widely shared *doxa* through the efforts of leaders, and negotiate strategies and tactics of political factionalism through the power of expression of local practitioners. Barber p. 109, this volume) further explains how, for at least three centuries, the Soconusco landscape was reshaped to "spatially concentrate community- and/or region-wide encounters with the divine." These public spaces were built and shared by the collectivity, and thus were imbued with their identity and purposeful actions across sites and perhaps the entire region. Public plazas and ballcourts delineated in deceivingly unstructured ways which spaces were dedicated to public gathering and communication with animate beings.

In contrast, Gruner (Chapter 2) describes a kind of enduring ritual landscape characterized by segregation – the Chacoan Great House. Just as Blackfoot painted tipis belonged to the individuals who dreamed about their designs and benefitted from the power designs afforded them (McClintock 1999), Great Houses belonged to "founders" or individuals from specific lineages or totemic associations, also possessing life histories that lent them political power. The Great House was such a self-contained heterotopic landscape that it could be "moved" from one place to another, as founding lineages left Chaco in search of new homelands where they built new Great Houses. Among the Blackfoot, even the most public of religious ceremonies entailed segregation of knowledge and liturgy as well as "closed doors" rituals of the participating esoteric societies (McClintock 1999). Yet, they maintained altars and bundles in their homes that kept them connected to the metaphysical world of their group.

In the Mississippian world, mounds, plazas, charnel houses, and townhouses were built above the surrounding landscape to create high places from bottomlands, to provide a vantage point over trails followed by incoming enemies, to segregate social groups, and to establish institutional domains (Alt and Pauketat, Chapter 3; Rodning, Chapter 4). As in the Central Valley of Mexico (Carballo, Chapter 6), these demarcated institutional domains were also political landscapes that perpetuated a cultural logic of inequality. Although commoners were often severed from the *inner sanctum* of a heterotopic landscape, for example, the top of a Maya temple (Hutson et al., Chapter 8), they also required of their leaders a successful ritual performance, and used their own rights to household ritual to maintain ties to the political life of their community. Both temples and domiciles, thus, were part of a unified ritual body practiced at different scales of authority.

Contributors touch on the temporality of heterotopic landscapes and the way these encapsulated metaphysical principles resonated through multiple generations of practitioners, even during times of political transformation (A. Joyce, Chapter 1). Just as religious institutions could outlive their founders, enduring contexts of practice reiterated ancient beliefs, commemorated significant events from the deep (often mythical) past, regulated the rhythms of movement and work across the landscape, and connected people to their ancestors. Physical permanence certainly stimulated the longevity of memories and practices attached to specific contexts and landscapes and contributed to the naturalization of religious ideologies (Swenson, Chapter 10); for mobile hunter societies such as the Blackfoot, the natural landscape became a permanent anchor of their cosmology (Oetelaar 2014).

Among the multiplicity of contexts of religious practice discussed in this volume, the household, the townhouse, the public building or plaza, the taskscape, and the natural place lend spatial scales against which the temporality of ritual practice can be measured. Each of these contexts, in turn, may be conceived of as a bundle in its own right, as Rodning (Chapter 4) explains. Take the household, for example, as the scenario of religious performances that not only fulfill commemorative and regenerative functions, but also help to maintain connections between different social and political realms (Hutson et al., Chapter 8). House foundation offerings, shrines, ancestor burials, altars, and imagery in household objects (e.g., Carballo, Chapter 6) could bring the essential elements of politically motivated, public religious practice down to the humblest of commoners. By the same token, the household could be the cradle of contestation and reform. In her study of outlying communities at Cahokia, Alt (2002, 2006) reminded us how important it is to look at households in order to assess the degree to which families held allegiances to the dominant ideology and expressed their heterogeneous cultural, ethnic, and religious identities. Likewise, in contemporary Blackfoot households, it is common to find elements of traditional religion, of modern pan-Indian religion, and of Christian worship (Zedeño et al. 2005). A minority of households, in fact, can claim to practice strict Blackfoot rituals, which are founded upon formal initiation and transfers as opposed to simple participation and, therefore, may be too expensive and time-consuming for the majority of economically depressed or poorly connected families.

The influence of economic and social inequality on religious practice clearly played out in other historical trajectories. In times of socio-political upheaval and demographic restructuring, such as the transition between Middle Mississippian (Cahokian) and Late Mississippian Periods (Alt and Pauketat, Chapter 3) or during the early years of European contact (Rodning, Chapter 4), community members might have found more than one option at hand that satisfied both the need to remain connected to familiar spiritual pursuits and to choose the best available survival options; these choices were materialized in household rituals. A similar case can be made for Honduran households who engaged in cosmopolitan networks as their religious spaces and assemblages indicate (R. Joyce, Chapter 7).

Religious principles that manifest outside the household may involve the quotidian "taskscape" (*sensu* Swenson, Chapter 10). Agricultural raised fields and hunting architecture are examples in point. Walker (Chapter 11) notes that the longevity and permanent character of Amazonian raised fields, forest islands, and causeways represent not only deep-time continuity in group ontologies that cross-cut linguistic and ethnic groups on a vast area, but also terrain-altering practices that influenced the ways in which people moved across the landscape and related to it. While not directly associated with materially-mediated religious practices (in fact, Walker cites ethnohistorical accounts of religious contexts segregated from taskscapes), these facilities nonetheless were highly influential in the rhythms and calendars of their builders.

A parallel case, profusely illustrated in early ethnographies (e.g., Duvall 1904–1911; McClintock 1999; Schaeffer 1978) and visible archaeologically (Zedeño et al. 2014), can be made for the massive bison hunting facilities built by Blackfoot ancestors across the northwestern Plains. Hunting knowledge, building knowledge, ecological and geographical knowledge, all were ritually regulated by esoteric societies, bundle groups, and painted tipi owners. These permanent facilities not only connected mobile hunters to the taskscape and regulated their movement, but also reflected ancient principles and practices that were reified and adjusted in each hunting event. Communal hunting complexes incorporated ritual liturgies and facilities (the black and yellow buffalo tipis) that, along with the Beaver bundle and certain ceremonial headdresses, were used to charm bison into their death (Allan Pard, personal communication 2016; Hellson, n.d.; McClintock 1999). In addition, rituals of renewal were carried out beyond the hunting complex during the segregated and public ceremonies of the *Okan*, where the bison drive was ritually reenacted by society leaders and participants (Witte and Gallagher 2008:435). Thus, communal bison hunting complexes integrated heterotopic landscapes and taskscapes, with each hunting event eliciting the accumulated knowledge and practice of multiple interacting generations (Zedeño et al. 2014).

Public architecture is yet another context of practice characterized by segregation, where a building, from construction to retirement, is singularized to represent a particular religious ideology. This much is clear in the Chacoan Great House, a highly distinctive kind of building that could be reproduced in more or less exacting detail (Gruner, Chapter 2). Piscitelli (Chapter 9) tells us that, while public buildings may have been dedicated to religious pursuits and used mostly by leaders and elites, they were nonetheless the product of a community of practice, one that often was deeply involved in the building process. Joyce and Barber (2015) make a strong case for the participatory nature of public architecture, where laborers were engaged in the sacralization or "ensoulment" of public buildings, thus becoming entrapped by their actions, a situation that promoted grassroots conservatism and resistance to political change (A. Joyce, Chapter 1). It is when communities of practice, while still providing labor, become segregated from the central locales of ritual activity – in particular, those that help perpetuate the ruling elite, as is the case of Mississippian mounds and mound burials (Rodning, Chapter 4), or the interiors and summits of Oaxaca, Maya, and Aztec pyramids (Carballo, Chapter 6; Hutson et al., Chapter 8; Joyce and Barber 2015) – that they are more amenable (or susceptible) to political manipulation. One could argue that the longer a community of practice is engaged in the production of heterotopias, the more independent it becomes from the trappings of would-be rulers . . . and vice versa.

Swenson (Chapter 10) points out a particular kind of context of religious practice, which embodies so much of the history of a place and a community that it becomes a "chronotope" – a symbol of, and a monument to, that historical trajectory. Through the case of Huaca Colorada, Swenson shows how chronotopes evolve just as the political milieu and religious makeup of communities do, but they do so at their own pace. Chronotopes are akin to elderly beings with singular biographies, who have witnessed continuity and change, becoming ever the wiser. Natural places – mountains and salient topographic features, in particular – often become chronotopes to particular communities of practice, regardless of their sociopolitical organization, but especially to mobile groups (Bethke and Zedeño 2014). Other kinds of chronotopes are commemorative monuments and places of inscription, such as stelae, stone effigies, geoglyphs, and rock art sites that have been visited and modified over the ages and continue to be meaningful to contemporary communities. Once again, these may be found across Amerindia.

Objects of practice

Objects of religious practice furnish a fine, but nonetheless far-reaching, scale for scrutinizing religious practice at the crossroads of political action. Ubiquitous in the archaeological record, they consist of modified and unmodified materials that indi-cate multifarious interactions among humans, nature, and the supernatural. These objects, too, can be manipulated for political gain. Two decades ago, William H. Walker (1995) classified objects by their life histories: singularized objects refer to those that, from conception to retirement, are dedicated exclusively to one or a few activities and appear in very specific contexts. A Mississippian shell mask, for example, would fit this category perfectly. Generalized objects, on the other hand, are those that, at some point in their life history, become segregated from their ordinary milieu and introduced into the religious realm through consecration. Per-sonal objects left as offerings (e.g., projectile points deposited under rock art panels in Wyoming, Francis and Loendorf 2002) would be considered generalized objects whose biographies took a sharp turn when they entered a ceremonial context.

While archaeologists tend to split artifacts into single classes for the purpose of analysis, objects of religious practice often come in complex or polythetic sets and usually belong in bundles that represent metaphysical concepts and actual prac-tices (Keane 2003; Pauketat 2013; Rodning, Chapter 4). Within these sets, there are singularized and generalized objects; I prefer to use the term "index objects" (Zedeño 2009) in reference to very specific objects and material representations that are widely recognized as having inherent power: red paint, crystals and cer-tain stones, fossils, tobacco, and spring water are examples in point. Other index objects are regionally and culturally specific, such as material representations of inherently powerful entities, including the thunderbird in the Great Plains, the feathered serpent in Mesoamerica, or the falcon in the American Southeast. Then there are accessory objects: those that are contextually associated with index objects and that embody specific knowledge and concepts; for example, in the Blackfoot bundles, certain mammals and birds tell the origin story of a bundle and their individual contribution to its power (Zedeño 2008). There are also biographical objects that indicate the identity and life history of the people who owned them. Variation in the composition and arrangement of complex objects, say, in founder shrines (Gruner, Chapter 2) and domestic bundles during Cahokia times (Alt and Pauketat, Chapter 3), may be the result of distinctive social biographies. Rodn-ing's (Chapter 4) discussion of the contents and structure of Cherokee mounds and townhouses at Coweeta Creek, where objects porting symbols of the Cherokee universe (ceramic vessels, shell gorgets) became entangled within buildings that incorporated the same symbols and principles in their layout, expands the com-plexity of material culture arrangements [bundles!] into ever-larger scales.

Moore (Chapter 12) makes a compelling case for the power of a single object to transform everything it touches. He examines the shell of the genus known as *Spondylus*, a polythetic index object that flowed across the natural, human, and spiritual realms of Andean America. Elaborating on Ingold's (2010:4) idea that a thing can act as a knot that joins together these realms, Moore explains how this shell created liminal spaces of communication between worlds. In certain circum-stances, *Spondylus* also was a proxis or agent of the state. Drawing from archaeo-logical associations, Moore further expands on the power of the shell to create contexts of practice by its very presence and through construction, sacrifice, and burial rites; to transform people and imbue elites with power and prestige and, as the quintessential rain-maker, to mediate between people and water through rituals associated with hydraulic systems and agricultural fertility. He notes that the acquisition, modification, and use of *Spondylus* were all part of the sacred realm and segregated from the manufacture of lesser objects; in fact, the manufacture of shell objects should be considered "an engaged metamorphosis of the inherent properties" of this index object (Moore, p. 270, this volume) – much like the manufacture of stone eccentrics by the Maya elite.

In societies with incipient forms of political authority, index objects served to demarcate places of power along gender and age. For example, Early Formative masks from coastal southwest Mexico, discussed by Barber in this volume (Chapter 5), are a unique kind of index object used by Soconusco elders to channel the power of spirit entities though which they could access a political authority (or recognition of the collectivity) that was not theirs when unmasked. In this case, a highly transformative object allowed the wearer to become another self; as Barber notes, a single human body could express multiple selves by virtue of possessing and wearing different portrait masks. Thus, the power channeled by the mask allowed certain individuals to differentiate themselves from others, thus promoting a visible (albeit somewhat transient) form of inequality in an otherwise fairly egalitarian society. Moreover, figurines arguably served as subtle age and gender markers among these communities, both within and outside the household.

One can neither overemphasize the importance of index objects in the perpetuation of cohesive religious networks, in the pledge of allegiance to certain ideologies, or in the contestation of politico-religious leadership, nor underestimate their power to bring about social prestige and economic prosperity to their owners. In fact, index and other objects of religious practice were not exclusively inalienable possessions (*sensu* Weiner 1992); on the contrary, as Moore (Chapter 12) indicates, polythetic objects such as *Spondylus* shells could also have economic value and circulate as currency, thus existing in an inalienable-commodity continuum, and representing diverse systems of valence. Eagles (particularly golden eagles) and eagle feathers provide a parallel case among the Missouri River tribes, particularly the Blackfoot and the Mandan. It is well known that among Plains groups, the eagle, a material incarnation of the thunderbird, is a celestial being of extraordinary power and thus occupies a high place in the cosmic order. Just like the shells, eagle feathers have transformative and consecratory properties and are icons of leadership and social prestige; eagle feathers also symbolize valor and courage in war. In the past, eagle trapping and feather handling was a holy activity steeped in mythology; a matter of utmost secrecy that belonged to specialists who had to be initiated and obtain rights to eagles at a great personal and economic cost (Murray 2011; Schaeffer and Schaeffer 1934).

Both among the Mandan and the Blackfoot, eagle trappers held a special place in society not only for their specialized knowledge and religious acumen, but also because of the privileged economic position that trade in eagle feathers provided and that often translated into political leadership (Chandler et al. 2017; Murray

2011). Before the arrival of Europeans, eagle tail feathers were the standard of value (Grinnell 1962:214) and were exchanged for religious rights as well as commodities. When horses were introduced into the northern Plains, they, along with eagle feathers, became the currency of the time. So precious were golden eagle feathers that three of them (and in rare cases, one feather) could buy a hunting horse (Zedeño 2017). Their place in the native market economy did not, however, in any way alter or diminish their inalienable properties as index objects.

In short, Moore's study illustrates the unique transformative and consecratory power of objects (natural or modified). Other contributions show how objects can imbue life and soul to a natural place, a house, or a public building (Barber, Chapter 5; Joyce and Barber 2015); define the identity and message of a network of religious practice (Alt and Pauketat, Chapter 3; Carballo, Chapter 6; R. Joyce, Chapter 7); unify or segregate commoner and elite sectors of a society (Gruner, Chapteer 2; Hutson et al., Chapter 8); and mark the passage of time in continuous or discontinuous trajectories and at various scales (Moore, Chapter 12; Swenson, Chapter 10).

Conclusion

This commentary has discussed five topics variously addressed by contributors: essence and experience, dynamics of religious practice, religious communities, contexts of religious practice, and objects of religious practice. In turn, these topics help to explore the three main tenets of the volume outlined by A. Joyce (Chapter 1): that there is an inescapable connection between religion and politics; that this relationship is founded upon ancient metaphysical principles; and that materially mediated practice validates, reproduces, contests, and transforms the fundamental relationship between religion and politics over time. Case studies illustrate how diverse contexts and objects of practice become entangled in a multiscalar fashion by the doings of a given religious community; how political agency is expressed through internal struggles underlying religious factions, and how cultural logic provides checks and balances to surmount the challenges of transformation or to maintain the *status quo*.

I would go as far as to suggest that politics and religion should be treated as a bundle in the broadest sense – one that encompasses nature, humans, and the cosmos, is regulated by the principles, potentials, and limitations of these realms of life, and is tailored to (and recursively, tailors) society in particular times and places. Yet, the core rules of the bundle's covenant are universal in Amerindia.

References Cited

Adams, E. Charles 1991 *The Origin and Development of the Pueblo Katsina Cult*. The University of Arizona Press, Tucson.

Alt, Susan 2002 Identities, Traditions and Diversity in Cahokia's Uplands. *Midcontinental Journal of Archaeology* 27: 217–236.

————. 2006 The Power of Diversity: The Roles of Migration and Hybridity in Culture Change. In *Leadership and Polity in Mississippian Society*, edited by Brian M. Butler and Paul D. Welch, Center for Archaeological Investigations, Occasional Paper No. 33. Southern Illinois University, Carbondale.

Arnold, Jeanne E. 1996 The Archaeology of Complex Hunter-Gatherers. *Journal of Archaeological Method and Theory* 3(2): 77–126.

Bethke, Brandi and María Nieves Zedeño 2014 *Chronotopes: The Parallel Biographies of Two Humanized Landforms*. Paper presented at the 79th Annual Meetings of the Society for American Archaeology, Austin.

Bowers, Alfred W. 2004 *Mandan Social and Ceremonial Organization*. University of Nebraska Press, Lincoln.

Carroll, Alex, María Nieves Zedeño, and Richard W. Stoffle 2004 Landscapes of the Ghost Dance: A Cartography of Numic Ritual. *Journal of Archaeological Method and Theory* 11: 127–156.

Chandler, Kaytlin, Wendi F. Murray, Maria Nieves Zedeño, Samrat Clements, and Robert Jones 2017 *Wingeds: A Missouri River Ethno-ornithology*. Anthropological Papers of the University of Arizona No. 78. University of Arizona Press, Tucson.

Crown, Patricia L. 1994 *Ceramics and Ideology: Salado Polychrome Pottery*. University of New Mexico Press, Albuquerque.

Duvall, David C. 1904–1911 Papers (vol. 1). Typed manuscripts. American Museum of Natural History Archives, New York.

Ewers, John, C. 1945 (1955) *The Horse in Blackfeet Indian Culture: With Comparative Material From Other Western Tribes*. Smithsonian Institution Bureau of American Ethnology, Bulletin 159. Government Printing Office, Washington, DC.

————. 1958 *The Blackfeet: Raiders of the Northwestern Plains*. University of Oklahoma Press, Norman.

Fowles, Severin 2013 *An Archaeology of Doings: Secularism and the Study of Pueblo Religion*. School for Advanced Research Press, Santa Fe.

Francis, Julie E., and Lawrence Loendorf 2002 *Ancient Visions: Petroglyphs and Pictographs of the Wind River and Bighorn Country, Wyoming and Montana*. University of Utah Press, Salt Lake City.

Grinnell, George B. 1962 *Blackfoot Lodge Tales: The Story of a Prairie People*. University of Nebraska Press, Lincoln.

Harrod, Howard L. 2000 *The Animals Came Dancing: Native American Sacred Ecology and Animal Kinship*. University of Arizona Press, Tucson.

Hellson, John n.d. The Black and Yellow Buffalo Tipis of the Blackfoot. Typed manuscript on file in the Bureau of Applied Research in Anthropology, University of Arizona, Tucson.

Ingold, Tim 2010 Bringing Things to Life: Creative Entanglements in a World of Materials. *Realities* Working Paper No. 15. Manchester. www.socialsciences.manchester.ac.uk/medialibrary/morgancentre/research/wps/15-2010-07-realities-bringing-things-to-life.pdf, accessed March 30, 2015.

Inomata, Takeshi 2001 The Power and Ideology of Artistic Creation: Elite Craft Specialists in Classic Maya Society. *Current Anthropology* 42: 321–349.

Joyce, Arthur A., and Sarah B. Barber 2015 Ensoulment, Entrapment, and Political Centralization: A Comparative Study of Religion and Politics in Later Formative Oaxaca. *Current Anthropology* 56: 819–847.

Keane, Webb 2003 Semiotics and the Social Analysis of Material Things. *Language & Communication* 23: 409–425.

McHugh, Chris 2014 *Siksika and Blackfoot Archaeology*. Paper presented at the Blackfoot and Archaeology Conference, Peigan Nation and University of Lethbridge, Lethbridge.

McClintock, Walter 1999 *The Old North Trail: Life, Legends and Religion of the Blackfeet Indians.* University of Nebraska Press, Lincoln.

Murray, Wendi Field 2011 Feathers, Fasting, and the Eagle Complex: A Contemporary Analysis of the Eagle as a Cultural Resource in the Northern Plains. *Plains Anthropologist* 56: 143–154.

Nugent, David 1993 Property Relations, Production Relations, and Inequality: Anthropology, Political Economy, and the Blackfeet. *American Ethnologist* 20: 336–362.

Oetelaar, Gerald 2014 Better Homes and Pastures: Human Agency and the Construction of Place in Communal Bison Hunting on the Northwestern Plains. *Plains Anthropologist* 59(1): 9–37.

Pard, Allan 2015 Repatriation Among the Piikani. In *We are Coming Home*, edited by Gerald T. Conaty, pp. 119–134. Athabaska University Press, Edmonton.

Pauketat, Timothy 2013 *An Archaeology of the Cosmos: Rethinking Agency and Religion in Ancient America.* Routledge, London.

Rodning, Christopher 2015 *Center Places and Cherokee Towns: Archaeological Perspectives on Native American Architecture and Landscape in the Southern Appalachians.* University of Alabama Press, Tuscaloosa.

Ruuska, Alex K. 2015 Social Investment in Regions of Refuge: Survival Strategies Among the Southern Paiute of Central Nevada. In *Engineering Mountain Landscapes: An Anthropology of Social Investment*, edited by Laura L. Scheiber and María Nieves Zedeño, pp. 75–98. University of Arizona Press, Tucson.

Schaeffer, Claude E. 1978 The Bison Drive of the Blackfeet Indians. *Plains Anthropologist* 23: 243–248.

Schaeffer, Claude E., and Mrs. [unknown name] Schaeffer 1934 Field Work among Blackfeet Indians, Montana. Correspondence and Field Notes. Glenbow Museum Archives, Calgary, Alberta.

Scriver, Bob 1990 *Blackfeet Artists of the Northern Plains.* The Lowell Press, Kansas City.

Thomas, David Hurst 2016 Materiality Matters: Colonial Transformations Spanning the Southwestern and Southeastern Borderlands. In *Transformations During the Colonial Era: Divergent Histories in the American Southwest*, edited by John G. Douglass and William M. Graves. University Press of Colorado, Boulder.

Walker, William H. 1995 Ceremonial Trash? In *Expanding Archaeology*, edited by James M. Skibo, William H. Walker, and Axel E. Nielsen, pp. 67–79. University of Utah Press, Salt Lake City.

Wenger, Etienne 1998 *Communities of Practice: Learning, Meaning, and Identity.* Cambridge University Press, Cambridge.

Wiener, Annette 1992 *Inalienable Possessions: The Paradox of Keeping While Giving.* University of California Press, Berkeley.

Wissler, Clark 1916 Societies and Dance Associations of the Blackfoot Indians. In *Societies of the Plains Indians*, edited by Clark Wissler, pp. 359–460. Anthropological Papers of the American Museum of Natural History, vol. XI. Trustees of the American Museum of Natural History, New York.

Wissler, Clark, and David Duvall 1912 *Social Organization and Ritualistic Ceremonies of the Blackfoot Indians.* AMS Press, New York.

Witte, Stephen S., and Marsha V. Gallagher, eds. 2008 *The North American Journals of Prince Maximilian of Wied, vol. II, April–September 1833.* University of Oklahoma Press, Norman.

Zedeño, María Nieves 2008 Bundled Worlds: The Roles and Interactions of Complex Objects from the North American Plains. *Journal of Archaeological Method and Theory* 15: 362–378.

―――. 2009 Animating by Association: Index Objects and Relational Taxonomies. *Cambridge Archaeological Journal* 19: 407–417.

————. 2013 Methodological and Analytical Challenges in Relational Archaeologies: A View From the Hunting Ground. In *Relational Archaeologies*, edited by Christopher Watts, pp. 117–134. Routledge, New York.

————. 2017 Rethinking the Impact of Abundance on the Rhythm of Bison Hunter Societies. In *Abundance: An Archaeological Analysis of Plenitude*, edited by Monica Smith, pp. 23–44. University Press of Colorado, Boulder.

Zedeño, María Nieves, Jesse A. Ballenger, and John R. Murray 2014 Landscape Engineering and Organizational Complexity among Late Prehistoric Bison Hunters of the Northwestern Plains. *Current Anthropology* 55(1): 23–58.

Zedeño, María Nieves, and Laura L. Scheiber 2015 People and Mountains. In *Engineering Mountain Landscapes: An Anthropology of Social Investment*, edited by Laura L. Scheiber and Maria Nieves Zedeño, pp. 186–194. University of Utah Press, Salt Lake City.

Zedeño, María Nieves, Lauren Jelinek, and Rebecca Toupal 2005 *Badger-Two Medicine Boundary Adjustment Study*. Final Report Prepared for the Lewis & Clark National Forest, MT, the Blackfeet Community College, and the Blackfeet Tribal Historic Preservation Office. Bureau of Applied Research in Anthropology, University of Arizona, Tucson.

INDEX